This is the first general history in English of the theatre in Vienna, the one German-speaking city which in the late eighteenth century and for most of the nineteenth sustained a theatrical life comparable to that of Paris or London. The book covers this theatrical culture from the beginnings of modern theatre in 1776 to the present day, relating it to social, political and intellectual history and charting how Viennese theatre has reflected political and social change (from the Josephinian reforms to Metternich, the rise of anti-Semitism and the collapse of the Austro-Hungarian monarchy, the Anschluss and the modern republic). It focuses primarily on the most important and productive theatres: the Burgtheater of the nineteenth and early twentieth century and the commercial theatres that housed Viennese dialect comedy and operetta. Particular emphasis is placed on the dramatists and composers from whom the lasting importance of the theatres chiefly derives, and on the ideological pressures reflected in the repertory, in censorship (to which one chapter is devoted) and in press reception. The book draws on original documents including diaries, memoirs and reviews, and is fully accessible to general readers as well as specialists.

CAMBRIDGE STUDIES IN GERMAN

THEATRE IN VIENNA

CAMBRIDGE STUDIES IN GERMAN

General editors: H. B. Nisbet and Martin Swales
Advisory editor: Theodore Ziolkowski

s. s. prawer: Frankenstein's Island: England and the English in the writings of Heinrich Heine

benjamin bennett: Hugo von Hofmannsthal: The theatres of consciousness

philip payne: Robert Musil's 'The Man without Qualities': A critical study

anna k. kuhn: Christa Wolf's Utopian Vision: From Marxism to Feminism

ernst behler: German Romantic Literary Theory

lesley sharpe: Friedrich Schiller: Drama, thought and politics

peter hutchinson: Stefan Heym: The perpetual dissident

j. p. stern: The Dear Purchase: A theme in German modernism

michael butler (ed.): The Narrative Fiction of Heinrich Böll: Social conscience and literary achievement

seán allan: The Plays of Heinrich von Kleist: Ideals and illusions

THEATRE IN VIENNA

A Critical History, 1776–1995

W. E. YATES

Professor of German, University of Exeter

CAMBRIDGE
UNIVERSITY PRESS

Published by the Press Syndicate of the University of Cambridge
The Pitt Building, Trumpington Street, Cambridge CB2 1RP
40 West 20th Street, New York, NY 10011–4211, USA
10 Stamford Road, Oakleigh, Melbourne 3166, Australia

©Cambridge University Press 1996

First published 1996

Printed in Great Britain at the University Press, Cambridge

A catalogue record for this book is available from the British Library

Library of Congress cataloguing in publication data
Yates, W. E.
Theatre in Vienna: a critical history, 1776–1995 / by W. E. Yates.
p.   cm. – (Cambridge studies in German)
Includes bibliographical references and index.
ISBN 0 521 42100 4 (hardback)
1. Theatre – Austria – Vienna – History.
I. Title.   II. Series.
PN2616.V5Y38   1996
792'.09436'13 – dc20   95–42994   CIP

ISBN 0 521 42100 4 hardback

For Barbara, Tom, and Paul

Contents

Illustrations

(Nos 3, 5, 9, 11, 16, 18, and 20 from the collection of
Peter Branscombe; nos 27 and 28 from the Schnitzler
Archive of the University of Exeter Library.)

MAP

Preface

In the late eighteenth century and for most of the nineteenth, Vienna was the one large cosmopolitan city in German-speaking Europe that sustained a theatrical life comparable to that of Paris or London. The evolution of the theatre there illustrates basic problems of theatre history as a discipline: the relation of the theatre to social change (reflected in changes in the public and its expectations), to political pressure (reflected most directly in censorship) and to the cultural climate (manifested most explicitly in press reviews). Vienna also provides a notable contrast to the English theatre: in the survival of the repertory system, in the practice of subscription (*abonnement*), in the level of state subsidy – all symptomatic of a culture in which the theatre and theatre-going have a central place in public and political consciousness. The importance of Vienna in the history of drama, opera, and operetta is such that anyone working on subjects connected either with international theatre history or with German-speaking drama needs information on the Viennese theatre; yet there is no general history of it in English to complement monographs on the main dramatists (Grillparzer, Raimund, Nestroy, Anzengruber, Schnitzler, Hofmannsthal) and composers (Haydn, Mozart, Beethoven, Johann Strauss, Richard Strauss).

When the most recent and fullest scholarly history of the Viennese theatre in German, Franz Hadamowsky's *Wien. Theatergeschichte*, appeared in 1988, I had the privilege of reviewing it in the *Modern Language Review* (Vol. 85 [1990], 515–18), and wrote that while it was admirably packed with facts, what he had 'deliberately omitted might properly be the subject of another account': he had provided a largely depoliticized history, and it might be possible to retell the story placing more emphasis on the wider context, giving more sense of swings in intellectual history and of the international scene, particularly the relation between Vienna and other theatrical centres. In a sense, this present book is an attempt to redress the balance, albeit with a different time-scale, and for English-speaking readers.

The history either of a single theatre or of the theatrical life of a whole city or nation is part of a wider cultural history; what I am attempting is to provide an account of the theatrical culture of Vienna since the late eighteenth century, relating it to the social, political, and intellectual history of the city, and keeping international comparisons in mind throughout. It is an attempt to chart how Viennese theatre has reflected the changing pattern of political and social life, and how those pressures have been played out in the politics of the theatre itself. The account treats both court (later state) theatres and commercial theatres and centres mainly on organisation, repertoire, and reception – that is, on the politics of the theatre, with developments in the theatre related to the political and social background. The subjects it covers include the building of theatres, their situation in an expanding city, and organizational change within them; the contrast and interrelation of court or state theatres and commercial theatres; theatre repertoires as reflections of developing tastes, with particular emphasis on the dramatists and composers on which the lasting importance of the theatres concerned rests; and ideological pressures reflected in the repertory and in reception.

I am aware that in taking 1776 as my starting-point I am cutting out some very interesting earlier material. The history of court entertainments, of strolling players, the building of the first permanent theatres in the seventeenth and eighteenth centuries, and the fashions for Italian opera and French drama would properly form the material for a companion volume. The significance of 1776 lies in the declaration by Joseph II of the so-called '*Spektakelfreiheit*', which made possible the building of the first permanent commercial theatres outside the old walled inner city and so provided the basis for the vivid theatrical life of the nineteenth century; it represents the beginning of the history of modern theatre in Vienna. The story is a rich one, both colourful and important.

There is no comprehensive factual reference book available on the Viennese theatres comparable to Nicole Wild's *Dictionnaire des théâtres parisiens au XIX* *siècle. Les théâtres et la musique* (Paris: Aux Amateurs de livres 1989) or Diana Howard's *London Theatres and Music Halls 1850– 1950* (London: The Library Association 1970). I have therefore tried to make the account as factually informative as possible, and I hope it will be useful in placing the major names in context; but my aim is not to provide a list of names and dates. It is impossible in the space available to cover every theatre, and I make no apology for the fact that most space is given to the most important theatres and the most productive periods: to the history of the Burgtheater in the nineteenth and early twentieth century, and to the commercial theatres that were the homes of Viennese dialect comedy and operetta.

Histories of Viennese theatre frequently concentrate largely on actors; writing for non-German-speaking readers, who may be expected to know many of the principal works performed but to be less concerned with individual performers, I have tried to avoid the danger of providing lists of performers' names (any Viennese reader will find glaring omissions) and to mention only the most important figures, concentrating more on repertory and management. While trying to present the story in a readable form, I have drawn as far as possible on authentic documents (including diaries, memoirs, and reviews) written by the participants. In using works of scholarship I have drawn particularly on those that themselves go back directly to original documents. Particularly important in this respect among older material are Karl Glossy's transcriptions of material on censorship, and among modern work a series of publications by Franz Hadamowsky, Franz Dirnberger, and above all by Johann Hüttner, whose searching examinations of the practical commercial problems of the nineteenth-century theatre have transformed our understanding of its workings.

Where both Hadamowsky's history and also the more popular account by Verena Keil-Budischowsky, *Die Theater Wiens* (1983), treat the material theatre by theatre, I have organized the material mainly by periods and genres, in an attempt to afford a broader historical perspective. Because I hope the story is of wide concern to those interested in the history of European theatre and in the history of drama and opera, as well as to those interested mainly in Vienna or in German and Austrian literature, quotations are translated into English (with the German occasionally given also where the phrasing is distinctive or problematic). Some longer passages in German which are of documentary value and are not widely accessible are reproduced in Appendix 1. German titles are given in the original language throughout; titles in other languages are given in their familar English forms (*The Marriage of Figaro, Orpheus in the Underworld*) except where the original is better-known (*La Belle Hélène*).

To keep the apparatus of bibliographical references within bounds, I have confined the notes to references for quotations and points of fact or judgement which derive from a single authority. For matters of fact, such as dates of productions and appointments, which are available both in contemporary newspapers and in reference works, individual references are not given. The works on which I have drawn are listed in the Bibliography, together with full details of works referred to in abbreviated form in the endnotes. There is such an enormous wealth of material, both printed and unprinted, on Viennese theatre that a comprehensive bibliography of the field would have constituted a book by itself; but though the Bibliography to the present study (pp. 291–314) is confined to the material on which I have principally depended, I hope that even in that truncated form it will serve as a useful reference tool, a guide of a kind that neither of the histories by Franz Hadamowsky and Verena Keil-Budischowsky provides.

Finally, a note on terminology: the word 'director' has become ambiguous in English, meaning both the theatre manager (German *Theaterdirektor*) and the 'stage director' (German *Regisseur*), for which the word 'producer' used to be used until the terminology was confused under the influence of the film industry. For the sake of economy and clarity, I have used 'producer' in the sense of 'stage director' (*Regisseur*) throughout, and reserved 'director' for the director of a theatre. I have also restricted the word 'première', when used without explanatory qualification, to refer only to the world première of a new work, as opposed to the first night of a new production.

Acknowledgements

It is a pleasure to acknowledge my gratitude for the help I have received from colleagues and friends. I am deeply indebted to two of them in particular. Professor Johann Hüttner (Vienna) gave me wise advice at an early stage and has also provided numerous further pieces of information; my bibliography and notes also give at least some indication of the reliance I have placed on his published work, especially on the nineteenth-century theatre. Professor Peter Branscombe (St Andrews) has also given me the benefit of his advice from the start and has unfailingly responded to a series of requests for information; furthermore he was kind enough to read through a late draft of the chapters on the eighteenth century and on opera and operetta, and I owe him a warm debt of thanks for generously making available material from his private collection for use in the illustrations.

I am also much indebted to Peter Back-Vega (Vienna), Dr Evelyn Deutsch-Schreiner (Vienna), Dr Mary Garland (Exeter), Professor Jürgen Hein (Münster), Dr John McKenzie (Exeter), Dr Walter Obermaier (Vienna), Professor Sigurd Paul Scheichl (Innsbruck), and Professor Friedrich Walla (Newcastle, NSW) for various pieces of advice, material, and information; to Jarmila Weissenböck (Österreichisches Theatermuseum) and Dr Wilhelm Deutschmann (Historisches Museum der Stadt Wien) for giving generously of their time to advise me on the selection of illustrations; to Trevor Learmouth (Exeter University Library) for careful scrutiny of the Bibliography; to John Saunders of the University of Exeter Photographic Unit for his skill and patience in providing photographs of a motley collection of originals; to Monica and Manfred Draudt (Vienna) for their kind hospitality at an early stage of my work on the book; and last but not least to my wife and my elder son, Thomas Yates, who both read drafts of the typescript and made numerous valuable comments and suggestions.

I must also express my gratitude to the British Academy for a Research Grant which enabled me to work in Vienna in 1994; to the University of Exeter for two terms' study leave in 1994; and to my colleagues in the Department of German who made that leave possible by unselfishly shouldering a lot of extra work at a difficult time.

Finally I would like to acknowledge my debt to various libraries and archives, both for the material I have been able to consult and for the helpfulness of their staff: to the Österreichische Nationalbibliothek in Vienna, in particular the Theatre Collection (Theatersammlung), now housed in the Österreichisches Theatermuseum; the Wiener Stadt- und Landesbibliothek; the Niederösterreichisches Landesarchiv; the Institute of Germanic Studies, London; and Exeter University Library, to which I am also particularly grateful for making available material reproduced from the Schnitzler Archive.

I am also indebted to all those at the Cambridge University press who have helped to bring the project to completion, in particular to Dr Katharina Brett, who has overseen it from the start, and to Dr Christine F. Salazar for her searching reading of the typescript.

VIENNA 1845
(The 'five theatres' and the site of other post-1776 foundations.)

1 Theater nächst dem Kärntnertor
2 Hofburgtheater
3 Theater in der Leopoldstadt [from 1847: Carltheater]
4 Theater in der Josefstadt
5 Theater an der Wien
6 Freihaustheater auf der Wieden [1787–1801]
7 Theater auf der Landstraße [1790–3]
8 Theater 'Zum Weißen Fasan', Neustift [1776–95]

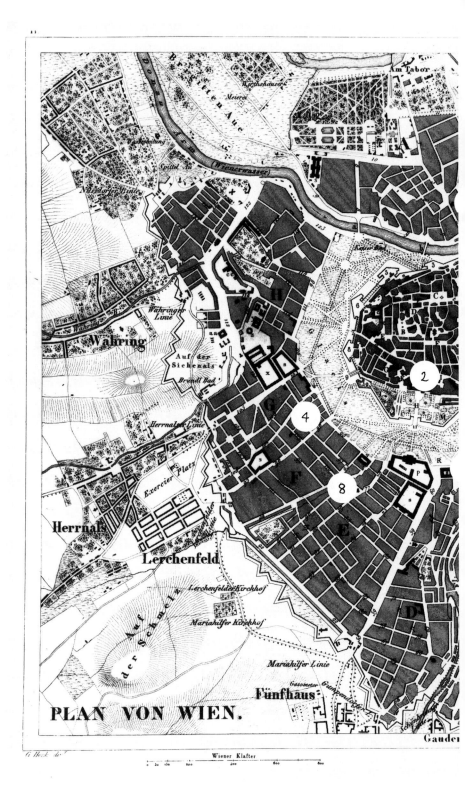

PLAN VON WIEN.

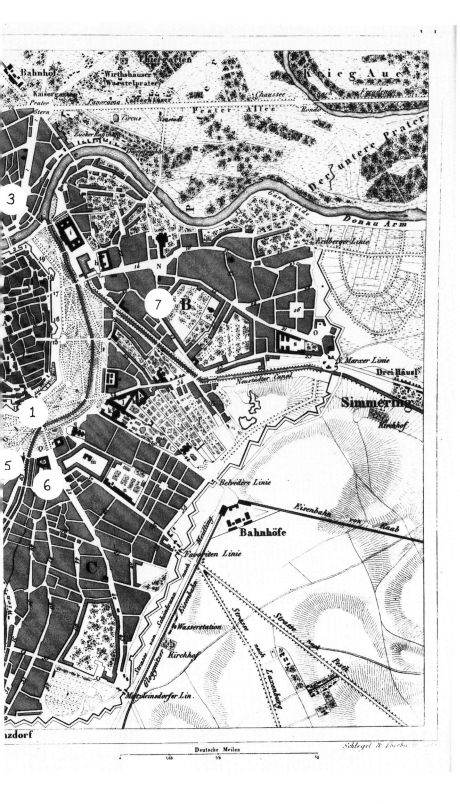

Deutsche Meilen

CHAPTER I

The establishment of the 'city of theatre'

I. THE TWO THEATRES IN THE CENTRE

The history of theatre in Vienna goes back a long way before 1776, but the date has passed into legend, celebrated in the centennial jubilees beloved of Austrian institutions. Its significance lies in two decrees that Joseph II, the reforming Emperor, issued on 23 March 1776 in an autograph instruction to the Master of the Imperial Household (*Obersthofmeister*), Johann Josef Fürst Khevenhüller-Metsch. One decree elevated one of the two court theatres to the status of a 'National Theatre'; the other, still more important, broke the monopoly hitherto enjoyed by the court theatres by establishing a new 'liberty for theatre' (*Spektakelfreiheit* or *Schauspielfreiheit*). This permitted the building of new play-houses outside the walled city centre and so paved the way for the flowering of Viennese theatre in the early nineteenth century. Both measures had their rationale in the cultural politics of the Enlightenment.

As a consequence partly of the Thirty Years War, partly of the fragmentation of the political map, the history of the stage in the German-speaking countries lagged behind that in France and England. Heinrich Laube, the most distinguished director of the Burgtheater in the second half of the nineteenth century, traced the idea of an 'educated' German theatre back to about 1730, when Gottsched's reforms enjoyed the support of Caroline Neuber's company in Leipzig.[1] But it was later still, in the 1760s and 1770s, that the first public theatres were founded in the German-speaking cities. Until then, most theatrical entertainments throughout German-speaking Europe took place either in court theatres or on the (often temporary) stages where itinerant troupes performed. The court theatres were often manned by Italian or French companies, and though the itinerant troupes performed in German, many of the works they acted were translated and adapted from other languages.

The theatrical life of Vienna had gone its own way since the Counter-Reformation, and in particular it had been spared the reforms that had taken place in Protestant Germany. Nevertheless, both court and popular traditions were strongly represented there. It had been one of the great European centres of court entertainments since the age of the Baroque. These had mainly been of Italian origin, with French comedy added in the eighteenth century. When Hofmannsthal has the Marschallin in the first act of *Der Rosenkavalier* receive an Italian tenor at her *levée*, that is an authentic reflection of the cultural and especially operatic flavour of mid-eighteenth-century taste.

The most famous of all the productions for festive occasions at court was Cesti's *Il pomo d'oro* (1668), one of the most lavish examples of Baroque opera in Europe, which was organized as part of the festivities celebrating the marriage in 1666 of Leopold I to Margarita Teresia, the younger daughter of Philip IV of Spain. The elaborate décor was by Lodovico Ottavio Burnacini, the libretto by Francesco Sbarra. The subject, the mythological Judgement of Paris, was tailored to the occasion: the Prologue ended with a celebration of Leopold as a victorious warrior, with the stage surmounted by La Gloria Austriaca borne by Pegasus; the conclusion of the opera twisted the traditional story to allow Jupiter to bestow the prize on the new Empress.[2] What ceremonial allegories of this kind lacked was comedy. In general, however, comic interludes were an integral part of operatic entertainment at court, and survived until about 1720. They centred on vulgar comic servants who bore Italian names but were descended from the comic figures of the German stage (the drama of the so-called *Englische Komödianten* of the seventeenth century) rather than from the *commedia dell'arte*. As late as 1792 Christian Gottlob Klemm, a playwright in Vienna, would stress how much of an advantage it was for the Viennese theatre that its comic figures were variants of an indigenous type belonging to the German-language theatre and not imported from Italian or French tradition.[3]

The production of *Il pomo d'oro* took place in a wooden opera house which Leopold I had had specially built by Burnacini on the Cortina, south-east of the Schweizerhof tract of the imperial palace (*Hofburg*), adjoining where the Josefsplatz now is. Half a century later

Lady Mary Wortley Montagu reported another operatic production in the Baroque tradition. The work was Johann Joseph Fux's *Angela Vincitrice di Alcina*, which she attended in 1716 in the gardens of the Favorita, the summer palace of Emperor Karl VI (on the site of what is now the Theresianum, in the fourth district of the city). The décor was by the celebrated Italian stage-designer Giuseppe Galli-Bibiena, and the report Lady Mary gave in one of her letters to Pope stresses the expensiveness and ingenuity of the scenic effects and the opulence of the costumes:

Nothing of that kind ever was more magnificent; and I can easily believe what I am told, that the decorations and habits cost the emperor thirty thousand pounds sterling. The stage was built over a very large canal, and, at the beginning of the second act, divided into two parts, discovering the water, on which there immediately came, from different parts, two fleets of little gilded vessels, that gave the representation of a naval fight. It is not easy to imagine the beauty of this scene, which I took particular notice of. But all the rest were perfectly fine in their kind. The story of the opera is the Enchantments of Alcina, which gives opportunity for a great variety of machines, and changes of the scene, which are performed with a surprising swiftness. The theatre is so large, that it is hard to carry the eye to the end of it; and the habits in the utmost magnificence, to the number of one hundred and eight. No house could hold such large decorations . . .[4]

The love of festivity on special occasions would never die in Vienna. Even in the commercial theatres of the early nineteenth century, which catered for a much humbler public, the enterprising director of the Theater an der Wien, Karl Carl, mounted a gala evening in March 1832 to celebrate the fortieth anniversary of the Emperor's accession, and followed it up the following year with a 'carnival' evening, for which the theatre was specially decorated and brilliantly illuminated with Argand lamps (the paraffin lamps that were the normal form of theatre lighting until they were gradually superseded by gaslight in the mid nineteenth century).

Lady Mary Wortley Montagu also visited a performance by the distant antecedents of Carl's company, the troupe led by Joseph Anton Stranitzky. This company had begun as one of many bands of strolling players which had visited Vienna regularly from the mid seventeenth century onwards. They enjoyed the facility of a permanent theatre, probably from the end of 1710. This was the Theater nächst dem Kärntnertor (Kärntnertortheater for short), which had been built by the city of Vienna close by the city wall and had opened on 30 November 1709, originally occupied by Italian players. Stranitzky's company performed blood-and-thunder dramas interspersed with short songs and interludes of broad comedy. These *Haupt- und Staatsaktionen* followed what by international standards was a primitive formula, and the scripts left room for comic extemporization. From those that survive (probably about a quarter of Stranitzky's repertoire) we know that the subjects included popular German material (e.g. a play on the damnation of Faust) but that most were derived from Italian opera. Stranitzky simplified the libretto texts and reduced the arias, though music, including ballet, remained an important element; indeed the 'good music' of his troupe was one of the factors advanced in 1709 by the Lower Austrian government in favour of according him the lease of the theatre.[5]

The principal appeal of his company to the Viennese public, however, lay in its comedy, which centred on the traditional German comic figure Hanswurst, played by Stranitzky himself in a stage version of a Salzburg peasant costume. The play that Lady Mary Wortley Montagu visited in 1716 was *Amphitruo*, which 'began', so she told Pope, 'with Jupiter's falling in love out of a peep-hole in the clouds, and ended with the birth of Hercules' but turned on the comic use made of Jupiter's metamorphosis. Her letter protests her shock at the vulgarity of the production ('I could not easily pardon the liberty the poet has taken of larding his play not only with indecent expressions, but such gross words as I don't think our mob would suffer from a mountebank'); but in view of the language barrier this may be taken with a pinch of salt. What her letter does not leave any doubt about is the entertainment value of the performance:

They have but one playhouse, where I had the curiosity to go to a German comedy, and was very glad it happened to be the story of Amphitrion, that subject having been already handled by a Latin, French, and English poet, I was curious to see what an Austrian author would make of it ... The way is, to take a box, which holds four, for yourself and company. The fixed price is a gold ducat. I thought the house very low and dark; but I confess, the comedy admirably recompensed that defect. I never laughed so much in my life.[6]

After Stranitzky's death in 1726 leadership of the company passed to Gottfried Prehauser, who also acted the Hanswurst role; later a rivalry developed between Prehauser and Joseph Felix von Kurz, who played another servant figure, Bernardon, in burlesque musical plays combining comedy with pantomime effects using allegorical figures, an inheritance from Baroque theatre tradition. For at least one of the thirteen Bernardon plays that have survived, *Der neue Krumme Teufel*,[7] it is known that the music was composed by Haydn. Another play, *Bernardon der dreißigjährige ABC-Schütz* (the text of which is lost), is an example of how such material lived on in the dialect theatre: adapted by later playwrights, first Karl Friedrich Hensler and then Friedrich Hopp, for a different comic figure, under the title *Thaddädl der dreißigjährige ABC-Schütz*, it was still playing in the Theater in der Leopoldstadt, with Nestroy in the main role, in the 1840s. Another work, the parody *Bernardon die Getreue Prinzeßin Pumphia*, published with a preface stressing its theatrical character and praising the skill of Prehauser's company (see document 1, p. 246), is an important forerunner of the tradition of parody in the nineteenth-century commercial theatres.

For whereas in Germany Harlequin as the representative of extemporized comedy was ceremonially 'banished' from the stage in 1737, in Vienna extemporization survived in the Kärntnertortheater until the 1770s, and far from dying out, the popular comedy associated with Hanswurst was able to move its base after 1776 to the new theatres built in the districts outside the walls. This whole tradition of vernacular entertainment was to become the most distinctive element of the theatrical culture of Vienna. The Kärntnertortheater was indeed long known as the 'German theatre' ('deutsches Theater'), by contrast with the court theatre attached to the imperial palace (Hofburgtheater), where in the mid eighteenth century the programme consisted of Italian opera and French drama.

This theatre is generally referred to for short as the Burgtheater, and that is the term I shall use. Its function as a court theatre was to provide entertainment for what, by contrast with the states in Protestant Germany, was a multinational court; hence the long-established dominance of Italian opera in the repertory. There had been a succession of theatres in the complex of the imperial palace since the mid seventeenth century. After one new theatre had burnt down in 1699 – the first of many fires that would feature significantly in the history of Viennese theatre – Emperor Joseph I had a big court theatre rapidly built by Francesco Galli-Bibiena, with two halls (one for operatic festivities, the other for Italian players and

Singspiele); this lasted till the 1740s, when the halls were turned into ballrooms. (Opened in 1748, these *Redoutensäle* survived until November 1992, when they too burned down.) In the meantime, Maria Theresia had granted Joseph Carl Selliers, one of the directors of the Kärntnertortheater, permission to build, at his own cost, a theatre in an indoor tennis-court (*Ballhaus*) attached to the palace. In March 1741 Selliers was given a contract to perform Italian operas in both theatres, with the Burgtheater earmarked for a double existence as opera-house and playhouse (*Opern- und Comoedienhaus*). The new *Comoedienhauß nechst der Königlichen Burg* opened in 1742, but it posed financial problems for successive licensees. In 1759 Maria Theresia sanctioned the opening of a casino in a new building alongside the auditorium: this made a regular profit, and it may be that the nobility were deflected from the theatre by gambling. (The same year the seating for the 'common people' in the pit was enlarged.) The theatre was reconstructed and extended several times, notably in 1748, in 1759-60 (when it was given a new façade on the Michaelerplatz and the stage area was substantially enlarged), in 1779, and again in 1794. The reconstructions in 1759 and 1779 established what would roughly remain the (rather barn-like) shape of the theatre until 1888. The original adaptation of the indoor tennis-court produced a narrow and high theatre (it was about 25.5 metres long, 10.4 metres wide, and 13 metres high); by 1748 the length was increased to 38 metres (the auditorium alone had a length of over 22 metres), the width to 15.2 metres. It protruded on to the Michaelerplatz at the stage end (see plate 1). Estimates of the capacity vary: there were boxes for members of the court and for their attendants; there were benches in the stalls and in the uppermost gallery (known in Vienna at this time, as in Paris, as 'paradise', a close equivalent to the English 'gods'); and there was also standing room. The most careful calculation based on the data for 1774 is that the auditorium may have held about 1350, with about 130 of the seats, according to the previous season's figures, committed to complimentary tickets.[8] The theatre was by no means always full: indeed, it has been calculated that in the mid 1770s, before Joseph II's reforms, the average audience was only about a fifth of the total capacity.[9] There were seasonal variations; in 1768 Joseph von Sonnenfels recorded that spring and summer were less favourable times for the theatre than autumn and winter, and that in winter the best period was Fasching (the weeks of carnival preceding Lent).[10] Seasonal

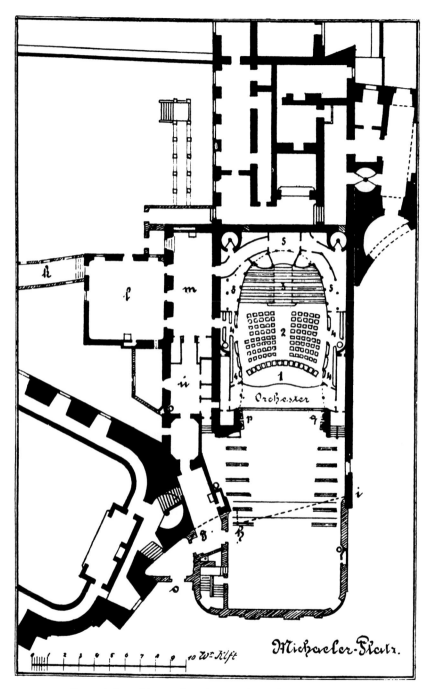

1 Ground plan of the old Burgtheater, drawn by Franz Segenschmid.

discrepancies of that kind were not peculiar to the eighteenth-century Burgtheater: in 1823, for example, the director of the court theatres, Count Dietrichstein, pointed them out to the then Emperor, and takings in the Wiener Stadttheater in 1878 show a similiar pattern, with the figures for May, June, and September (the theatre was closed in July and August) less than half of those for the other months.[11] The problem may, however, have been particularly intractable in the Burgtheater because the atmosphere tended to be stuffy, so that the audience in the upper galleries were glad when the annual six-week break was moved from Lent to summer in 1786. Nevertheless the narrowness of the theatre produced a distinctive atmosphere, facilitating a sense of close contact between the stage and audience which would eventually underlie the characteristic style the company developed in the nineteenth century.

2. ENLIGHTENMENT REFORM

The battle over extemporization, sparked off at least as much by the popularity of Bernardon as by Prehauser's Hanswurst but never-theless generally called the *Hanswurststreit*, was fought out in Vienna in the period 1748–70. The move to suppress extemporized comedy in favour of controlled performance of written comedy was part of the same process of enlightened despotism that also saw the introduc-tion in 1751 of a centralized system of censorship for printed books. At the same time, the *Hanswurststreit* was both a sign of growing interest in the theatre and a stimulus for progress. With the exception of the work of one gifted playwright, Philipp Hafner, the popular drama of the dialect stage was still crude in mid-century, and this underlined the need for reform in the spirit of the Enlightenment. Hafner was not a supporter of extemporization, the unpredictability and potential vacuity of which he satirized in a parody of a scenario,[12] but he was very much a theatrical dramatist, opposed to the tyranny of literary theorists. He died after only two years' writing for the stage, and his total output was only eight plays, but in adaptations by Joachim Perinet some of them continued to be performed until the mid nineteenth century. In works like the satirical *Die bürgerliche Dame*, about a bourgeois woman who gives herself aristocratic airs, the lighter *Etwas zum Lachen im Fasching*, centring on a loose-living philanderer (both of which contain roles for Hanswurst), and the parody *Evakathel und Schnudi*, a burlesque of bombastic tragedy, Hafner anticipated important strands in the later development of Viennese popular drama, though his achievement as one of its founding fathers was recognized only when Grillparzer's uncle, Joseph Sonnleithner, published an edition of his works in 1812.

The reformers were led by the influential Joseph von Sonnenfels, who was appointed the first professor of cameralistics in the University of Vienna in 1763 and also engaged actively in journalistic debate from the mid-1760s. It was his *Briefe über die wienerische Schaubühne* (1768) that brought the controversy to a head. Sonnenfels's instincts were inevitably moulded by French models, but his aim, in keeping with parallel developments in Germany, was to establish in Vienna a legitimate German-language drama, cleansed of vulgarities (at the end of the *Briefe über die wienerische Schaubühne* he makes clear that he saw the death of Prehauser as presenting a particularly favourable opportunity for reform),[13] and without the artificialities of the foreign plays associated with the court theatre.

In 1761, in the middle of the dispute, the Kärntnertortheater was destroyed by fire, and as a consequence the German actors were temporarily housed in the Burgtheater. This makeshift arrangement opened up the possibility of consolidating the two theatres, and the site of the Kärntnertortheater was bought from the city. In the event Maria Theresia had the theatre rebuilt by Nikolaus Pacassi as an opera house and reopened in July 1763, in a form nearly identical to that of the previous building, with seats on five floors; but from this point on, both theatres, though often leased to private directors, were court property, subject to strict supervision in keeping with the aesthetics and the pedagogic idealism of the reformers. No longer was the theatre perceived as serving the glory of the ruler and the amusement of the populace; rather its function was specifically that of enlightenment. The intention to educate and improve necessitated strict control of the repertoire, so that, as Sonnenfels put it in his *Grundsätze der Polizey, Handlung und Finanzwissenschaft* (1765–7), plays might become a 'school of manners, courtesy, and language' ('eine Schule der Sitten, der Höflichkeit und Sprache').[14]

For the same pedagogic reason censorship was extended in 1770 to the theatre and extemporization banned. Joseph II's definition of the function of the censor was based on a memorandum written by Sonnenfels, who was himself briefly appointed censor in 1770. The responsibility of the censor was to exclude from the stage everything 'that offends in the slightest against religion, the state, or good manners, all obvious nonsense and coarseness, that is, everything unworthy of a capital city and the seat of a court'.[15] The principle that censorship was essentially intended to make the theatre conform to Enlightenment values in respect both of moral standards and of aesthetics was most fully set out in a long memorandum written in 1795 by Franz Karl Hägelin, who worked as a censor from October 1770 (when he succeeded Sonnenfels) to December 1804. The memorandum was drawn up for the guidance of censors in Hungary, and defined the theatre as being intended to function as 'a school of manners and taste'.[16] The story of how censorship, intended as an instrument of Enlightenment principles, became a political device used to suppress Enlightenment ideas, will be pursued in Chapter 2.

Another measure for which Sonnenfels argued in his *Briefe über die wienerische Schaubühne* was the establishment of a 'national theatre' (*Nationalschaubühne*). The immediate model was the Hamburg theatre, founded in 1767; it was from Hamburg that Friedrich Ludwig Schröder came to the Burgtheater in 1781, bringing with him his interest in Shakespeare adaptations. But the idea was generally in the air; a 'national theatre' was also opened in Mannheim in 1779. These theatres were conceived as being financed out of state or court funds, even if that was not always maintained, and were under state or court authority. In Mannheim, where the repertory centred on sentimental plays by Iffland and Kotzebue, and Iffland was also the principal actor till 1796 (when he went to Berlin to manage the 'National Theatre' there), what can be seen is in fact the beginnings of middle-class commercial theatre in Germany. The ultimate exemplar of the true 'national theatre' idea was in fact the Comédie-Française in Paris, which had been established as long ago as 1680, and which would remain the yardstick of achievement even for Laube in the mid nineteenth century.[17]

The idea took hold in the 1770s for three main reasons. First, the development of an educated bourgeoisie had produced a need for permanent theatres in the big towns, which could appeal to the whole community (unlike court theatres which supported foreign companies) while also offering fare superior to the crude entertainment of the touring companies. Secondly, the perceived need was for non-commercial (that is, subsidized) theatres, in keeping with the Enlightenment aim of cultural education. And thirdly, this cultural intention had a political subtext, in the spirit of cultural nationalism, namely, the improvement of the German *Kulturnation* by the promotion of German plays, and also by the systematic training of actors, improving their conduct and raising the status of the acting profession. The fundamental rationale, then, of the idea of a more literary theatre for a middle-class audience, essentially divorcing non-court theatre from commercial considerations, was driven by social and educational politics, though economic and financial factors also played a considerable part in every practical realization of the idea.

In Vienna, the element of cultural nationalism was an important factor. In the years 1752–72, the repertory of the Burgtheater had been dominated by French drama and *opéra comique*; the Kärntnertortheater was still the 'German theatre'. But in 1762 Gluck's *Orfeo ed Euridice* was given its première in the Burgtheater; and five years later, after a long closure following the death of Emperor Franz I, the first production after the reopening was Gluck's *Alceste*, which was enthusiastically reviewed in Sonnenfels's *Briefe über die wienerische Schaubühne*.[18] It was an important advance in the whole programme of cultural reform, Sonnenfels stressing that the principal singer was German; it was followed rapidly by the ousting of French drama from the Burgtheater, where the Hamburg experiment and the theoretical reflections in Lessing's *Hamburgische Dramaturgie* had created a climate suitable for creating a 'national' theatre playing literary drama written in German.

When the post of *Musikgraf*, effectively responsible for the administration of court entertainments, fell vacant in 1772, the duties were assumed by the elderly Khevenhüller, who served as *Obersthofmeister* from 1769 to 1776. Khevenhüller, whose diaries would later form one of the principal sources for the libretto of *Der Rosenkavalier*, was unable to devote himself to the theatre, and Joseph II seized the opportunity to intervene personally, with the support of his mother, the Empress Maria Theresia, until her death in 1780. After Khevenhüller's death in April 1776, the theatre was administered under the authority of the court chamberlain (*Oberstkämmerer*), Franz Xaver Wolf Graf Rosenberg-Orsini; but Joseph II himself remained actively involved in overseeing its policies and direction.

The timing of the 1776 decrees was determined partly by the growing discontent of theatre audiences, and partly by financial pressure resulting from unsatisfactory management by the lessees of the two existing court theatres. The decrees led to a reorganization of the theatres, with the German players to play in the Burgtheater. Joseph's memorandum to Khevenhüller dated 23 March 1776 bestowed on the Burgtheater the title 'German National Theatre' ('das Theater nächst der Burg, so hinführo das teutsche National Theater heißen solle').[19] Joseph was no doubt driven to choose the term 'national theatre' partly because the most obvious alternative, 'German theatre' ('deutsches Theater'), was associated with the Kärntnertortheater; but introducing the title 'das teutsche National Theater' carried with it two clear implications.

First, it signalled Joseph's reformist intentions: the theatre should function as a national theatre in the Enlightenment sense, moving away from what had been a predominantly French repertory. Joseph kept abreast with developments in Hamburg; in September 1776 he sent a senior member of the Burgtheater company, Johann Heinrich Friedrich Müller, on a four-month mission to Hamburg and other North German cities. Müller's journey is documented in a record which he published in 1802. His brief was not only to report on the leading German companies but also explicitly to secure the engagement of actors to strengthen the Burgtheater company, which at the time numbered only twenty-two.

Secondly, more pragmatically, the German players were the least costly to maintain, and the Burgtheater was the less costly of the two theatres; although a clear separation of opera and spoken drama had to wait till 1810, by choosing the Burgtheater as his 'national theatre' Joseph II removed from his purse the most costly enterprises, including both ballet and Italian opera. Of these considerations the financial one was the more pressing; indeed, the title 'Nationaltheater' was ephemeral (it was no longer being used consistently by as early as 1780).

Artistically, the new developments brought changes (some of them short-lived) and also problems of adjustment. Partly because the Burgtheater was physically a lower building and more intimate in atmosphere than the Kärntnertortheater, the 'German players' had difficulties in adjusting (just as there would be difficulties in adjusting to a larger and *less* intimate house in 1888); what became known as the characteristic Burgtheater style was eventually formed by incomers, in particular by performers who came to Vienna with experience in Hamburg behind them: Johanna Sacco, whose appearance in the Burgtheater in June 1776 in Beaumarchais's *Eugénie*, according to Müller, gave the theatre 'new impetus'; Franz Hieronymus Brockmann, who had been the primary target of Müller's visit to Hamburg;[20] and then Schröder, who first appeared in the Burgtheater as a guest star in April 1780 in *King Lear* and who was regarded as the leading representative of the modern theatre of enlightened Germany. The acquisition of Schröder and his wife in 1781 amounted to a programmatic commitment to reform, and it is revealing that the terms of their contract provided for a salary twice that of Sacco, who had hitherto been the main star attraction.[21] The company was organized on democratic lines (the so-called '*Wahlsystem*'), with the artistic management in the hands of a committee of five who were elected annually from the company and whose rights included the selection of the repertory. This system, enlightened in theory, produced conflict and lack of discipline in practice, and was ended by the Emperor in 1789, when Brockmann assumed sole charge of the artistic management.[22]

Hiving off the Kärntnertortheater also proved problematic, and Joseph II decided in 1785 to return it to court administration. The purely German repertory in the Burgtheater lasted even less long. By June 1776, Italian opera was back, and so by July was ballet; that is, the theatre in effect retained the mixed repertory of a traditional court theatre. More long-lasting was a prohibition on curtain-calls; this, however, was not a product of idealism but was related to the status of actors as officials. (For similar reasons a playwright such as Grillparzer, who earned his living mainly as a minor civil servant, was unable to appear on stage to accept applause for his plays in the nineteenth century.) The ban on curtain-calls for actors in the Burgtheater became a strong tradition, and was indeed ended only in the 1980s.

The repertory in the late 1770s was still extremely limited, especially in respect of modern plays. The same principles that informed the censorship laws cast a heavy shadow. Even Lessing's *Nathan der Weise*, one of the great classics of the Enlightenment spirit, which was published in 1779 and first performed in Berlin in 1783, was not seen in Vienna until 1819, and even then only in a bowdlerized version. Shakespeare evenings were rare; *Romeo and Juliet*, which was produced in Weisse's adaptation, was given only two performances in 1776 because Maria Theresia did not wish to have plays performed which featured deaths and funerals.[23] The following year the theatre received a formal instruction in similar terms, informing it that Joseph II did not wish to see plays in which funerals, cemeteries, graves, and similar sad scenes occurred, and specifying that on these terms *Romeo and Juliet* would have to be 'forbidden for ever'.[24] It was not till the early 1780s, under Schröder, that the basis of a standard repertory began to be established, a tradition to be strengthened in the early nineteenth century when Joseph Schreyvogel built up an international repertory.

In 1778, however, Joseph II established in the Burgtheater a German 'national *Singspiel*', a programme which was inaugurated in February 1778 with Ignaz Umlauff's one-act *Die Bergknappen*[25] and directed from 1779 by Gottlieb Stephanie ('the younger'). This was a time of excitement in the musical theatre; it was on 4 July 1781 that Mozart wrote to his sister that the theatre was his 'sole entertainment',[26] and the creation of the 'national *Singspiel*' led directly to the commissioning of *Die Entführung aus dem Serail*, with a libretto by Stephanie (première 1782). But partly because the available performers were essentially singers as opposed to actors able to sing, and partly because of the taste of the predominantly aristocratic audience, the *Singspiel* proved unable to hold its own against the Italian operatic style. Italian *opera buffa* was restored to supremacy from 1783, and though the 'national *Singspiel*' was reopened in the Kärntnertortheater in 1787, there too it lasted only a year. A similar pattern continued under Emperor Leopold II in 1790–2. Dittersdorf, it is true, achieved some successes in the German idiom, with texts by Stephanie; but in the court theatres all the major premières were in the Italian idiom: *The Marriage of Figaro* (1786), which did nothing to dissuade Joseph II from his view that Mozart's music was too difficult for performance,[27] *Così fan tutte* (1790), Cimarosa's *Il matrimonio segreto* (1792).

This is a fair reflection of the balance of power between the rival idioms; German opera tradition was in effect banished to the commercial theatres. From the mid-1790s *Singspiele* began to reappear, with Franz Xaver Süssmayr celebrated as 'the second Mozart';[28] but in the main Salieri (court composer since 1774) effectively continued to dominate operatic taste for the best part of three decades until his withdrawal from the stage in 1804. (It was at that time that Joseph Weigl began to enjoy a series of successes with *Singspiele* in the vernacular.)

Despite the victory of Italian opera over the notion of a 'national *Singspiel*', the organization of theatrical life as a whole was still informed by the same Enlightenment ideals of cultural nationalism and of aesthetic and moral education as had been implicit in the foundation of a 'national theatre'. The criteria enshrined in the

conception of the theatre as 'a school of manners and taste' had
inhibiting effects on the repertory. That the one avant-garde play
produced under Joseph II, Klinger's *Die Zwillinge*, was forbidden
after a single performance is indicative of the obstacles in the way of
original German pieces; even Kotzebue and Iffland became stock
features of the repertory only later. In general, the standard of acting
was ahead of the quality of the repertoire. This had the effect of
establishing an order of priorities that long remained distinctively
characteristic of the expectations of the Viennese theatre public, in
that what was regarded as being of prime interest and importance
was not the play but the actor. Writing as late as 1907, Max
Burckhard, director of the Burgtheater in the 1890s, was still
categorical that in the theatre interest centres not on the dramatist
but on the performer.[29] Moreover, from the engagement in 1776 of
Johanna Sacco, who specialized in comedy, a style developed in the
Burgtheater which favoured not declamation but rather a more
conversational naturalness. In 1779 the idiom appropriate to comedy
was defined as a language drawn from Nature, but not from the
common mob.[30] Actors expected to model their bearing, too, on fine
society,[31] and so began another tradition: the Burgtheater became a
model of manners. The theatre imitated society; society in turn
imitated the theatre.

3. THE FIRST COMMERCIAL THEATRES

Until 1776, the lessees of the two court theatres held exclusive licences
for all public entertainments, including masked balls and firework
displays as well as theatrical performances. Any one else wanting to
mount an occasional entertainment required their permission and
had to pay a licence fee. The effective monopoly functioned as a
form of compensation for the losses sustained by the lessees as a
result of the court hold over their operations – allocations of free
boxes, for example, and days of enforced closure for reasons of state.
The *Spektakelfreiheit* declared by Joseph II established a new freedom,
for those deemed suitable, to provide entertainments both within the
walled city and outside it, subject only to permission from the police,
who came under the jurisdiction of the administration of Lower
Austria. Responding to one application for permission to perform in
the districts outside the walls, Joseph II confirmed that the 'liberty'

had been granted 'permanently for the pleasure of the public' ('auf beständig für des Publici Ergötzung ertheilet').[32]

The effect was not just a boom in occasional entertainments in taverns and halls but the foundation of the first private (that is, commercial) theatres in Vienna. There had been a small wooden theatre on the outskirts of the city, in Penzing, near Schönbrunn, from 1770, where performances were given from time to time by a number of companies until the early 1780s. (There would be other small theatres in Penzing from 1792 to 1804.) Penzing lay beyond the outer ring of fortifications (*Linienwälle*) which demarcated the limits of Vienna proper; what now sprang up was a series of new foundations in districts within the city limits, between the outer fortifications and the walled city centre.

The first was in the Neustift district in 1776, the theatre 'Zum Weißen Fasan', which opened in 1776 and despite its distance from the centre survived (albeit with interruptions) for nearly twenty years, with an erratic programme, from high drama and *Singspiel* down to crude popular comedy. In a way typical of these small theatres, a whole gallery of names were associated with it, mostly briefly. These included the dramatist Franz Xaver Karl Gewey, who headed a company of amateurs in 1781; an experienced director, Georg Wilhelm, who moved in that same autumn, remained there till 1786, with a company including at one stage Anton Hasenhut, later a very popular comic actor, and returned in 1790–1 with a programme of variable quality centring on *Singspiele*; Karl Mayer, later director of the Theater in der Josefstadt, whose company took over the Fasantheater in the autumn of 1786; and Franz Scherzer, a native Viennese, whose company had played in Penzing in 1776 and appeared briefly in the Fasantheater in 1794.

Other theatres followed: in 1781 in the Leopoldstadt district, in 1783 in Mariahilf, in 1787 in Wieden, in 1788 in the Josefstadt, in 1790 in Landstrasse, and in 1792 in Rossau. Of these, three were of long-lasting importance: Karl Marinelli's Theater in der Leopold-stadt, the theatre founded in the Freihaus near the River Wien, and the Theater in der Josefstadt.

The entrepreneurs concerned were granted 'privileges' (patents) which specified certain exclusions, including the performance both of ballets and of operas in foreign languages. That is, performances in German were promoted and the two court theatres were protected, especially in respect of musical productions. At the same time, the continued Enlightenment emphasis on education and taste in the court theatres meant that responsibility for providing entertainment (not just for the poorer classes) fell mainly on the commercial theatres, where the dialect comedy inherited from the old 'German theatre' took root. In the course of Sonnenfels's reforms extemporization had disappeared, but the new commercial theatres were subject to continued official watchfulness. That they were 'privileged' and supervised meant that they were much more part of the cultural establishment than the itinerant players of the mid-to-late eighteenth century; but they did not succumb to the main danger inherent in the supervision imposed by enlightened despotism, the danger that drama could become an instrument of the state; for in Viennese dialect drama there was always a tendency towards irony, even satire: this is the mode adopted by Hafner, which lived on later in Kringsteiner and Meisl.

The oldest of the main commercial theatres was that in the Leopoldstadt, a district separated from the city centre by an artificially regulated arm of the Danube (the so-called 'Danube Canal'). In 1780 Karl Marinelli, who had been a member since 1761 of a touring troupe that played regularly in Vienna, applied for permission to build a theatre there. It opened on 20 October 1781, and was under his sole direction from 1783 until his death in 1803. In large part, as was usually the case, the company was drawn from interrelated families, supplemented by various recruits from outside. These included Hasenhut, who joined in 1787 and made his name in the role of a childishly comic figure, Thaddädl. But the most important comic figure was Kasperl, a character descended directly from Hanswurst and played by Johann Laroche (or La Roche). Laroche, who had played in Vienna since 1769, was the cornerstone of the Leopoldstadt company from the foundation of the theatre in 1781 onwards. Other members engaged by Marinelli included the composer Wenzel Müller (1786), the prolific dramatists Hensler (1786) and Perinet (1790), and the actor Ignaz Schuster (1801). Müller and Perinet specialized in *Singspiele*, Hensler and Schuster in local comedy – the two genres that formed the mainstays of the repertoire. Perinet provided parts for Kasperl in comedy partly based on Hafner, with *Singspiel* elements; the best-known of his *Singspiele* was *Kaspar der Fagottist*, which was first performed on 8 June 1791 and was probably based on one of the same sources as *Die Zauberflöte* (produced just under four months later, at the rival Freihaustheater).[33] The form later developed into a musical fairy-tale, e.g. the two parts of Hensler's *Das Donauweibchen* (1798), based on a local version of the Melusina legend, with music by Ferdinand Kauer. *Das Donauweibchen* was performed all over German-speaking Europe and long remained popular in Vienna – Nestroy played the central comic role of 'Kaspar Larifari' in the Theater an der Wien as late as 1835. It also had numerous sequels, the most successful – also containing a part for Laroche – being Hensler's *Die Teufelsmühle am Wienerberg* (1799), with music by the prolific Wenzel Müller, who enjoyed sustained popular success and would later compose for Raimund also.

What was distinctive about the Theater in der Leopoldstadt was that it maintained a popular character, and never attempted rivalry with the court theatres. Hence its uniqueness as the quintessential popular theatre of Vienna, which enjoyed a European reputation for comedy: as late as 1837 Murray's *Handbook for Travellers in Southern Germany* reported that it was still 'the true national theatre of Austria'.[34]

The Freihaustheater auf der Wieden was founded by Christian Rossbach, an itinerant player who came originally from Fulda but who had been in Vienna since 1778. He received permission to open a theatre in the Freihaus, a large complex near the right bank of the River Wien – 'the biggest tenement house of Vienna'[35] –, from its owner, Prince Starhemberg, in 1787; he applied for an official concession that February, received it from the Lower Austrian authorities on 16 March, and the theatre opened on 14 October 1787. It was 15 m. wide, with a stage 12 m. deep; its capacity was about 1,000, similar to that of the Theater in der Leopoldstadt. (Both theatres were larger than the Theater in der Josefstadt.) Rossbach was succeeded in March 1788 by Johann Friedel, and after Friedel's death the following year by Eleonore Schikaneder, whose husband Emanuel had in February 1786 already received imperial permission to build a theatre beyond the green belt of open land that separated the city centre from the *Vorstädte* beyond it. The Schikaneder era began in July 1789 with a performance of *Der dumme Gärtner aus dem Gebirge oder Die zween Anton*, centring on a comic role played by Schikaneder himself, a counterpart to the Kasperl of the Leopoldstadt. (Unfortunately the texts of Schikaneder's seven 'Anton' plays have not survived.) In November there followed an opera, *Oberon, König der Elfen*, drawn from Wieland. The major successes in the theatre were headed by *Die Zauberflöte*, Mozart's last opera, with a libretto by Schikaneder himself. There being no prospect of preferment for Mozart under Leopold II, the work was composed specifically for Schikaneder's company (he himself played the main comic part, Papageno); the première took place on 30 September 1791, and it was performed no fewer than 223 times between 1791 and the closure of the theatre in 1801. The next most successful production was Schikaneder's *Der Tiroler Wastel*, a musical play contrasting city ways with those of the country, which was given 118 performances from 1796 onwards; other major additions to the repertoire included another *Singspiel* with a libretto by Schikaneder, *Der Spiegel von Arkadien* (1794), the music for which was by Süssmayr.

The Theater in der Josefstadt, though it has twice been substantially rebuilt, is the only one of the eighteenth-century foundations that still stands on its original site. Its early history was not, however, very distinguished. Karl Mayer, whose company had appeared in the Fasantheater in Neustift in 1786–7, retained the licence (*Privileg*) from 1788 until 1830; but throughout that period it functioned for the most part as a 'feeder' for the other two commercial theatres.

Of the shorter-lasting foundations resulting from the *Spektakelfreiheit*, the most ambitious, and the most nearly successful, was the theatre in Landstrasse (the current third district), south-east of the city centre. It was not a heavily populated district, and had no great record of cultural activity; and the theatre itself seems to have been fairly primitive, with most of the seating in the form of benches. Nevertheless, it survived for three and a half years with a mixed programme that spoke eloquently of Enlightenment pretensions. The opening production on 11 April 1790 was Haydn's *La vera constanza*. Drama was provided by the well-known touring company of Franz Scherzer, and opera was organized separately by one of his partners, a man of letters (also well-known), Johann Rautenstrauch. The enterprise was dogged by misfortune from start to finish. The very opening had to be postponed because of the death of Joseph II in 1790. Two years later the death of Leopold II in March 1792 led to a further enforced closure for eight weeks. In 1793 two of the principals died suddenly within four months of each other; and finally a member of the company embezzled the theatre's funds. Nevertheless, under successive partners and directors a programme was offered that included Shakespeare, Goethe, Schiller, Molière, and Kotzebue, and while it was under the management of Josef Kettner, a respected actor, it even attracted a visit from Emperor Leopold II in August 1791.

The 'liberty' lasted only till 1794, when the court theatres were again leased out by Emperor Franz II. The contract went to a banker, Peter von Braun, and stipulated explicitly that no permission would be given for further theatres to be built, either within the city walls or outside them. Braun ran four separate companies: German actors, Italian opera, German *Singspiel*, and ballet, and in the Burgtheater he established the position of literary adviser and *Dramaturg* (*Theatersecretär*), a post to be filled by influential men of letters. The first of these was Johann Baptist von Alxinger, who was appointed in January 1797 but died a few months later. The responsibilities and authority of the position varied over the years. As Alxinger's successor Braun appointed none other than Kotzebue; though he left again at the end of 1798, after his resignation (in December 1798) he was granted a pension of 1,000 fl. per annum, and in return undertook to submit all his new plays to the Burgtheater. The première from this period that is recorded in all the history books is that of the verse version of Goethe's *Iphigenie* in January 1800; but the production was given only three performances. By contrast, no fewer than forty-five of Kotzebue's plays were staged in twelve years, and one in particular, *Die deutschen Kleinstädter* (1802), was to exercise an important influence as the first play set in the fictional small town Krähwinkel, which in the hands of Bäuerle and later of Nestroy would function as a satiric reflection of the capital itself. Kotzebue's successors as *Theatersecretär* included, briefly, Joseph Schreyvogel, who worked in the theatre in 1802–4, and then from 1804 till 1815 Joseph Sonnleithner; but the office became a position of significant influence only when Schreyvogel took it over again in the 1814–15 season.

Braun had extended the seating capacity, adding extra boxes, and had opened his programme on 1 September 1794 with an Iffland comedy, *Die Aussteuer*. By establishing Iffland (who gave visiting performances in 1801 and 1808) and Kotzebue at the heart of the repertory, he laid the foundations for what became one of the distinctive genres of the Burgtheater, the *Konversationsstück*, a kind of comedy of manners in which special weight was placed on the art of social conversation. The cultivation of this type of play depended on a natural style of acting, which from the time of Schröder and Brockmann onwards was regarded as one of the hallmarks of the Burgtheater company and which was further cultivated by later generations of actors, including notably Maximilian Korn in the early nineteenth century. The Emperor so approved Braun's work that he made him a Baron in 1795, and his contract, which was originally for twelve years, was renewed for a further fifteen years in 1804, with the condition preventing the building of new rival theatres repeated. (It lasted in fact till 1806.)

Thereafter (apart from the replacement of the Freihaustheater by the Theater an der Wien in 1801 and the rebuilding of the Leopoldstadt theatre in 1845) there were no new theatres in Vienna until 1860. The building of the Theater an der Wien on a site on the left bank of the River Wien which had been acquired by a businessman, Bartholomäus Zitterbarth, was allowed to go ahead – despite a protest from Braun – because it was regarded not as a new theatre but as a substitute for the Freihaustheater, which was too small for Schikaneder's purposes; indeed Schikaneder took most of his company, including the orchestra, with him. On 12 June the final performance took place in the Freihaustheater, with an afterpiece *Thespis*; the next evening the first performance took place in the new theatre. The main work was again an opera, but to emphasize the seamless continuity between the two houses it was preceded by an introductory piece, *Thespis' Traum*, a continuation of the previous evening's afterpiece. The Theater an der Wien was distinguished by its modernity and its size: Murray's *Handbook for Travellers in Southern Germany* called it 'the largest and most handsome house in Vienna'.[36] Estimates of its capacity vary widely. Including standing room, it may have held over 2,000 (more or less double what it holds today); certainly it was the biggest of all the Viennese theatres until the new Opera House opened in 1869.

Schikaneder's repertoire included operas and dramatic spectaculars, and also comedies, both Viennese and French. His official tenure of the licence passed to Zitterbarth in 1802, but he remained unofficially in charge until February 1804, when Zitterbarth, impoverished by continuing losses from expensive opera productions that failed to appeal to the local public, sold the theatre for one million Gulden to his main competitor, Braun, who was backed financially by the Emperor himself, dealing under a pseudonym.

Under Braun, it was initially Sonnleithner who was in charge. He built links with Beethoven, who indeed lived for a time in the building and was closely linked with it until 1808. A number of Beethoven's works were given their first public performances in the

Theater an der Wien, including the Eroica Symphony in 1805, the violin concerto in 1806, the Fifth Symphony and the Pastoral Symphony in 1808. The most significant in theatrical terms was *Fidelio*, for which Sonnleithner himself provided the libretto and which was first performed on 20 November 1805, shortly after Vienna had fallen to the French. It did not take hold in the repertoire in that version, and underwent two later revisions.

Sonnleithner's direction, plagued by continuing financial problems, lasted only just over six months, whereupon Braun reinstated Schikaneder. Control eventually passed to a group of nine noblemen who had followed the example of the Emperor in taking an interest in the theatre and indeed in art and culture in general. The group was formed in 1806, with a view to taking over monopoly control of the largest theatres. When their negotiations with Braun broke down in August 1806, and Braun declared his intention to close the Theater an der Wien, Franz II himself stepped in, and forbade the closure in an edict of 30 August. He stressed the usefulness of the theatre as a political vent: if the audience were safely being entertained, they could not be on the streets hatching revolution. The Theater an der Wien in particular provided the 'favourite entertainment of the upper and middle classes', and 'even the lower classes' attended it.[37] Nevertheless, the Emperor prudently rejected Braun's suggestion that the theatre should be purchased from court funds.[38] The truth of the matter is that the size of the Theater an der Wien always spelt trouble for its directors. It was difficult to fill, particularly because the commercial theatres drew their audiences largely from the district immediately around them. The bigger the theatre, the more new plays were needed to attract full houses. The problem was spelt out as late as 1847 by a reviewer in one of the Viennese journals (see document 7, p. 249): the Theater an der Wien had been built for opera and spectaculars and had always been too big to function as a true popular stage.

Ownership of the theatre finally passed to the *Gesellschaft der Kavaliere* on 30 December 1806, and their programme began with the new year 1807. The direction of the Burgtheater, the Kärntnertortheater, and the Theater an der Wien was now in the same hands, though individual members of the *Kavaliersdirektion* had responsibility for particular areas. Ferdinand Graf Pálffy von Erdöd, a highranking official in the administration of mining in Hungary and the most significant of those involved, was responsible for spoken drama, and Joseph Fürst Lobkowitz for opera. This part of the story will be taken up again in Chapters 3 and 4.

The history of theatrical performance in eighteenth-century Vienna turns on the contrast in levels between the court theatres (with their strong operatic tradition) and the rough and tumble of the low comedy offered by the German players and institutionalized, following the *Spektakelfreiheit*, in the commercial theatres outside the city walls. The seminal importance of *Die Zauberflöte* in the cultural history of the city lies partly in its expression of the humane idealism of the Josephinian Enlightenment, partly in the fact that in it the two idioms came most completely together, the musical sophistication of the operatic composer blending with the comedy of simple figures rooted in the dialect theatre. Vienna did not produce the kind of politically charged comedy that Beaumarchais provided in pre-revolutionary Paris; it is characteristic that the Viennese work which most fully reflects the humanitarian ideals of Illuminist Freemasonry was not overtly political at all but an opera.

In the decade between its first production in the Freihaustheater and the opening of the Theater an der Wien, the political climate changed: the Austrian response to the revolutionary movement of the 1790s was suppression, notably in the 'Jacobin' trials of 1794–5 and the dissolution of the Masonic Lodges. Until 1848 Austria remained a police state. That the unchanging pattern of five established theatres (see map) was preserved for over half a century, so that despite the proverbial enthusiasm of the Viennese for the theatre, the number of theatres did not increase while the population of the city was doubling, is a reflection of the social conservatism that was imposed under Metternich's régime; it was one of the established facts of Viennese life, and it is in that sense that in 1845 Nestroy included a joking allusion to there being 'five theatres' (and those not always full) in a satirical song in *Unverhofft*.[39] As well as the central strategy of maintaining tight control over public entertainments for political reasons, there were no doubt financial reasons why greater pressure was not generated for an expansion of theatrical provision. These included the economic crisis that induced a state bankruptcy in the second decade of the century, with a massive devaluation of the currency.

The institutional stability provided a basis for the most remarkable half-century of theatre in the history of German-speaking Europe. Throughout that period, though Berlin was growing fast, Vienna was the one metropolitan centre capable of sustaining a lively theatrical culture. The competition and interaction of the two court theatres and the three commercial theatres allowed it to enjoy a paramount position as the principal theatrical centre in the German-speaking countries throughout the first half of the nineteenth century – the theatrical equivalent of the musical golden age associated with the First Viennese School.

CHAPTER 2

Censorship

1. CENSORSHIP UNTIL 1848

From the late eighteenth century onwards, certainly until the end of the Metternich régime in 1848, it was axiomatic that censorship was even more strictly exercised in the theatre than it was on the printed word. This is because performance could make an immediate impact on people of all classes, whereas books were in effect restricted to the educated classes. This general principle was enshrined in Hägelin's 1795 memorandum, and the passage puts the point so clearly that it is worth quoting verbatim. One of Hägelin's considerations is that beside the court theatres there were now other licensed theatres (he uses the revealingly condescending term 'Nebentheater', 'subsidiary theatres'), from which the same standards in taste could not be expected.[1] In that context he spells out, in a passage reproduced on pp. 246–7 (document 2):

It is beyond question that censorship of the theatre must be much stricter than the normal censorship of printed reading matter, even if the latter may consist of dramatic works. This is a consequence of the different impression which can be made on the minds and emotions of the audience by a work enacted with the illusion of real life, by comparison with that which can be made by a play that is merely read at a desk. – The impression made by the former is infinitely more powerful than that of the latter because the former engages the eyes and ears and is intended even to penetrate the will of the spectator in order to attain the emotional effects intended; this is something that reading alone does not achieve. Censorship of books can restrict their circulation and make them accessible only to a certain kind of reader, whereas the playhouse by contrast is open to the entire public, which consists of people of every class, every walk of life, and every age.

The dangerous influence that might be exercised by stage performance became an established orthodoxy, and was for example restated in 1820 by Friedrich Wilhelm Ziegler, himself a senior

Burgtheater actor (a member of the company since 1783) as well as a minor playwright, in a paper proposing a reform of the court theatres which would involve the introduction of unified censorship laws throughout German-speaking Europe: spoken drama was a 'political force' working against 'religion, law, and monarchy', which had done more damage than 'all the political pamphlets' together, 'since the inspiration of the spoken word, heard by many thousands, strikes more deeply than any cold political writings read only by a few'.[2]

As outlined in Chapter 1, theatre censorship existed in Vienna before the *Schauspielfreiheit*, and was originally intended to underpin the educative and moral function of the theatre. It was only after the French Revolution that it acquired political teeth. The political climate was transformed by the reverberations of the Revolution in Paris, and was made even more uncertain by the death of Joseph II in 1790. This is the turning point in the development of what had been intended as a mechanism of didactic enlightenment into an instrument of political repression. Schiller's *Fiesko*, for example, had been staged in the Burgtheater under Joseph II in a version close to Schiller's text; reviewing the history of its performance in 1803, the censor commented that times had then changed, so that though it had been performed again in 1794 it had not been well received, and had subsequently been much altered before being resubmitted, cleansed of everything politically offensive ('von allen politischen Anstößigkeiten gereinigt').[3]

New regulations issued on 16 January 1795 had formalized the tightening of political criteria, and these are reflected in Hägelin's memorandum, drawn up in the same year: the very words 'liberty' and 'equality' were not to be mentioned on the stage, nor even was 'Enlightenment'.[4] The new climate attracted the scorn of the Josephinian intellectuals, who saw their principles being suborned: in September 1796 Alxinger wrote to Friedrich Nicolai with contempt of the censorship and clericalism that were being taken as the sole defence against the perceived threat of a 'Jacobin' revolution.[5] But the suspicion of the very term 'liberty' was deep-rooted and long-lasting, and extended even to opera libretti: right up to the 1848 revolution, the lines 'Es lebe die Freiheit, / Die Freiheit soll leben!' in the finale from Act One of *Don Giovanni* had to be sung as 'Es lebe die Fröhlichkeit, / Die Fröhlichkeit soll leben!'[6] – the idea of freedom reduced to meaningless 'jollity'.

When day-to-day administration of censorship was taken over by the police in 1801 and a unified office of 'police and censorship' was created, the machinery of a fully-fledged police state was complete. From 1817 to 1848 – that is, to the end of Metternich's rule as Austrian Chancellor – the operation of censorship came under the jurisdiction of the Chief of State Police (president of the *Oberste Polizei- und Zensurhofstelle*), Count Sedlnitzky. The regulations were revised and further tightened in 1810, especially in relation to printed books; hence, no doubt, Grillparzer's recollection in 1844 that at about this time censorship had been the political question of most interest to him.[7] Furthermore, censorship became tighter throughout Europe after the Carlsbad conference in August 1819, which followed the murder of Kotzebue, at that time in the service of the Tsar, by a radical student. But in Austria the state already had one of the strictest censorship systems in Europe, which protected the Establishment in every way, including not just political interests but also the interests of the church; and modifications undertaken in the early nineteenth century only confirmed the principles that were already set out by Hägelin in 1795. By the mid-1830s the petty restrictions had become a standing joke. A satirist from outside Austria such as Adolf Glassbrenner made fun of the censors' tampering with textual detail in his *Bilder und Träume aus Wien* (1836);[8] in the same year, so the actor Carl Ludwig Costenoble records, when Bauernfeld's satire *Der literarische Salon* was offered to the Burgtheater and doubts about the censor's reactions were voiced, the company were quick to joke about the 'Intimidation, Cuts and Rejection Office' ('Schreckens-, Streich- und Verwerfungsstelle').[9] Discussing the effects of censorship with members of the company two years earlier, Johann Ludwig Deinhardstein, then 'Deputy Director' of the Burgtheater, insisted that Sedlnitzky was a man of insight and intelligence, and that the impenetrable arbitrariness of the system was the fault of minor officials.[10] But that it was a major hurdle was never in dispute. In the case of *Der literarische Salon*, the company's fears were well-founded: Costenoble records that the censor not only made cuts in the text but also intervened while it was in rehearsal to insist that the central comic character, a journalist and reviewer called Morgenroth, must not be acted as a recognizable imitation of the reviewer M.G. Saphir.[11]

Throughout the first half of the nineteenth century, the censors continued to work in conformity with the criteria set out by Hägelin. It was quite usual for those appointed to include men of letters, though they could not act in respect of their own area of writing; even Schreyvogel, for example, who was in charge of the artistic administration of the Burgtheater from 1814 to 1832, was appointed a part-time censor in 1818 – not in the theatre but in the field of journalism ('Belletrie'). This involved him in censoring the theatre sections of the Viennese journals. That Deinhardstein was in exactly the same position in the mid-1830s was cited by Glassbrenner as an example of the corruption of the system;[12] following the bitterness caused by the production of *Der literarische Salon* Adolf Bäuerle, the editor of the *Theaterzeitung*, even applied direct to Sedlnitzky to have Deinhardstein taken off the job of censoring his paper.[13]

One of the basic duties of the theatre censor being to safeguard morality, the language of any play submitted had to be purified of indecent expressions (including any mention of adultery); plots might not include the depiction of an immoral act or such reminders of immorality as illegitimate births. There must be nothing offensive to the church: religious subjects were excluded, and priests were never shown on the popular stage. As late as 1819 the Archbishop was still insistent that any biblical material was unsuitable for stage performance,[14] and three years after that Schreyvogel's version of *The Merchant of Venice* was banned because it did not accord with the standards of the times in 'religious and moral' respects.[15] The list of restrictions was particularly severe in the political field. Not only was nothing permitted that belittled the monarchy (or the institution of monarchy) or portrayed rebellion against the ruling house: it was not even permissible to treat political liberty as a subject. Not just terms like 'liberty' and 'equality' had to be avoided but also 'tyrant' and 'despotism'.[16] Under Metternich, as Grillparzer observed in an essay of 1839 (which, of course, remained unpublished), the chief aims of government policy were conservative, the repression of liberalism and the preservation of the *status quo*.[17] In keeping with this principle, the censorship laws were designed to protect the whole fabric of society. The treatment of violent and shocking crimes was forbidden. Criticism or satire of nationalities was not allowed. Individuals could not be mentioned by name; neither the aristocracy nor even groups of citizens – a whole trade or craft – could be attacked.[18] As late as 1851, when Nestroy's comedy *Mein Freund* was submitted for approval, one passage was adjudged injurious to the peasantry as a class – a verdict against which the dramatist protested (see document 10, p. 252).

There is no systematic survey of censorship in the Viennese theatre to compare with John Russell Stephens's study of censorship in nineteenth-century London.[19] But the way the system worked is well documented. Right up till 1848, all texts to be performed had to be approved in advance. In the Burgtheater the final authority lay with the office of the court chamberlain (*Oberstkämmereramt*). This arrangement was not envied in the commercial theatre,[20] since the court chamberlain was advised by the police censor, who was watchful that in the Burgtheater both text and performance must be in accordance with strict standards of propriety. In 1828, for example, Schreyvogel's adaptation of *King Henry IV Part Two* was approved on the explicit condition that the inn scene featuring Mistress Quickly (Frau Hurtig) in Act Two be 'acted with decency'.[21] Certainly the system of controls seemed to compare badly with Berlin, where in 1799 Iffland took over a national theatre free of external censorship; but from the late eighteenth century onwards every theatre in German-speaking Europe was subject to control of one kind or another. The lack of formal censorship in Berlin depended on the maintenance of tight self-discipline within the theatre itself, and when Iffland wrote his much-quoted letter of 10 February 1799 to Schiller that 'the theatre has no censorship', he was in fact writing to explain why he was not prepared to risk producing *Wallensteins Lager* for fear of offending powerful military interests.[22]

The commercial theatres, where the repertory changed rapidly, relied on the censors to deal with their manuscripts expeditiously. Surviving manuscripts give a good idea of the normal time span. A version of Grillparzer's *König Ottokars Glück und Ende* submitted by the Theater an der Wien in February 1825 was dealt with in twelve days.[23] Plays submitted on behalf of the same theatre by the next director, Karl Carl, include three by Nestroy for which the manuscripts censored have survived. In 1833 *Der böse Geist Lumpacivagabundus* was submitted on 5 March and returned eleven days later; in 1837 a manuscript of *Das Haus der Temperamente* was with the censor for three weeks, being submitted on 20 October and returned with corrections on 11 November. Seven years later *Die beiden Herrn Söhne* took a similar time, being submitted on 18 December 1844 and returned on 8 January 1845.[24]

What the theatre would submit was a specially prepared manuscript written out by a copyist. The censor read it, keeping a particularly watchful eye open for indecent double-entendre, for anything that might offend religious susceptibilities, and for turns of phrase that could be construed as having political implications. He would delete offending words, phrases, or whole speeches with a black crayon, and the manuscript was then returned to the theatre with a seal of approval, subject to these corrections. No manuscripts were kept in official archives as was the case in London (where even autograph manuscripts have been preserved in this way).[25]

The official attitude to the theatre was ambivalent. On the one hand, if the audience were safely being entertained, they could not be on the streets hatching revolution; this is a recurrent strand in official thinking, and as late as the 1820s the Theater in der Leopoldstadt seems to have been allowed considerable licence. Tieck, who as newly-appointed *Dramaturg* at the court theatre in Dresden toured the leading theatrical centres in the southern German-speaking states (Vienna, Munich, Stuttgart) in the early summer of 1825, called it the 'only free theatre in Germany',[26] and three years later Charles Sealsfield (the exiled Moravian priest Karl Postl), observing that as 'the Government' had 'taken every precaution to debar' the Viennese 'from serious or intellectual occupation, the Prater, the Glacis, the coffee-houses, the Leopoldstadt theatre, are the only objects of their thoughts and desires', and that since the farces provided by Bäuerle and starring the actor Ignaz Schuster 'are innocent in the Austrian sense of the word, – viz. contain only obscenities, – they pass the censor unmolested'.[27] On the other hand, because the whole theory of censorship was based on the potential influence of the theatre, the dialect theatre had to be screened since it was accessible to a wide audience; moreover, the censors in Vienna had to be doubly watchful because plays that had been passed in the capital were normally passed more or less automatically in the provinces also (but not *vice versa*). To enforce the decisions of the censor, so-called *Kommissäre* (police spies) attended dress rehearsals, premières, and as many other performances as possible of all productions in the commercial theatres from 1803 until 1848, charged with checking that the regulations were properly observed and that any parts of the text deleted by the censor were really omitted in performance. An early example of the instructions the *Theaterkommissäre* worked to was published by Karl Glossy in 1915;[28] many similar documents have survived in the Niederösterreichisches Landesarchiv. This practice of police inspection was not confined to Vienna;[29] but it was only of limited effectiveness. Checking the text was no bar to the use of suggestive gesture or emphasis of delivery; and indeed there were long-standing complaints against the alleged obscenity that actors lent to their gestures, and Hägelin's memorandum of 1795 concedes the impossibility of controlling that kind of effect, or indeed of controlling surreptitious additions to the approved text.[30]

Extemporization (that is, straying from the approved text, whether genuinely *ex tempore* or not) was punishable by imprisonment. The most famous case concerns Nestroy, who in 1835 reacted to a hostile review of *Zu ebener Erde und erster Stock* published by the young critic Franz Wiest in the journal *Der Sammler* on 3 October. Nestroy inserted in his role as the servant Johann a comment to the effect that it was remarkable that the cleverest English card-game should have the same name as the stupidest man in Vienna. Nestroy had already made an official complaint about Wiest and requested an injunction preventing him from reviewing any more of his plays;[31] now he received a warning from the police *Kommissär* in attendance[32] and Wiest in turn lodged an official complaint. The continuing ill feelings in the company against the press can be gauged from the fact that on 16 December Wenzel Scholz included in a satirical song in another play two extra strophes, one of them ridiculing reviewers who wrote carping reviews but could do no better themselves. Scholz was hauled over the coals the next day for delivering a text that had not been passed by the censor;[33] in January Nestroy paid for his sally against Wiest with five days' incarceration.

Some of the decisions of the censor were both trivial and ridiculous. In 1823, for example, Friedrich Joseph Korntheuer (one of the leading actors in the Leopoldstadt company, who had prominent roles in Raimund plays), wrote a comedy entitled *Alle sind verliebt*, in which mention was made of 'böhmische Dalkerl' (a food, as standard a phrase as 'Yorkshire pudding'). Because the meaning could also be 'Bohemian idiots', the censor, Alois Zettler, reduced it to 'Dalkerl', so undoing the idiom altogether.[34] But there were also much more damaging consequences of the censorship laws, affecting both the commercial theatre and the Burgtheater. A few examples concerning the work of major classics may serve to illustrate the point.

Schreyvogel's adaptation of *King Lear*, which preserved the tragic ending of the play, ran foul of the convention that the downfall of monarchs was an impermissible subject, and was banned in 1822.

This was a play whose 'moral' had been defined by Hägelin as being that a ruler must never abdicate; the tragic ending had to be replaced by an ending in which both Lear and Cordelia remained alive.[35] Tieck, while particularly impressed by the performance of Heinrich Anschütz in the title role, condemned the revision of the ending as 'barbaric'. The sixth chapter of Stifter's novel *Der Nachsommer* includes an account of a performance of the same version, which similarly stresses the powerful emotional impact made by the play but also the lack of conviction carried by the happy ending.[36]

Some of the most striking examples of intrusive censorship concern Schiller, who was long regarded as the embodiment of dangerous libertarian trends. It was perhaps inevitable that *Die Räuber* was not acted at all in the Burgtheater until 1850; but his later plays also ran into all manner of difficulties. From 1795, when the new tighter regulations came into force, until about 1805 (the year of the French invasion and the battle of Austerlitz, when liberty suddenly became a more attractive idea), his plays practically disappeared from the Viennese stage. During that time it is true that *Die Jungfrau von Orleans* was submitted to the censor in 1802, but in a version so radically bowdlerized that the censor passing it recorded that what he was approving was in effect 'a new play'.[37] It was performed under the title *Johanna d'Arc*. *Don Carlos* was not staged till 1809, and then only in a much-cut version which remained in the repertory until 1847; it was still impossible to stage the first two parts of the *Wallenstein* trilogy in the mid-1820s, so that it had to be adapted for performance in a single evening, with scenes from the last two acts of *Die Piccolomini* serving as an introduction to a much-condensed *Wallensteins Tod*.[38] As for *Maria Stuart*, one of the principles Hägelin noted was that the execution of royalty could not be shown in a monarchist state,[39] and he explicitly mentions Mary Stuart as a case in point; an application by Pálffy to stage a version of Schiller's tragedy in 1810 was summarily rejected, and an appeal to the Emperor on the grounds of the eminence of the play, which merited performance on one of the leading German stages, also failed.[40] It was not until 1814 that Pálffy finally succeeded in getting permission for *Maria Stuart* to be produced in the Burgtheater, and even then only in a modified version strictly overseen by the then director of the censorship office, Baron von Hager.[41] *Wilhelm Tell*, which treats political liberty within the context of a rebellion against Austrian rule, fell victim to some of the most sensitive political clauses; it could not be produced in Vienna at all until the censorship began to be slightly more relaxed some twenty years after the French Revolution. Then an anonymous adaptation was staged in the Theater in der Leopoldstadt and another adaptation by the actor and producer Karl Franz Grüner, in which the whole of the final act was left out, was performed in the Theater an der Wien, with Grüner in the title role. In 1824 even a ballet on the same subject was forbidden 'for political reasons'.[42] Schiller's play was not seen in the Burgtheater until 1827, when it was given a lavish production with new music by Adalbert Gyrowetz and costumes by the theatre's chief stage designer Philipp von Stubenrauch, but still in what was basically the same emasculated version. Eduard Genast, who appeared as a guest in 1847, was appalled to find the final act still omitted and found it 'irresponsible towards the dramatist and the public'.[43] *Wilhelm Tell* is a work that is particularly vulnerable to political pressures. After the Anschluss in 1938, it was performed both in the Burgtheater and in the Deutsches Volkstheater on Hitler's birthday, 20 April, as an expression of patriotism; three years later it was banned on Hitler's personal command as a document of political freedom.[44] A hundred years earlier, when Schiller's dramas, together with Grillparzer's, drew higher attendance figures per performance in the Burgtheater than those of any other dramatists, *Wilhelm Tell* was second only to *König Ottokars Glück und Ende* in this respect[45] – a revealing statistic which explains the censor's extreme watchfulness.

Things were no easier for Lessing's verse drama *Nathan der Weise*, which offended not political susceptibilities but clerical interests. When the Burgtheater wanted to produce it in 1815, the Archbishop of Vienna objected that its moral, enshrined in the famous allegory of the three rings, was 'offensive' to the Christian religion ('jene anstößige Allegorie'). In 1818 it was resubmitted in a revised version which had been prepared, according to Costenoble's diary, by a former Burgtheater prompter, and this version was passed since it now contained 'nothing contrary to religion' ('nichts Religionswidriges'). When the play was finally produced in 1819, then, it was in a version in which all the passages to which the archbishop had objected, including the parable of the three rings, had been doctored to meet his requirements; and it remained in the repertory in this form until 1846.[46] The Patriarch had been transformed into a commander of a military order, the monk into his servant (a role played by Costenoble).

The list of plays which suffered similarly radical adaptation in order to conform to the conventions could readily be extended. Just two months earlier, Deinhardstein's version of *Tartuffe* had been produced, and Costenoble blamed his own disappointing performance in the title role on the adaptation, in which Tartuffe was not a priest.[47] When Goethe's *Götz von Berlichingen* was finally performed in the Burgtheater in 1830, it was in an adaptation by Schreyvogel in which the Bishop of Bamberg was transformed into the 'Landgraf von Franken' (another role played by Costenoble).

Clearly the proscriptions ruled out much of the usual subject-matter of serious drama. The treatment of the German classics in particular made nonsense of the original intention that the Burgtheater should function as a 'national theatre'; and the rule that historical material treated must not include events that cast an unfavourable light on any part of the Habsburg dynasty made it practically impossible to develop an indigenous tradition of Austrian historical drama in the theatre.

The best-documented case in the field of historical drama concerns Grillparzer. His first two plays for the Burgtheater treated subjects drawn from classical antiquity, against which there was no objection; but as soon as he tried his hand at historical drama, attempting the Austrian equivalent of the Shakespearian 'history', the problems started.[48] The text of *König Ottokars Glück und Ende* was submitted by Schreyvogel on behalf of the Burgtheater in late November 1823. The memorandum produced in the police censorship office the next month recommended that it was unsuitable 'both from the police point of view and politically', drawing attention in particular to the dissension between various nationalities within the Empire on which the plot turned. Both the newly-appointed court chamberlain Count Czernin and the director of the court theatres, Count Dietrichstein, tried to intervene on Grillparzer's behalf,[49] and Grillparzer himself wrote direct to Sedlnitzky – one of the most remarkable documents of the period, the leading dramatist of the nation reduced to pleading for his very livelihood to the head of the police service.[50] All these efforts were, however, unavailing: the official ban followed in January, and indeed the text offended against so many of the conventions that it is remarkable that it was ever let through. A historical drama by Kotzebue on the same subject, *Rudolph von Habsburg und König Ottokar von Böhmen*, had, it is true, been performed with some adaptation in the Theater an der Wien in

August 1815 (under the title *Ottokars Tod*, which removed the open allusion to the House of Habsburg); but the task of working on it had led Schreyvogel to complain about the 'incredible' difficulties the censorship placed in the way of everything new, and to beg Kotzebue that in choosing his subjects in future he should bear the political and clerical pressures in Vienna in mind.[51] It was not in fact until April 1824 – according to Grillparzer's own account, after the Empress had taken an interest[52] – that Wallishausser was granted permission to publish *König Ottokars Glück und Ende*.

Wallishausser was the main specialist publisher of theatrical literature in the Biedermeier period; in that respect the position in Vienna was less complicated than that in Paris or in London, where a whole network of independent bookshops published play-texts. One consideration that the authorities had to take into account when considering Wallishausser's application was that while the printed text of a play was likely to make a less vivid impact than a stage performance, once it was printed it would be harder to prevent its performance in the provinces, including in Hungary.[53] Nevertheless, Wallishausser got the go-ahead for the printed edition, and in December 1824 it was finally followed by permission for performance, subject to numerous alterations that removed so far as possible all mentions of specific nationalities. The delay since the text had first been submitted amounted to thirteen months. In his autobiography, written in 1853, Grillparzer recounts that a few years later he met the censor responsible, asked what had been found objectionable or dangerous about his text, and received the answer 'Nothing, but I thought to myself: one never can tell'[54] – quite possibly an apocryphal anecdote, but one which conveys his frustration at the inscrutability and apparent arbitrariness of the system.

Wallishausser shrewdly timed the publication of *König Ottokars Glück und Ende* to coincide with the première on 19 February 1825; though estimates of the sales varied, it seems to have sold over five hundred copies that same day, so that the first print run was sold out by the end of the month, and the edition had to be reprinted in the autumn. The première was very well attended, and though the critical reception was mixed, the whole occasion provided (as Grillparzer himself was well aware) an example of the way scandal tends to generate interest, so that the protracted affair with the censor contributed directly to the play's success.[55]

No sooner was the play published than Pálffy's Theater an der

Wien, in severe financial straits, attempted to cash in with a rival production. Only four days after the première in the Burgtheater, Count Dietrichstein, technically head of the court theatre direction (*Hoftheater-Direction*), lodged an objection with the police censorship office against this proposed rival production, requesting that it be postponed for a year.[56] The outcome of the dispute was to establish the principle that although a text was generally available once it was published, every new production still required renewed censorship. The manuscript submitted by the Theater an der Wien has survived; the censor, Zettler, insisted on emendations, along the lines of the standard principles, in a total of 125 passages.[57] The eventual production, premièred on Easter Monday, was clearly designed to make the play as inoffensive as possible. Grillparzer recounts in his autobiography that the actor Moritz Rott, who played Ottokar, enquired immediately after the Burgtheater première how Anschütz had played the role there, and when told that he had been harsh and forceful, immediately said that he would play him 'mildly'.[58] This was probably not just an attempt to be different; Rott's more moderate playing of the role looks suspiciously like an attempt at political correctness, in keeping with the interests of the censor,[59] and was embedded in a production which depended largely on spectacular stage effects.

The pressures on dramatists were not limited to the official censorship system. The orthodoxies were further entrenched by reviewers who wished to avoid alienating the authorities. This point has been made about the reviewers of the Burgtheater production of *König Ottokars Glück und Ende* in 1825, including Joseph Sigmund Ebersberg in *Der Sammler* and Paul Thorn in the main specialist paper, Bäuerle's *Theaterzeitung*;[60] a similar suspicion exists later about the most polemical theatre critic of the 1830s and 1840s, Moritz Gottlieb Saphir, editor of *Der Humorist* from 1837 onwards, who angled for a position in the Burgtheater in the early 1840s and whose reviews maintained an anti-radical line that had unmistakable political overtones. Another form of pressure is evidenced in the fate of *Ein treuer Diener seines Herrn*, Grillparzer's next tragedy after *Ottokar*, which is set in Hungary and presents a tragedy caused by an unreasonable ruler. After three successful performances, two of which the Emperor himself had attended, Grillparzer was informed by Sedlnitzky that the Emperor wanted to acquire sole ownership of the piece – in effect an edict that it must be withdrawn from circulation. (In this case Grillparzer got round the problem by arguing that copies had already been made so that it might be impossible to secure its complete withdrawal:[61] the Emperor reversed his decision after three more weeks, but the play disappeared from the programme a year later.)

Well may the theatre directors and dramatists alike have felt hemmed in by pressure to toe an orthodox line. Immediately following the discussion of Grillparzer in Sealsfield's *Austria As It Is* comes the lament:

A writer in Austria must not offend against any Government; nor against any minister; nor against any hierarchy, if its members be influential; nor against the aristocracy ... What would have become of Shakspeare had he been doomed to live or to write in Austria?[62]

It is not surprising that censorship was one of the central discontents of the *Vormärz* Liberals. In March 1845 Eduard von Bauernfeld, the leading writer of society comedies for the Burgtheater, drafted a petition demanding reform (*Denkschrift über die gegenwärtigen Zustände der Zensur in Österreich*); it was signed by ninety-eight other prominent authors (including the Burgtheater dramatists Grillparzer and Halm, the dialect dramatists Castelli and Friedrich Kaiser, and the critic Saphir). It was a mild document, which did not even request the abolition of censorship but limited itself to demanding correct implementation of the established codes to counter arbitrary practices.[63] Neither Nestroy nor Karl Carl was among the signatories. This may be because they were unwilling to sign any document to which Saphir had put his name; or it may have been the result of commercial circumspection (no theatre director could afford to alienate the authorities); or they may have deemed the petition insufficiently radical; or they may have realized that even this rather tame petition was doomed to be unsuccessful, as indeed it was.

Part of the answer to Sealsfield's rhetorical question about what would have become of Shakespeare if he had lived in Austria may be gauged from the effect that censorship had on Grillparzer. It certainly contributed to his abandoning work in about 1840 on his drama *Esther*, which is based on the Book of Esther and treats sensitive questions of religious tolerance and the relationship of religion and politics; it must also have been one of the factors that led him to withhold his late tragedies, including *Ein Bruderzwist in*

Habsburg (which he finished in 1848–9 and which in effect dramatizes many of his concerns about the 1848 revolution), from performance.

In respect of the comedies of the commercial theatre, the kind of alteration the censor would insist on is particularly well documented in a manuscript of *Das Haus der Temperamente*.[64] In this case the censor intervened in over fifty places in the text. None of the passages had a political connotation (it is not that kind of play), though it is striking that a reference to the university was struck out. An exclamation 'Höll und Teufel' had to be altered to 'Donnerwetter'. (It was normal for words like 'himmlisch', 'Gott', 'heilig', and 'Teufel' to be rejected; hence the frequent use of the dialect form 'Teuxel' instead of 'Teufel'.) But in *Das Haus der Temperamente* the censor's eye was mostly on possible sexual innuendo. In this respect the standards adhered to in Vienna were very comparable to those in Victorian England. An allusion to how things would 'get going' after a wedding ('dann wird's gehen') was narrowed down to a reference to dancing ('dann wird getanzt'), a suggestion that a girl 'might be innocent' (''s Madl kann ja unschuldig seyn') was made more specific: she 'might perhaps not know anything' about the matter at issue (''s Madl kann vielleicht nichts davon wissen'). At one point a male character casts a longing look at his neighbour's daughter, whose hand he is hoping for, and says, 'I know what I have to do' ('Ich weiß, was ich zu thun hab'): this had to be changed to 'I know what I have to hope' ('Ich weiß, was ich zu hoffen hab'). The suggestive French words *lit de repos* and *Kanapee* had to be changed into the reassuringly everyday *Schlafsessel*; even a reference to 'pleasure' was changed into 'joy'. And true to the spirit of Hägelin's memorandum, which sets out the principle that the censor must make sure that two lovers never leave the stage together,[65] the censor in 1837 was still concerned to avoid any suggestion that two unmarried figures, even servants, could be left alone together out of sight, and deleted a line drawing attention to the fact that a chambermaid was being locked in in the same room as the central comic figure (played by Nestroy). The petty prurience of the censor's eye was eventually countered by Nestroy, after the revolution, when he appealed in 1851 against the censor's treatment of his play *Mein Freund*: 'If one is determined to find smutty jokes, then every sentence is a smutty joke: the words "father, mother, son, daughter" are smut, because if one is determined one can associate them with the act of procreation, which is a precondition for the meaning of every one of them' (see document 10, p. 253).

The power of the censor to tamper with texts of plays which were waiting to be performed presented problems for theatre managements as well as for playwrights. In the commercial theatre, writers were contracted to provide an agreed number of acceptable texts a year; financial self-interest consequently dictated that there had to be a considerable degree of self-censorship, cautious avoidance of themes and situations that were likely to be objected to. In the Burgtheater too, while there was no such financial pressure on contracted playwrights, the director still had to meet the same standards: even after the 1848 revolution, Heinrich Laube was explicitly charged in the mid-1850s with the responsibility of submitting for production only texts that had been purged of any passages offending 'against politics, religion, and morality'[66] – that is, exercising an internal censorship, following the same principles as had applied since the end of the eighteenth century.

In the commercial theatres, however, the discipline of 'self-censorship' is only part of the story. When in his autograph manuscript of the first act of *Das Gewürzkrämer-Kleeblatt* (1845)[67] Nestroy changed the line 'When stealing wives one makes a fool of oneself if one makes a noise' ('Beym Frauendieb blammiert man sich, wenn man ein Lärm macht') to 'when expropriating wives one makes a fool of oneself if one shouts' ('Bey der Frauenentwendung blammiert man sich, wenn man ein G'schrey macht'), it is fairly easy to guess that the linguistic revision was at least partly motivated by a calculation of what he could not possibly get away with. The same kind of calculation even more clearly underlies an alteration in the second scene of the next act, when he first had the wife of the main comic figure leaning on the shoulder of a shop assistant ('sich auf seine Schulter lehnend') and changed this so that she bent over his chair ('sich über die Stuhllehne neigend'). But that kind of modification went only some way to meeting the objections the censor might raise in detail; and since speed of production was important, Carl's theatres ingeniously circumvented the official censorship by submitting doctored manuscripts.

What the censor was likely to object to could, after all, be foreseen; all the suspect phrases that he might spot were therefore thinly 'ringed' in the manuscript, and blander alternatives inserted. Once again a few examples must serve.[68] Much of the material ringed is of the kind that might carry more or less obvious sexual innuendo. In *Weder Lorbeerbaum noch Bettelstab* (1835), a wife's complaint about 'having nothing to wear' was rephrased so that she merely had 'nothing new'; in *Der Kobold* (1838), where the garrulous comic figure Staberl refers to himself as having once been a bride, but 'of the male sex' ('männlichen Geschlechts'), the phrase 'of the male sex' was cut out; in *Das Gewürzkrämer-Kleeblatt* (1845) the argument that a woman must not be condemned for a single indiscretion ('wegen einen Fehltritt') was toned down by turning the 'indiscretion', a word which carries a clear suggestion of a moral peccadillo, into an 'ill-considered action' ('wegen einer Unüberlegtheit'). In the same play, the reflection of the main comic figure 'A woman like that is young, and may still improve for the better – well, anything is possible' ('So ein Weib is jung, kann sich noch bessern – na ja, möglich is All's') was deleted entirely for the censor's eye. Political sensitivities can be glimpsed behind the alteration in *Müller, Kohlenbrenner und Sesseltrager* (1834) of an 'Italian singer' ('das schönste is schon ein wällischer Sänger') to a 'great singer' ('ein großer Sänger'); in *Der Kobold*, where the ruler of the Underworld, Brennroth, says 'we powerful figures are just poor fools when we're up against Fate' ('Gegen das Schicksal seyn wir mächtige Wesen alle nur arme Narren'), 'powerful figures' was ringed and 'spirits' ('Geister') entered as a substitute. The most successful of all Nestroy's plays, *Der böse Geist Lumpacivagabundus*, contains in Act Three a solo scene in which Nestroy, in the role of the cobbler Knieriem, sings about the imminent coming of a comet, each of the two strophes ending with the refrain: 'Da wird einem halt Angst und bang, / Die Welt steht auf kein Fall mehr lang' ('So fears creep up on one fast; / This world cannot possibly last'), which Nestroy is reputed to have delivered with a meaningful stress on the first word of the last line ('*This* world cannot possibly last'), suggesting a reference to the particular world of Metternich's Austria. The refrain was left out in the precautionary 'pre-censorship', so one of the best-known passages in the play was presumably never approved by the official censor.

The scribe preparing the manuscript to be submitted to the censor's office had to copy out the doctored version; this helped get approval quickly, as there was normally next to nothing left that the censor could possibly object to. (Certainly in Nestroy, the extent of official intervention in *Das Haus der Temperamente* was unusual.) For obvious reasons, published memoirs of the time do not contain accounts of this precautionary 'pre-censorship', so that the practice has to be pieced together from surviving manuscripts. It is best documented in respect of Nestroy.

Nestroy generally wrote in the 'precautionary' rings and alternative wordings in his own autograph fair copy of the text. They could involve copious alterations, especially if the subject of the play was by the standards of the time *risqué* (as in *Das Gewürzkrämer-Kleeblatt*, which centres on three grocers who suspect each other's wives of infidelity) or bore on contemporary political or social questions (as in *Der Schützling*, one year before the revolution). His revisions – rings and alternatives – were copied into the manuscript used by the producer or the prompter, for use at rehearsals; this is exemplified in manuscripts of *Müller, Kohlenbrenner und Sesseltrager, Weder Lorbeerbaum noch Bettelstab*, and *Der Kobold*. But only the revised text was written out for the censor; this is confirmed by *Die beiden Herrn Söhne*, of which both a manuscript with Nestroy's autograph 'pre-censorship' and the manuscript submitted to the censor (and approved without any further alteration) have survived. In *Der böse Geist Lumpacivagabundus*, Nestroy added notes to the copyist specifying that a revised version of the song-texts was to be submitted to the censor; at one point in the second act he also spelt out that the wording deleted with rings must be copied out for the prompter.[69] It seems, then, that all the passages omitted in the text submitted to the censor were smuggled back for performance; confirmation of this can be found in the way such passages recur in later copy-manuscripts. The police spies attending the performance can, of course, only have been checking that what the censor had rejected was definitely left out; but still it seems incredible that they should not have noticed that the text being performed was radically different from that which had been approved, and it may well be that they were venal and could be deflected from over-scrupulous supervision.

Be that as it may, the device worked, and by the late 1830s new plays were regularly performed within a few days of the censor's official approval. In 1840, for example, the censor released the manuscript of *Der Talisman*, with corrections, on 9 December;[70] the première took place seven days later, on 16 December; or again *Die beiden Herrn Söhne* was approved on 8 January 1845 and performed on 16 January.

2. CENSORSHIP AFTER THE 1848 REVOLUTION

Revolution broke out in Vienna on 13 March 1848; the very next day the Emperor, Ferdinand I, declared an end to censorship of the press. The day after that, Sedlnitzky resigned (he spent the next four years in Troppau, in Austrian Silesia), and on 29 March the *Oberste Zensur- und Polizeihofstelle* was dissolved. The most important immediate consequence in the theatre was Nestroy's writing of *Freiheit in Krähwinkel*, a satiric review of the first stage of the revolution. First performed on 1 July in the Carltheater, a new theatre which stood on the site of the old Theater in der Leopoldstadt, the play was controversial: some perceived it as 'ultra-liberal', celebrating the revolution; others thought that on the contrary Nestroy had betrayed the libertarian cause. (This was the view taken by a rival playwright wholly committed to the revolutionary cause, Friedrich Kaiser, who saw the play as 'a satire of every libertarian aspiration'.)[71] But there is no gainsaying the forthrightness of the attacks on censorship that Nestroy incorporated in the central role: it was 'the younger of two vile sisters, the name of the elder being "Inquisition"'; a censor was a 'man reduced to a pencil, a personified stroke through the products of the mind'.[72] The revolution was defeated in Vienna on 1 November; censorship was quickly reimposed by Prince Windischgrätz, the commander of the imperial troops, and began operating again on 11 November, headed by representatives of the army, supported by civilian staff, and concentrating at first mainly on the press. It was not until 14 November 1850 that a new decree regulating the supervision of theatres (*Theaterordnung*) was approved by the Emperor and came into effect. In the meanwhile, from the end of 1848 onwards, the military censorship (*Säbelzensur*) remained in place. In the theatre it was generally less strict than the old police censorship had been; only that can explain how Nestroy got away with the amount of political allusion he worked into *Lady und Schneider* and *Judith und Holofernes* in 1849. However, a further unofficial control was operated by so-called *Vertrauensmänner*, a self-appointed group of watchdogs who reported any offensively libertarian passages that came to their notice,[73] and one consequence of the events of 1848 may have been that treatment of the armed forces was even more vigilantly controlled than before: in 1851 the theatre agent Adalbert Prix warned a playwright that on the orders of the Emperor himself no soldiers other than musicians might appear on stage.[74]

The 1850 decree survived the commitment to freedom of speech enshrined in article 13 of the basic state law (*Staatsgrundgesetz*) of 21 December 1867. It remained in place, in effect determining the broad outlines of censorship, until the end of the monarchy. Section 3 of the decree required that every production had to be approved in advance (being accorded an *Aufführungsbewilligung*) by the governor (*Statthalter*) of the province in which the performance was taking place: in Vienna's case that was Lower Austria. The authorities continued to make their recommendations on the basis of reports from official censors; but the 1850 decree was accompanied by an instruction defining the importance of the theatre as an institution of cultural education and establishing advisers to assist the *Statthalter*. This system remained in place until 1881, when the whole censorship procedure reverted to the *Statthalterei*.

Two indications from the early 1870s of how much the rules had in practice been relaxed are that Ludwig Anzengruber's *Der Pfarrer von Kirchfeld*, which deals with liberalism in the church, was approved for production in the Theater an der Wien in 1870 subject only to relatively minor emendations to the text,[75] and that after Grillparzer's death *Ein Bruderzwist in Habsburg*, centring on two Habsburg Emperors at the time of the outbreak of the Thirty Years War, could be shown in September 1872 both in the Wiener Stadttheater and in the Burgtheater.

In broad terms, what was still excluded from performance from 1850 onwards was anything directed against the ruling house, anything that might threaten law and order or that offended public decency, anything that intruded into the private lives of individuals, and anything offensive to religion or morality: clerical sensibilities underlay, for example, the problems that Anzengruber's comedy *Die Kreuzelschreiber* (Theater an der Wien, 1872) and his tragic drama *Das vierte Gebot* (Theater in der Josefstadt, 1877) ran into; it was not even possible for the latter play to be performed under its correct title (in English it would have to be translated 'The Fifth Commandment', that is, 'Honour thy father and thy mother'), and it appeared on the theatre-bills simply as *Ein Volksstück*. But that both plays were performed at all is an illustration of the greater liberalism shown by the *Statthalter* by contrast with the police censors.

The most fascinating example of the workings of police censorship in the commercial theatre in the years following the new decree was the treatment of Nestroy's comedy *Mein Freund* in 1851. The censor's objections to the play included an attack on Nestroy's moral and political influence, with *Freiheit in Krähwinkel* adduced as evidence, and amounted to an attempt to preserve all the political as well as moral control typical of censorship under Sedlnitzky, defending religious susceptibilities, crossing out any conceivable allusion to public figures or political issues, and even arguing that any suggestion of social conflict was unsuitable for comic treatment. It provoked a detailed, point-by-point rebuttal by Nestroy, in a manuscript which has survived in the Lower Austrian archives (see document 10, pp. 250–5). Another notable production that brought the censor into play was the first Viennese production of Offenbach's *La Belle Hélène* in 1865, one of the milestones in the history of operetta in Vienna. The censor found fault with the libretto as 'offending against morality and decency';[76] against his advice, the Lower Austrian authorities allowed the performance but their permission was conditional on a considerable number of cuts of possibly suggestive matter, including the whole of Helen's account of the episode of Leda and the swan.[77]

For the court theatres the responsible office was still ultimately that of the court chamberlain, but the system was cumbersome. Its administration varied, but from 1867 there was a system of semi-official censorship conducted by a senior civil servant; the authority to whom he reported was the official management authority (*General-intendanz*) that came into being in 1867, itself subordinate to one of the Masters of the Imperial Household (*Oberhofmeister*). By the end of the century the official advice, though conservative in respecting the established conventions of the Burgtheater as a court theatre, was generally sympathetic and understanding; but up to the end of the monarchy there continued to be cases of friction or even court intervention. In 1889 the director of the Burgtheater, August Förster, failed to get permission to mount productions of Ibsen's *Ghosts* and *The Wild Duck*;[78] in 1899 Schnitzler's *Der grüne Kakadu*, a one-act comedy set in revolutionary Paris but with obvious implications for *fin-de-siècle* Vienna, was banned by the responsible *Oberhofmeister*, Prince Alfred Montenuovo; in 1904 Gerhart Hauptmann's *Rose Bernd* was withdrawn from the repertoire after six performances, apparently after an objection by a member of the imperial family,[79] and six years after that Schönherr's *Glaube und Heimat* enjoyed a big success in the Deutsches Volkstheater only after it had been deemed unsuitable for the Burgtheater.[80]

In one form or another, censorship remained in force in the court theatres till 1918, and longer in the commercial theatres. It affected the development of satirical cabaret: in 1910, for example, the cabaret 'Die Hölle' was forbidden to represent public figures from political life, and also to show anything that could be construed as an attack on the institution of marriage.[81] The cabarets were, indeed, forced into self-censorship just as the satirical playwrights of Metternich's time had been.

In the conventional theatre, discontent with the workings of the censorship laws surfaced particularly in two public controversies. The first centred on a light satirical comedy set in military circles, *Der Feldherrnhügel* by Roda Roda and Karl Rössler, which was staged in December 1909 in the Neue Wiener Bühne and well received, but had to be withdrawn in January 1910 because the uniforms were insufficiently different from those of the imperial army and the play could be taken as alluding to Austria. Despite protests, a question asked in the Lower Austrian parliament, and modifications proposed by the theatre, the ban was upheld by the advisory committee (*Theaterbeirat*),[82] which had been reinstituted, against resistance from the Lower Austrian authorities, in 1903. The second controversy was sparked off when a production of Schnitzler's *Professor Bernhardi* which was planned in the Deutsches Volkstheater was forbidden in October 1912. It was widely assumed that the reason for the ban was Schnitzler's treatment of anti-Semitism in Austrian political life; the official reason, more vaguely phrased and not published, was the play's allegedly 'tendentious and distorted' depiction of public life. (This formulation occurs in a memorandum to the police authorities in Berlin, where the world première took place in the Kleines Theater on 28 November 1912.)[83] In this case the censor had at least grasped the implications of the play accurately, perceiving that its depiction of rivalry and deception within the hospital that Bernhardi heads and of opportunism in the politician Flint presents the very currency of Austrian political life as corrupt. In both cases the matter was taken up in the press, whose reactions followed ideological lines. In 1910 the Liberal *Neues Wiener Journal* argued that the decision by the *Statthalter* showed the need for old-fashioned censorship to be abolished altogether.[84] In 1912, the *Arbeiter-Zeitung* similarly argued that the ban on *Professor Bernhardi* showed up the deficiencies of the system and the urgent need for reform, while on the Right, the *Reichspost* published an article supporting the censor.[85]

The picture of intellectual corruption in *Professor Bernhardi* was so specifically rooted in Vienna that it was bound to run into difficulties with the authorities; in other respects, including the adjudication of plays treating contentious questions in the sphere of sexuality, the censors and their advisers were, from about 1900 onwards, much more inclined to hold back from draconian bans and open confrontation: Max Halbe's *Jugend* in 1901, Wilde's *Salome* in 1903, and Wedekind's *Franziska* in 1913, for example, were approved for performance in the Deutsches Volkstheater – in the case of *Jugend* and *Salome* only after a thorough revision of the text, in the case of *Franziska* subject only to some cuts, avoiding giving the work what would, as the censor shrewdly saw, have been the added mystique associated with an outright ban.[86]

On 30 October 1918 the provisional National Assembly of the infant republic passed a decision ending all censorship on the grounds that it was contrary to the basic rights of the citizen and therefore illegal.[87] The next day Schnitzler drily noted in his diary that nothing now stood in the way of a Viennese production of *Professor Bernhardi* – albeit at the price of world war and the collapse of the empire.[88] The production duly took place in the Deutsches Volkstheater the same December. But just how much censorship had ended was unclear. The next sentence of the National Assembly's decision specified the ending of censorship of the press, and this opened the way to what was essentially a rerun of the dispute that had been fought out in Paris in the last twenty years of the nineteenth century:[89] the Lower Austrian provincial government took the line that the new dispensation applied only to the press and not to theatre or film, and continued to apply the 1850 law. The issue came to the constitutional court in December 1919 in connection with a production of Wedekind's *Die Büchse der Pandora* in the Neue Wiener Bühne; by the casting vote of the president the court upheld the submission of the Lower Austrian government and in effect confirmed that the ending of censorship was limited to the press, so that theatres continued to have to seek approval of productions and (in accordance with a law of 1911) the authorities had to be represented at dress rehearsals.

The device of an advisory committee, reinstituted in 1903, continued in existence until 1926, when its members were Friedrich Engel, Ludwig Tils, and Karl Glossy, the last two of whom had served since 1903. How liberally they performed their task can be seen from the fact that in 1921, when a production of Schnitzler's *Reigen* was mooted, they raised points about the propriety that would be necessary in performance (not at all an unusual caveat in the period, and not just in Vienna),[90] but recognized the artistic merit of the work and unanimously agreed to recommend that performance be permitted.[91] Indeed Johannes Schober, chief of police in Vienna (and also a past and future Chancellor), would argue in 1926 that from 1918 onwards censorship was in effect over; most reports of alleged censorship from then on, he wrote, were in fact entrepreneurial stunts, trying to gain publicity for a play or an author.[92]

Nevertheless, as was predictable amid the social and political upheaval after the First World War, there was continued uncertainty about where authority really lay. The theatres still had to get permission through the police authorities, as under the monarchy, with the final decision in case of dispute lying with the provincial or city government. (From the beginning of 1922 Vienna was a separate province.) When the Ministry of Internal Affairs closed down performances of Schnitzler's *Reigen* in 1921 after the public disorders to which the production gave rise, this led to a formal objection from the Mayor of Vienna.[93]

Censorship was finally declared illegal by the constitutional court in a judgement of 22 March 1926. The next day this judgement made the main headline on the front page of the *Neue Freie Presse*; the article beneath the headline traced the history of the law back to 1850, admitted that the practice of censorship under the guidance of advisers had in the recent past been very benevolent, but affirmed that any control was irreconcilable in principle with the democratic system. Twelve days later the same newspaper carried the article by Schober already referred to, in which he reviewed the legal position and reminded readers that even after the ending of censorship, neither illegal material nor anything that might be construed as an incitement to public disorder could be performed. Section 3 of the 1850 decree was now clearly superseded; but not, he argued, Section 6, which spelt out the responsibility of the police to preserve public order and decency. The police would continue to have that responsibility. Schober saw the 'preparatory' censorship exercised by the advisory groups as a 'safety valve', whose removal would lead to legal disputes. The report in the *Neue Freie Presse* twelve days beforehand had put it differently, pointing out that the new decision in effect shifted responsibility to theatre directors to make proper use of the liberty that had been gained. The point is directed against financial opportunism; but the responsibility also weighed heavily on Franz Herterich, director from 1923 to 1930 of the Burgtheater (technically a theatre not directly affected by the change in the law). The administration of the state theatres was wary of the artistic autonomy of their directors, and Herterich had to defend his decision to mount a production of Schnitzler's *Komödie der Verführung* in 1924; part of his self-defence was a demonstration of the circumspection he had shown in refusing to produce Shaw's *St Joan* because of satirical elements that he adjudged politically and clerically sensitive.[94] This illustrates how hard it was for the national theatre in the republic to shake off the constraints under which it had operated during the monarchy.

CHAPTER 3

The 'old' Burgtheater

I. FROM PÁLFFY TO SCHREYVOGEL

The monopoly of the largest theatres by the art-loving nobles who formed the *Gesellschaft der Kavaliere*, nine of them to begin with, lasted from 1807 to 1814. The association was quick to dissolve, partly because of a financial crisis which was caused by the war against Napoleonic France in 1809: the Emperor, always resistant to appeals for financial support, rejected appeals for compensation out of the public purse, except in respect of décor in store which had been lost during the French invasion of Vienna in May 1809. For two years inflation raged and the value of the Gulden sank. The crisis ended with the state itself in effect bankrupt, and with an enforced devaluation of paper money in 1811. The currency was eventually stabilized with 100 Gulden (fl.) in the traditional silver currency, known as *Conventionsmünze* (C.M.), worth 250 Gulden in paper money (known as 'Schein' or 'Wiener Währung', W.W.). This arrangement remained in force until 1857, and as both currencies remained in circulation together, financial calculations are often subject to imprecision.

The financial crisis of the Napoleonic period led to a reorganization of the court theatres in the autumn of 1810, the two houses being given distinct functions. The Kärntnertortheater was designated the home of opera and ballet, with higher prices charged in all parts of the house, and the Burgtheater, whose 'dilapidated state and poor condition in other respects' made it 'wholly unsuitable for large-scale productions',[1] was designated the home of German drama.

This change, dictated by practical exigency, was to prove much more significant than Joseph II's short-lived and opportunistic elevation of it to the status of a 'national theatre' in 1776. It is in 1810 that

49

the history of the Burgtheater as the true national theatre for spoken drama really began.

Within a few months, Pálffy was named director of the court theatres – a position that remained subordinate in the court hierarchy to that of Count Wrbna (Rudolph Graf Wrbna-Freudenthal), who as court chamberlain since 1806 remained 'supreme director of the court theatres' (*Oberster Hoftheaterdirektor*). In the summer of 1812 Lobkowitz took over the lease of the court theatres, but his period in charge ended the following year in insolvency, and from the beginning of 1814 Pálffy was back in charge. In May he appointed Joseph Schreyvogel to the post of *Präsidial-Sekretär* – in effect, as a day-to-day administrator, but also responsible for assisting Sonnleithner in planning the repertoire and casting.[2]

At the same time Schreyvogel was also appointed deputy director of the Theater an der Wien, which Pálffy had purchased in January 1814. Schreyvogel's function there was soon limited to that of *Dramaturg*, with the actors Siegfried Gotthelf Koch and Karl Franz Grüner – the latter trained by Goethe in Weimar – taking over responsibility for production. Pálffy's attempt to rebuild the kind of theatrical empire the original *Gesellschaft der Kavaliere* had intended led him into substantial financial losses: so much so that in the autumn of 1814, in an attempt to extract support from the exchequer (*Ärar*), he threatened a total closure of the theatres. In April 1817 the direction of both court theatres finally returned technically to the exchequer, being administered through the Ministry of Finance, while Pálffy devoted himself entirely to the Theater an der Wien.

Overall responsibility for the court theatres still lay with the court chamberlain (Wrbna, then Czernin from 1824); but the financial power lay with Count Johann Philipp Stadion, the Finance Minister from 1815 until his death in 1824, who was given the task of putting the finances of the court theatres back on a sound footing – a task which led him to advance a strong case for increased funding in the interests of maintaining the standards appropriate to the imperial capital. Day-to-day administration was overseen by a senior civil servant in the Ministry, Claudius von Fuljod. Fuljod, to whose department of the Ministry Grillparzer was posted as a junior official in the summer of 1818, is remembered in Grillparzer's autobiography as a small-minded man without any understanding of artistic matters.[3] Stadion by contrast was a generous supporter. Towards the end of his life, according to Auguste von Littrow-Bischof, Grillparzer even recalled having read his manuscript version of *König Ottokars Glück und Ende* to him in what must have been the late summer or early autumn of 1823[4] – a remarkable tribute to Stadion's interest if the report is accurate, for that is after the time when Stadion's Ministry was directly involved in the running of the Burgtheater, since a new director of the court theatres, Moriz Graf von Dietrichstein, was appointed from Easter 1821. Dietrichstein remained in this position, under the court chamberlain, until the end of May 1826.

Various schemes to rebuild the old theatre having come to naught, it was in urgent need of modernization. On her first visit in 1836, Frances Trollope observed that it was 'much better fitted by its shape and proportions' for its former function as a tennis-court than for its present function as a theatre, and also that it was 'very dingy'[5] – a fact all the more conspicuous because, as remained the custom in every theatre until the late nineteenth century, the oil lamps that lit the auditorium remained on throughout the performance. (Gas lighting was not introduced in the Burgtheater until 1867.) At the beginning of Dietrichstein's period of office, there were still benches in the rear stalls (as opposed to the 'Parterre noble', or orchestra stalls, which contained a mainly aristocratic clientèle). Wlassack's list of the seating gives a capacity of 1314 in 1822, including standing places but excluding boxes;[6] that would probably mean a total capacity of about 1,600 in all; an official document from 1828 gives an even higher total, 1,800 when 'absolutely full';[7] but these figures clearly depended on cramming in the very maximum of standing customers, and the normal capacity was lower.[8]

The years 1814–32 are usually thought of as Schreyvogel's period in charge of the Burgtheater. He was never, however, its 'director'. What he took over in 1815, when Sonnleithner retired, was the role of the 'Theatersecretär' as *Dramaturg* and literary adviser (his diaries of that year and the next show him assiduously reading manuscripts, grumbling at the time spent on weak plays),[9] and as administrative secretary to the director. Just how far-reaching his responsibilities became is not wholly clear. Zedlitz, writing three years after his death, spoke of Stadion as having selected him for the 'direction' of the theatre as a *Dramaturg* ('zur speciellen dramaturgischen Leitung der Anstalt'),[10] and the actor Heinrich Anschütz, who joined the company in 1821, recollected that part of the power of the senior actors who functioned as producers (*Regisseure*) had passed into Schreyvogel's hands.[11] Schreyvogel himself insisted in 1825 that practical details of production were in the hands of the actors, though the phrasing (he says he was using his resulting 'free time' in building up the repertory)[12] suggests that it was not always so. Certainly his diaries show that he took an active interest in rehearsals. Plays were not very long in rehearsal: the première of Schreyvogel's version of *Romeo and Juliet* in December 1816, for example, took place just eighteen days after the parts were distributed; he had reckoned with a gap of only fourteen days, and the first rehearsal on stage took place just four days before the première.[13] But the work was all the more time-consuming as a result, as he confided to his diary more than once.[14] Eduard von Bauernfeld, whose first comedies were performed towards the end of Schreyvogel's period of office, recalls him as having still conducted rehearsals personally then.[15] Nevertheless, some of the responsibilities that would normally fall to an artistic director remained the province of the producers: in theory these included adjudicating on manuscripts submitted (though Schreyvogel did at least some of that work himself) and also making proposals for casting.[16] Nor can Schreyvogel be given all the credit for improving the Burgtheater by securing the engagement of major actors, including Anschütz. His advice was no doubt influential, and his diary testifies to his admiration of Anschütz's gifts and accomplishments; but Anschütz records negotiating with the 'direction', and it was Stadion, not Schreyvogel, who was responsible in 1820 for getting authority to recruit him.[17] Certainly Schreyvogel's powers were restricted, even though he immediately established good working relations with Dietrichstein when the latter took over as director: Czernin made it clear that the ultimate power of decision, even in matters of casting, remained with himself.[18] The limited scope of Schreyvogel's authority makes his role in establishing the reputation of the Burgtheater as a theatre that might 'be said to correspond with the Théâtre Français in Paris'[19] all the more remarkable an achievement.

Schreyvogel was a true product of the Josephinian Enlightenment, trained in a cultural tradition inherited from Weimar classicism (and especially versed in the work of Goethe, whom he had met in the course of two years he spent in Jena and Weimar in the mid-1790s), and with international horizons. In 1816, while working on his adaptation of *Romeo and Juliet* and shortly after reading *King Lear*, he committed to his diary the idea of providing the theatre with new adaptations of all the finest works of Shakespeare,[20] his ambition being to build up a collection of between twelve and fifteen plays. In fact during his period as *Dramaturg* there were new productions of seven Shakespeare plays, adapted in accordance with the taste of the time and providing major roles for Anschütz, who played the title part nearly fifty times in his adaptation of Voss's translation of *King Lear* (this is the bowdlerized version with a happy ending tailored to the censorship laws), and who also played Falstaff in Schreyvogel's version of *Henry IV*. Schreyvogel was steadily constructing a repertoire of international drama commensurate with the position of the Burgtheater as the principal serious theatre of the multinational empire.

Equally important in this were his free translations from the Spanish, all written under the pseudonym Carl August West and published by Wallishausser: versions of Calderón's *La vida es sueño* (*Das Leben ein Traum*) and *El médico de su honra* (*Don Gutierre*) and of Moreto's *El desdén, con el desdén* (*Donna Diana*). The first of these, *Das Leben ein Traum* – based, as Schreyvogel made clear in the foreword to the first edition (1816), on a version by Johann Diederich Gries that had appeared in Berlin the previous year – was first performed in the Theater an der Wien in June 1816 and in the Burgtheater in 1822; this is the play which first brought Schreyvogel and Grillparzer together when Wilhelm Hebenstreit, the editor of the *Modenzeitung*, published a fragment of Grillparzer's translation of the same play in an attempt to discredit Schreyvogel's freer version. *Don Gutierre*, first performed in the Burgtheater in January 1818, was a tragedy in which Anschütz appeared both as a guest performer in 1820 and as a full member of the company in 1821. *Donna Diana*, a lively comedy, was first performed in November 1816, with the actress Julie Löwe, a personal friend of Schreyvogel's, in the title part, and established itself firmly in the repertory (it was performed over a hundred times in the old Burgtheater, remaining in the repertory until 1882); over fifty years later Bauernfeld would generously say that it read and played like an original and could still serve as a model of verse comedy.[21] In building up the repertoire Schreyvogel had from the first been aware of the shortage of suitable comedies, and when Julie Löwe was well received in a version of Marivaux's *Les Fausses Confidences* in May 1815, he congratulated himself on having presented her with the opportunity of a new career in a genre better suited to her talents.[22]

In the same period two new Molière productions, *Tartuffe* in

Deinhardstein's translation in 1818, and *Les Femmes savantes* in Kotzebue's version in 1819, were unsuccessful; but numerous other French comedies, by Picard, Scribe, and others, were added to the repertory; the translators included Theodor Hell, the editor of the *Abend-Zeitung* in Dresden, who was also a prolific translator. Schreyvogel also promoted the fashionable German dramatists of the day. Adolph Müllner's fate-tragedy *Die Schuld*, which had already been produced in 1813, retained its niche in the repertory; the first drama by Raupach, who became one of the main staples of the programme, was added in 1819 (this was *Die Fürsten Chawansky*), and the most popular of all, *Der Müller und sein Kind*, in 1830.

Over and above all these imports, Schreyvogel was active in encouraging indigenous talent. Castelli testified to the debt numerous young writers owed him for his advice and stimulus.[23] He lavished attention on young Viennese dramatists: not just Grillparzer but also Zedlitz, Deinhardstein, and Bauernfeld. Bauernfeld found a thriving tradition of society comedies on which he could build: in 1825 Tieck called the Burgtheater the best of all German theatres for comedy.[24] It was a tradition partly schooled on French models but also with strong local roots in the work of the prolific Johanna Franul von Weissenthurn. A member of the Burgtheater company from 1789 to 1842, she was admired by Tieck for her comic acting;[25] her work had first entered the repertory in 1800 (a one-act comedy, *Das Nachspiel*), and she continued to provide it with plays almost until the end of her life.

Schreyvogel's encouragement of Grillparzer is well known. It started with *Die Ahnfrau*, which he cajoled him into writing. After some difficulties with the censor (the reasons for which are unknown, as no documentation has survived), it was performed on 31 January 1817 in the Theater an der Wien, in a revised text, which Schreyvogel had persuaded Grillparzer to write in order to strengthen the motivation and make the dialogue livelier – typical aims of a competent *Dramaturg*. Grillparzer, upset by critical perceptions of the play as a mere romantic fate-tragedy, was never reconciled to this version, which expanded the role of the eponymous ghost; nevertheless, it established his reputation. Why it was produced in the Theater an der Wien rather than in the Burgtheater is not clear. Both theatres were still in Pálffy's hands, and though in his autobiography Grillparzer says that the reason was the actors available there,[26] the main role, that of the young heroine Bertha, was played

2   Sophie Schröder as Sappho, after a portrait by Moriz Daffinger.

3 Julie Rettich (formerly Julie Gley) in Raupach's *Crowells Ende*.

by Sophie Schröder, who had been a member of the Burgtheater company since 1815. Grillparzer later accounted for his own initial hesitation about writing the play by saying that he had recognized that the material seemed 'at best suitable for the suburban theatres',[27] and though it is true that Müllner's fate-tragedy had been in the Burgtheater repertory for nearly four years, *Die Ahnfrau* was the work of an unknown and Schreyvogel may well have found it easier to persuade Pálffy that it represented an attractive box-office prospect in the Theater an der Wien than that it was a safe venture in the court theatre.

In the autumn of 1817 Grillparzer began writing *Der Traum ein Leben* – a work still more clearly influenced by the drama of the commercial theatres. But by this time he had also completed a tragedy in classical form, *Sappho*, which was performed in the Burgtheater on 21 April 1818, with Sophie Schröder in the title role (see plate 2). An instant success, it brought Grillparzer a five-year contract as house dramatist (*Theaterdichter*). Over the next thirteen years all his completed plays passed through Schreyvogel's hands and were performed in the Burgtheater. The last Grillparzer production of the Schreyvogel era was Grillparzer's first failure with the critics: this was the love-tragedy on the Hero and Leander theme, *Des Meeres und der Liebe Wellen*, which fell victim to weak performance. The actress who would naturally have played Hero, Sophie Müller (the original Kunigunde in *König Ottokars Glück und Ende*), had died the previous year, and her replacement, Julie Gley, was not up to the part. Known after her marriage as Julie Rettich, she remained a leading member of the company into the 1860s (see plate 3, showing her in the stately style of the court theatre in a Raupach drama added to the repertory in 1839). Frances Trollope greatly admired her in Shakespeare, judging her voice as being 'almost of as sweet and rich a tone' as that of Mlle Mars in Paris. But it is significant that Laube would later write that her undoubted intelligence outstripped her artistic talent, and Speidel would describe her as intelligent but unsensuous.[28]

Des Meeres und der Liebe Wellen was given only four times. The last play Grillparzer submitted to Schreyvogel was *Der Traum ein Leben*; Schreyvogel cautiously recommended that it still needed further work,[29] and the final version was not produced until 1834.

One of the principal tests of a theatre is the new drama that is generated within it, and this is a test that Schreyvogel's Burgtheater passes with flying colours. In the spring of 1828, at the height of his powers, Grillparzer described his own dramatic work as half-way between Goethe and Kotzebue,[30] that is, combining poetic and genuinely theatrical effects. To the end of his creative life he would continue to insist, both in his written notes and in conversation, that genuine drama must be theatrical, must be seen on stage, and that a drama that is merely read cannot be more than a lifeless 'book'. 'I was an Austrian born and bred', he wrote, looking back over his own career in 1853, 'and for every one of my plays I had in mind its performance, and indeed specifically its performance in my native city.'[31] In all of this he echoed the views of Schreyvogel, and indeed Zedlitz saw the liveliness of Schreyvogel's 'unpedantic' adaptations of Calderón, Moreto, and Shakespeare as deriving from the very same distinction between the needs of the stage and those of the study.[32] A collection of Schreyvogel's writings published in 1829 includes a long attack on the 'separation between dramatic literature and the theatre' which he presents as characteristic of German drama of his time; all the great international dramatic literature, he argues, arose organically from practical work in the theatre and fed on indigenous tradition, whereas, with the exception of the popular stage, German drama was divorced from practice. 'A play is written to be seen on the stage', he affirmed; hence the German word *Schauspiel*. 'From Aeschylus and Aristophanes to Gozzi and Beaumarchais it has never occurred to a dramatic genius to write for the study rather than for the stage.' He cites Schiller's development in *Fiesko* and *Kabale und Liebe* as showing the beneficial effect of practical contact with the theatre, and regrets that that contact did not last longer.[33] Grillparzer would place weight on the advantage he had in writing for first-class actors and a knowledgeable audience; in 1853 he too drew the contrast between the conditions he had enjoyed in these respects in Vienna and those under which Schiller had worked, observing that Schiller would have been an even greater dramatist if he had had a real public and good actors to work for.[34]

Certainly Grillparzer had the benefit of a strong company, including Sophie Schröder to play Sappho, Medea in the trilogy *Das goldene Vließ* (1821), Margarethe in *König Ottokars Glück und Ende*, and Gertrude in *Ein treuer Diener seines Herrn* (1828), and Anschütz to play Ottokar, Bancbanus in *Ein treuer Diener seines Herrn*, and the Priest in *Des Meeres und der Liebe Wellen*. Anschütz was endowed with a resonant voice and was greatly respected as a speaker of dramatic verse, combining in Laube's view the best of the formal and natural traditions of acting going back to Goethe's Weimar theatre and to Schröder and Iffland respectively;[35] it was also he who spoke Grillparzer's funeral oration for Beethoven and the oration at the unveiling of the monument by Beethoven's grave. No less a judge than Tieck, who saw him as Lear in 1825, was hugely impressed by the 'poetic truth' in his depiction of Lear's madness.[36] Other prominent members of the company included Maximilian Korn, who was the first Phaon in *Sappho* and Zawisch in *König Ottokars Glück und Ende* – a distinctive contribution to the theatrical texture of both plays, for Korn was best known as a comic actor (he was a central component in the urbane style of the *Konversationsstück*, and according to Anschütz never shed a Viennese tinge to his accent).[37]

In 1832 Schreyvogel was summarily dismissed by Czernin and replaced by Deinhardstein, who was given the title 'deputy director' (*Vicedirektor*). Schreyvogel was awarded a pension of 1,000 fl. per annum[38] – half his salary – after eighteen years' service in which the reputation of the Burgtheater as the premier theatre of German-speaking Europe was established. He died of cholera in July of the same year. Bauernfeld recalls him in his memoirs as 'a serious-minded man of upright character, learning, taste, and good judgement; propriety itself in business matters; reliable, impartial; a man to whom any intrigue was alien'.[39] Costenoble saw his dismissal and the consequent loss of his guidance as a matter for regret,[40] and according to Bauernfeld, looking back in 1849, throughout the company his advice and leadership were missed.[41] Four years after his death Grillparzer wrote sadly in his diary that there was no longer anyone in Vienna with whom he would care to discuss artistic matters.[42]

Despite the constant struggle in which successive directors had to engage in order to protect their funding, the Burgtheater budget was lavish by comparison with that of the commercial theatres. At the end of the 1820s the subsidy it received from the exchequer amounted to about a quarter of its total income. The financial position of playwrights, however, was less than secure. There was no equivalent to the Société des auteurs et compositeurs dramatiques which existed in France from the late 1820s (the successor to Beaumarchais's Société des auteurs dramatiques, which had first sought to regulate acting rights in the Comédie-Française before the Revolution) or the Dramatic Authors' Society which existed in England from 1833. There was also no equivalent at this stage to the French system whereby the author received a proportion of the net receipts from performances: in the Burgtheater a scheme of royalties was proposed by Lobkowitz in 1813, but in the event the first Viennese theatre to introduce such payments was the Theater in der Josefstadt under Franz Pokorny in 1839, and the Burgtheater did not follow suit until 1844, under Holbein. Nor was there any kind of profit-sharing system such as was introduced in the English theatre by Boucicault in the 1860s. Grillparzer was fortunate to be given a contract in 1818 after the success of *Sappho*. It guaranteed him an income of 2,000 fl. W.W. for five years. (This may have meant as little as 400 fl. C.M., as the relationship between silver and paper money was not stabilized until 1820.) He was bound to offer any new plays to the court theatre; any that were accepted would carry a further honorarium but could not appear in print for a year.[43]

What a leading dramatist might hope to earn from a successful play can be pieced together from his returns on *König Ottokars Glück und Ende*, which he finished outside the period of his contract. He received 200 Dukaten (that is, 900 fl. C.M.) honorarium for its first production, paid after three performances, plus a further 100 Dukaten (450 fl.) as a gift from Prince Liechtenstein.[44] He also earned at least 2,600 fl. C.M. from the first edition, including the reprint.[45] Other fees came in from performances elsewhere – there is a record of 50 Taler (100 fl.) received after the first performance in Berlin in 1830, for example – and also for later performances in the Burgtheater: a receipt for 93 fl. has survived for a performance on 18 January 1862.[46] This was not big money; Grillparzer still needed to earn his living as a minor civil servant. His income from his (relatively few) plays compared very well with that of the journeymen playwrights who had to provide the commercial theatres with a new play every two months or so (see pp. 107–8, below); but his earnings bear no comparison with Nestroy's in the commercial theatre. In the years 1839–42, for which Nestroy's private records survive, his income averaged 6,000 fl. C.M. per annum; in the one month March 1842, at the height of his powers, he had an income of a total of 1,317 fl.[47] But he was a more prolific dramatist; the month concerned included performances of five of his own plays, including the première and thirteen further performances of one of the most successful, *Einen Jux will er sich machen*; and he was also an extremely hard-working star actor.

A more revealing comparison is that Schreyvogel was paid 300 fl. in 1816 for his adaptation of *Romeo and Juliet*, and that in 1822 his salary was 2,000 fl.; this might be supplemented by *ad hoc* honoraria, as it was in 1831, when Czernin accorded him a sum of 300 fl., and also by earnings from his publications, as when Wallishausser paid him 200 fl. for the second edition of *Donna Diana* in 1822.[48] Also in

1822, Stubenrauch, whose décor and costumes did much to attract paying customers and boost the box-office takings, was paid 1,300 fl. It is indicative of Viennese priorities that those with the highest incomes were the principal actors. Dietrichstein had set a ceiling on salaries of 3,000 fl. (a ceiling that remained in force until 1848),[49] but various personal allowances were payable on top of that. In 1822, the senior actors who were also *Regisseure* (including Korn) were paid 4,500 fl.; Sophie Müller and Julie Löwe were each paid 4,000 fl., Anschütz 3,800 fl., Costenoble 3,600, and the star actress Sophie Schröder no less than 5,000 fl.:[50] when first she was taken on in 1815, Schreyvogel had noted in his diary that she was 'very expensive'.[51]

The emphasis on acting and actors was not confined to the court theatres, though their companies enjoyed especial prestige, and it could certainly be overdone. Writing in 1853 about the commercial theatres since the death of Raimund, Bauernfeld would complain that the plays performed no longer seemed to matter and that the only thing anyone was interested in was the personality of the actors; in 1887, in a piece celebrating the silver jubilee of the actress Charlotte Wolter's first appearance in the Burgtheater, Ludwig Speidel felt he had to emphasize that actors are only reproductive artists, not creative ones; also in the 1880s Juliette Adam, writing under the pseudonym 'Comte Paul Vasili', reported that the Viennese, like the Parisians, were more interested in gossip about the private lives of their actresses than in seeing them perform; Stefan Zweig, writing about the Burgtheater at the very end of the nineteenth century, recalls an 'almost religious cult of personality' at that time; and in 1907 Egon Friedell remarked that the Burgtheater was unlike every other great theatre in that the actor was regarded as more important than the play.[52]

The persistence of this kind of priority means that historical records need to be scrutinized for distortion. At the end of 1835, for example, *Griseldis* by Friedrich Halm (the pseudonym of Baron Eligius Franz von Münch-Bellinghausen) was received better on the second night than on the first. In 1868 Laube, who had not been in Vienna in December 1835, recounted what must have become a word-of-mouth orthodoxy in the country, namely that the reason for the improved reception was that on the first night the title part was played by one actress, Therese Peche, and on the second night by another, Julie Rettich (the former Julie Gley). Costenoble's diaries show that while indeed Julie Rettich's performance was rapturously received, Therese Peche had also been warmly applauded, and that an additional factor the second night was that the dramatist had shortened the text by strategic cuts. What passed into Burgtheater legend was, then, a simplified version of events, and it is typical that the simplification took the form of reducing everything to the rivalry of two actresses.[53]

Intense interest in the leading performers is, however, symptomatic of the perception of drama as an essentially theatrical art which is at the heart of the vitality of Viennese tradition. A corollary for dramatists was a conviction of the function of drama as entertainment and of the authority of the public as the ultimate arbiter of theatrical success – a point made frequently both by Schreyvogel and by Grillparzer, who first wrote of the public as a 'jury' in his diary in 1821 and still stood by that view in 1849.[54]

The audience attracted by the Burgtheater at this time was, however, still drawn mainly from the aristocracy and wealthy bourgeoisie. Murray's *Handbook for Travellers in Southern Germany* (1837) records that the stalls in the 'first or noble parterre, corresponding with the orchestra seats in an English theatre', were 'frequented by ladies as well as gentlemen', and adds: 'Servants in livery (distinguished by figures in their hats, and hence called numeros) supply the audience with ices and other refreshments betwen the acts.'[55] One of those who worked as a *Numero* in his youth was Ferdinand Raimund, who became the most popular actor-playwright in the commercial theatre in the 1820s: the son of a suburban craftsman, he was apprenticed in his teens to a confectioner and part of his work was to sell refreshments in the Burgtheater. But the audience contained few members from a similarly humble background. It was still fashionable for the aristocracy to maintain a box, subscribed for a whole year; indeed most boxes and stalls remained in the same family from 1750 onwards well into the nineteenth century, and Glassbrenner drew a mocking picture of an audience most of whom were there because it was the done thing rather than out of interest in the play.[56] Certainly the audience was conservative in its tastes; the compensation was that because aristocratic families were brought up in an expectation of attending, the whole theatre culture was imprinted in successive generations of the ruling class, in a way that helped to guarantee its survival and continuity.

2. THE LAUBE ERA

The names Schreyvogel and Laube are often linked as the two figures who brought the Burgtheater to its peak, maintaining the quality of an evolving company and at the same time building up the repertoire, so realizing the spirit of Joseph II's original conception of a 'National Theatre'. But the seventeen and a half years that separated their periods in office saw a decline, so that when Laube took over he was engaged in a rescue operation.

Deinhardstein, who began by having to overcome the hostility of Schreyvogel's many admirers,[57] was fortunate in having among the plays on the stocks Grillparzer's highly stageworthy *Der Traum ein Leben*: one of the best examples of the influence of the popular Viennese stage on the drama of the Burgtheater, it was immediately a big box-office success when it was produced in October 1834, remained the most successful of Grillparzer's plays throughout his lifetime, and was indeed the Grillparzer play most frequently played in the Burgtheater (and latterly the Akademietheater) until the mid-1960s. He was also fortunate in that just over a year later the first drama of Friedrich Halm, *Griseldis*, was produced – another cornerstone of the repertoire for thirty years. But the first full-length new play to be premièred under Deinhardstein was one of his own comedies, *Garrik in Bristol*, with Ludwig Löwe (Julie Löwe's brother) in the double role of Garrick and Johnson; it too was well-received – because of his official position, Deinhardstein was unable to appear on stage to respond to the applause, and an actor had to appear in his stead[58] – and indeed proved a good box-office draw. This set the pattern for the development of a lighter repertory, with an increasing number of comedies. The playwright on whom Deinhardstein most depended in this respect was Bauernfeld, who had had his first success under Schreyvogel (*Leichtsinn aus Liebe*, 1831) and now produced a series of light-hearted society comedies influenced by Molière, Scribe, and Kotzebue, which dominated the comic repertory from the early 1830s onwards. Deinhardstein – perhaps influenced by Czernin – rejected one play, *Fortunat*, which Bauernfeld had written in the late 1820s, using the fifteenth-century *Fortunatus* chapbook as his source, and which he hoped might match the success of *Der Traum ein Leben*; nevertheless, in the course of his long career, no fewer than fifty of his plays were produced in the Burgtheater.

Some, including a number of single-act plays, were flops; but thirteen of his plays were performed thirty-five times or more, and in all the tally comes to 1,200 performances up to 1912, making him at that point the sixth most frequently performed author in the Burgtheater,[59] after which his name disappeared for good from the programme.

Box-office records show that this kind of comedy did not in fact produce returns comparable to those generated by works by Schiller, Grillparzer, and Halm.[60] But they were simpler to stage and became a speciality of the theatre. Laube would later write of Bauernfeld that he was the 'foster father' of a whole tradition of gracefully witty dialogue peculiar to Vienna.[61] As a consequence, the Burgtheater acquired a new social function: as its audience became less exclusively aristocratic and more bourgeois (especially after the creation of the Dual Monarchy in 1867, when the Hungarian aristocracy largely disappeared and their place was taken by the new industrial barons), the acting of the company came to be regarded as a model of conduct and aristocratic bearing. Julie Löwe in particular established herself as the embodiment on stage of elegant and 'aristocratic' behaviour.[62] Recalling performances of *Konversationsstücke* in the theatre on the Michaelerplatz, Ludwig Speidel wrote that the audience lost all sense of being in a theatre and simply felt they were moving in the best of society.[63] The Burgtheater retained this role as a model of manners and polished conversation, and even of elegant dressing, at least until the late nineteenth century.[64]

It was also a comedy, however, that in 1838 provoked the most sensational failure under Deinhardstein, Grillparzer's one verse comedy, *Weh dem, der lügt!*. Again the performance seems to have been weak, but over and above that the play fell victim to a rivalry with political overtones, which went back to 1835. After being rejected by the Burgtheater, Bauernfeld's *Fortunat* had been performed in the Theater in der Josefstadt on 24 March 1835, and sharply criticized by Saphir in a two-part review in the *Theaterzeitung*. Bauernfeld's next play was a comedy, *Bürgerlich und Romantisch*, which included a caricature of Saphir in the person of a reviewer-turned-servant named Unruh. It was premièred in the Burgtheater on 7 September 1835 and attacked for its lack of a 'basic idea' by Saphir, who attributed its success to the excellent performance. The next shot in the feud was fired by Bauernfeld: a polemical satirical comedy, *Der literarische Salon*, directed against Saphir and the editor of the *Theaterzeitung*, Adolf Bäuerle. The première on 24 March 1836 was well received, according to Costenoble's account, by Bauernfeld's 'supporters'. Two days later the *Theaterzeitung* published a witty review by Saphir criticizing it for having colourless characterization and insufficient action. The play was performed only once; both Bäuerle and Saphir appear to have objected formally, and according to Costenoble, the Emperor himself decided that he was not going to put up with an open squabble in his theatre.[65]

This was a petty feud, a clash of personalities rather than of significant principles. But it had far-reaching consequences, which affected the whole temper of public debate in the years leading up to the 1848 revolution. It was not just in the suppression of *Der literarische Salon* that victory went to Saphir. Bauernfeld was a figure of liberal opinions; Saphir, whose attempts to establish his own journal in Vienna since 1834 had been frustrated by opposition at court, was now given permission to launch *Der Humorist*, which appeared from the beginning of 1837 (at first three times weekly, rising to six times weekly by 1844) and provided a vehicle for his outspoken criticism of dramatists of satirical stamp. These included both Nestroy and Bauernfeld, between whom he claimed to detect an 'undeniable similarity'.[66] Bauernfeld's standing as a dramatist was not hurt by the affair; *Bürgerlich und Romantisch*, indeed, was performed more often in the Burgtheater than any other of his plays (a total of 155 performances up to 1912). But when the theatre announced a comedy by Grillparzer, a friend of Bauernfeld's, the very title *Weh dem, der lügt!* ('Woe betide liars!') aroused expectations that another salvo in the feud was going to be fired. A clique of Saphir's supporters led the audience in noisy disapproval. Press criticism turned in part on the designation 'comedy' (*Lustspiel*), which the performance had not lived up to. That the critical voices included Saphir, who wrote a damning review in *Der Humorist*, probably had less impact on Grillparzer than the rejection of the play by the first-night audience, since he had always insisted on the authority of the audience's verdict as 'the voice of general humanity'.[67] Coming on top of the disappointment he had suffered with *Des Meeres und der Liebe Wellen* four years earlier, this new failure led to his withdrawal from the stage. There were reverberations in the commercial theatre also: Nestroy's *Glück, Mißbrauch und Rückkehr*, which had its première in the Theater an der Wien four days after that of *Weh dem, der lügt!*, was billed not as a *Posse* but as a *Lustspiel* (probably at Carl's instigation, for there is no corroboration in the surviving manuscripts); the play was a hit, but the term *Lustspiel* drew considerable critical flak, both in *Der Humorist* and in other journals, and Nestroy responded by making fun of critical pedantry, calling his next play, *Gegen Torheit ist kein Mittel*, a 'comic tragedy with music' ('lustiges Trauerspiel mit Gesang').[68]

Deinhardstein never succeeded in imposing his authority strongly on the theatre. After the death of Emperor Franz in 1835 he resigned himself to having insufficient support to realize his aspirations, and though Czernin withdrew from day-to-day decision-making on health grounds in 1835, he maintained an irksomely close super-vision.[69] In 1841 a new artistic director was appointed. Franz von Holbein was a native Viennese who had had sixteen years as director in Hanover, where he had made his name by balancing the budget and leaving the theatre in surplus.[70] He set in motion a programme of sounder financial planning, cutting back on the distribution of free seats, and systematically economizing on outgoings. New plays added to the repertory under Holbein included three of the highest earners in the first half of the century: in 1842 Friedrich Halm's romantic verse drama *Der Sohn der Wildnis*, in 1844 Bauernfeld's *Ein deutscher Krieger*, a historical drama set at the end of the Thirty Years War and treating the theme of German unity, and in 1846 Bauern-feld's *Großjährig*, a thinly-disguised albeit fairly mild satire of the rigidity and stasis of the Metternich era, whose brief success (it lasted on the repertory only four years) led to a marked sharpening of critical hostility towards Bauernfeld in conservative reviewers.

But although Holbein succeeded in improving the theatre's finances, he was over-bureaucratic in his management and tended to be overshadowed by the court chamberlain Count Dietrichstein. One consequence of his financial stringency was that when Laube took over in December 1849 he needed to secure a massive injection of cash, in particular to get new blood into the company, which needed regeneration.[71]

The succession was a matter of prolonged speculation. In the changed political climate in the second half of the 1840s, three names who had been associated with the radical 'Young German' move-ment were much canvassed. One of them, Franz von Dingelstedt, had long been converted from his former radical views. He had first visited Vienna in the early 1840s and had written reports for the Stuttgart *Morgenblatt für gebildete Leser*; his time would come later.

Another, Karl Gutzkow, probably destroyed any chances he may have had by publishing his *Wiener Eindrücke* (1845), in which he described the Burgtheater as being reduced to ineffectiveness by the combination of a narrow-minded censorship and the corrupt taste of its aristocratic patrons;[72] his plays were banned by an imperial edict dated 14 November 1845.[73] The other candidate, Heinrich Laube, proved a much shrewder political operator, though lengthy negotiations were required to secure his appointment. Revolution broke out in mid-March, toppling Metternich and bringing an end to censorship. Even though the Austrian delegation, including Bauernfeld, failed to reach the Frankfurt *Vorparlament* before it had broken up in early April, the notion of an enlightened united Germany which it represented stimulated strong German nationalist enthusiasm in Vienna. It was associated especially with the students of the Academic Legion, who sported the German colours, and was reflected in the theatre in the success of a production in the Theater an der Wien on 1 April of Benedix's play *Das bemooste Haus* – not a new work, but staged for the first time in Vienna – in which German students appeared as characters on the stage[74] (see plate 4, an illustration that also shows the typical illumination of the stage by a row of footlights, which would be supplemented by sets of further Argand lamps behind the wings, as shown in plate 5). That same evening the Carltheater mounted the first night of a production of Laube's comedy *Gottsched und Gellert*; by the time of the fourth performance the ever-opportunistic director Carl had the black, red, and gold flag symbolizing German unity flying from the front of the theatre, and after the final curtain the German flag was brought on stage and Carl, who had played the role of Gellert, made a speech extolling the ideal of a united Germany stretching from the North Sea to the Adriatic.[75]

In late May, the first barricades were erected in Vienna following the government's decision to dissolve the Academic Legion and close the university. One of them was in the Michaelerplatz, directly in front of the Burgtheater (see plate 6). Meanwhile on 24 April Laube's prose drama *Die Karlsschüler*, which centres on the triumphant first performance of Schiller's *Die Räuber* and had been banned by the censors until the revolution, was given its first Viennese performance in the Burgtheater, and became another focus of libertarian enthusiasm: Anschütz reports that jubilation broke out in the audience at

4   Performance of Roderich Benedix, *Das bemooste Haus*, in the Theater an der
Wien, 1848.

5 Set for Josef Kilian Schickh's comedy *Die Localsängerin und ihr Vater*. Theater in der Josefstadt, 1839.

6   Barricade in front of the Burgtheater on the Michaelerplatz, May 1848.

every mention of Schiller and of liberty and justice.[76] In response to curtain-calls for the actor who had played the part of Schiller, Carl Albrecht Fichtner, Laube himself appeared on the stage.

Dietrichstein pressed to have him appointed artistic director, with the aim of achieving 'organic reform' in the theatre.[77] This plan failed at first on financial grounds, but the next year Laube (who in the meantime had served as a delegate to the Frankfurt parliament), returned to Vienna to direct a production of another of his own plays, the tragedy *Struensee*. That was in October 1849; Baron Münch (Friedrich Halm) and others pressed Laube's case, and by then a new court chamberlain, Karl Graf Lanckoronski, had been appointed by the young Emperor Franz Joseph. The office still carried with it ultimate responsibility for the direction of the court theatres, and Lanckoronski succeeded in getting Laube appointed director, the Emperor signing the decree on 25 December 1849. The next day Laube took over, and on 1 January 1850 the *Theaterzeitung* carried an announcement by Holbein himself to the effect that Laube had been nominated 'artistic director' (*artistischer Director*). The appointment was initially subject to confirmation in five years' time (Holbein's disappointing record prompted caution), but was confirmed in July 1851.

In order that Holbein's financial skill should not be wasted, he retained a post as 'economic director (*ökonomischer Direktor*), and remained in that office until 1855. This was not helpful to Laube's reforming intentions: for instance, Holbein tried to oppose the engagement of the first young actor whom Laube selected to strengthen the cast in tragedy, Bogumil Dawison, because of the cost envisaged. But most of Holbein's interest was directed at the opera (Kärntnertortheater), which he directed from 1849 to 1853, gaining a reputation there too for concentrating on economical management,[78] so that his influence in the Burgtheater was in practice limited.

Holbein had been the first non-aristocrat to be given the title of 'director', but had been politically timid, in a way that Laube scorned; he had regarded even the end of censorship in 1848 as a worry.[79] Though the revolution had been quashed in October and November 1848, Laube's appointment was a concession towards the new libertarian spirit. But it was also dictated by practical exigence. Laube found the company in bad shape, and the problems in respect of artistic standards were compounded by financial problems. The success of his direction turned on his skill both in managing the theatre and in squeezing adequate subsidies from the exchequer. The subsidy he received from 1850 onwards (100,000 fl. per annum) was double that under the previous direction. At the same time prices were raised, pushing up the takings. By the beginning of the 1850–1 season the Finance Ministry wanted to claw back some of the subsidy; and Laube's reply, arguing that on the contrary the financing was still inadequate, is the fullest summary both of his policy and of the plight of the theatre as he saw it.[80]

The principal costs, he explained, lay in the company, but it had to be supported by comparable excellence in costume, décor, and music. The stock of costumes was minimal, and no efficient control had been imposed; the costumes even of plays still in the repertory had been used to provide costumes for other plays. He had already stopped the use of musicians. In décor, he argued, Vienna was thirty years behind Paris or Berlin; his own expenditure on décor had been modest, and the only innovation he had made had been to make use of Moritz Lehmann from the Carltheater, from whose engagement as stage designer he promised a solid practical advance in the form of sets for the new box stage, which would be of considerable advantage in the *Konversationsstück*. As for the actors, a company needed to be constantly renewed, and this had not happened for twenty years, so that the personnel he had taken over – a company just over forty strong – were aging and inadequate. Of the men Laube took over, the central figure, Anschütz, was over sixty-five; others were sickly or of limited use (Ludwig Löwe, for example, the original Otto in *Ein treuer Diener* in 1828, Rustan in *Der Traum ein Leben* in 1834, and Leon in *Weh dem, der lügt!* in 1838, was nearly sixty); he had engaged Josef Wagner (who would be a member of the company till 1870) as a young romantic hero. There were too many inadequate actresses who could not be got rid of; he was working for the engagement of Marie Bayer-Bürck from Dresden (who would in fact never join the company, though she appeared frequently as a guest). What he needed was not only a higher annual subsidy but five years of extra supplementation for a 'period of regeneration'; and he justified this by comparing the outlay in Vienna with the figures expended in smaller courts in Germany. The choice was clear: either the subsidy as before, with a mediocre theatre, or the best theatre in German-speaking Europe, which required an appropriate subsidy.

Laube did not succeed in getting the subsidy raised but he succeeded in preventing it from being reduced until 1859 (the year of the Franco-Austrian War and the disastrous Italian campaign). By 1862 he was still pointing to the small number of actors and the inadequate stock of costume and décor, and complaining that takings were limited by the small capacity of the theatre and further reduced by the number of free tickets dispensed. Nevertheless, partly by his regeneration of the repertoire, partly by careful housekeeping, and partly by increasing the income through raised admission and subscription prices, he kept the Burgtheater in the black, and when he finally tendered his resignation in September 1867 he was able to claim that in the eighteen years of his directorship the theatre had not had a deficit.[81]

Laube's declared intention in respect of the repertory was that anyone who spent a year in Vienna should be able to see in the Burgtheater all the German classics and other dramas of lasting vitality from the last hundred years, plus the legacy of Shakespeare and the Romance countries to the German stage.[82] He set about revitalizing the programme with great energy, adding a whole succession of new productions from his first year in charge: major new productions of Goethe, Schiller, and above all Shakespeare (still adapted to fit contemporary taste), successful revivals of Grillparzer, and modern plays, with a special emphasis on comedies and light *Konversationsstücke*. In this Laube was responding to the established tastes of the audience: he observed that there was 'no public that laughs as readily and as well as the Viennese public': it had for a long time not been an 'audience for tragedy'.[83] Notable successes in the field of comedy included Freytag's *Die Journalisten*, which Laube staged in 1853, the year after its first performance in Karlsruhe; but a considerable share of the programme – about a quarter – was taken up by translations from French, both comedy and social drama. Laube defended this by arguing that the plays were all thoroughly absorbed into the Burgtheater idiom, and that it was essential to cultivate modern drama in order to maintain the skills of the actors.[84]

He was also shrewdly aware that to keep up its attractiveness a theatre must offer its audience varied fare, and looking back in 1868 in a book reviewing his years in charge of the Burgtheater, he was able to claim that it had offered the most comprehensive programme in Europe, outdoing its only rival, the Comédie-Française, precisely in its international coverage.[85] By comparison with the Schreyvogel era, Laube's programme was weakest in nurturing young dramatists from Vienna; its strength lay rather in contemporary French drama and in the proven classics. Schreyvogel had discovered and encouraged Grillparzer; Laube rediscovered him. The revivals included a successful new production of *Des Meeres und der Liebe Wellen* in 1851, with Marie Bayer-Bürck playing the main role to Laube's complete satisfaction,[86] and with Wagner as Leander and Anschütz as the Priest; but the vindication came too late to coax Grillparzer to put his late plays (he had just finished the last of them, *Die Jüdin von Toledo*) forward for performance. In 1849, Grillparzer had had doubts about Laube's appointment, seeing him as too politically involved;[87] but Laube it was who re-established his standing, finding that his plays retained an attraction for the 'educated' part of the public which a contemporary such as Friedrich Halm could not match.[88]

That comparison, as Laube phrased it in 1868, may be harsh on Münch, who had been involved in toppling Laube from his post the previous year, and with whom he did not make peace until about 1871.[89] The issue that triggered Laube's resignation was the creation of a *Generalintendanz*, an official administration (run by Münch) to which the director was directly responsible. Laube pointed to theatres in Germany where the creation of such administrations had led to interference in artistic matters; he stressed the danger that opportunistic criteria would prevail; and he saw the artistic director reduced to a mere head of production.[90] His resignation was on this matter of principle, in defence of the autonomy of the director, whose responsibilities he set out in a long resignation letter.[91] The court view, as recorded in a memorandum by the Master of the Imperial Household, Prince Hohenlohe, was that Laube was motivated by personal ambition.[92] What Laube, by contrast, suspected lay behind the whole manoeuvre was political pressure: he claimed to have heard that he had lost his position because of the liberal plays he had taken into the repertory, including Bauernfeld's *Aus der Gesellschaft*, a miniature portrait of Viennese society;[93] and certainly there had been mounting disquiet that he was presenting polemical dramas on current social issues, many of them translated from the

French, to an extent that was incompatible with the function of the Burgtheater as a court theatre.[94]

Laube put up with working in a theatre that was notoriously cramped and uncomfortable.[95] He did not lavish money on décor; he would later sum up his guiding principle in the motto 'Sparing in décor, rich in performance!'[96] By comparison with later producers who went in for elaborate stage effects (including Dingelstedt, the most important of his successors) he was remembered rather for 'aesthetic spartanism'[97] – and indeed the argument was advanced that his frugality in staging helped to prompt the lavishness of Dingelstedt's productions as a reaction.[98] The one innovation he made in staging was to introduce the box set. Since the seventeenth century, the standard stage construction in the European theatre had been the wing and flat system, with the side scenery in a series of flats which were not joined up and could be moved by being rolled on grooves. The effect was completely unrealistic: actors often did not enter through working doors, and from the boxes at the side of the stage the audience could see through the gaps between the flats. The box set, with closed walls, functioning doors and windows, and a ceiling piece, had been in use in Paris and London since the early 1830s (Grillparzer had admired the realism of the sets on his visit to Paris in 1836) and in Vienna had first been introduced in about 1840 in the Theater an der Wien by Karl Carl, who visited Paris in July of that year. By comparison with the traditional open wings and painted back-drop, it offered important acoustic advantages and permitted a more informal manner of delivery. In fact the size and shape of the old Burgtheater had long meant that the style of speaking there was less declamatory than elsewhere, even in classical tragedy, where convention dictated a style of rhetorical pathos. Eduard Genast, for example, found on his visit in 1847 that when playing Tell he had to assume a simpler manner of speaking than in Berlin; and while Tieck twenty-two years earlier had had the impression that the tempo of performance in the Burgtheater, even in comedy, was slower than he was used to in Dresden, more weight should probably be given to the report of Genast, based on his experience acting with the company: his verdict was the opposite of Tieck's, namely, that he found himself having to fit in with a faster tempo than he was accustomed to.[99]

Certainly the use of the box set was part and parcel of Laube's concern to refine this tradition by cultivating an intimate speaking style in modern drama. The spoken word was his central artistic concern: in his writings on theatre history he revealingly uses the term '[das] rezitierende Schauspiel' (a 'recited play').[100] He saw his main responsibility as lying in production, conducting rehearsals, and instructing the actors, with what he regarded as the added advantage of being an experienced playwright as well.[101] He was not always tactful: at the outset he had a trial of strength with six senior actors with the rank of producers (*Regisseure*), in particular with Ludwig Löwe; when he had problems with the individualistic Dawison he did not shirk from dismissing him to preserve the harmony and balance of his company. His greatest lasting achievement lay in building up that company, recruiting a series of outstanding younger talents, including most notably the elegant Adolf von Sonnenthal and the tragedienne Charlotte Wolter, who made her début in 1862 as Iphigenie and was a central figure in Laube's Grillparzer revival, famous for her melodious and powerful voice. Laube left an indelible imprint on the shape, the style, and the standards of the company until the end of the century; one of the most perceptive critics of the period, Ludwig Speidel, who was in Vienna from 1853 onwards and covered the Burgtheater for the *Neue Freie Presse* for nearly forty years, wrote in 1888 that of all the directors of the Burgtheater so far he was the one to make the deepest mark on it.[102]

3. THE LAST YEARS IN THE 'OLD' BURGTHEATER

The name that had for some time been canvassed as a likely successor to Laube was Franz von Dingelstedt; he was being discussed as a less pushful alternative as early as 1864.[103] He had been director of the court theatre in Munich in the early fifties, then from 1857 director of the theatre in Weimar, the climax of his achievement there being a spectacular cycle of the Shakespeare histories in 1864. In Munich he had been a member of the 'Munich circle', who included Heyse and Geibel, and he had been in close contact with the fashionable Shakespeare translator Friedrich Bodenstedt, who became director (*Intendant*) of the Meiningen Court Theatre in the years 1866–9. The Meiningen company were celebrated for their attention to accurate historical settings, costume, and properties, and for disciplined production, especially of crowd scenes (Georg II of Meiningen, the patron of the Court Theatre, had been among those who went to Weimar to see Dingelstedt's Shakespeare cycle in 1864); and Dingelstedt brought similar characteristics to the Burgtheater.

In 1867 he was appointed not to the Burgtheater but to the Kärntnertortheater; but in December 1870 he was transferred – not without regret on his part, as he had not only committed himself to ambitious opera productions but had also become interested in ballet.[104] His principal precondition was that the antiquated theatre on the Michaelerplatz must be replaced, and the original intention was that as a stop-gap solution the company should temporarily take over the Kärntnertortheater, which had fallen vacant when the new Opera House on the Ringstrasse was opened in May 1869, though this scheme proved too expensive to realize.[105]

Dingelstedt remained director of the Burgtheater until his death in 1881. He was experienced, and financially shrewd – indeed according to his eventual successor, Adolf Wilbrandt, he was particularly proud of his financial skill,[106] and it was an important quality in view of the costly productions he mounted. His whole approach to production was dominated by his emphasis on rich décor: he would even interrupt actors at rehearsal to transfer his attention to some element of the setting.[107] This shift of emphasis caught the taste of the times (there are obvious affinities with the pictorialism of the Victorian theatre in England), appealing to the *nouveaux riches* who were increasingly prominent in the Burgtheater audience. His attention to detail in his extras reflects the interest in historical realism in the painting of the time (his direction coincided with the domination of Viennese painting by Hans Makart) and is also a key indicator of his affinities with the Meiningen style. Indeed, his anticipation of that style may explain why the Meiningen company received a mixed reception when they played in the Theater an der Wien in 1875: Speidel, for example, reviewing their productions in the *Neue Freie Presse*, found them over-elaborate and lacking in emotional focus.[108] The Meiningen productions seemed less innovative in Vienna than elsewhere simply because theatrical historicism was not a novelty there.

Dingelstedt's attention to elaborate detail in setting and costumes transformed Burgtheater practice, and not just in reaction against Laube: even in Schreyvogel's time, as Anschütz testifies, it had been axiomatic that the extras had been sketchily kitted out.[109] He enjoyed the great advantage of being able to concentrate on the visual side of production because he did not have to rebuild the acting strength as Laube had had to do. New actors were of course added, including Hugo Thimig for comic roles, but basically the company Laube had assembled continued to mature under Dingelstedt; he reaped the benefit of Laube's groundwork. Charlotte Wolter became a dominantly central figure. She offered what in 1887 Speidel summed up as a 'feast for the ears and the eyes'; Hevesi wrote in 1894 of her 'Makartism'.[110] In his obituary in 1894 Speidel took the same point even further:

> She had not only lived through but helped to shape the decorative period of the Burgtheater under Dingelstedt. Only through her was Hans Makart brought to life, because she added both the breathing moving body and the soul to decorative costume and colour... Long after Makart's death she continued what he had achieved in painting, but with more genius than he had commanded.[111]

The repertory continued to contain modern French plays, in response to the taste of the paying public; indeed, the biggest box-office success of Dingelstedt's direction was a translation of the dramatized version of Alphonse Daudet's popular novel *Froment jeune et Risler aîné*, with Sonnenthal and a gifted young actor who was a member of the Burgtheater company off and on in the 1870s, Friedrich Mitterwurzer, in the title parts. But the prestige productions were of Shakespeare; the most celebrated event in the Dingelstedt years was a Shakespeare week in 1875, presenting again (as in Weimar) the cycle of Shakespeare histories in Dingelstedt's adaptations, with casts including Sonnenthal as Richard II.

A bonus that fell into Dingelstedt's lap was that after Grillparzer's death in 1872 the three completed plays he had withheld from the public, *Ein Bruderzwist in Habsburg*, *Libussa*, and *Die Jüdin von Toledo*, became available; and in 1879 Dingelstedt also ventured a revival of *Weh dem, der lügt!*, with Mitterwurzer as Galomir. This was a play that even Laube had not risked, judging it a difficult work in terms of theatrical effectiveness.[112] But it is *Ein Bruderzwist in Habsburg* that is most revealing about the contrast in style between Dingelstedt and Laube, for there was a race between them to stage it first. Laube was at this point the director of the new Wiener Stadttheater, which had opened on 15 September 1872. The performance in the Burgtheater of a play about 'fraternal strife' in the House of Habsburg was a major departure from tradition. But Grillparzer's death as a revered elder statesman had come just a year after the unification of Germany; he was already being seen as the great Austrian national poet, and both *Ein Bruderzwist in Habsburg* and *Libussa*, which is about the foundation of Prague, the second great Habsburg city, fitted credibly into the role. Dingelstedt planned to have the première on 18 October, then to bring it forward to mid-September,[113] then he reverted to October. Laube took advantage of this leisurely timetable and announced the Stadttheater production for 24 September; as soon as this announcement broke Dingelstedt rearranged his première for 28 September. The rival performances took place, then, within four days of each other: Laube's production deriving its psychological impact from the spoken text, Dingelstedt's a *Gesamtkunstwerk*, the spoken text illustrated at every step by visual effects. Both were well received; if Dingelstedt's carried the day, it was not just because of the greater means he had at his disposal but also because of the star-studded cast he was able to field, including Josef Lewinsky as Rudolf II, Sonnenthal as Mathias, Ludwig Gabillon as Klesel – all of them recruited for the Burgtheater company by Laube.

Four months later the Burgtheater mounted the first Viennese production of *Die Jüdin von Toledo*, which had had its first performance in Prague in November 1872. Again Dingelstedt assembled a very strong cast: Sonnenthal as the tempted King Alphons, Mitterwurzer as his courtier Garceran, and Charlotte Wolter in the title part, the unreflectingly seductive Rahel. Dingelstedt had found the text 'strange' when he had first read it, and had predicted that it would not go down well; it was held together by a strong sensual element, but had a 'cold' ceremonial tone.[114] The critical reception was mixed: conventionally respectable attitudes were as strait-laced in Vienna as in Victorian London, and Dingelstedt's production was found 'unedifying' ('unerquicklich') in its effect because the play centres on a character with no depth or spiritual nobility.[115] That is, the critics tried to apply criteria applicable to classical tragedy: the tragic figure must have a nobility of spirit. Such criteria were not appropriate, for though Grillparzer had developed as a disciple of Goethe, this was a very modern play, a long way ahead of its times, and anticipating themes characteristic of the Schnitzler period: in particular the concentration on frankly sexual attraction. Charlotte Wolter, herself schooled as a classical tragedienne, seems to have

been unable to adjust; certainly Speidel, defining both playfulness
and sensuality as essential to Rahel's character, observed that these
were effects that Charlotte Wolter did not achieve and that were
indeed alien to her.[116]

After Dingelstedt's death in 1881, Adolf Wilbrandt was appointed
as his successor. He was respected both as a dramatist and for his
personal integrity; when he resigned in 1887 it was because the
work had proved so exhausting that it was preventing him from
getting on with his creative writing. By comparison with Laube and
Dingelstedt, Wilbrandt was very much the poet in the theatre, and
was concerned to enlarge the repertory of poetic drama. Premières
included his own translations of *Electra* (1882) and *Oedipus Rex* (1886),
the latter very favourably reviewed by Speidel,[117] so bringing into
the repertory two works by Sophocles that would later be adapted
by Hofmannsthal.

In the six years in which Wilbrandt was in charge the company
remained a stable one. When his arrangement of both Parts of
Goethe's *Faust* was staged on three successive evenings at the
begining of 1883, so realizing what had been one of his 'first dreams'
on his appointment,[118] he was able to call on Sonnenthal as Faust,
Lewinsky as Mephistopheles, and Charlotte Wolter as Helena – all
three members going back to Laube's time. Newcomers to the
company included the comic actress Katharina Schratt: when the
new Burgtheater on the Ringstrasse was built, the curtains would
feature her as the representative of the comic muse, the counterpart
to Charlotte Wolter's tragic muse. Rudolf Tyrolt, on the other hand,
a local actor with a comic touch, did not fit in well. These were in
fact years of consolidation rather than of innovation, in the repertory
as well: Ibsen's name was becoming known internationally, but
Dingelstedt had rejected *The Pretenders* in 1872,[119] and not one of his
problem plays had been seen in the old Burgtheater by the time it
closed in 1888.

The closure came while Sonnenthal was acting as temporary
('provisional') director. That the old theatre on the Michaelerplatz
was destined to close had long been decided, but the construction of
the new theatre on the Ringstrasse, designed by Gottfried Semper
(who died in 1879) and by Karl Hasenauer took fourteen years –
nearly twice as long as was taken on the Opera House. The
disadvantages of the old theatre were well known: they included

antiquated facilities, lack of space, and a high level of fire risk (not least on the single spiral staircase that led to the upper galleries). But when the time came, parting was hard. The final performance was Goethe's *Iphigenie*, with Charlotte Wolter as Iphigenie; then Sonnenthal spoke a closing epilogue that had been written for the occasion by the new artistic secretary, Alfred von Berger, expressing the sadness of the final curtain and optimism at the future that beckoned in the imposing new building: the audience would find 'in the new house the Burgtheater of old' ('Im neuen Haus das alte Burgtheater').[120]

But the move from the Michaelerplatz to the new theatre on what was then the Franzensring (now the Dr.-Karl-Lueger-Ring) proved much more difficult than moving the opera had been. The acoustics of the new theatre were alien – the auditorium was nearly half as high again (17.5 m.) as in the old Burgtheater, and the differences in acoustics were so great that it was necessary to rehearse every play afresh.[121] On the exterior of the building busts of the great dramatists – rather in the style of Garnier's Opera House in Paris, which had opened in 1875 – symbolize the pretensions of the foundation, and specifically its rivalry with the Comédie-Française (see plate 7): at the north end the international classics, Calderón, Shakespeare, and Molière; in the centre the German classics, Lessing, Goethe, and Schiller; at the southern end the tragic dramatists of the nineteenth-century Burgtheater, Hebbel, Grillparzer, and Friedrich Halm. The internal décor is lavish: the young Gustav Klimt was one of those who worked on the ceiling paintings illustrating the history of theatre over the ornamental main staircases at the north and south ends of the building. But precisely all the sumptuous appointments exemplify the difference that Adolf Loos would later hammer home between functional effectiveness and decorative effect. The auditorium was in an unpractical lyre-shape, which gave poor vision from many of the boxes (this is clearly shown in plate 8), and it was widely perceived as too ostentatious – a demonstration, as Tyrolt put it in his diary, of the egoism of the architect, who had created a monument for himself at the expense of the tradition of the theatre.[122] What Tyrolt defined as having been lost was the immediacy of contact between stage and public. (In this, exactly the same mistakes were made as had also been made in the new Opera House.) The new Burgtheater held an audience almost

7 New Burgtheater showing sculptures on façade.

8   Original interior of the new Burgtheater.

half as big again as the old house (1653 places, as against 1125 in the old Burgtheater in 1887). Even before the opening Ludwig Gabillon, another veteran of Laube's company, noted in his diary that the acoustics were poor and that the actors had been a secondary consideration in designing the building; a month after the opening he confirmed his fears: the old 'intimacy' had been lost.[123] The result was that the company inevitably found themselves facing a choice between adopting a strenuously declamatory style and reconciling themselves to inaudibility. Declamation won the day, and so a new artifice developed, the style that became known as 'Burgtheaterpathos'. Hence the all-out attack mounted by Speidel in the *Neue Freie Presse* on 6 January 1889: the new building had been constructed with total disregard for the whole tradition of the Burgtheater; the proportions and construction of the new building, with its large stage and high auditorium, were such that from many parts of the house the actors were inaudible; they were forced to speak louder, and as a result the art of subtle conversational speaking with which which the Burgtheater was associated had been lost, the whole tempo of dialogue slowed down (see document 13, p. 257).

The social changes that had taken place in the expanding city since 1848 and were reflected in the composition of the Burgtheater audience coincided with the development in aesthetic taste that was represented both by Dingelstedt's production style and by the architecture of the new Burgtheater and the other 'monumental' buildings on the Ringstrasse. It was inevitable that a long period of adjustment was going to be required in the theatre. Meanwhile the most hostile critic of the company under successive directors, Karl Kraus, would continue to look back nostalgically on the old Burgtheater and its company as an ideal.[124] After Hasenauer's death in 1894 improvements were made in the auditorium in 1897, but as late as 1910 Schnitzler's diary records a conversation with Max Burckhard, the director of the theatre for most of the 1890s, and Hugo Thimig (himself a future director) about its 'huge defects'.[125] Years later Thimig learnt from Katharina Schratt, who was the Emperor's confidante, that Franz Joseph had been prepared to build another smaller theatre as soon as the new Burgtheater was opened, and had been deterred only by Prince Hohenlohe, who as Master of the Imperial Household objected that the tacit admission that the building on the Ringstrasse was unusable would make him look foolish.[126] A plan to add a second house was eventually put forward formally in 1907 by Burckhard's successor, Paul Schlenther,[127] but was not realized until after the First World War.

CHAPTER 4

Commercial theatres in 'Old Vienna'

I. THREE 'POPULAR THEATRES'

The Vienna of the Biedermeier period was by modern standards a compact city, though it was begining to grow fast (the population increased from about 230,000 in 1800 to just over 400,000 in the mid-1840s). Musical and theatrical circles overlapped (both Schubert and Beethoven were friends of Grillparzer), and there were also many connections on a personal level between playwrights and actors from the Burgtheater and those connected with the commercial theatres. Indeed one of the distinctive features of this period was the interplay of court and commercial theatres – a parallel amid the political stagnation of Metternich's Austria to the interplay between 'private' and 'public' theatres in what had in other respects been the very different cultural climate of Elizabethan London.

The commercial theatres were regularly referred to as 'popular' theatres (*Volkstheater*), that is, theatres for ordinary people, as opposed to the court. The Viennese shared with their contemporaries both in Paris – the public of the Boulevard du Temple – and in Victorian London a liking for melodrama and for spectacle, which especially the Theater an der Wien catered for throughout the first half of the nineteenth century. But at the heart of the repertory was comedy of various kinds, in Viennese dialect. How far the commercial theatres functioned either as theatres for the lower classes or (at least until Nestroy's time) as 'oppositional' theatres, offering a subversive counter to the norms of the court theatres, is doubtful. Social and political conformism was enforced by the censor. Classical plays and grand opera were parodied; indeed, the commercial theatres nurtured a notable tradition of parody. But one of their functions, even in parodies, was essentially a popularizing one. For the audience they attracted came mainly from their immediate locality. Public transport from one part of the city to another was difficult; that the city centre was still walled was a barrier both practically and psychologically. As late as 1859, when plans for a new theatre on the quay along the Danube Canal were being considered, the authorities judged that it was unlikely to create difficulties for the Carltheater since the audience of the Carltheater was mainly resident in the Leopoldstadt.[1] It is true that numerous records from the Biedermeier period show that members of the nobility and aristocracy sometimes attended the commercial theatres, but just as the Burgtheater and Kärntnertortheater catered principally for the aristocracy and the wealthy bourgeoisie of the inner city, so the commercial theatres catered mainly for the population in their own districts. To this extent they drew in a more restricted audience than that of the *petits théâtres* of Paris. It was drawn essentially from the petty bourgeoisie, artisans, shopkeepers, minor officials and what Friedrich Kaiser, describing the public in the Theater an der Wien in the 1830s, called 'those of the workers who were interested in something other than merely sensual pleasures':

Even the boxes and stalls were filled more by the families of manufacturers and other business people than by the nobility...The second and third tiers were occupied by less well-off people for whom the pleasure of theatre-going at least once a week was made possible by the cheap prices. Up in the gods people were to be seen...in shirtsleeves, making themselves comfortable in the oppressive heat.[2]

Originally built to accommodate Schikaneder's operatic ambitions, the Theater an der Wien was considerably larger than the two other commercial theatres founded in the 1780s. Capacities of theatres everywhere keep changing, usually decreasing as facilities are improved, comfort enhanced, and safety regulations enforced: by 1912 the published capacity of the Theater an der Wien was only 1,359. But in 1828, at its fullest, it was reckoned to hold twice as many as that, whereas the Theater in der Leopoldstadt and the Theater in der Josefstadt each held no more than 1,400.[3] In 1807–13, while it was under the *Gesellschaft der Kavaliere* and in the same hands as the Burgtheater and the Kärntnertortheater, the Theater an der Wien did not really function as a 'popular' theatre, and dialect comedy was not established at the heart of the repertoire there until it was run by Karl Carl from the mid-1820s onwards.

The Theater in der Leopoldstadt was the theatre with the most closely-knit audience, because its setting on the other side of the

Danube Canal from the city centre gave it a clearly demarcated catchment area. After Marinelli's death in 1803 the direction passed to two dramatists in succession: first to Hensler, then in 1816 to Leopold Huber, whose insolvency in 1821 led to several years of dispute and uncertainty in the management. Nevertheless, throughout the first three decades of the nineteenth century this was the theatre *par excellence* of unpretentious entertainment, centring on a succession of comic figures, from Laroche's 'Kasperl' to 'Staberl', created by Ignaz Schuster in plays by Bäuerle. It was often known as the 'Kasperltheater', and preserved an unbroken comic tradition. The repertory included the distinctive Viennese 'play with magic' (*Zauberstück*), combining dialect comedy with the use of fairies or magicians (a reflection of the Romanticism still dominating European literature), and often involving spectacular stage effects descended from Baroque tradition (with *Die Zauberflöte* an important intermediary influence). It developed into its most subtle form after the actor-dramatist Ferdinand Raimund joined the company in 1817, having established his reputation as a comic actor during three years in the Theater in der Josefstadt.

The latter theatre remained the Cinderella among the commercial theatres throughout the nineteenth century. In 1812 the licence-holder, Karl Mayer, leased it to Joseph Huber (Leopold Huber's brother), who employed the architect Joseph Kornhäusel to refurbish the auditorium. Joseph Huber also refashioned the acting company (it was he who recruited Raimund). But the theatre was constantly in the red. When Joseph Huber was overtaken by financial ruin in 1818, the lease passed to his brother, until he in turn was bankrupted, and eventually to Hensler, who following his years in the Leopoldstadt had been director of the theatres in two provincial towns near Vienna, Pressburg (now Bratislava) and Baden. Over the summer of 1822 Hensler had the theatre completely rebuilt to a design by Kornhäusel, replacing the original building with a new and considerably larger one – the core of the theatre that still survives today (see plate 9). It reopened in October 1822, the curtain-raiser being a piece by Meisl, *Die Weihe des Hauses*, for which Hensler had commissioned an overture by Beethoven (*The Consecration of the House*, op. 124).

The Theater in der Josefstadt had a mixed programme, with drama, dialect comedy (generally plays that had already enjoyed a success at one of the other theatres), and even opera. One of the

9   Theater in der Josefstadt, interior, 1826.

highlights in Hensler's last year, for example, was a production of Weber's *Der Freischütz* in August 1825.[4] But it is typical that the Theater in der Josefstadt was not the first Viennese theatre to stage the work, nor even the second: it had been performed in the Kärntnertortheater in 1821 and the Theater an der Wien in 1822.

Hensler's death in November 1825 fell at a time of flux in the commercial theatre, with managements changing and the Theater an der Wien even closed for a time. Eventually the Theater in der Josefstadt passed in 1826 to the company of Karl Carl, who had been director of the Isartor-Theater in Munich and as an actor was a well-known Staberl (see plate 10). Financially the shrewdest operator of all in the first half of the nineteenth century, even he reported a 'significant loss' during his first year in the Josefstadt.[5]

Almost the only really important dramatic première in the Josefstadt in the first forty years of the nineteenth century was *Der Verschwender*, Raimund's last play (1834), which he wrote after his contract with the Theater in der Leopoldstadt had expired in 1830, and the music for which was provided by Konradin Kreutzer, *Kapellmeister* of the theatre from 1833 to 1840.

After the death of Marinelli in 1803 (when Hasenhut left the company) and of Laroche in 1806, the Leopoldstadt theatre had undergone a period of regeneration under Hensler's direction (1803–16). Ignaz Schuster, a member of the company since 1804, established himself as the central comic actor, supported by a team that also included a versatile actress, Katharina Ennöckl, who was first engaged in 1804 and served as a member of the company until 1829, when she left to marry Bäuerle. In the first half of Hensler's period in charge the repertory was enriched by comedies by Josef Ferdinand Kringsteiner, but increasingly it was dominated by three prolific playwrights, Carl Meisl, Joseph Alois Gleich, and Adolf Bäuerle. Between them they wrote nearly 500 plays of various kinds, mostly between 1804 and 1838. Most involved some music, which throughout the early nineteenth century remained one of the most important elements of Viennese popular drama.

Three or four particularly characteristic genres developed. Kringsteiner took up the contrast of city and country, albeit (by contrast with Schikaneder) in plays without songs; but his most significant contribution to the development of dialect comedy lay in his parodies, resetting the action of literary originals in a dialect-speaking milieu. *Othello, der Mohr in Wien*, first produced in 1806, with

10   Karl Carl as Staberl.

music by Schuster, remained in the repertory until 1823: in that year, with Katharina Ennöckl in the role of Desdemona, it was shown two days after the Burgtheater première of Schreyvogel's adaptation of Shakespeare's tragedy in Voss's translation. Six years later it was reworked by Meisl, to music by Adolf Müller (*Othellerl, der Mohr von Wien*), and in this form has survived as a repertoire piece into modern times: the most recent production, by Klaus Kusenberg, was in 1990 in the Burgtheater – one of many examples of the tenaciousness of Viennese theatre tradition.[6]

A liking for parody was not peculiar to Vienna: in London, for example, John Poole's *Hamlet Travestie* (1811) ushered in a tradition of Shakespeare burlesques. There is a particularly close parallel to the Viennese Othello parodies, making comparable use of localization, in Charles Mathews's *Othello, the Moor of Fleet Street*, which was performed in the Adelphi Theatre in 1833.[7] But in Vienna the flourishing of the genre is particularly characteristic of the symbiotic relationship between the court theatres and the commercial theatres, which exploited successes in the court theatres by putting on comic counterparts. The Burgtheater production of *Maria Stuart* in December 1814 was the spur for Bäuerle's *Maria Stuttgartin*, performed in May 1815 in the Theater in der Leopoldstadt; similarly the success of Grillparzer's *Die Ahnfrau* led to Meisl's *Die Frau Ahndl* (1817, with music by Wenzel Müller). *Sappho* was parodied in the Theater in der Josefstadt by F.X. Told (*Seppherl*, 1818), and so the tradition continued, down to Nestroy's parodies of Hebbel's *Judith* and of Wagner's operas *Tannhäuser* and *Lohengrin*. Even productions in the commercial theatres were not immune from parody if they were perceived as being pretentious: Raimund's *Moisasurs Zauberfluch*, for example, produced in the Theater an der Wien in September 1827, provoked a response in the Theater in der Leopoldstadt less than six weeks later in Meisl's *Moisasuras Hexenspruch*.

The strategy of localization on which this tradition of theatrical parody depended was also the basis of the 'mythological caricature', a reworking of ancient myths in Viennese dialect verse, with local allusions. The form had sprung up in the late eighteenth century; Meisl adopted it as a vehicle for Ignaz Schuster, playing a henpecked Jupiter (*Orpheus und Euridice, oder: So geht es im Olympus zu*, 1813, with music by Kauer; *Die Entführung der Prinzessin Europa, oder: So geht es im Olymp zu!*, 1816, with music by Wenzel Müller), and it not only fitted in with the development of local satirical comedy but also, half

a century later, provided a link with the subject-matter of Offenbach's operettas.

The key work in the development of comedy set in contemporary
Vienna, with at least the germ of social satire but often also with a
strain of rather sentimental local patriotism, was Bäuerle's *Die Bürger
in Wien* (1813), with the main figure (Staberl, played by Schuster)
established as a Viennese craftsman, a down-at-heel umbrella-
maker. In 1842, thanking Bäuerle for a favourable review of *Einen Jux
will er sich machen* that had appeared in the *Theaterzeitung*, Nestroy
acknowledged that he looked on Bäuerle as a 'model', the 'founder'
of the type of comedy he himself wrote.[8] There is an element of
hyperbole in this courtesy from a working dramatist to the editor of
an influential reviewing journal; nevertheless, together with Meisl,
Bäuerle was one of the most influential playwrights who shaped the
development of satirical dialect comedy before Nestroy. A work of
particular importance was *Die falsche Primadonna* (1818), a play set in
Krähwinkel, the fictitious small provincial town first popularized by
Kotzebue's *Die deutschen Kleinstädter*. Bäuerle used the setting to reflect
the popular enthusiasm surrounding the soprano Angelica Catalani,
who gave a concert that year in the Theater an der Wien with tickets
sold at five times the normal price; the success of the play ushered in
a succession of 'Krähwinkel' comedies, which would culminate thirty
years later in Nestroy's satire of the 1848 revolution, *Freiheit in
Krähwinkel*.

Bäuerle also contributed to the vogue for the *Zauberspiel*, the most
important form of which has come to be called the *Besserungsstück*: a
character with a besetting fault is cured by magic or a magically
induced dream. The pattern was established in 1818–19 by Meisl's
Der lustige Fritz, a parody of a play by Carl Franz van der Velde, and
Gleich's *Der Berggeist*, in which the role Raimund played was the very
embodiment of disgruntlement, a figure emblematically named Herr
von Missmuth. The moral, built into the convention, is an acceptance of the *status quo*; if that accords with the social policy of
Metternich's régime, then by the same token the very topic of
discontent has social and political implications. The 'curative' moral
was reduced to overt loyalism by Bäuerle, as in *Wien, London, Paris
und Constantinopel* (1823, with music by Wenzel Müller), which ends
with a celebration of the superiority of Vienna over the other capitals
and involves the recreation on stage of well-loved Viennese settings;
so too does *Aline, oder: Wien in einem andern Welttheile* (1822, also with

music by Wenzel Müller); at the same time both plays appealed to an interest in exotic settings which had been a feature of Viennese taste since *Die Entführung aus dem Serail*. By the early 1820s Raimund was growing discontented with the standard of plays he was being offered[9] and began to write his own, beginning with *Der Barometerma-cher auf der Zauberinsel* in 1823. The best-known are all variants on the *Besserungsstück* pattern: *Das Mädchen aus der Feenwelt oder Der Bauer als Millionär* (1826), *Der Alpenkönig und der Menschenfeind* (1828) (see plate 11, which shows the first magical appearance of the spirit Astragalus to the misanthrope's family), and later *Der Verschwender* (1834).

Throughout the 1820s he was the central star in a strong company. The other principal attraction was the actress Therese Krones, whose best-known part was that of Youth in *Das Mädchen aus der Feenwelt*. On the stage she was regarded as the very personification of *joie de vivre* – the 'Viennese Déjazet'.[10] Off stage she had a reputation for loose living (Castelli called her one of the two most dissolute women in Vienna);[11] but that needs to be seen in the context of the time, when acting – particularly on the commercial stage – was not regarded as a respectable pursuit for a young woman. (For much of the nineteenth century, the theatre was one of the few places where women were able to pursue an independent career; yet as late as 1927 a Viennese gynaecologist, Bernhard Bauer, published a work arguing that the opportunity for sexual licence might be a major factor in attracting them to acting.)[12]

The *Besserungsstück* pattern of discontent, a curative dream, and an exotic setting is reproduced in Grillparzer's *Der Traum ein Leben* – a further example of the creative interaction between the court and commercial theatres. Raimund himself recognized the close parallel, in particular with *Das Mädchen aus der Feenwelt*, and is reported to have described his own work as falling short in lacking the beauty of Grillparzer's language.[13] This sense of disappointment is indicative of the pretensions which he brought to the dialect theatre and which distinguish his work from that of the less complicated journeyman playwrights who provided most of the plays on the repertoire. Acute observers regarded his influence as having been decisive in changing the complexion of the commercial stage, disturbing the balance of what had been simply a theatre of unpretentious entertainment and destroying the naivety that had made for genuinely popular theatre. In 1835, Saphir accused him of having invented a new genre, allegorical plays that were 'not *Volksstücke*'; eight years later a

11   Ferdinance Raimund, *Der Alpenkönig und der Menschenfeind* 1, 18 (Theater in der Leopoldstadt, 1828).

reviewer in the *Sonntags-Blätter* similarly referred to his 'upside-down tragedies' and asked the rhetorical question what was 'popular' ('volksthümlich') about them.[14] The same considerations underlie Bauernfeld's view, first expressed in 1853 and repeated in his memoirs, that the Theater in der Leopoldstadt had reached its peak before Raimund.[15]

The period of most rapid decline, however, came at the end of the 1820s, and coincided with Raimund's two years as director (1828–30). In 1829 Katharina Ennöckl retired and another leading actor, the gangling Friedrich Joseph Korntheuer, died; in 1830 Therese Krones died and both Schuster and Raimund himself left the theatre. Within two years the very heart of the company had been lost, just at the time when the productivity of Meisl, Gleich, and Bäuerle was tailing off. This rapid change of fortune in the Leopoldstadt explains why within a few years the leadership in dialect comedy could pass to the Theater an der Wien.

From 1807 until 1813 the Theater an der Wien was run by the *Gesellschaft der Kavaliere*; when the partnership – by now reduced to only three members – was dissolved at the end of September 1813, Count Pálffy took over the sole direction of the theatre, reopening it on 1 October with *Don Giovanni*, and purchasing it at the beginning of the following year. Under the *Gesellschaft der Kavaliere* it had been thoroughly renovated in 1812, and the repertoire had been enlarged to include a number of plays by Schiller, hitherto proscribed: *Die Räuber* (1808), *Wilhelm Tell* (1810, in Grüner's adaptation), *Die Jungfrau von Orleans* (1811). Grüner's adaptation of Goethe's *Götz von Berlichingen* – another play which had still not been done in the Burgtheater – was staged in 1809. Other significant events included the appearance of Iffland in *King Lear* in 1808 and the première of Kleist's *Das Käthchen von Heilbronn* in 1810, in an adaptation by Heinrich von Collin that provided spectacle for the audience but was poorly received by the critics.[16] A speciality of the theatre that also catered for the taste for spectacle was musical dramas on biblical themes, two of the most successful being *Saul, König von Israel* (1810) and *Moses* (1813), both with music by Ignaz von Seyfried.

After the theatre had passed into Pálffy's sole control there were more dramas, including others by Schiller that had been seen in the Burgtheater (*Wallenstein*, 1817; *Die Braut von Messina*, 1819; *Maria Stuart*, 1821), and also the ghost play *Die Ahnfrau* which made Grillparzer's name. By the time *Die Ahnfrau* was performed at the end of January

1817, Pálffy had just appointed Hensler as director; but this arrangement lasted only eight months. His debts were now rapidly mounting. As a profitable attraction he had cultivated children's ballets, which were arranged by Friedrich Horschelt, a member of the court ballet company in the Kärntnertortheater; the young Fanny Elssler was probably among those who appeared, and Grillparzer's playful short poem 'Therese Heberle' (1820) commemorates another young dancer who was subsequently taken on by the Kärntnertortheater.[17] But when the children's ballets were banned in 1821 (the Empress suspected that the morals of the children were at risk) and the musical dramas on biblical themes were also stopped, Pálffy was soon facing financial ruin.

The dependence of the commercial theatres on a mainly local audience meant that the Theater an der Wien, which was bigger even than the Carltheater when that opened in 1847, was always difficult to fill, flops had to be instantly dropped, and the theatre director kept on needing new plays. Even Schikaneder had depended on exploiting the potential of the large stage and elaborate machinery for spectacular scenic effects, and Pálffy spared no expense in following the same policy. In a production of *Die Jungfrau von Orleans* in 1824, for example, over four hundred extras were involved.[18] The taste for spectacle, including equestrian display on stage, was long-lived in the Viennese commercial theatre. Jürgen Hein has documented an example in Carl's 'arrangement' of Grabbe's *Don Juan und Faust* for the Theater an der Wien in January 1838, in which Nestroy played the role of Leporello: the text was considerably cut, and the production was enlivened by supernatural apparitions and magical effects.[19] The fondness for spectacle was also a feature of the rise of melodrama in London, and indeed one of the most successful plays of the kind in the Theater an der Wien (it lasted in the repertory till 1841) was a melodrama called *Timur der Tartar-Chan* (1822) after an English original, Monk Lewis's *Timour the Tartar*, which had first played at Covent Garden in 1811. (*Timur der Tartar-Chan* is a further work that provoked a parodistic reaction in another commercial theatre, in this case Gleich's *Timur, der große Tartar-Chan oder Die Cavallerie zu Fuß*, produced in November 1822 in the Theater in der Josefstadt and revived there in 1830.)

The expense involved in the lavish productions Pálffy indulged in proved impossible to recoup. He tried to wipe out his debts in 1819–20 by means of a lottery; the main prize was the theatre itself, but the winner, a wine-merchant in Hungary, chose the option of taking money instead and the theatre remained in Pálffy's hands. He tried other devices. In 1821 he reached agreement with the lessee of the Kärntnertortheater, Domenico Barbaia, for the joint running of the Theater an der Wien; but that lasted only five months. In November 1824 he appealed to Sedlnitzky to lift the ban on biblical dramas, but in the following February this notion was rejected by the Archbishop of Vienna,[20] and by late March 1825 Sedlnitzky warned the Emperor that Pálffy's bankruptcy was imminent.[21] The production of *König Ottokars Glück und Ende* in April 1825 was a last desperate attempt to cash in on the success the play had enjoyed in the Burgtheater: contemporary reports suggest that an experiment was made with a 'conversational' style of speaking, to good effect in the scenes between Kunigunde and Zawisch in Act Two; but the main emphasis in the production was on spectacle, to appeal to the cruder tastes of the audience of the Theater an der Wien.[22] At the end of May, Pálffy was forced to close the theatre, the last performance being one of *König Ottokars Glück und Ende.*

When Karl Carl and his company took over the theatre, the period of ambitious amateurism came to an abrupt end and was succeeded by a much more realistic commercial grasp. Carl drove a characteristically hard bargain with Pálffy, leasing the theatre in the first instance for three months. His company began its 'guest performances' ('Gastvorstellungen') on 19 August 1825. What he promised, in a manifesto published in the *Theaterzeitung*, was a 'théâtre de variétés, in the best sense of the term', that is, the widest possible range of plays, including romantic drama, high comedy, and dialect comedy, all to be carefully produced (see document 3, p. 247). After two extensions of the lease, Pálffy finally went bankrupt in December 1826, the theatre was sold by auction, and in February 1827 Carl negotiated a new lease for the next six years, at a cost of 15,500 fl. per annum.[23] At this stage he was running both the Theater an der Wien and the Theater in der Josefstadt; but the latter was only a springboard, and the use he put it to has been likened to 'asset stripping'.[24] It was to the Theater an der Wien that he moved the strongest members of his company (including the actor Wenzel Scholz, who had made his début in the Josefstadt in April 1826), and it was there that he used the composer Adolf Müller, who was appointed director of music (*Kapellmeister*) in 1828 and remained in that post until 1847. In 1831 Carl gave up the Theater in der

Josefstadt altogether, having negotiated another six-year lease of the Theater an der Wien for 11,200 fl. a year,[25] and he remained director there until April 1845.

2. KARL CARL

In 1828, when Carl was running both the Theater in der Josefstadt and the Theater an der Wien, the Emperor requested Sedlnitzky for a report on him. The police accounts, based on inquiries in Munich as well as in Vienna, added up to a mixture of positive and negative, in ways that anticipate the mixed reactions Carl provoked to the end of his life. In the practice of running a theatre he was experienced, energetic, and attentive to detail in rehearsals, which often went on until 3 a.m. There was nothing against him politically, though he seemed to adhere to police regulations only in so far as it was not in his interest to break them: he not only held rehearsals on Sunday mornings but also – the arch-offence against the censorship laws – indulged in extemporization in his Staberl plays. (The Emperor commented that it was up to the police authorities to see that the rules were enforced.) Carl's principal concern, the reports made clear, was with financial profit, not with artistic merit, and he was disliked, even within his company, as being autocratic and as generally paying badly. His moral reputation was also dubious: a womanizer, he would suggest to actresses who complained about low pay that they did not have to depend on their income from acting alone. The conclusion was that although he was competent to run a theatre of low status, he was unsuitable to run a court theatre.[26]

Carl's skill as a producer was uncontested; there is a case for seeing him as an early precursor of modern *Regietheater*, establishing the authority and control of the producer over the performance of the individual actors. This mastery was often referred to in newspaper reviews as something that could be taken for granted. On Nestroy's *Das Haus der Temperamente*, a complex piece to stage in that the action takes place in four rooms, the stage being split both horizontally and vertically, a report in *Der Wanderer* informed readers simply: 'The production was as is to be expected from Director Carl, who in this respect cannot be surpassed'.[27] His production strategy placed considerable weight on visual effects. In this he was influenced by Grüner, who in 1803–4 had worked in Goethe's theatre in Weimar and in 1814–16 under Pálffy in the Theater an der Wien, being removed by Pálffy from his function as producer in May 1815 only against Schreyvogel's better judgement,[28] and had then been in charge of the court theatre in Darmstadt (1816–30) and had also worked in Frankfurt (1832–6) before returning to Vienna. Grüner's handbook *Kunst der Scenik in ästhetischer und ökonomischer Hinsicht*, published in Vienna in 1841, was dedicated to Carl, and Carl seems to have learned particularly from his expert marshalling of crowd scenes. Carl's reputation as a producer strong on visual impact may be gauged from Raimund's choice of the Theater an der Wien for the first production of *Moisasurs Zauberfluch* in 1827 – a work singled out in the reports on Carl that Sedlnitzky submitted to the Emperor the following year as being one of the few plays of merit that he had staged so far.

Carl's competence in production was achieved by tight discipline, which was essential in view of the speed with which new plays were performed, often only a few days after the text was approved by the censor (see p. 41, above). There is no sign that he tolerated the kind of perfunctoriness in rehearsal that was widespread in the London theatre before Macready, but the rapid turnover of plays meant that, as in London, rehearsal time was often only a few days. This imposed considerable strains not just on the actors but on the whole staff of the theatre, including the director of music, for whom Carl would draw up a precise list of detailed requirements for his productions.[29] One document has survived from May 1832 setting out a week's tasks for Adolf Müller, including preparation for the planned première of Nestroy's parody *Zampa der Tagdieb* at the end of the week, only five days after the première of Hérold's opera *Zampa* in the Kärntnertortheater: the music '*must* therefore be composed *very quickly*' and rehearsed daily.[30] (In this case the première of the parody did not in the event take place until over six weeks later: either Nestroy or Müller may have failed to meet Carl's deadline.)

Carl's commercial acumen meant that his first priority in his programme was that a play must be entertaining, in order to pay its way. This clarity of purpose is what most distinguished him from his main rival in the 1830s and 1840s, Franz Pokorny, who took over both the Theater in der Josefstadt and later the Theater an der Wien after him and allowed himself an ambitious programme of opera. When in December 1845 Carl produced a Staberl play, *Staberl als Freischütz*,[31] in the Theater in der Leopoldstadt at the same time as Pokorny was putting on Weber's opera in the Theater an der Wien, the rivalry between the two men and the contrast in their ambitions were clear to see: on the one hand a serious opera producer, on the other a commercial entertainer. Carl was a showman, with considerable skill in advertisement. He missed no opportunity to tag speeches to the audience on to performances. In 1838, for example, after a period in which he had not acted much while Scholz and Nestroy had established themselves, he took over a part at short notice in Nestroy's *Glück, Mißbrauch und Rückkehr*, and used his curtain call to promise not only that henceforth he would be acting again more but also that he would spare no effort to raise the standards in his theatre.[32] When his company gave their final performance in the Theater an der Wien in 1845, the show ended with the sentimental farewell chorus 'So leb denn wohl, du stilles Haus' from Raimund's *Der Alpenkönig und der Menschenfeind*, and then Carl appeared with the assembled company (the men in black, the women in white) to deliver a speech appealing to the audience's loyalty and promising to transform the rather dilapidated Theater in der Leopoldstadt into a veritable 'temple of gaiety'.[33] When he closed the Theater in der Leopoldstadt two years later, he made a similar speech, satirically summarized by one commentator as boiling down to saying that he had now made so much money that he could afford to build a new theatre.[34] The opening that December of the new Carltheater provided another occasion for a speech, Carl dedicating the theatre to the service of the public as a monument to his gratitude.[35]

Spectaculars and melodramas, as well as comedies, continued to enjoy considerable popularity in the commercial theatres; but Carl's success in Vienna was largely built round Nestroy, who for over twenty years wrote exclusively for his theatres, and predominantly in comic vein. In the late 1840s, more than half of the takings in the Theater in der Leopoldstadt and Carltheater came from Nestroy plays (these included one of his biggest box-office successes, *Der Schützling*), and some three quarters of the takings came from performances in which he appeared as a comic actor.[36]

Nestroy began making burlesque use of the *Zauberstück* (the biggest hit of his early plays was *Der böse Geist Lumpacivagabundus*, 1833), then made a decisive move away from magic effects in 1835 in *Zu ebener Erde und erster Stock*, with a bold use of a two-level stage to represent the social contrast of rich and poor. The logical move from this greater realism towards explicit satire of Vienna led to a major theatre scandal, when *Eine Wohnung ist zu vermieten* was roundly rejected both by the audience in the Theater an der Wien, whose aggressive stamping and whistling left Nestroy himself visibly 'dismayed', and by the press critics.[37] Though it was in London that audiences were notoriously noisiest, there is abundant evidence throughout the Biedermeier period that the audiences in the Viennese commercial theatres were also capable of making themselves heard in no uncertain manner. In 1820, for example, the audience in the Leopoldstadt barracked Raimund when he was dragging his feet about marrying Gleich's daughter Luise;[38] in 1842, in the Theater an der Wien, when a two-act comedy by Eduard Breier, *Die falschen Engländer*, had been billed as being in three acts, the audience was not to be pacified after the final curtain until Carl agreed to play the first act of *Einen Jux will er sich machen* as compensation.[39]

After the failure of *Eine Wohnung ist zu vermieten* in 1837 Nestroy took refuge in more stylized experimentation, presenting humanity reduced to the types of the four humours, each with its own quarter of the stage, in *Das Haus der Temperamente*. It was in *Glück, Mißbrauch und Rückkehr* (1838) that he found his way towards his characteristic formula, the *Posse mit Gesang*, a farcical comedy in which the action is driven by chance and the satire is highlighted by a small number of solo scenes with monologues and songs (*Couplets*) for the central comic figures played by Nestroy himself, Scholz, and the singer Marie Weiler. The success of the play established what would become the pattern of his biggest hits in the years 1840–5, from *Der Talisman* to *Unverhofft*; and Carl's return to acting also encouraged Nestroy to write his very next play, *Der Kobold* (1838), a parody of a Romantic ballet, round Carl's old role as Staberl.

At the end of 1838 Carl bought the Theater in der Leopoldstadt, which had been in decline since the period of Raimund's direction. It had been run since 1831 by Franz von Marinelli, the second son of Karl von Marinelli, and the state of affairs was accurately reported in Murray's *Handbook* of 1837: it had 'much fallen off of late years in its actors and the pieces brought out in it'.[40] For the six and a quarter years between his purchase of the Theater in der Leopoldstadt and the expiry of his lease in the Theater an der Wien, Carl had a commanding position in the Viennese commercial theatre. He ran the Theater in der Leopoldstadt as his second-string theatre: the main premières were in the Theater an der Wien; when their potential there had been exhausted, plays moved to the Leopoldstadt to catch a different audience. In the 1841–2 season, for example,

Nestroy's *Das Mädl aus der Vorstadt* was performed twenty-seven times in just over three months in the Theater an der Wien and then relaunched (with the same cast, including Nestroy) in the Theater in der Leopoldstadt in April 1842.

Nevertheless, taking on a second theatre increased Carl's need for plays. This pressure came close on the heels of a change in the *Zeitgeist*, signalled politically by the July Revolution in Paris in 1830, and exemplified in the Viennese theatre in the contrast between the rather sentimental work of Raimund in the 1820s and the utterly unsentimental style of Nestroy, both as dramatist and as actor. The desperate need for new plays to satisfy the ever-hungry public was articulated by Saphir in May 1841 in a review of a play by Haffner: long runs were not enough, the public wanted variety, and that is just what Carl's programme provided (see document 6, pp. 248–9). He would put on attractions such as visiting acrobats (commemorated in occasional plays provided by Nestroy: *Der Affe und der Bräutigam* in 1836, for a popular mime, Eduard Klischnigg, and *Moppels Abenteuer* the following year, when the English acrobats Lawrence and Redisha appeared). He also put on romantic drama, including plays by Charlotte Birch-Pfeiffer, providing roles for Wilhelm Kunst, an actor who had briefly been married to Sophie Schröder and whom Carl had first brought with him to Vienna in 1825. He had performances from visiting stars, including the comic actor Friedrich Beckmann from Berlin. But above all he cultivated a form based on the Parisian *comédie-vaudeville*, a form of comedy interspersed with a large number of songs sung to well-known popular airs, which had been adopted by Scribe and others and had established itself as the dominant form of light entertainment in the Parisian popular theatres in the 1820s. Friedrich Kaiser rightly objected that the term *vaudeville* was not quite appropriate for the Viennese adaptations, which were just light comedies with more songs than was customary in the local *Posse mit Gesang* (see document 12, pp. 256–7). An important factor in the popularity of these pieces in Vienna was Carl's engagement of the singer Ida Brüning-Wohlbrück, a member of a well-known German theatrical family (her father had been an actor in Weimar), who combined comic acting skills with musicality. Carl, incidentally, was known to have more than a professional interest in her;[41] developments in the theatre have often been determined as much by personal entanglements as by aesthetic or political movements. She made her début in the Theater an der Wien on 25 November 1842 in

Chonchon, die Savoyardin, oder: Die neue Fanchon, a three-act *vaudeville* based on a French source and with music by Adolf Müller. The review in the *Theaterzeitung* praised her, saying that she lacked only command of Viennese dialect to be 'the second Krones'; as it was she could undoubtedly be better dubbed 'the German Déjazet'.[42] Kaiser would describe Carl's cultivation of Ida Brüning-Wohlbrück as a stab in the back to the local dialect comedy on which his fortune had been based (see document 12, p. 256); but even before her arrival his repertory had included an increasing amount of material based on *comédies-vaudevilles*. Of eleven full-length comedies by Nestroy that were premièred between December 1840 and Carl's vacation of the Theater an der Wien at the end of April 1845, eight, including *Der Talisman*, *Das Mädl aus der Vorstadt*, and *Der Zerrissene*, were based directly on *comédies-vaudevilles*. Friedrich Kaiser, who at the peak of his powers dominated Carl's programme together with Nestroy (it has been calculated that in the years 1848–53 they filled two-thirds of the repertory),[43] was another who adapted a succession of Parisian sources in the 1840s and early 1850s.[44] This absorption of French material is symptomatic of a crucial period of transition both for Vienna as a rapidly expanding city and for its theatrical life: local 'popular' comedy for a stable indigenous community was starting to give way to international entertainment for the rising bourgeoisie. A similar openness to French influence was a phenomenon that could be observed both in London and in Berlin, where Louis Angely also used *comédie-vaudeville* sources; in Vienna, where a unique local tradition seemed under threat, it provoked an extended critical argument (see pp. 118–20, below).

When Carl's company moved its base to the Leopoldstadt, Nestroy provided box-office successes in *Der Unbedeutende* (1846) and *Der Schützling* (1847), but the run of the latter play was interrupted when Carl decided to demolish the theatre and rebuild it. One of the early excitements after the summer break was the opening of the new Carltheater on 10 December 1847. Completed in seven months, the building had 804 seats and the total capacity, including boxes, benches in the upper tiers, and standing room, may have approached 2,000. The process of purchasing and renovating the Theater in der Leopoldstadt, then of demolishing and building the new Carltheater in its place, was credibly reported to have cost Carl over 500,000 fl., a huge outlay of risk capital;[45] but the new theatre turned out to be less profitable than the old one, as it was more expensive to run and

12   Friedrich Kaiser proclaiming the new constitution, 15 March 1848.

attendance dropped rather than rising.[46] Kaiser reports that while the interior décor was much admired, there were complaints about poor visibility and echoing acoustics, and Ferdinand von Seyfried too recounts that the interior was a disappointment, decorative but unpractical.[47] These are both hostile witnesses, but the issues they raise would recur repeatedly in the new theatre buildings of the later nineteenth century.

In 1848, the commercial theatre was no more immune than the Burgtheater from the tensions of the Revolution. When the promise of a democratic constitution was published on 15 March, it was one of the commercial playwrights, Friedrich Kaiser, who rode through

13   Scholz and Nestroy on sentry duty, March 1848.

the streets with the proclamation (see plate 12). Carl, ever the
opportunist, saw a chance of making advertising capital. He formed
a company of the National Guard in the Leopoldstadt district and
had the members of his company (including both his star actors,
Nestroy and Scholz) appear in uniforms from his stock of theatrical
costume guarding one of the bridges over the Danube Canal (see
plate 13). There were heated arguments about the implications of the
satire in *Freiheit in Krähwinkel*.[48] The crushing of the revolution – from
11 October to 10 November 1848, all theatres were closed – brought
the run of Nestroy's play to an end; but in March 1849 he returned
to the subject of the revolution in *Judith und Holofernes*, combining his
satire with parody of Hebbel's tragedy *Judith*, which had been
produced in the Burgtheater on 1 February. The self-vaunting

Holofernes (Ludwig Löwe in the Burgtheater production, the corpulent Scholz in Nestroy's parody) is contrasted in *Judith und Holofernes* to the everyday material concerns of the ordinary Jewish population. These function as a gauge of everyday good sense by comparison with Holofernes's militaristic boastfulness; at the same time the satire of the rhythms of Jewish speech coincided with what was to become a rising tide of anti-Semitism in Vienna. The play was a box-office success; so too were *Mein Freund* (1851) and *Kampl* (1852); a new leading comic actor, Carl Treumann, was added to the company – not without tensions between him and Nestroy – in 1852, and the theatre was in good shape when Carl died, a very rich man, in 1854.

Carl kept tight control over his dramatists' production: Karl Haffner's contract even specifies that Carl could determine how many and which comic actors he might devise roles for in a new play.[49] Nestroy, under less contractual pressure than the run-of-the-mill dramatists (though under no less time pressure because of his commitments as a star actor) was able to revise his manuscripts with meticulous attention to detail; but lesser playwrights, particularly younger ones, had to deliver material to a tight schedule. The contract that Haffner was given for one year in 1837, with provision for an extension for a further two years, committed him to providing eight new full-length plays, acceptable to Carl and passing the censor. He was tied to writing exclusively for Carl, and forbidden to publish his plays within three years of their passing the censor. He had a wage of 40 fl., with an added fee of 20 fl. for the first, seventh, thirteenth, twentieth, and twenty-fifth performance, and was also allowed one benefit evening.

These 'benefit performances' were also allotted to leading actors in the company – a system familiar in London since the early eighteenth century. In Vienna, actors awarded a benefit would appear in a work of their choice and receive half the net takings. (They also had the right to act as ticket agents, extracting extra profit from selling tickets from their own homes.)[50] Benefit evenings could be lucrative: the actor Wenzel Scholz averaged 346 fl. for his benefits in 1847, and in the five years 1847–51 Nestroy earned just under 3,000 fl. (i.e. 600 fl. per year) from his; but for lesser lights and in unfavourable circumstances – bad weather, or an unattractive choice of play – the income could be very small, even down to as little as 10 fl.[51] The big names could also supplement their earnings by touring in the summer (see pp. 112–14, below) and also by occasional

appearances in private performances in wealthy houses: according to
Friedrich Kaiser's account Scholz was paid 48 ducats (= 216 fl.) in
August 1832 for appearing in the private theatre of Baroness
Geymüller, which Castelli was running.[52]

Haffner's contract stipulated that for his benefit evening he had to
provide a ninth play, and would not receive a fee for the first
performance. The first contract that Friedrich Kaiser was given in
1840 committed him to providing six acceptable plays a year; his
salary was 24 fl. per month, which rose the next year to 40 fl. and to
50 fl. thereafter.[53] Playwrights would also receive royalties from
publication of their plays, though these might come through slowly if
the publication were delayed, and were likely to be subject to
deductions for an agent's commission (see p. 112, below). Carl's
employees resented the tough terms he imposed, and Kaiser in
particular poured out that resentment after Carl's death in a memoir
accusing him of 'unscrupulousness'.[54]

The details of these and other contracts were assembled by Otto
Rommel in 1930, but he tends to accept Kaiser's view and to
interpret the material in a way hostile to Carl.[55] The other side of
the coin is that dramatists of proven competence were paid more
handsomely. In 1840 Carl paid Bäuerle a total of 500 fl. C.M. for
what would prove to be his last two successful plays, *Rococo* and *Der
Sonderling in Wien*; yet even when dealing with so well-established and
influential a figure as Bäuerle he was strict in setting his conditions:
Bäuerle must make alterations already agreed between them, the
plays must be approved by the censor, and Bäuerle might neither
publish them nor offer them to any other Viennese theatre director
for three years from the date of their first performance by Carl's
company.[56] As the leading actor-dramatist of the company Nestroy
earned well. By 1847, when Carl drew up a new contract with him,
his income was about 10,000 fl. per annum; by then the flat-rate fee
for performances of his own plays had given way to royalties of 6 per
cent of net takings other than for premières and benefit performances.[57] (Kaiser, the only other playwright to whom Carl seems to
have paid royalties, was granted only 3 per cent.)[58]

Carl was certainly not generous; this can be seen, for example,
from the terms on which he employed even his *Kapellmeister* Adolf
Müller. In 1836–9, at a time when he was composing the music for
all Nestroy's plays, Müller was contracted to write two operas (or
scores for musical plays) plus twenty other pieces of music (which

might take the form of one further opera), against a salary of 1,000 fl. C.M. per year, plus a benefit (for which he had to provide the music and pay for its being copied), the total to be augmented by an extra 40 fl. C.M. for every additional full-length 'opera'.[59] In 1832, according to Friedrich Kaiser, Scholz was offered 3,000 fl. (more than double the salary Carl was paying him at the time) to join the Kärntnertortheater to play in comic *Singspiele* there, and was prevented from accepting because he was contractually tied to Carl's company.[60] Kaiser is too biased against Carl to be the most reliable witness; but certainly, though Scholz was immensely popular and had a crucial function as the foil to Nestroy's satire (a function akin to that of a 'lightning conductor', as Seyfried observed),[61] in the 1852–3 season, after over a quarter of a century in Carl's company, he was still on a salary less than a third of that paid to Carl Treumann (1,940 fl. against Treumann's 6,000 fl.);[62] and though Carl left him an annuity of 500 fl. in his will,[63] Scholz lived to enjoy it for only three years.

On 3 August 1854, a week and a half before his death, Carl went to Bad Ischl, supposedly to convalesce. The day before he left he signed a letter to two senior *Regisseure* in his company, Grois and Lang, handing over responsibility for the day-to-day running of the Carltheater. (He put Grois in charge of organizing the programme, Lang in charge of rehearsals.)[64] The *Theaterzeitung* reported that he was fit and merely needed to get back his strength;[65] but the signature on the letter is in a shaky hand unlike his usual confident scrawl. What is striking about the document, however, is that even on the brink of death, Carl emphatically reserved all decisions concerning both personnel and finances to himself. And when his will (which he had written in 1852) was published, it included a reminder to his heirs and successor that all the members of the company other than Nestroy held contracts which allowed them to be dismissed at short notice and that all his contracts were so framed that they could be broken at once after his death or retirement, together with an enjoinder to his heirs to make judicious use of this to maximize the terms they might get for letting or selling the theatre (see document 11, pp. 255–6).

In general, however, what Carl paid was not out of line in his time. How depressed wages were may be gauged from the fact that whereas nowadays wages and salaries may amount to 75–80 per cent of a theatre's outgoings, even in Nestroy's last year as director of the

Carltheater (1859–60) the figure was under 50 per cent.[66] The figures for playwrights and actors need to be set against other wages: in 1850 the annual income of a schoolteacher was about 150–250 fl., and that of a tailor working in the Theater an der Wien under Pokorny – an average wage of 45 Kreuzer a day – was similar.[67] Certainly Carl paid no worse than Pokorny,[68] and the answer to Kaiser's complaint that 'by a good play he understood only one that made money'[69] is that he carried both the financial and the legal responsibility for the whole enterprise. Kaiser, recalling that Carl was given to emphasizing that the welfare of three hundred families depended on him, would counter sourly that it was only thanks to the work of his employees that he had become a millionaire.[70] But the terms of his contracts with his playwrights and actors reflected his responsibilities: he needed a regular supply of new plays that would pass the censor and run in the repertory, and needed to be able to count on actors to perform them; and if the playwrights and actors in his employ had little contractual security, in practice they were securely employed in a successful company. To that success Carl himself contributed not only managerially but also artistically as an actor and especially as a producer.[71] The suspicion with which he was viewed was clearly tinged with envy of his success (by contrast with Pálffy and others), and also with anti-Semitism;[72] in fact much of his supposed ruthlessness was essential to responsible commercial management.

There is a revealing passage in his will (see document 11, p. 256) in which he defines his work as directing not a theatre but a 'theatre business' ('die Leitung eines Theater-Geschäftes'). The Biedermeier age was one of political stability, but not of financial stability. Sudden changes in wealth were a standard theme of comedy from the 1830s onwards (*Der Verschwender, Zu ebener Erde und erster Stock*), and the example of men like Pálffy and Pokorny (and of Schikaneder and the Huber brothers before them) can only have confirmed Carl's caution. It is precisely the risks of the 'theatre business' that his will stresses: 'Through my many years of experience I have learnt to recognize that directing a theatre business is the hardest, most uncertain and consequently most dangerous commercial business.' This passage may shed some light on the costliest mistake in Carl's career, when he failed to purchase the Theater an der Wien at auction in April 1845. According to Kaiser, he was confident that no other purchaser would emerge and he would then be able to buy it himself below the asking price,[73] but it may well be that he was also inhibited by sheer commercial caution. The result was that his rival, Franz Pokorny, acquired it at auction for 199,000 fl.[74] – less than 40 per cent of what the acquisition and reconstruction of the Leopoldstadt theatre cost Carl.

3. THE CULTURAL CLIMATE AND WORKING ENVIRONMENT

It had long been accepted that once a play was in print it could be performed without payment, so that in effect, plays were in the public domain once printed, as had been the case in France until the French Revolution and as was still the case in London. The practice grew up of printing texts with a rider on the cover or title page to the effect that in relation to theatres they retained the status of manuscripts (a common formulation was 'den Bühnen gegenüber als Manuscript gedruckt'), or more explicitly in the case of work by dramatists contracted to Carl that all rights remained Carl's property. But what generally happened was that publication was delayed, especially in the case of the most successful plays that could still be expected to be box-office draws. Haffner's contract with Carl barred him from publishing his plays for three years; in the mid-1840s, Nestroy appears to have been tied to a similar clause preventing publication for eighteen months.[75] Popular musical numbers might be published separately in piano reductions: musical excerpts from over thirty of Nestroy's plays were published in this way, mostly in Anton Diabelli's series *Komische Theater-Gesänge*, but only seventeen complete play texts appeared in print in his lifetime, most of these published by Wallishausser. When they were reprinted (as was the case with *Der böse Geist Lumpacivagabundus*, *Eulenspiegel*, and *Einen Jux will er sich machen*) this was in Wallishausser's series *Wiener Theater-Repertoir*, which had a function similar to that of the *Magasin théâtral* in Paris, from which many Viennese plays were adapted. Titles in the series ranged from verse plays produced in the Burgtheater (Schreyvogel's *Donna Diana* was no. 11) to texts of dialect dramatists (Friedrich Kaiser was a prominent contributor). It appeared from the early 1850s until the late 1870s, and in the end ran to nearly four hundred titles.

The main losers from the system were the playwrights, and not only those who worked for the commercial theatres. When Bauernfeld's *Großjährig* was published in 1849, he added as a foreword an 'Open Letter' to theatre directors and the management of court theatres, protesting against the 'sacred theatrical axiom' that once a text was in print it could be performed without further payment: the result was that directors would pay only for manuscripts, and that an author had to wait years before he could have a successful new play published.[76] Because plays circulated mainly in manuscript or in printed editions that claimed manuscript status, theatrical agents played an important part in their dissemination, and not just in Vienna itself: cities such as Graz and Linz and others which now lie outside Austria (and indeed outside the German-speaking area) but were then important centres of German-speaking theatre (Prague, Brünn, Pressburg, Laibach, Lemberg, Pest) – were dependent on Vienna for a large part of their programme, much as French provincial theatres depended on Paris. The most prominent agent in Vienna was Adalbert Prix, who acquired the rights for plays by Nestroy and Kaiser: letters survive recording Nestroy's either having sold rights outright in respect of productions of his plays in Germany and the Austrian provinces, or else using Prix as his agent against an agreed share of the proceeds;[77] and several of Kaiser's plays carry announcements that Prix similarly held performance rights outside Vienna. Prix, who also worked in Carl's office for some years (1839–43), was a key figure in shaping the theatre programme, for his activities included translation of texts from the French, and he also functioned as a publisher from the mid-1840s till 1863.[78] Nestroy's second-last play, *Frühere Verhältnisse*, is based on a one-act farce by Emil Pohl, *Ein melancholischer Hausknecht*, which had been performed in the Wallner-Theater in Berlin in July 1861 but had not been printed, and can have come into Nestroy's hands only through an agency, presumably Prix.[79]

The inter-city activity exemplified in Prix's agency is part of the growing internationalization of the commercial theatre from the 1830s. This extended to the actors. The frequency of guest appearances made by star actors was a phenomenon that had been developing steadily throughout German-speaking Europe since the early years of the century, and figures from the mid-1840s show that Vienna was by some way the most important centre from which the touring actors were drawn.[80] Raimund played in the major German centres (Berlin, Munich, Hamburg) as well as in Prague in the years 1831–6. In the 1840s it was usual for actors to go on tour in the summer, when (as in Paris) the theatres in Vienna closed because there were other competing attractions in hot weather. Nestroy, a

14 Wenzel Scholz in the title role of Nestroy's *Eulenspiegel*.

workaholic, went on tour every summer from 1839 to 1854, playing in Hamburg, Breslau, Berlin, Munich, Frankfurt am Main, and Leipzig; also in Brünn, Linz, Pest, Graz, Lemberg, and repeatedly in Prague, where in 1842 both he and the Burgtheater actor Fichtner were to be seen (the leading actors of the court theatres were always particularly sought after as guest stars), and where on 24 May 1847, in a performance of *Der Schützling*, he notched up his hundredth appearance – a feat approched only, according to the leading Prague reviewer, by his colleague Wenzel Scholz.[81] In 1844, they both appeared there in *Einen Jux will er sich machen*; when Nestroy went on to Berlin and appeared as Weinberl there too, reviewers were keen to compare his performance with that of Friedrich Beckmann, who had played the part in 1842 (he also appeared frequently in *Der Talisman*), and who had himself visited Vienna in 1841 and 1842.[82]

In mid-century, Vienna had a stronger influence on the expanding theatrical life in Berlin than *vice versa*. A particularly influential figure was Franz Wallner, who had been a member of Carl's company in the Theater an der Wien at the end of the 1830s and the beginning of the 1840s. He appeared in Berlin for the first time in 1845 in the Königsstädtisches Theater on the Alexanderplatz (the theatre where Beckmann worked), became director of that theatre in 1855 and then opened his own theatre in 1858, setting out to create a Berlin equivalent to the dialect theatres in Vienna, with David Kalisch as his principal comic dramatist. But the influence was not just one-way. Even Nestroy's debt to sources deriving from Berlin extended beyond the one-act comedy by Pohl: *Eine Wohnung ist zu vermieten* was based on a play by Louis Angely, *Wohnungen zu vermieten!* (1832), and in 1858 he adapted Kalisch's one-act farce *Ein gebildeter Hausknecht*. (Kalisch's play had been performed in the Königsstädtisches Theater on 2 May and published that same year in Berlin; the Viennese version, with music by Carl Binder, was first performed in the Carltheater on 11 September.) The Angely play itself was based on a French source, a *vaudeville* entitled *Appartements à louer* by Duflot and Roche, first performed in the Théâtre du Vaudeville in 1832; the piece by Kalisch seems to have derived from a Viennese comedy, Korntheuer's *Alle sind verheiratet* (1823).[83] It is characteristic of the theatrical life of the period that there was a constant interchange of material between the great international centres. In London, Raimund's *Der Alpenkönig und der Menschenfeind* was adapted in 1831 by John Baldwin Buckstone as a romantic drama entitled *The King of the Alps*; In Paris, Nestroy's *Zu ebener Erde und erster Stock* was adapted by Mélesville and Carmouche under the title *Du haut en bas* and performed in 1842 in the Théâtre du Palais-Royal, one of the *petits théâtres*.

For the Viennese dramatists ever in search of new material (see document 6, pp. 248–9), London was a productive source of material. Grillparzer, visiting in 1836, was particularly impressed by the comedy to be seen there;[84] Nestroy's plays include three adapted from English originals (*Einen Jux will er sich machen*, *Liebesgeschichten und Heiratssachen*, and *"Nur keck!"*, based on plays by Oxenford, Poole, and Boucicault respectively), and Bulwer-Lytton's *Money!* was adaped as a three-act comedy by Kaiser and staged under the title *Geld!*, with music by Adolf Müller, in the Theater an der Wien in 1841.

But it was Paris which, as for the playwrights in London, was the most prolific source of material to adapt, and which consequently exerted the strongest influence. In the late summer of 1840, Carl himself went to Paris on an extended visit, accompanied by senior colleagues, in order to glean practical tips that could be applied to his own theatres; he was away from Vienna for nearly seven weeks,[85] and among the material he returned with was probably a copy of *Bonaventure*, a *comédie-vaudeville* by Dupeuty and F. de Courcy which had been performed in the Théâtre du Vaudeville in late June, with the comic actor Étienne Arnal in the title role, and which provided Nestroy with the source of *Der Talisman*. *Der Talisman* was produced in the Theater an der Wien on 16 December 1840; a month later a rival (and less free) version, *Rot, braun und blond oder Die drei Wittfrauen* by Joseph Kupelwieser, was premièred in the Theater in der Josefstadt. A similar example is provided by a *comédie-vaudeville* by Duvert and Lauzanne, *L'Homme blasé*, which was performed in the Théâtre du Vaudeville on 18 November 1843, again with Arnal in the title part: within a few months it had been adapted in London by Boucicault and Charles Mathews (this version, entitled *Used up*, was performed in the Theatre Royal, Haymarket, on 6 February 1844), while in Vienna two versions in *Posse* form received their première on the same evening, 9 April 1844: in the Theater in der Josefstadt Kupelwieser's *Überdruß aus Überfluß oder Der gespenstige Schlosser*, with music by Carl Binder; in the Theater an der Wien Nestroy's *Der Zerrissene*, with music by Adolf Müller.[86]

Importation of material from Paris was, of course, by no means limited either to the 1840s or indeed to the commercial theatre; as late as the 1870s the Burgtheater was just as quick off the draw in putting on its version of *Froment jeune et Risler aîné* (see p. 78, above): the French play, which was adapted from Daudet's novel by Daudet himself in collaboration with Adolphe Belot, had first been performed in the Théâtre du Vaudeville on 16 September 1876; the German version by Ludwig Doczi, *Froment junior und Risler senior*, was produced in the Burgtheater just under eleven weeks later, on 29 November.

But it was in the commercial theatres that the influx of French material took on epidemic proportions in the late 1830s and early 1840s. One factor was the lack of an effective system of copyright. In England, this was a burning issue, the distinction between the right to reprint and the right to mount a dramatic performance being gradually defined in Acts of Parliament passed in 1833 and 1842.[87] In Austria, by contrast, things were much laxer. (The Dual Monarchy did not even sign the Berne Convention of 1887, and copyright law was not brought into line with international standards until 1920, when Austria was required to sign the Berne Convention by Article 239 of the Treaty of Saint-Germain-en-Laye.)[88] There was free use of borrowed material in the Viennese theatre, and this included free pillaging of novels, without any concern for copyright – the issue that vexed Dickens in London.[89] The popular novels of Paul de Kock, Eugène Sue, and Frédéric Soulié were widely available in translation and provided the commercial dramatists, Nestroy among them, with ready-made plots; Nestroy even attempted a dramatization of Dickens's *Martin Chuzzlewit* (*Die Anverwandten*, 1848).

Though journalistic reviewers bewailed the dependence on French sources, the press was in fact one of the means by which such sources came to the attention of Viennese directors, playwrights, and agents. Reports on theatrical events elsewhere appeared regularly; the huge success of *L'Homme blasé* in Paris, for example, was at once reported at length in Vienna in the *Theaterzeitung* and *Der Wanderer*.[90] Because the tight censorship made anything like modern political journalism impossible, until 1848 theatre, opera, and the other arts were the central concerns of the Viennese press. For that reason the theatre coverage too was kept under particularly tight official scrutiny: when Schreyvogel was relieved of his position as censor of theatre reviews in 1823, following complaints from Dietrichstein about an account in *Der Sammler* of a production of a minor comedy in the Burgtheater, his immediate successor, Johann Baptist Rupprecht, received instructions from Sedlnitzky that he must exercise 'ruthless strictness' to ensure that reviews remained not only unpartisan but also moderate in tone, avoiding any polemics that might detract from the 'honour of the literature of the nation'.[91]

The longest-running journal devoted mainly to the theatre was the *Theaterzeitung*, edited by Bäuerle, which appeared under various titles from 1811 to 1859. Its coloured illustrations, some of them engraved after water-colours by Johann Christian Schoeller, together with a 'gallery' of coloured engravings which Bäuerle published separately (e.g. plates 3, 5, 11, 19, and 20), are among our most important sources of information about stage costume from the mid-1820s until the early 1840s. In the 1830s and 1840s the *Theaterzeitung* tended to be so supportive of Karl Carl's theatres that malicious observers regarded Bäuerle as venal and in Carl's pocket.[92] In 1846 a sequel by Louis Grois to *Einen Jux will er sich machen* was produced in the Leopoldstadt, and one of the songs sung by Nestroy in the leading part included satirical reference to reviewers who praised bad plays – almost certainly a mischievous oblique allusion to venality, though not necessarily with the *Theaterzeitung* in mind. (The *Theaterzeitung* review ignored that implication but was strong in condemning the play,[93] and it was given only four performances.) Among other long-running papers specializing in theatre and the arts, *Der Wanderer* (1814–73) was informative but had few aspirations to critical authority; the most combative journal was Saphir's *Der Humorist* (1837–62). Saphir's polemical and self-indulgently wordy reviewing style was not calculated to win over those he wrote about; there may also have been an element of anti-Semitism in the hostility with which he was widely regarded in theatre circles. A more sober form of aesthetic and ideological conservatism was represented by the *Wiener Zeitschrift für Kunst, Literatur, Theater und Mode* (1816–48, edited from 1836 to 1844 by Friedrich Witthauer), which tended to apply moralistic and didactic criteria and regularly referred to Raimund as a standard for popular theatres. There were also of course shorter-lived journals, some of them edited by influential figures, such as W. Lembert's *Der Telegraph* (1836–8), A.J. Gross-Hoffinger's *Der Adler* (1838–43), and Ludwig August Frankl's *Sonntags-Blätter* (1842–8); plays with a substantial musical component were often covered in the *Allgemeine Wiener Musik-Zeitung* (1841–8); and there were also newspapers with wider coverage which had important reviewing sections, notably the *Österreichisches Morgenblatt* (1836–48), founded and edited first by Frankl, then from mid-1841 edited by Johann Nepomuk Vogl, and *Die Gegenwart* (1841–8). After the revolution the most informative specialist journal was *Der Zwischen-Akt* (1858–71); by this time there were also an increasing number of general newspapers with coverage of the theatre, including the *Ostdeutsche Post* (1848–66) and the *Fremdenblatt* (1847–1919).

The role of the press was particularly influential in the 1830s and 1840s, for reviews of individual plays and discussions of the commercial theatre in general often turned not only on matters of aesthetic judgement but also, at least implicitly, on political issues, which could not be hammered out openly because of the censorship. In a society in which public meetings were forbidden, debate about the theatre functioned as a covert forum for discussion of society as a whole.

4. THE DEBATE ABOUT 'POPULAR DRAMA'

After the death of Raimund, a recurrent subject of discussion was the supposed decline of Viennese popular drama. This debate became sharper after the 1830 July Revolution in Paris, as fears grew in conservatively-minded circles that the very fabric of society was under threat: as a 'moral institution' the stage had an educative function and could bolster social and political continuity. By the late 1830s, there was a critical consensus in the Viennese newspapers: Viennese popular theatre, and particularly dialect comedy (the *Lokalposse*), were going rapidly downhill[94] – a view that was passed on outside Vienna as unquestioned fact in Cotta's influential *Morgenblatt für gebildete Leser* (Stuttgart).[95] Criticism was intensified when in December 1838 Karl Carl took over the Theater in der Leopoldstadt, the time-honoured home of dialect comedy, where Raimund had spent most of his career.[96]

The contrast between Nestroy's sceptical view of the world and the more sentimental quality of Raimund's comedies led to frequent critical reproaches. Reviewers confused the satirist (who was both dramatist and chief actor in his own plays) with his subject, and criticized him for representing the very qualities in life (crudeness, pettiness, self-seeking, philistinism) that he was satirizing. The issue surfaced in 1833 in a cautious review in the *Wiener Zeitschrift für Kunst, Literatur, Theater und Mode* of Nestroy's first major success in Vienna, *Der böse Geist Lumpacivagabundus*, and of his own acting in the role of Knieriem;[97] and in the years that followed he was repeatedly criticized for coarseness in characterization and language, and a lack of any edifying moral teaching.[98] Since he was acknowledged to be the outstanding dramatist of his generation, a considerable weight of expectation was placed on him, and he was at the centre of sustained controversy throughout the 1840s. In the *Österreichisches Morgenblatt* in particular, his achievement was repeatedly measured against the responsibility he bore for the future of popular theatre, and the attacks on his alleged failings were all the harsher when he did not conform to critical demands.

In the early 1840s the controversy fought out in the review columns of the Viennese press centred on two issues. One was the perceived threat to indigenous dialect comedy (the *Posse*) presented by the imported *vaudeville*. In defence of local tradition, critics had long pressed the case that dramatists should use 'original' material rather than plots adapted from French sources, and with the vogue for the *vaudeville* the commercial stage in Vienna seemed to face the same risk of becoming a satellite of Paris as the London theatre also did (or also seemed to) a decade or so later. Underlying the argument was a moralistic rearguard action against 'indecency', which was openly associated with French material. For example, Nestroy's *Das Mädl aus der Vorstadt* (1841), based on a *comédie-vaudeville* by Paul de Kock and Charles-Victor Varin, *La Jolie Fille du faubourg*, was criticized both for being based on a French source and for the alleged indecency of the situations and coarseness of language and ideas.[99] Another object of this kind of attack was Nestroy's *Das Gewürzkrämer-Kleeblatt*, a comedy about imagined infidelity which was first performed in the Theater an der Wien on 26 February 1845. It was based on a *vaudeville* by Lockroy and Anicet Bourgeois, *Trois Epiciers*, which a visiting French company had performed in December 1844 in the Kärntnertortheater and which had been favourably received.[100] But Nestroy's version was greeted with a chorus of disapproval, and was criticized above all for its supposed indecency.[101]

Notions of what constitutes decency and indecency are in constant flux. By modern standards Nestroy's plays are far from obscene. Moreover, as he himself would later say in his protest about the censoring of *Mein Freund* in 1851, risqué jokes – or what counted as risqué jokes – were not in fashion in 1851 but had been in fashion earlier (see document 10, p. 253): that is, to the extent that he included any risqué element he was probably responding to the taste of the time rather than offending against it. The real thrust of the objections of critics such as Saphir, who accused him of corrupting taste by establishing an expectation of indecency,[102] was directed not at matters of taste but rather at increasing radicalism in the popular theatre, of which Nestroy's satire was symptomatic.

This political thrust underlies still more clearly the second principal demand voiced around 1840. This was for a new kind of play, to which the term *Volksstück* was applied. It should be 'humorous' rather than 'witty' in tone (Raimund was frequently invoked as a model); it should have a moralistic intention, and it should present an idealized view of everyday life. This part of the debate came to a head following the première in the Theater an der Wien in September 1840 of Friedrich Kaiser's *Wer wird Amtmann?*, with Nestroy in the main part (see plate 15). In this play Kaiser tried to launch a new genre, the *Lebensbild*. The term, meaning 'picture of life', implied a realistic presentation of life by contrast with the distortion of which Nestroy's satire was constantly accused. Kaiser's aim was also to undo what he saw as a trend to comic trivialization by achieving just the blend of sentiment and morality that the critics were demanding. The *Österreichisches Morgenblatt*, which defended the *Posse* against the *vaudeville*, was bound to disapprove of plays such as *Das Gewürzkrämer-Kleeblatt* as alien to local tradition;[103] but it was equally critical of *Wer wird Amtmann?*, with its incongruous mixture of effects. Elsewhere, however, that play was praised precisely for its combination of morality and sentiment.[104] Nestroy's next play, three months after *Wer wird Amtmann?*, was *Der Talisman*. It includes an open attack on the *Lebensbild* genre, which the central comic figure defines as a 'sad farce' ('eine traurige Posse').[105] Tensions developed within the company, and Carl insisted that his playwrights, including Kaiser, must adhere to Nestroy's style.[106] But what was at issue was not just a rivalry between individual playwrights or between contrasting kinds of comedy; this is confirmed by the fact that most of the passage satirizing the *Lebensbild* was deleted by the censor,[107] who clearly wanted to defend the new genre against radical attack. And when in 1846, a year after *Das Gewürzkrämer-Kleeblatt*, Nestroy himself provided in *Der Unbedeutende* a play that could be seen as more than mere farce and as presenting a clear 'moral', it was praised for having struck out in a 'healthy' new direction.[108]

In the following year the debate about the 'decline of the popular theatre' reached a new intensity. When the German theatre in Pest was destroyed by fire on 2 February 1847, a twenty-page pamphlet *Ueber den Verfall der Volkstheater* appeared, sold in aid of members of the theatre who had lost their jobs as a consequence of

Richter: *Marsch! unter die Maß!*
Florian: *Ich—ich hab' gar keine Maß,*
ich war immer ganz unmaßgeblich—

15   Nestroy as Florian Langbaum being measured by a recruiting sergeant in
      Friedrich Kaiser's *Wer wird Amtmann? oder Des Vaters Grab.*

the fire. Emphasizing the moral function of the popular theatres, the anonymous writer presents their decline as incontestable: the popularity of the *vaudeville* showed the extent to which, by contrast with the past, they were now devoted to mere amusement. This argument provoked disagreement, not as regards the decline but as regards its cause. K. Arnold, the theatre critic of the *Österreichische Blätter für Literatur und Kunst, Geografie, Geschichte, Statistik und Naturkunde,* placed the blame on obscenity in performance ('die Zotenreißerei der Schauspieler'); the actors got round the censorship by suggestive gesture and as a consequence alienated the more cultivated part of the theatre public ('das eigentlich gebildete Publikum'). His article cites two examples, *Zwölf Mädchen in Uniform* (adapted by Nestroy from an original by Angely) and Grois's *Eine Dorfgeschichte, die in der Stadt endet,* and since Nestroy played the main part in both there could be no doubt whom he was blaming. Arnold's article does not deny that reform was needed, but his main attack is directed at trivial and ill-constructed comedies built round 'a few *Kouplets'* (satirical songs).[109] The argument continued in the reviews devoted to Nestroy's next play, *Der Schützling* – his last full-length play before the 1848 revolution. Much of the critical discussion centred on what was perceived as the crisis in the popular theatre.

The central character in *Der Schützling* has ambitions as a factory manager, and some critics compared the play to *Der Unbedeutende* as evidence of Nestroy's determination to develop the *Lokalposse* in a new direction, blending comedy with serious treatment of present-day reality.[110] He was even congratulated on having entered the world of polemical high comedy.[111] But precisely this sense that he was embarking on a new genre also provoked critical dissent, in particular on two counts. First, the play lacked a genuinely 'popular' quality; it contained fewer major characters from the poorer classes ('Charaktere aus dem Volke') than *Der Unbedeutende.*[112] Secondly, Nestroy depended for his effect not on cosy 'humour' but on politically loaded wit, what one critic dubbed 'Zeitungswitze'.[113] Saphir took up this point in December, comparing Nestroy's 'polemical' manner to that of Bauernfeld,[114] and it provided Friedrich Kaiser with a theme for the next few years. Kaiser regularly worked in allusions to the theatre in his plays: for example, to the overworking of playwrights by directors in *Der Rastelbinder* (Theater an der Wien, 1843), or to the miserliness of theatre directors in *Sie ist verheiratet* (Theater in der Josefstadt, 1845); by 1850 his target in *Junker und Knecht* (Carltheater) was 'political' wit in comedy.[115] As with the earlier dispute about the *Lebensbild* and the *Volksstück*, it is clear that attacks on Nestroy for writing 'wittily' instead of 'humorously' were politically charged; his critics were concerned with the defence of the social and political *status quo*. It is indicative that exactly the same arguments would be used three-quarters of a century later against operetta, with Nestroy then quoted as an example of the traditional qualities that had been sacrificed.[116]

The lucrative run of *Der Schützling* in the Theater in der Leopold-stadt was interrupted when Carl closed the historic theatre on 7 May to have it demolished and rebuilt. This event sparked off renewed debate about the uncertain state of the dialect theatre. Saphir published a three-part essay, 'Des Wiener Volksstücks Glück und Ende', arguing that the decline in popular drama was manifest: the general enthusiasm for *Der Schützling* proved that truly popular, 'humorous' drama was at an end, its place usurped by a stilted hybrid form with polemical intentions ('Tendenzstreben').[117]

When the new and much larger Carltheater opened on 10 December 1847, the daily *Die Gegenwart* printed a celebratory poem by Ludwig Eckardt, dedicated to Carl and welcoming the advent of a new home for 'popular theatre'.[118] At the end of March, Arnold had made the point that popular drama belonged essentially in small theatres, and that for that reason the Theater an der Wien had never been suitable for it (see document 7, p. 249); so now Saphir, using the opening as an opportunity for further discussion of the decline of popular theatre since Raimund's death, raised shrewd questions about the likely character of Carl's new theatre, forecasting that he would run a broader repertoire, cultivating both *vaudeville* and large-scale drama there (see document 9, pp. 249–50). Even while *Der Schützling* was still running in the old Theater in der Leopoldstadt, a critic in the Leipzig journal *Die Grenzboten* recorded that the character of the audience was changing: the theatre had increasingly been attracting a more up-market public, with the poorer strata of society no longer to be seen there (see document 8, p. 249). That could be explained in part by the increasing poverty of the time; but the removal of standing room behind the stalls of the new theatre (the *Stehparterre*) confirms that Carl was deliberately aiming to attract a more prosperous audience. The architects of the Carltheater were Eduard van der Nüll and August Sicard von Sicardsburg, who would later also design the new Opera House; and like the Friedrich-

Wilhelmstädtisches Theater in Berlin, the theatre looked like a bourgeois imitation of a grand opera house (see plate 16). When we bear in mind that just over ten years later the Theater an der Wien was known as the 'meeting place of the *beau monde*',[119] it is clear that the character of the commercial theatres had decisively altered, reflecting the changing character of the expanding city.

5. POKORNY, TREUMANN, AND THE DECLINE OF DIALECT COMEDY

Franz Pokorny, who ousted Carl from the Theater an der Wien in 1845, had run the Theater in der Josefstadt since 1837. There he had introduced a system of royalties in 1839; and in February 1842 had mounted one of the biggest hits in the whole history of the commercial dialect theatre, a sentimental *Zauberspiel* by Franz Xaver Told entitled *Der Zauberschleier*, which was based on a source drawn from Scribe and was produced with lavish décor by Theodor Jachimovicz depicting scenic views of the Danube valley: the admiration aroused by the sets made Jachimovicz, so an envious rival noted, 'the man of the hour'.[120] The play centres on the love of a fairy for a poor painter (a basic situation similar to that in Raimund's *Der Verschwender*, which had been staged in the same theatre eight years earlier), and it was generally praised by conservative critics for its 'poetic' qualities (in implicit contrast to the satirical comedies of Nestroy offered by Carl's company in the other two commercial theatres).[121] *Der Zauberschleier* ran and ran: 100 consecutive performances by the beginning of June 1842, 200 performances by February 1843, over 375 performances up to the time of Pokorny's death in 1850.

Pokorny's successful bid for the Theater an der Wien, made possible by box-office profits from the run of *Der Zauberschleier*, came as a surprise – not least to Carl, who seems, as Seyfried suggests, to have underestimated him.[122] Once he had taken it over, Pokorny invested 70,000 fl. in having the theatre renovated, both outside and inside. A new balcony was constructed above the famous Papageno door, the depth of the stage was increased, new stage machinery and a new heating system were installed, the auditorium was newly decorated, and gas lighting was introduced (in this the Carltheater followed suit two years later). Pokorny's intention was to restore the standing of the Theater an der Wien as an opera theatre. It reopened

16　Carltheater.

on 30 August with a production of Flotow's *Alessandro Stradella*, with the Emperor himself attending,[123] and within a couple of months, the frequent changes in the operatic repertory (as many as four operas in a fortnight) and in the casts were drawing press comment.[124] Pokorny concentrated on building up the strength of his company in opera. The celebrated bass Joseph Staudigl – a 'bass nightingale', as Glassbrenner had dubbed him[125] – joined the company from the Kärntnertortheater in 1845; for two years (1846–8) Albert Lortzing from Berlin worked in tandem with Suppé as *Kapellmeister*. Special attractions included performances by the Swedish soprano Jenny Lind in May 1846 and January-April 1847, including the première of Meyerbeer's *Vielka* (a revised version of *Ein Feldlager in Schlesien*), performed in February 1847 with Jenny Lind in the title role. In 1846 Pokorny applied unsuccessfully to take over the lease of the court Opera House,[126] and he probably hoped to be appointed as its director after the revolution; but that was a vain hope, and the predictable result of his ambitious programme was in fact financial ruin.

By April 1846 the press was lamenting that the Theater an der Wien had turned into an opera theatre, so that the *Posse* was now to be found only in the Leopoldstadt.[127] In fact Pokorny also continued to put on some dialect drama, specializing in didactic dramas with realist pretensions, provided by Friedrich Kaiser and others, including one of the most talented younger minor playwrights, Carl Elmar. Once again a fire played an influential role, in this case the burning-down of the German theatre in Pest in February 1847. Pokorny seized the opportunity to engage promising actors from the Pest company: Carl Matthias Rott, who became one of the main stars in the Theater an der Wien in the 1850s, and the brothers Carl and Franz Treumann. When Pokorny died in August 1850 and the theatre – heavily in debt – was taken over by his twenty-four-year-old son Alois Pokorny, Franz Treumann soon moved to the Carltheater, and in consequence of the rivalry between Rott and Carl Treumann the latter followed in 1852. This turned out to be a considerable coup for the Carltheater in its competition with the Pokornys, for Carl Treumann would play a central part in the creation of Viennese operetta.

What first prepared the ground for the arrival of French operetta in Vienna was a series of performances of musical scenes given in March and April 1856 in the Carltheater by a French company headed by Levassor (from the Théâtre du Palais-Royal) and Mme Teisseire (from the Théâtre du Gymnase-Dramatique). One of the items was *Les Deux Aveugles*; it was Vienna's first taste of Offenbach. Following the departure of Levassor and his company, Carl Treumann appeared in a similar show, performed in German; and in October 1858 he chose for a benefit performance Offenbach's early one-act operetta *Le Mariage aux lanternes*. He translated the text himself and it was billed as a 'komisches Singspiel' under the title *Hochzeit bei Laternenschein*. At this time the theatre was under the direction of Nestroy, who had taken over after Carl's death in 1854, though for the day-to-day management he depended heavily both on Marie Weiler, who was effectively in charge of administration by the end of 1856, and on Ernst Stainhauser, who had been Carl's chief accountant in the Leopoldstadt since 1845. Despite the affection in which Nestroy was held personally, his six years in charge were not free of contention. Speidel would later accuse him of having allowed indecency to flourish unchecked.[128] In fact fundamental changes were taking place in the repertory. The rise of Carl Treumann, who became the principal comic actor beside Nestroy following the death of Scholz in October 1857, coincided with a trend towards one-act plays (there was a similar tendency in the Burgtheater at the time); and the introduction of Offenbach operetta – the part of Jupiter in the Carltheater adaptation of *Orpheus in the Underworld* was one of Nestroy's most popular roles in his final season there – further undermined the position of indigenous comedy as the principal ingredient of the repertoire.

Between 1800 and 1855, though the number of theatres had not increased, the population of the city had doubled. The incoming population from the far-flung provinces in the early stages of industrialization had no attachment to local genres of dialect comedy, and it is one of the marks of Carl's acumen that he saw this coming as early as the 1840s, arguing openly that local comedy had had its day (see document 12, pp. 256–7), and trying first to replace it by *vaudevilles* starring Ida Brüning-Wohlbrück, and later engaging Carl Treumann in the hope of establishing a new convention of farcical comedy in standard German.[129]

When new theatres finally began to be built it was mainly to provide homes not for indigenous comedy but for operetta, light vaudeville comedy, even variety. One important exception was the Theater am Franz-Josefs-Kai, which opened in 1860 – the first new professional theatre to have been opened within the city limits since 1801 – and had dialect comedy as well as operetta in the repertory (it was, indeed, where Nestroy made his final appearances in 1862 after his retirement), but which burnt down in 1863. The building of the Theater am Franz-Josefs-Kai was an early product of the massive programme of building that went with the rapid expansion of the city. The demolition of the ramparts encircling the city centre was approved by an imperial decree signed on 20 December 1857. The subsequent scheme of town planning, approved just under two years later, centred on the construction, on the open space outside the old walls, of the Ringstrasse, a modern boulevard with large-scale public and commercial buildings. The demolition of the old walls and the extension of the city centre gave Treumann an opportunity to apply for permission to build on the area of the Gonzaga-Bastei a theatre specializing in the *Posse* (with music and dancing), drama, comedy, pantomime and *Singspiel* (but not opera). The proposal, submitted in November 1859, was a welcome response to the anomalous position whereby there were still only five permanent theatres available during the main season but seven in summer, including two outdoor *Arenabühnen* (see below, pp. 132–3); and the planned position of the new house seemed to pose no immediate commercial threat either to the Carltheater or to the court theatres.

What Treumann proposed was a substantial modern theatre in an extended complex, to include shops, cafés, and residential accommodation. As a short-term solution he applied for permission to build a temporary theatre on the former Fischmarkt, on part of the proposed site. There were protests from local residents against this compromise, and specifically against the fire risk associated with what was basically to be a wooden building; but since it would enable Treumann to keep together Nestroy's company, which would otherwise be disbanded, approval was given subject to strict safety conditions. These included the construction of a lead roof, the provision of exit stairways in stone or wrought iron, and acceptance of official requirements concerning fire-fighting appliances – the last a particularly important point since the temporary theatre, which opened in November 1860, was a sizable construction, with three tiers, thirty-two boxes, 318 seats at stalls level and five hundred in the galleries. The contract spelt out that the sole function of the licence was to give Treumann time to have a permanent theatre built, that it must be completed by November 1863, that the licence for the temporary theatre would on no account be extended beyond October 1863, and that it must be completely demolished by the end of November 1863. When Treumann did apply in March 1861 for an extension of the licence, his application was turned down, but as successive applications were submitted to modify the plans for the permanent theatre its possible completion date steadily receded.

Treumann's theatre lasted only three years, but it was well attended and profitable, and had an enviable reputation for high standards of production, playing an important part in popularizing the box set. (Moritz Lehmann was in charge of stage décor in the theatre's first season.) Above all it provided an important element of continuity between the Carltheater under Nestroy and the Carltheater of the 1860s – continuity not so much in respect of local dialect comedy (which was mainly limited to two visits by Nestroy and after his death to occasional performances with Carl Rott in Nestroy parts) as rather in the production of Offenbach. This was a source of criticism, which Friedrich Kaiser was happy to repeat: Treumann had undertaken to maintain a high-quality popular theatre but instead had provided frivolous French musical entertainment.[130] The repertory was dominated by one-act productions and by operetta; it was in this theatre that the company from Offenbach's Théâtre des Bouffes-Parisiens gave the first operetta cycle in Vienna in June-July 1861, and they returned again in June-July 1862. The repertory of German-language operetta, too, was dominated by adaptations of Offenbach, though it also included three one-act comic operettas by Suppé, the most successful of which was *Zehn Mädchen und kein Mann*; and one of the highlights in the programme in 1862 was the production of Nestroy's last play, *Häuptling Abendwind*, an adaptation of an Offenbach operetta that had been performed in Vienna in the summer of 1861, with Nestroy and Treumann in the main parts.

It was on the evening of 9 June 1863, after a performance of a one-act farce by Anton Bittner (*Eulenspiegel als Schnipfer*), which had been taken over from the old Carltheater repertory, and of Suppé's *Zehn Mädchen und kein Mann*, that fire broke out in the roof of the temporary theatre. There was no loss of life, but the building was gutted. Treumann abandoned his project for a permanent theatre and took over the lease of the Carltheater, which was vacant following the failure of two successive directors – the second was Lehmann – to follow his example in cultivating operetta. The availablity of the

Carltheater was so convenient a coincidence that Friedrich Kaiser, recounting the story of the fire in his memoirs and listing all its advantages for Treumann, all but accused him of arson: the ever-malicious Seyfried repeated the same rumours of Treumann's complicity, albeit without supporting them.[131]

Treumann's contract for the lease of the Carltheater was for fifteen years, but he completed only three (1863–6). The success he had achieved on the quayside was not repeated, partly because he did not keep his company together (Rott, for example, returned to the Theater an der Wien), and partly because there was competition from a 'Singspielhalle', a wooden theatre for musical entertainments, which Johann Fürst founded in 1862 in the nearby Prater, and for which several of the established dialect writers (including Elmar, Haffner, and Alois Berla) wrote. Nevertheless, Treumann established the reputation of the Carltheater as an operetta theatre. Nestroy plays became more prominent again when Anton Ascher, a member of Treumann's company on the quayside, took over the direction of the Carltheater in 1866, but the true 'rediscovery' of Nestroy did not get fully under way until 1881.

In the transition from dialect comedy to operetta, the Theater an der Wien was consistently outflanked by Carl Treumann's theatres. Having failed to keep Treumann in his company, Alois Pokorny was beaten by the Carltheater and the Theater am Franz-Josefs-Kai in the race to present Viennese productions of Offenbach. He tried to engage the Bouffes-Parisiens for a season in 1858, and tried to negotiate with Offenbach again in October 1858, but nothing came of the schemes[132] (the climate was not propitious; in the next spring the Franco-Austrian War in Italy would break out), and the Carltheater retained its monopoly of French operetta. He also failed in 1858 to engage one of the later stars of operetta, Marie Geistinger. She had acted in 1852–4 in the Theater in der Josefstadt (let by Franz Pokorny in 1850 to Georg Wilhelm Megerle) and enjoyed consider-able success in parodies of the Spanish dancer Señora Pepita de Oliva, who gave over fifty performances in the Carltheater in 1853 (and would also appear in the Theater in der Josefstadt in the first half of 1857); but she moved to northern Germany in 1854, in the first instance to Berlin, to the Friedrich-Wilhelmstädtisches Theater in the Schumannstrasse (the site that would later be that of the famous Deutsches Theater), and did not return to Vienna until 1865. It was in the Theater an der Wien that what is generally considered the first

Viennese operetta, Suppé's *Das Pensionat*, was produced in November 1860; but it had no immediate imitators, and Alois Pokorny's programme consisted mainly of dialect dramas by minor dramatists. His period as director ended, as in so many other cases, in insolvency proceedings in 1862. The theatre was closed, and passed to a new lessee, Friedrich Strampfer.

This was the turning of the tide. Though Strampfer continued to run a programme in which dialect plays predominated, he succeeded in concluding in 1864 a contract with Offenbach, which he renewed in 1867 with an added clause restricting Offenbach's relations with the Carltheater: he was allowed to offer the Carltheater only one full-length operetta per year.[133] The first full-length Offenbach production in the Theater an der Wien was *La Belle Hélène*. It had been performed in Paris in December 1864; the opening night in the Theater an der Wien on 17 March 1865, with a cast headed by Marie Geistinger, was the work's German-language première. The success of the production ushered in the operetta age (see Chapter 5) and opened the way for the Theater an der Wien to become the main operetta theatre in Vienna. In 1869 Strampfer was succeeded by Maximilian Steiner, an actor and producer (and also his long-serving administrator). Steiner ran the theatre, for the first six years in partnership with Marie Geistinger, until his death in 1880, maintaining some dialect drama in his programme (Kaiser, later Anzengruber) as well as operetta; when he was succeeded by his son, Franz Steiner (director until 1884), dialect drama finally disappeared almost completely from the programme.

The map of the popular commercial theatres in Vienna had radically changed in some thirty years. The opening of Treumann's theatre on the quayside had broken the long deadlock that had limited the number of Viennese theatres to five, and it was quickly followed by other new ventures. The first was the Harmonie-Theater in the Wasagasse, north of the centre, which was opened in 1866 with a capacity of about 1,300, including standing room for 400, and which was at once greeted as 'Vienna's sixth theatre';[134] but it quickly changed into a music-hall, and is remembered mainly as one of the earliest buildings designed by Otto Wagner. Another short-lived venture was opened in 1870 in the Tuchlauben in the city centre: it was in the former hall of the Gesellschaft der Musikfreunde, whose new building on the other side of the Ringstrasse was completed in 1869. The hall was reconstructed in 1871 to form a theatre with 28 boxes and in all 600 seats: known at first as the Vaudevilletheater, then from 1871 as the Strampfertheater, it played mainly operettas and comedies and lasted only until 1875, but is notable because two of the most celebrated performers of the operetta era, Alexander Girardi and Josefine Gallmeyer, appeared there, Josefine Gallmeyer also functioning as co-director (with Julius Rosen) in the 1874–5 season.

One reason for the decline of dialect drama in the old commercial theatres that had been its traditional home was that as the city expanded, less well-off theatre-goers seem to have gone increasingly to outdoor summer theatres (*Arenabühnen*) beyond the outer walls, to variety theatres (in the Prater and elsewhere), and to a more conveniently-located theatre in the working-class district of Rudolfsheim, which was opened as a speculative venture by Carl Schwender in 1867 as the Colosseumtheater, was renamed the 'Volkstheater in Rudolfsheim' in 1870, and lasted until 1897, albeit with a very variable programme under a series of different directors. The first of the *Sommerarenen* were both associated with the indefatigable Franz Pokorny. One was in Hernals, to the west of the city centre; built in 1848, it was taken over a year later by Pokorny and was used in the summer until the end of the 1854 season. Pokorny's other outdoor theatre, which he opened in July 1849, was in Fünfhaus, further to the south, on the way to Schönbrunn: the Braunhirschen-Arena, in what had been the park of Baroness Henriette von Pereira-Arnstein. It held an audience of over 3,000 and had a stage double the depth of those of the standing theatres in the city. Not for nothing did Nestroy build into the opening song of his comedy *Kampl* (1852) a satirical allusion to 'arenas' springing up everywhere in summer-time;[135] they presented the permanent theatres with dangerous competition, and were disapproved of by those who looked to the theatre for more than light entertainment.[136]

A related development was the opening in 1856 of the Thalia-Theater, a large mainly wooden theatre, by Johann Hoffmann, then lessee of the Theater in der Josefstadt, beyond the outer fortifications to the west of Vienna. Unheated, this too was designed for summer productions, but though it was run with a mixed repertory, Hoffmann used it from 1858 onwards to present operas, which he discontinued in the Josefstadt. (The theatre survived until the end of the 1860s, and was demolished in 1870.)

The programmes in the outdoor summer theatres typically involved spectacular effects (including fireworks and animal acts), but several leading actors also appeared there: Carl Rott and Carl Treumann in the Braunhirschen-Arena, for example, and the young Marie Geistinger in Hernals. Their dependence on good weather made them risky ventures, despite their capacity, and even the Braunhirschen-Arena, initially a success, finished up by losing money and was given up by Alois Pokorny after the 1861 season. There were similar later ventures, but all were short-lived. The tradition of dialect comedy which had been driven out of the commercial theatres nearer the centre of the city did not take lasting hold further out as the city grew beyond its old limits.

The process of expansion and industrialization brought with it severe social consequences: there was a long-lasting housing shortage (conditions in the outlying newer suburbs, where the working classes mostly lived, were squalid); alcoholism and prostitution were rife. It was inevitable that the most notable playwrights who contributed to continuing the tradition of dialect drama after Nestroy were informed by political and social concerns: most notably Ludwig Anzengruber in the 1870s and 1880s, but also Kaiser and Elmar before him. Anzengruber made his name with *Der Pfarrer von Kirchfeld*, performed in the Theater an der Wien in 1870 while it was jointly directed by Steiner and Marie Geistinger; he would later recount that he was motivated by the urge to improve on the 'rubbish' being performed, which he saw as betraying the educative mission of the theatre.[137] But in his later dialect plays of the 1870s, also set in the country, he found himself in competition with the operettas of Johann Strauss the younger: the comedy *Der G'wissenswurm*, for example, premièred in September 1874, had to compete with *Die Fledermaus* – an unequal battle. The result was that while some of his later plays, including notably the comedy *Ausm g'wohnten Gleis* (1879), continued to be staged in the Theater an der Wien, his finest work, *Das vierte Gebot*, a tragic drama set in the city, was produced not in the Theater an der Wien but in the Josefstadt (29 December 1877), and the most typical of his light Viennese comedies, *Alte Wiener*, in the Ringtheater in September 1878.

Indeed, of the three old commercial theatres, only the Theater in der Josefstadt remained loyal to dialect drama; the Theater an der Wien was dominated by operetta and the Carltheater either by French operetta or by light French comedies. Just as the Burgtheater under Laube and Dingelstedt cultivated contemporary French drama and comedy, so when Franz Jauner, an actor and producer who came to Vienna from the Court Theatre in Dresden, took over the Carltheater in 1872, some of his biggest successes were with translations of hits from Paris: Sardou's *Fernande* in October 1872, *Tricoche et Cacolet* (by Offenbach's librettists Meilhac and Halévy) in January 1873, the Lecocq operetta *La Fille de Madame Angot* in January 1874, and Dumas's *Monsieur Alphonse* two months later. In the course of this development, leading comic actors associated with dialect drama were increasingly taking starring roles in imported comedy – Karl Blasel, for example, in *Tricoche und Cacolet* and *Madame Angot*, Josefine Gallmeyer in *Monsieur Alphonse*.

That operetta was likely to exercise a powerful influence on dialect comedy had been clear from the outset, *Häuptling Abendwind* being a case in point. One effect was the prominence assumed by female stars: an early reflection of this is Friedrich Kaiser's comedy *Localsängerin und Postillon*, with music by Anton M. Storch, which was produced early in 1864 in the Theater in der Josefstadt, starring Josefine Gallmeyer. What failed to materialize from the competition between dialect drama and operetta was any fusion of the two forms into a new satirical genre. It is characteristic that the one event of importance involving local comedy in the last quarter of the nineteenth century was the commemorative Nestroy cycle in the Carltheater in 1881. The veteran Adolf Müller composed an overture which he conducted himself; Bauernfeld provided a suitably nostalgic prologue which was delivered by Franz Tewele (who had succeeded Jauner as director of the theatre in September 1878);[138] and what had been planned as a week's programme proved so successful that it expanded to a festival lasting seven weeks, in which no fewer than twenty-seven plays were performed. But an attempt to repeat the recipe with a further cycle of local comedies failed.

The failure to rejuvenate the tradition can be seen in the subjects that were treated in its later stages. Some familiar old themes were reworked, including the traditional satire of the follies of pretension and snobbery, which went back to Hafner: examples included two plays by O.F. Berg, *Der Modeteufel* (Carltheater, 1860) and *Der närrische Schuster* (Theater an der Wien, 1877). The Krähwinkel theme was reworked by Theodor Flamm in a one-act comedy *Die Rekrutierung in Krähwinkel* (Carltheater, 1857), in which Nestroy and Treumann (see plate 17) played two draft-dodgers feigning incapacities to evade recruitment by a board including the traditional figure of the

17 Carl Treumann as Samuel Flekeles in Theodor Flamm, *Die Rekrutierung in Krähwinkel*.

commandant Rummelpuff; this slight piece was performed nearly sixty times in three years, and Nestroy appeared in it sixty-five times in all. New subjects included events connected with the 1848 revolution, as in Anton Langer's *Ein Wiener Freiwilliger* (Theater an der Wien, 1855) and O.F. Berg's *Der letzte Nationalgardist* (Theater an der Wien, 1871). The example of Nestroy's *Der Schützling* (1847) in treating the coming of industry was followed by Carl Elmar in *Unter der Erde* (Theater an der Wien, 1848) and *Das Mädchen von der Spule* (Theater an der Wien, 1852) and by Kaiser in *Eine neue Welt* (Theater an der Wien, 1860). And religious tolerance and intolerance provided a subject for Berg in *Einer von unsere Leut'* (Carltheater, 1859; Theater in der Josefstadt, 1861; later revised as *Isaak Stern*, Theater an der Wien, 1871), for Kaiser in *Neu-Jerusalem* (Theater in der Josefstadt, 1867), and for Elmar in the naively tendentious *Die Tochter des Gottlosen* (Theater in der Josefstadt, 1874), as well as for Anzengruber in *Der Pfarrer von Kirchfeld*. But even such plays as these, which pretended to social topicality, were for the most part lacking in substance or satirical bite. Following the exclusion of Austria from the German Confederation in 1866 and the creation of the German Empire under Prussian domination in 1871, Friedrich Kaiser provided the Theater in der Josefstadt with a series of patriotic historical plays, heavy-handed exercises in populist mythopoeia: *Pater Abraham a Sancta Clara* (1873), *General Laudon* (1873), *Sonnenfels* (1873). What was also increasingly common was nostalgic evocation of theatre and music history, as in Kaiser's *Der letzte Hanswurst* (Carltheater, 1853) or Haffner's *Therese Krones* (Theater an der Wien, 1854 – a play in which Josefine Gallmeyer took over the title role in 1862, and which remained in the repertory until 1879 and was given 120 performances in all), *Wenzel Scholz* (Theater an der Wien, 1859) and *Scholz und Nestroy* (Theater in der Josefstadt, 1866).

Nestroy himself had treated the theatre as a theme in two late comedies, *Theaterg'schichten* and *Umsonst*, the former including a satirical view of a performance of Grillparzer's *Sappho* in an open-air summer 'arena'; but with increasing frequency fascination with show-business degenerated either into sugary sentimentality, as in Elmar's *Ferdinand Raimund* (Theater an der Wien, 1851) and Anton Langer's *Strauß und Lanner* (Theater an der Wien, 1855, revived in the Josefstadt in 1884), or else into utter triviality, as in *Heißes Blut* by Leopold Krenn and Carl Lindau (Theater an der Wien, 1892), a play about a Hungarian country girl dreaming of success in the theatre in Vienna. The self-indulgence of this trend, producing plays that were either backward-looking or inward-looking, is a sure indication of a tradition that had burnt itself out.

CHAPTER 5

Opera and operetta

I. OPERA AND BALLET IN THE BIEDERMEIER PERIOD

When the Ringstrasse was built, the placing both of the new Burg-theater and of the new Opera House in central positions on it – the Burgtheater opposite the new Town Hall, the Opera House on the intersection of the Ringstrasse with the wealthy Kärntner Strasse, very close to the old Kärntnertortheater which it replaced, which had nestled close to the city walls – had an obvious symbolical function, signalling the importance of the two theatres among the central institutions of the capital. By the late eighteenth century Vienna was celebrated for the vitality of its musical life. Within a month of arriving there in 1781, Mozart was convinced that it was for his profession 'the best place in the world';[1] Charles Sealsfield's highly critical account of the repressively ruled Austria of the late 1820s still records a Vienna in which on a Sunday, 'wherever you go, the sound of musical instruments will reach your ears';[2] and in the mid-1830s Frances Trollope was persuaded that 'strains of music ... seem to form as necessary a part of the existence of an Austrian as the air he breathes'.[3] Yet if one applies to the court opera houses after Mozart's death the test suggested above (p. 57) for Schreyvo-gel's Burgtheater and asks how much new opera of distinction was generated within them, the record is much less impressive. Haydn's considerable operatic output was associated mainly with premières at Esterháza, and even Mozart's operas were not all performed first in Vienna. There were premières in the Burgtheater of *Die Ent-führung aus dem Serail* in 1782, *The Marriage of Figaro* in 1786, and *Così fan tutte* in 1790; but the production of *Die Zauberflöte* in the Freihaustheater in 1791 was a direct consequence of the effective relegation of German opera to the commercial theatres, while both *Don Giovanni* (1787) and *La Clemenza di Tito* were given their premières not in Vienna at all but in Prague (1791), which had received *The Marriage of Figaro* with much more undivided acclaim than Vienna.[4] It was in Schikaneder's Freihaustheater that *Don Giovanni* received its first Viennese performance in German in 1792, and following the demise of the 'national *Singspiel*' in the Kärntnertortheater in 1788 it was in the Theater in der Leopoldstadt that Wenzel Müller established himself as a composer of *Singspiele* and other light operatic works.

Given the importance of theatre in the cultural life of the city in the early Biedermeier period, it was inevitable that a composer such as Schubert should have aspired to making his name in the opera house. His *œuvre* includes the music for two spectacular entertainments performed in the Theater an der Wien, the opera *Die Zauberharfe* (1820), the libretto for which has been lost, and Helmina von Chézy's play *Rosamunde, Fürstin von Cypern* (1823), neither of them a success either with the critics or at the box-office.[5] Only one of his operatic works was performed in the Kärntnertortheater in his lifetime, *Die Zwillingsbrüder* (1820), and that too achieved only a moderate success; the romantic opera *Fierabras*, with a libretto by Joseph Kupelwieser, was announced as an imminent production in 1823 but then dropped. As for Beethoven, the first production of *Fidelio* (the outstanding product of a vogue for 'rescue operas') was prepared under the composer's direction by Ignaz von Seyfried, the *Kapellmeister* of the Theater an der Wien, but neither of the two productions it received there in 1805–6 (the first with 'Leonore no. 2' as the overture, the second with 'Leonore no. 3') was successful at the box-office; and though Grillparzer wrote a libretto for him on the popular Melusina theme in 1823, to which Beethoven responded with a letter of warm thanks expressing his pride in the honour he felt Grillparzer had bestowed on him,[6] he never composed a score for it, and it was eventually set to music by Konradin Kreutzer. (The completed work was first performed in 1833, in Berlin.) The account of the Kärntnertortheater of the 1830s in Murray's *Handbook for Travellers in Southern Germany* reported that 'Operas and ballets are got up here in a very splendid style, not surpassed by any theatre in Germany, and the orchestra and singers are usually of first-class excellence',[7] but from the reviews in the Viennese press it seems that for much of the first half of the century the standard of operatic performance was variable. Nevertheless in its function as court Opera House from 1810 onwards the Kärntnertortheater enjoyed a position of great prestige among the theatres of the city. This is reflected both in the prominence given in the reviewing journals to its productions, and also in the good attendances it generally attracted. With five tiers rising above the stalls (see plate 18), it had a total capacity of about 2,400 in 1828, and Frances Trollope was assured that this was insufficient to meet demand,[8] though certainly there are records of ill-attended premières, as in the case of a new production of *Die Zauberflöte* in 1847.[9] At the same time there was also a continuing tradition of opera in the old commercial theatres. In the Theater an der Wien, as we have seen, first Schikaneder and then Pálffy were driven to financial ruin by mounting costly opera productions. It was there that the Italian soprano Angelica Catalani appeared in 1818 and that Schubert's *Rosamunde* was produced in 1823. In the Theater in der Leopoldstadt, Marinelli put on works by Gluck, Dittersdorf, Salieri, Cherubini, and Weber. In the Theater in der Josefstadt opera became one of the most important components of the repertory in the early 1830s, when it was directed by Johann August Stöger (himself originally a tenor, who came to the Josefstadt after nine years as director of the theatre in Graz). During his period in charge (1832–4), with Kreutzer as *Kapellmeister*, the theatre was in direct competition with the Kärntnertortheater, with no fewer than twenty-nine operas being produced in twenty months; mostly these were works which had already been performed in the Kärntnertortheater, but they also included the successful première of Kreutzer's *Das Nachtlager von Granada* in January 1834. Opera was also central to the policy pursued by Franz Pokorny, especially after 1845 in the Theater an der Wien, where Lortzing's appointment as *Kapellmeister* bore immediate fruit in the première of *Der Waffenschmied* in May 1846.

That indigenous composers filled a relatively small proportion of the opera repertory in the Biedermeier period is at least in part explained by the continuance of tensions between discrete national traditions of opera. The taste of the time (in Vienna as in London) was for Italian opera, and Vienna provided far less resistance than London to Italian influence. This contrast may be illustrated by the different reactions to Angelica Catalani: in London she was accused in 1809 of having contaminated the English-speaking theatre by importing Italian opera;[10] in Vienna the adulation she attracted when she performed in the Theater an der Wien in June 1818 reached such uncritical extremes that Bäuerle was moved to satirize

18 Theater nächst dem Kärntnertor, interior.

it in his farce *Die falsche Primadonna*, first performed in the Theater in der Leopoldstadt in the following month.

The foundation for the dominance of Italian opera in the Biedermeier period was laid by performances by a visiting Italian company in the Kärntnertortheater in the autumn of 1816, and was cemented during the eight years (1821–9) during which the impresario Domenico Barbaia was lessee of the Kärntnertortheater, bringing Rossini himself to Vienna in 1822. Between 1816 and 1825 no fewer than twenty-five Rossini operas were performed in Vienna, and Sealsfield records that a new Rossini opera in the Kärntnertortheater would 'produce quite as much and even more excitement than the opening of the Parliament in London'.[11] After the vogue for Rossini, which lasted nearly twenty years, the Italian influence remained strong: in 1842 Donizetti was appointed court composer, and he provided two new operas for premières in the Kärntnertortheater, *Linda di Chamounix* (1842) and *Maria di Rohan* (1843). These were both adapted from French material, and French operas were also strongly represented in the programme of the Kärntnertortheater during the Biedermeier period: there were productions of works such as Hérold's *Zampa* (in 1832, a year after the première in Paris) and Meyerbeer's *Robert-le-diable* (1833, a year and a half after the Paris production, and in this case also two months after the first Viennese production in the rival Theater in der Josefstadt); and in particular the Meyerbeer enjoyed sustained success.

Among German works, *Der Freischütz* was performed in 1821, the same year as the Berlin première, and was such a success that Barbaia also put it on in the Theater an der Wien the next year; a rival production followed in Hensler's Theater in der Josefstadt in 1825, which stimulated so much interest that for a time that theatre seemed to be establishing itself as the city's second opera house. But *Euryanthe*, commissioned by Barbaia for the Kärntnertortheater in an attempt to repeat the success of *Der Freischütz*, was less well received in 1823. (Indeed, Barbaia's decision not to risk a performance of Schubert's *Fierabras* was probably a direct consequence of the failure of *Euryanthe*.)[12] In the 1830s and 1840s, operas by German composers such as Spohr and Lortzing as well as by Kreutzer did of course feature in the programme of the Theater in der Josefstadt and the Theater an der Wien, but it was only in the late 1840s that interest in the subject of German union (the interest which had also been reflected in Bauernfeld's drama *Ein deutscher Krieger*) provided a more propitious climate for German operas. Flotow's *Martha* was given its première in the Kärntnertortheater in November 1847; then in the 1850s came the first Viennese performances of operas by Wagner on medieval German themes: *Tannhäuser* in 1857 in the Thalia-Theater (the censors had been unwilling to have it performed in the court Opera House),[13] *Lohengrin* in 1858 in the Kärntnertortheater, where Carl Eckert was director from 1857 to 1860 – the first conductor to hold the post.

Perhaps the best indicator of how comprehensively the fashions for Italian opera and Romantic opera took over in the Biedermeier period is the relative lack of interest in Mozart. The press paid lip-service to his standing as 'the Shakespeare of music', 'the master among all the composers';[14] but the amount of Mozart in the opera repertory was limited. *Die Entführung aus dem Serail* was not performed for ten years between May 1829 and July 1839. *Così fan tutte*, which had been performed in the Kärntnertortheater in 1819 and 1820, was revived in 1840, when it was sung in German under the title *Mädchentreue*; but it received only seven performances. *Die Zauberflöte*, to be sure, was established as a staple classic; the frequency with which the comedies of the dialect theatres include quotations both from the libretto and from the score shows that the composers and playwrights could count on its being well known to their audience. Yet when it reappeared in the programme of the Kärntnertortheater in October 1827 after an interval of four years, it was only as a stopgap, forced on the management because several Italian singers in the company had fallen ill.[15] In January 1842, when there was a new production, with Staudigl as Sarastro, the reviewer in the *Theaterzeitung*, who wrote explicitly as an admirer of 'German music', assumed that the management of the theatre must have been reduced to putting it on as a *pis aller* because there were no new operas that commended themselves,[16] and the reviewer in *Der Humorist* took it for granted that the number of Mozart lovers was generally reckoned to be very low – an assumption that made the full house attending on this occasion all the more gratifying.[17] In Mozart's case it should be added that his Italian operas fared little better. In the 1830s, both *The Marriage of Figaro* and *Don Giovanni* were performed in the Kärntnertortheater; but *Idomeneo*, given just five performances in 1819, was not seen again in any of the Viennese theatres till 1879, while after 1809 (the final performance of a production in the Theater an der Wien) *La Clemenza di*

Tito was not given in any of the major Viennese theatres for a century and a half.

The particular fondness of the Viennese public for Romantic opera during the political repression of the Metternich era was no doubt in part motivated by escapism, just as the vogue for the *Zauberspiel* had been in the commercial theatre. A similar escapist tendency can be seen in the success of Romantic ballet in the same period. Since the age of Gluck in the second half of the eighteenth century, dance as a component of opera had been dominated by foreign artists, the most prolific choreographer being Gluck's celebrated collaborator Jean-Georges Noverre. Notable ballets around the turn of the century included Beethoven's *Die Geschöpfe des Prometheus* (Burgtheater, 1801), choreographed by Salvatore Viganò, who was an influential figure in Viennese ballet in the period 1793–1803; but the importance of ballet was re-established during the Congress of Vienna, when it made accessible entertainment for foreign guests. The principal dancers in the Kärntnertortheater at that stage were still mainly French or Italian. There was also a considerable dance component in the repertoire of the Theater in der Leopoldstadt in the second half of the 1820s, when Paolo Rainoldi mounted burlesque pantomimes there. But ballet in nineteenth-century Vienna was always subordinate to opera. In 1817 the Emperor even decided to abandon it altogether as a measure to combat Pálffy's accumulated debts, and though that was successfully resisted by Stadion, ballet was then restricted explicitly to its function as an 'auxiliary' element in opera performances.[18]

In the second half of the 1830s, when the waltz craze inspired by Johann Strauss the elder and Josef Lanner was sweeping Vienna, dance briefly became more prominent. The Romantic ballet was at its height, and a number of star dancers were as popular in Vienna as in the other great capitals: Jules Perrot, Carlotta Grisi, Marie Taglioni, whose career had been launched in Vienna in 1822 but whose most famous role in *Sylphide* was first seen in Paris, and her Viennese rival Fanny Elssler, who rose to fame in the 1820s and achieved huge success in the fiery Spanish *cachucha* in 1833 (see plate 19) in Jean Coralli's ballet *Le Diable boiteux* (music by Casimir Gide) – a performance whose popularity inevitably led to parody, in this case by Wenzel Scholz in *Die Cachucha*, a farce by Grois with music by Adolf Müller (Theater an der Wien, 1837), in which Scholz appeared costumed in an imitation of the great ballerina (see plate 20),

Costume Bild zur Theaterzeitung. №48.

Fanny Elßler in der Cachucha.

19 Fanny Elssler in the *cachucha*.

20   Wenzel Scholz in the *cachucha*.

achieving an effect of comic incongruity that can best be gauged by comparing his appearance with his normal earthy roles such as Eulenspiegel (plate 14). Fanny Elssler, her dramatic projection always contrasted with the more lyrical and ethereal effects of Marie Taglioni, was fêted in long international tours. Much of her fame was gained outside Vienna, but her tours were reported on regularly in the *Theaterzeitung* and other journals. She gave her last performance in the Kärntnertortheater in June 1851 in a *Faust* ballet by Perrot (music by Hector Panizza) that had been premièred the previous month.

Within a month of the opening of the new Opera House the public were offered an ambitious and expensive ballet production, *Sardanapal* by Paul Taglioni, the Vienna-born brother of Marie Taglioni, to music by Peter Ludwig Hertel; the takings of 3,508 Taler at the première made only a modest dent on the outlay of 25,000 Taler that had gone on the décor.[19] But as with all the international stars of the period, Paul Taglioni's fame as dancer and choreographer was built up mainly outside Vienna, in his case in Berlin and London. In the second half of the century the ballet company in Vienna retained its own traditions and continuity, most strikingly embodied in the long career of Josef Hassreiter, who worked in the company for half a century: he had appeared on stage with Fanny Elssler as a young child, spent twenty years as a dancer in the new Opera House, being best remembered for the long-lasting success of *Die Puppenfee* (1888) which he conceived in collaboration with the painter Franz Gaul to music by Josef Bayer, and he finally served as *Ballettmeister* and principal choreographer there in the years 1890–1919. (The best-known Viennese dancer of the early twentieth century, Grete Wiesenthal, danced with the company under Hassreiter in 1902–7 before launching her solo career.) Nevertheless, after the brief fashion for Romantic ballet, dance reverted to a secondary role in the Opera House, and the standards of dancing and choreography were generally regarded as being below those obtaining in all the other branches of music and drama.[20]

The widespread interest in opera and, especially in the 1830s, in ballet is reflected in the parodies mounted by the commercial theatres of works performed either in the Kärntnertortheater or in other theatres. Even *Die Zauberflöte* was not safe against parody: in August 1818 the programme of the Theater in der Leopoldstadt included *Die travestirte Zauberflöte*, with music by Wenzel Müller and a text by Meisl. Adolf Müller made his name with music to *Die schwarze Frau* by Meisl (Theater in der Josefstadt, 1826), a parody of Boieldieu's *La Dame blanche* (Kärntnertortheater, 1825), and he also provided the scores to Nestroy's parodies of Hérold and Meyerbeer, *Zampa der Tagdieb* (Theater an der Wien, 1832) and *Robert der Teuxel* (Theater an der Wien, 1833). The case of the Meyerbeer provides a particularly good example of the wide interest in opera, the whole theatrical life of Vienna being drawn in. Müller and Nestroy were not even the first in the field in parodying it: the Meyerbeer original was performed in the Theater in der Josefstadt on 20 June (a production for which Stöger was much praised), and on 13 July *Der Wanderer* published the first announcement of Nestroy's parody; but on 18 July the première of a rival parody, *Robert der Wauwau* by Josef Kilian Schickh with music by Andreas Scutta, took place in the Theater in der Leopoldstadt; and it was only after the Meyerbeer had been produced in the Kärntnertortheater (31 August) that Nestroy and Müller completed their work, which was finally staged on 9 October. The success of Perrot's *Der Kobold* (Kärntnertortheater, 3 March 1838) can similarly be measured by the parodies that were mounted, in this case in all three commercial theatres, that in the Theater in der Leopoldstadt (more a light-hearted imitation than a critical parody, to judge from contemporary reviews) being written by Told, that in the Theater an der Wien by Nestroy, and that in the Theater in der Josefstadt by Schickh.[21]

The escapism underlying the vogue for Romantic operas and ballets made them easy targets for Nestroy's parodies, which set out to show up their unreality; in the same spirit he would also parody Wagner's early operas in the 1850s, the scores to his *Tannhäuser* (Carltheater, 1857) and *Lohengrin* (Carltheater, 1859) being provided by Carl Binder. It is clear that often what the commercial theatres offered were essentially popularizations, cashing in on the curiosity of their local public about hits in the Kärntnertortheater (as also about hits in the Burgtheater) that most of that local public would not themselves see. But in the case of opera the composers in the commercial theatres could also rely on their audience for considerable knowledge of the best-known operas. This is clear from the frequent allusive quotation of operatic music in the drama of the commercial theatres, particularly in the parodistic medleys (*Quodlibets*). These medleys were a speciality of Nestroy's; he had begun his theatrical career as an operatic bass, singing Sarastro in a production of *Die Zauberflöte* in the Kärntnertortheater, and himself recognized that they were a special attraction, not least in his appearances as a guest star outside Vienna.[22] They also provided a vehicle for the singing of Marie Weiler, who was one of the leading singers in dialect comedy and was acknowledged as surpassing her rivals in her 'bravura singing'.[23] The development of the *Quodlibet* to accommodate her is one of many examples of the importance of actors in determining the development of the repertory.

2. THE RISE OF OPERETTA

Industrialization came late to Austria. But there as elsewhere, people abandoned the land in search of new employment, flooding into the capital from all corners of the Empire. The population of Vienna, which had been a mere 317,000 in 1830, steadily rose. By 1872 it had doubled and was still growing, reaching nearly 750,000 by 1885, and over a million counting the outlying districts beyond the city boundaries. The years 1860–90 saw an increase of over 160 per cent (the comparable figure for London and for Paris was around 60 per cent); in the ten years from 1880 to 1890 alone, the total rose by over 300,000. In the theatre, the increase in population brought with it a change in tastes. The socio-economic character of the theatre-going public may not have changed greatly, for the main increase lay in the poorest classes, whereas the public that attended the 'five theatres' was mainly drawn from the middle and lower middle classes. But the changes in the social climate affected the cultural climate: in particular dialect comedy was vulnerable to competition from a less localized genre like operetta, which appealed to an audience increasingly drawn from a population new to Vienna.

In Viennese operetta a range of influences came together: Offenbach, the Viennese waltz, and the local tradition of satirical comedy, in which formal musical numbers including overtures as well as songs were established ingredients. Before Offenbach the term 'operetta' meant simply a one-act comic opera; what developed in Vienna was a larger scale of work, in imitation of opera, designed for an upwardly mobile public who found in it not just easily accessible entertainment but also a form of release from the pressing social and financial realities of a society being transformed by industrialization. The more acute urban poverty became, and the more unsettled the financial climate became, the more the theatre-going public took refuge in the fantasy world of operetta.

Before the emergence of Johann Strauss in the 1870s, operettas (usually French) were produced mainly in four theatres: the Carltheater, the Theater am Franz-Josefs-Kai (1860–3), the Theater an der Wien (occasionally from 1860, more systematically from 1865), and the Harmonie-Theater (1866–8). As we have seen in Chapter 4 (pp. 126–30), the driving force behind the introduction of operetta, at first in the Carltheater under Nestroy's direction, was Carl Treumann, who also played a seminal role as actor, producer, and translator. One of the landmarks in the conquest of the Viennese stage by the new genre was his performance of *Hochzeit bei Later-nenschein* in October 1858. The instrumentation of the (pirated) score was done by Carl Binder, who himself made this public in a letter to the *Theaterzeitung*.[24] In the three seasons of Treumann's Theater am Franz-Josefs-Kai, that became the acknowledged operetta centre; and when Treumann took over the Carltheater after the Kai-Theater fire, one of the highlights of his direction was his own adaptation of *La Vie parisienne* (1867).

Although the Viennese critics had long been very suspicious of French influence on the indigenous dialect comedy with which operetta was in competition, the new genre was absorbed in the Viennese repertory rapidly and with ease, not least because the long-established traditions of parody and burlesque on the Viennese stage (including earlier nineteenth-century burlesque treatments of mythological subjects) meant that actors were available who had no difficulty in adopting a style appropriate to operetta. The cast of the 1858 production of *Hochzeit bei Laternenschein*, for example, included Treumann himself and two female singers schooled in local comic tradition, Elise Zöllner and Anna Grobecker.[25] Similarly the production of *La Belle Hélène* in the Theater an der Wien in 1865, the first important product of Offenbach's contract with Strampfer, had not only Marie Geistinger in the cast but also the popular dialect actors Karl Blasel and Carl Matthias Rott; and all the star performers in the 1870s and 1880s – Girardi, Marie Geistinger, and Josefine Gallmeyer – worked in dialect drama as well as in operetta, which contributed to preserving links between the two genres. So too Karl Haffner, the older of the two librettists of *Die Fledermaus*, had been a prolific writer of sentimental comedies for the commercial theatre since the 1840s. Since music, moreover, had always been a fundamental part of the drama of commercial theatres, there was a sense that this tradition of popular theatre music was living on in operetta;[26] and certainly as Viennese operetta developed, an element of continuity was ensured by the experience that the operetta composers such as Suppé and Millöcker had of working in dialect drama: Millöcker, for example, had written the music for O.F. Berg's *Der letzte Nationalgardist* (1871) and *Der närrische Schuster* (1877).

Offenbach himself first visited Vienna in 1861 to conduct in the Kai-Theater at the end of January, and again in June and July, when his company were appearing there; and he returned in 1864, when his romantic opera *Die Rheinnixen* was given its première in the Opera House (Kärntnertortheater). It is on this visit that he is reported to have encouraged Johann Strauss the younger to try his hand at writing operettas.[27] By this time the balance of power between the competing theatres had shifted decisively in favour of the Theater an der Wien. In November 1860, barely a month after Nestroy's retirement from the direction of the rival Carltheater, the première of Suppé's *Das Pensionat* had been staged there. Two years later, in September 1862, Strampfer had taken over the Theater an der Wien. It was there that he secured a contract with Offenbach and began to cultivate full-length operetta in 1864 (in contrast to the one-act pieces in which the now defunct Kai-Theater had specialized); and it was there that he engaged Josefine Gallmeyer, whose acting style Speidel regarded as coming closest to Nestroy's in spirit[28] and who would vie with Marie Geistinger as the leading lady of operetta in Vienna – a rivalry so open that it passed into folklore and was one of the standard highlights of theatre history commemorated on popular postcards well into the twentieth century (see plate 21). By the 1870s, under Maximilian Steiner, the Theater an der Wien was established as the undisputed home of Viennese operetta.

The decisive turning-point was the production of *Die Fledermaus* in 1874, starring Marie Geistinger in the role of Rosalinde. (She had sung the famous *csárdás*, which the disguised Rosalinde sings in Act Two, in a charity concert the preceding October.)[29] *Die Fledermaus* was given forty-nine performances in sixty-five days – a huge success, built not only on its music but also on its subtle blend of light-hearted satire and sentimental escapism. The whole action turns on Orlofsky's *grand souper*, keeping up the old myth of Vienna as a city of self-indulgent good living, an idealized world into which we are transported by the waltz at the opening of Act Two, conjuring up an

Geistinger als
Schöne Helena

Josefine Gallmeyer und Marie Geistinger

Gallmeyer als
Gebildete Köchin

21   Josefine Gallmeyer and Marie Geistinger.

atmosphere of frothy hedonism amid the masks and disguises at Orlofsky's ball. Yet unlike most operettas it was recognizably related to the Vienna of 1874. Indeed it stands out in the history of operetta by its closeness to reality. Many of the social stresses of the time are reflected in it: financial insecurity (Eisenstein is a *Rentier*, one of the speculative capitalists in a city full of *nouveaux riches*, whose fortunes were made in the boom that had ended in the financial collapse of 1873), moral laxity (Falke's tempting of Eisenstein with the ballerinas at Orlofsky's ball), hedonism (the celebration of champagne at the end of Act Two), social deception (the 'Hungarian countess'). Even the *csárdás* in praise of Hungary reflects a nostalgia for lands effectively lost with the creation of the Dual Monarchy in 1867.

Die Fledermaus is not an aggressively critical or polemical work. The depiction of infidelities and deceptions clearly belongs to the traditions of French farce, and the libretto draws on stock devices of international comedy – for example in the parody of legal jargon (Blind's 'Rekurrieren, Appellieren, / Reklamieren, Revidieren...' in Act One). The libretto was indeed based on a French source (a piece by Henri Meilhac and Ludovic Halévy, the librettists of *La Belle Hélène*), and that in turn was based partly on a comedy by the German dramatist Benedix, *Das Gefängnis*, which the Viennese public had been able to see in the Burgtheater since 1851. Yet within the conventions of its genre, *Die Fledermaus* presents hypocrisies and corruption in a recognizable contemporary world, in a blend of farce and reality that has unmistakable links with the satirical tradition in Viennese dialect comedy.

During the first run of *Die Fledermaus*, the company of the Theater an der Wien was enriched by the arrival of Alexander Girardi from the Strampfer-Theater in the Tuchlauben, and he took over the role of Falke in *Die Fledermaus* in September 1874. When Steiner became director the following summer, Girardi, still not twenty-five, was given a new contract securing him a minimum income of 11,200 fl. (already not much short of the 15,000 fl. which Marie Geistinger had been drawing).[30] He would remain in the company for twenty-two years, and figured centrally in a succession of further major operetta hits, starting with Johann Strauss's *Cagliostro in Wien* in February 1875, and continuing through works such as Millöcker's *Der Bettelstudent* (1882), in which Marie Geistinger would return to the theatre as co-star in 1884, Strauss's *Der Zigeunerbaron* (1885), in which he played the booty-laden pig-breeder Zsupán (see plate 22), and Zeller's *Der Vogelhändler* (1891).

22   Alexander Girardi in Johann Strauss, *Der Zigeunerbaron*.

When the Theater an der Wien was bought by Franz Jauner at the end of 1880, it was almost exclusively an operetta theatre. Jauner, one of the most energetic figures in the theatrical life of Vienna in the last two decades of the nineteenth century, had the misfortune to take over the lease of the Ringtheater in October 1881. This was one of a number of new foundations which sprang up from the 1870s onwards, a phenomenon that will be treated mainly in Chapter 6. It was originally named the Komische Oper, in imitation of the Opéra-Comique in Paris, and opened on 17 January 1874 (just under three months before the première of *Die Fledermaus*) with a production of Rossini's *Barber of Seville*. A rather narrow and high building (there were seven tiers of boxes), with a capacity of 1,700, it stood on the new Schottenring, diagonally opposite the Stock Exchange, and was renamed the Ringtheater in 1878. The first new opera production under Jauner's régime was *The Tales of Hoffmann*, which was success-fully launched on 7 December 1881. Just before the second perfor-mance the following day, a fire started in the gas lighting system, and the theatre burnt down – one of the great disasters of theatre history, in which at least 386 people lost their lives. Both Jauner and the mayor of Vienna, Julius von Newald, who had responsibility for safety arrangements, were among those charged with criminal negligence; Newald was cleared of blame in a long court case, but Jauner was one of those found guilty and sentenced to a short term of imprisonment. Though strict new controls on theatre construction were introduced in 1882, theatre superstition was such that *The Tales of Hoffmann* was not performed again in Vienna for nearly twenty years, until Mahler, characteristically scornful of superstition, put it on in the Opera House in 1901. Jauner, moreover, though pardoned by the Emperor, was barred from taking over control of the Theater an der Wien. Though by 1884 he had succeeded in forcing Franz Steiner out of his position as director, he was still refused a licence himself, and he passed the ownership of the theatre, at least nominally, to Alexandrine von Schönerer, who would function as director or co-director for nearly sixteen years (1884–1900).

In 1917 Karl Kraus published in *Die Fackel* a poem, 'Jugend',[31] in which he looks back nostalgically on the theatre of the 1880s as a kind of lost golden age: the Burgtheater of Sonnenthal and Charlotte Wolter, and a series of French operettas, all performed in German versions. Most were by Offenbach, whom Kraus greatly admired. It is possible that in some cases he had productions in the Carltheater in mind: *La Belle Hélène* and *La Grande Duchesse de Gerolstein* were produced there in 1886, and *Barbe-bleue* in 1887, but all these had also been well established in the repertoire of the Theater an der Wien since the 1860s; Andran's *Gilette de Narbonne* was produced solely in the Theater an der Wien (1885); and though both the other operettas alluded to, *La Princesse de Trébizonde* and Lecocq's *La Fille de Madame Angot*, had been produced in the Carltheater in the 1870s, it was in the Theater an der Wien that there were new productions in the 1880s (in 1885 and 1886 respectively). If one recalls that the premières in the 1880s also included *Der Bettelstudent*, *Eine Nacht in Venedig*, *Der Zigeunerbaron*, and a version of *The Mikado* (1888), it is clear how strong the position of the Theater an der Wien was in competition with all the other houses which mounted operetta productions.

The main competition came from the Carltheater, which had a varied programme under a rapidly changing succession of directors. Suppé, who composed music to over two hundred stage works and who had begun his career as *Kapellmeister* in the Theater in der Josefstadt and Pokorny's theatres in the provinces (Baden, Pressburg, Ödenburg), was *Kapellmeister* at the Theater an der Wien for seventeen years, sharing the duties with Lortzing (1846–8) and then with Adolf Müller. Müller continued as musical director in the Theater an der Wien until 1878, but Suppé moved to the Carltheater in 1865, and premières there included *Leichte Kavallerie* (1866), the overture to which is still played quite often, and *Boccaccio* (1879). The Carltheater also beat the Theater an der Wien to staging *La Princesse de Trébizonde* (1873) and *La Fille de Madame Angot* (1874), and operetta was dominant in the programme in the 1870s and again from the 1890s onwards. By the 1880s and 1890s, operetta had developed into theatrical big business, and its triumphal takeover of a succession of Viennese theatres is part of the story to be treated in Chapter 7.

The foundation stone of the new Opera House to be built on the Ringstrasse by van der Nüll and Sicardsburg was laid in 1863; in 1865 part of the Ringstrasse was opened; and in 1869 the new Opera House (*Hofoper*) was inaugurated with a performance of *Don Giovanni*. Two years previously Dingelstedt, the last director of the opera in the Kärntnertortheater, had been passed over for the position of director of the Burgtheater because priority was given to the task he had been set of rescuing the Opera House from 'anarchy'.[32] The huge new neo-Renaissance building was ideally suited to his style. Built on a large site (8,709 m²), it had a capacity of 2,324, which could be increased to 3,100; and it seemed that as in the Carltheater two decades earlier the architects had again overdone the décor at the expense both of the acoustics, which were very different from those in the Kärntnertortheater, and of visibility (from some seats the view was poor). Certainly at first there were exactly the same problems of adjustment as would also arise in the new Burgtheater some twenty years later; the leading conservative music critic of the time, Eduard Hanslick, writing in the *Neue Freie Presse* a month after the opening, noted the loss of 'intimacy' between the performers and the audience: the building was 'a splendid house but an imperfect instrument'.[33] However, the elegance and opulence of the décor, the ornateness of the main staircase and of the auditorium blended with the lavish style of production that Dingelstedt established.

One of the notable opera productions in 1870 was the first Viennese production of *Die Meistersinger* under the conductor Johann Herbeck. Wagner had cultivated his connections with Vienna, and had conducted three midday concerts in the Theater an der Wien as early as December 1862 and January 1863. When Herbeck succeeded Dingelstedt, his works became increasingly prominent in the repertory of the Opera House, albeit in the teeth of opposition from Hanslick. Franz Jauner, who succeeded Herbeck in 1875 after three years as director of the Carltheater (for three years he remained in charge of both houses) visited Wagner in Bayreuth in the summer of 1875, and the ties grew closer. As pan-German nationalism grew in Austria, contemporary reports became increasingly partisan, so that their objective reliability is suspect; it is only fair to remember that Verdi too, at Jauner's invitation, conducted performances of *Aida* in June 1875, and that Jauner also put on a successful production of *Carmen* later that year, less than eight months after its failure in Paris. But certainly he worked particularly hard to ensure Wagner's support. Wagner produced *Tannhäuser* and *Lohengrin* in Vienna; he conducted *Lohengrin* himself in 1876; and he even permitted the performance in 1879, under the baton of Hans Richter, of the first *Ring* cycle to be seen outside Bayreuth.

Jauner's period as director of the Opera House was brought to an end by financial difficulties. What followed under Wilhelm Jahn was an incumbency of record length (1880–97), free of scandals and sustained by Jahn's successful management of the theatre finances. A notable première was that of Massenet's *Werther* in 1892; it was also under Jahn that the first operetta – *Die Fledermaus* – was performed in the Opera House in October 1894, and other new additions to the repertory included Smetana's *The Bartered Bride*. This is an opera which had had its première in Prague in 1866. The first performance in Vienna was given in an open-air theatre in the Prater in 1892; the following year it was to be seen in the Theater an der Wien, and finally in 1896 in the Opera House – almost the whole gamut of theatrical possibilities open in the Vienna of the late nineteenth century.

CHAPTER 6

The late nineteenth century: new foundations

I. THE WIENER STADTTHEATER

By the 1870s the Viennese theatre was in the throes of change, as the city itself was. The demolition of the old walls round the inner city had begun in 1858, and the first section of the new Ringstrasse had been opened in 1865; but construction work continued throughout the 1870s, and some of the big new buildings, including the new Burgtheater, were not completed until even later. When Laube returned to Vienna in late 1870, he found that even after his relatively brief absence he 'hardly recognized' it.[1] Not only was it a permanent building site; its whole social and cultural life was in flux. The population had been about 500,000 in 1860; by 1880 it was nearly half as much again, and over a million including outlying suburbs which were eventually incorporated in the city in 1891. By the end of the century the total was over 1,600,000, and with an industrial area across the Danube, including Floridsdorf, being incorporated in 1904, the 2,000,000 mark was topped by 1910 – a fourfold expansion in just half a century.

Of the old dialect theatres, the Carltheater and Theater an der Wien were by the 1870s targeting a predominantly middle-class audience by concentrating mainly on operetta; the Theater in der Josefstadt remained closer to the old idea of a 'popular' local theatre but was increasingly run-down. (When in the 1890s Schnitzler chose to make Weiring, the father of the heroine of *Liebelei*, a musician in the Theater in der Josefstadt, he did so because it sent a clear social signal: Weiring's professional life is one of disappointment.) When Anzengruber, the one serious dramatist who tried to adapt the tradition of dialect comedy to treat contemporary problems (and who in Berlin would be recognized as an important precursor of naturalism) had his tragedy *Das vierte Gebot* performed in the Josef-

stadt in 1877, it was indicative of the defeat his work had met in the
Theater an der Wien at the hands of operetta over the previous
seven years.

The growing population of the city had significant consequences
for the commercial theatres. The size of the potential public did not
swell as fast as the city did, for much of the expansion was in the
industrial proletariat, who were largely excluded not only by low
wages but also by punishingly long working hours (up to thirteen
hours a day in 1890, with business hours not ending until 9 or even
10 p.m.); nevertheless, demand increased enough to create an
opportunity to construct theatres in different parts of the expanding
city. That audiences still tended to be drawn largely from the
immediate locality of the theatre is indicated by Hüttner's analysis of
the casualties of the 1881 Ringtheater fire, which shows that the
audience was predominantly made up of inhabitants of the First
District (the city centre) and relatively prosperous districts nearby;
and as the occasion was a public holiday, it can be assumed that, as
had long been characteristic of Sunday performances, the audience
had if anything a more popular character than the regular Ringtheater audience.[2] To draw in the public from other districts,
theatres nearer to hand were needed.

At the same time there were also changes in tastes to accommodate, reflecting the influx of newcomers from outlying parts of the
monarchy. Even before the rise of operetta there were signs of a
greater acceptance of international horizons in the kind of entertainment offered in the commercial theatre, specifically what one
journalist, writing in 1855 about the model offered by Paris, called
'the cosmopolitan popular muse'.[3] By the end of the century the
development of a modern city culture would show in the growing
prominence of light boulevard comedies from the German-language
centres: works by Paul Lindau (Berlin), Franz von Schönthan
(Vienna), Otto Ernst (Hamburg), and the like.

The growth of the bourgeoisie also presented an opportunity for
new 'serious' theatres additional to the court theatres. Saphir had
foreseen something of this coming change when he forecast in 1847
that Carl would need to run a broader repertoire, including large-
scale drama, and that the Carltheater was too showy a building to be
a natural home for 'popular' dialect drama alone (see document 9,
pp. 249–50); unease about the unprecedented showiness of the décor

is also reflected in the criticisms voiced by Kaiser and Seyfried (see above, p. 105) to the effect that show had been given precedence over practicality, producing problems of visibility and of acoustics. The priority given to the appearance of the building and the auditorium is clearly indicative of the rising social pretensions of the public Carl had to aim at. Other signs of change in the nature of the potential public include flourishing series of play-texts (Wallishausser's *Wiener Theater-Repertoir*, which lasted into the 1870s, was supplemented in the 1870s and 1880s by another series, L. Rosner's *Neues Wiener Theater*, which itself grew to almost half the size of Wallishausser's original); like the cheap paperbacks of the classics available in Reclam's 'Universal-Bibliothek', which was founded in 1867, these reflected the growth of a middle-brow public, as did the equivalents in London (the series of acting editions published by Lacy and by Dicks) and in Berlin (Eduard Bloch's *Theater-Gartenlaube*). A related phenomenon – again paralleled exactly in Berlin – is the substantial coverage of cultural and theatrical matters in the arts section of new newspapers across the whole political spectrum, including the Liberal *Neue Freie Presse* (founded in 1864), *Neues Wiener Tagblatt* (1867), and *Wiener Allgemeine Zeitung* (1880), the *Deutsche Zeitung* (founded in 1871), originally Liberal but increasingly in the pan-German nationalist camp, the Social Democrat *Arbeiter-Zeitung* (1889), and the *Reichspost* (1894), the main organ of the anti-Semitic Christian Social party. The style of the new theatres built in Vienna in the last three decades of the nineteenth century reflected their pretensions to meet the expectations of the time, what we would now call their marketing strategy: they had imposing exteriors and ornate interiors, with boxes (though in one case, the Deutsches Volkstheater, there were no boxes at the stalls level). The ill-fated Komische Oper (later Ringtheater) on the Schottenring was an example of the pattern; so even was the more popular Fürst-Theater in the Prater, rebuilt as a full-scale theatre in 1873 (see plate 23). The older theatres had to be modernized to conform to the new standards: when Jauner took over the direction of the Carltheater for the second time in 1895, he had the whole interior reconstructed, closing the topmost gallery, lowering the ceiling, and installing electric lighting. By then, however, the Leopoldstadt district was declining in smartness, and the more prosperous public was increasingly drawn to the theatres in and around the Ringstrasse.

23   Fürst-Theater.

The most imposing example of all the new theatres was one in the Seilerstätte, in the heart of the old city, whose ornate exterior combined statuary and columns in true historicist style (see plate 24). The principal moving force behind the foundation of this enterprise was Max Friedländer, the chief editor of the *Neue Freie Presse*, who devised a scheme for raising the necessary capital by advance sales of boxes and stalls as inheritable property (a full box cost 25,000 fl., a seat in the stalls 5,000 fl.) and formed a company of interested supporters, who were won over not least by his success in persuading Laube to accept appointment as the first director. The shortfall in the capital required was made good by a loan; and on this basis the Wiener Stadttheater was completed, designed by the architect Ferdinand Fellner, with a second loan helping to cover the building costs. It was an adventurous experiment, born of the cultural idealism and commercial optimism of the Liberal era: a theatre with a capacity of 1,292, without any standing room, and intended to present an ambitious dramatic programme, which could include works of merit that were judged unsuitable for the court theatre,[4] and so to offer the prosperous middle classes a viable and attractive alternative to the Burgtheater (which until 1888 was still in its old home attached to the imperial palace). The Komische Oper, planning for which began in the summer of 1872, was conceived in very similar terms as a middle-class rival to the Opera House.[5]

The opening production in the Wiener Stadttheater in September 1872, Schiller's fragment *Demetrius*, with Laube's ending, served notice of the theatre's ambitions. Its foundation amounts to the nearest parallel in Viennese theatrical history to Adolph L'Arronge's illustrious Deutsches Theater in Berlin; the only question mark hung over its financial position. According to Laube he was worried about this from the outset but was persuaded by Friedländer's enthusiasm; in the event the interest on the initial loans of just over 400,000 fl., combined with the restriction on box-office takings arising from the advance 'sale' of boxes and stalls, amounted to a crippling handicap. The Stock Exchange crash of 9 May 1873 struck at the very middle and commercial classes the theatre was aiming to cater for, causing an immediate fall-off in attendance, which particularly affected the dearest seats. The history of the Wiener Stadttheater illustrates very clearly the dependence of the commercial theatre on the economic climate: as Rudolf Tyrolt, a leading member of the company, put it in his lively 'chronicle' of the theatre, 'the Wiener Stadttheater was

24 Wiener Stadttheater.

brought into being by the economic boom and received its first mortal blow from the Stock Exchange crash'.[6]

Reviewing the state of affairs after the first full season, Laube assessed the artistic health of the theatre as stronger than the health of the national economy;[7] but in fact not even his energies could compensate for the lack of an established company in which major acting talents could be nurtured in such a way as to provide genuine competition for the Burgtheater, where the company built up by Laube himself was still largely intact. Laube had not departed from his principle that 'speaking is the chief medium of the actor';[8] in his concern about the poor level of speaking on the stage – not just in his new company but in the German theatre altogether[9]– he took the practical step of appointing Alexander Strakosch as instructor in speaking and elocution (*Vortragsmeister*). It was a controversial appointment. That Tyrolt was critical of it is perhaps not surprising, since from Laube's own account of the first two years of the theatre it is clear that he was one of the actors whose diction Laube judged to need coaching; but Speidel also took the view that Laube was over-dependent on Strakosch, and Wilbrandt judged that Strakosch's influence on the actors was too strong, and that his systematic training in diction tended to produce a monotonous effect.[10]

Laube himself, though overworked, devoted himself with all his old intensity to rehearsals, of which there were on average between six and eight for each new production.[11] He had at his disposal individual actors of merit, including Theodor Lobe, who had previously been director of two theatres in Breslau and who played Rudolf II in Laube's production of *Ein Bruderzwist in Habsburg*, and a number of strong comic actors: Franz Tewele would later become director of the Carltheater, and both Rudolf Tyrolt and Katharina Schratt were later members of the Burgtheater. Katharina Schratt, who made her début in March 1873 in Kleist's *Das Käthchen von Heilbronn*, established herself in roles including Katharina (Kate) in *The Taming of the Shrew*, and quickly became the most popular comic actress in the company. But Laube's critics thought the whole notion of rivalry with the Burgtheater, in which he was encouraged by Strakosch, a fundamental tactical error;[12] for the company he commanded could not compete with the Burgtheater in Shakespeare, Schiller, or Lessing. Consequently he was reduced to depending increasingly on contemporary French drama, and was indeed criticized for that from the first.[13]

In sum, the Wiener Stadttheater was equipped neither financially nor in personnel to withstand the prolonged crisis that followed the 1873 crash. Laube himself had recognized that so long as Vienna was prosperous, the Burgtheater alone did not meet the demand for theatre of literary pretensions, but that as soon as the prosperity vanished the demand shrank and was insufficient for one such theatre, let alone two; now he could not but cast envious glances at the subsidies and subscriptions that allowed the Burgtheater, with lower takings, to weather the economic storm.[14] A box-office failure that seemed particularly significant was that of Wilbrandt's tragedy *Giordano Bruno* (2 March 1874): the Viennese, concluded Tyrolt, 'had more than enough sadness in real life by day; what they wanted from the stage, and in particular from the Stadttheater, was cheering entertainment'[15] – precisely the same escapism, that is, as underlay the popularity of operetta in the Theater an der Wien. Crisis meetings before the summer breaks in 1873 and 1874 endorsed further borrowing to see the theatre through, but plunging the enterprise even further into debt was no long-term solution, and the next step, as Laube foresaw in 1873, had to be a change of strategy, constructing a programme of lighter entertainment. Under those circumstances it would not be appropriate for him to stay on as director.[16]

In September 1874, after two years in which over a hundred plays had been staged, he resigned, and the most exciting period in the history of the theatre ended. He was criticized for resigning: the theatre was generally referred to as the 'Laubetheater' and its fate seemed inseparable from him, so that his announcement had an immediate depressing effect on the whole company.[17]

Lobe, who had in effect acted as Laube's deputy, took over the direction, but there was no improvement in the position, and in 1875 Laube, having in the meantime published an account of his first two years in the theatre (*Das Wiener Stadt-Theater*, 1875), took it on again. He introduced cut-price matinées (the first in Vienna), and guest stars included Marie Geistinger, who appeared in unfamiliar guise in February 1876 as a tragic actress in plays by Dumas and in Laube's *Graf Essex* – with mixed critical success, partly because her image was fixed as that of an operetta star. Tours by the company outside Vienna included a successful three-week appearance in Budapest in May and June 1876. (This was the year after the first visit of the Meiningen company to Vienna: the fashion for elaborate staging made it desirable to take entire productions on tour, and the development of railway transport made it possible.) But losses mounted again in the two seasons 1877–8 and 1878–9; the first Viennese production of Ibsen's *Pillars of Society* in February 1878 lasted only for five performances; the theatre was burdened financially by the high salaries it paid to keep its star actors, including Katharina Schratt;[18] and in June 1879 Laube resigned for the second time. For four and a half months a collective of actors, including Lobe and Tyrolt, were in charge; the theatre plunged still further into the red; Laube was then reappointed for a further three years. This time he too lasted only four and a half months, having been reconciled to making economies but having failed to reverse the theatre's financial fortunes and refusing to change the whole character of its repertoire.

The last years of the Wiener Stadttheater were under the direction of Karl von Bukovics, who had been an actor in the company, and who leased it for four years, with his brother-in-law Eduard Theimer as a partner responsible for the financial administration. The company was immediately strengthened by the addition, both as actor and as producer, of Mitterwurzer from the Burgtheater, though his was a restless membership, in that he left first for the Ringtheater (returning after the fire) and then to take over the Carltheater. Important productions included the first Viennese production of another Ibsen play, *A Doll's House*, in September 1881, but the classics had now disappeared from the programme, and the repertory consisted mainly of superficial comedies.

On 16 May 1884, Anzengruber's *Der Meineidbauer* was on the programme. In the late afternoon a fire broke out in the upper reaches of the auditorium; it blazed until 3 a.m., and the whole interior was gutted. A proposal to rebuild the theatre completely on the same site was turned down by the Lower Austrian authorities on the basis of new regulations for theatre buildings introduced after the Ringtheater fire, and in March 1887 the ruin was sold for 350,000 fl. to Anton Ronacher, who had the shell restored and reconstructed, under the supervision of the original architects, as a variety theatre, with tables where the stalls had been, and with well-appointed restaurants and hotel accommodation in the complex. The 'Etablissement Ronacher' was one of a series of variety theatres that sprang up in the last three decades of the century. The Harmonie-Theater in the Wasagasse, renamed the Orpheum, had become one such theatre in the early 1870s under the ownership of Eduard Danzer. The Wiener Colosseum in the ninth district, which opened in 1898, eventually became a cinema, as did the Apollotheater in the sixth district (Gumpendorfer Strasse), another big complex which was opened in 1904 with a hotel as well as a variety theatre. But Ronacher's was the most ambitious enterprise of all of these. The reconstruction cost 2,000,000 fl., an enormous investment in modern comfort. It was the first Viennese theatre with electric lighting, and although that broke down at the opening in April 1888 and Ronacher would never recoup his investment and indeed withdrew as director in January 1890, the 'Etablissement Ronacher' was by then well established and became notorious for the frivolous triviality of its programme. It survived as a variety theatre for some sixty years, and still stands, having recently been renovated (1993).

2. NATIONALIST SENTIMENT: THE DEUTSCHES VOLKSTHEATER AND THE RAIMUNDTHEATER

The loss of the Wiener Stadttheater left a gap. The idea of creating a serious theatre, free from court influence and aimed at a middle-class audience, had taken root. But by 1886–7, when it was clear that it was not going to reopen, the political climate had changed; in particular pan-German nationalism (anti-Slav and anti-Semitic) had been fanned by a series of events: the loss of the Six Weeks War in 1866, the creation of the Dual Monarchy in 1867 and of the united German Empire in 1871, the Stock Exchange crash in 1873. The growth of this nationalism was now such that it coloured future planning in the theatre.

In 1885 Adam Müller-Guttenbrunn, a critic of pan-German persuasion who had been born in Guttenbrunn (in what was then Hungary and is now in Romania) and who had come to Vienna in 1880, published a polemical booklet – hardly more than a pamphlet, only 34 pages of text – entitled *Wien war eine Theaterstadt*. (The stress falls on the verb in the past tense: 'Vienna used to be a city of theatre.') The argument advanced, that the Viennese theatre had declined into a state of 'intellectual bankruptcy' which betrayed the ethical and didactic purpose of the theatre as an institution,[19] was coloured by Müller-Guttenbrunn's ideological position, which combined xenophobic nationalism with scurrilous anti-Semitism. He presented the taste of the 1880s as being corrupted by imported

French farces and operettas, which dominated the repertory. 1885 was the year of Johann Strauss's *Der Zigeunerbaron*, but Müller-Guttenbrunn's attack is also directed at Jauner's direction of the Carltheater and of the Ringtheater. Operetta was an 'artistic bastard, which might have been conceived by a stock exchange jobber and a Parisian *cocotte*'.[20] Even in the Burgtheater, Dingelstedt was putting on material that ought to have been limited to the commercial theatres; and the Burgtheater was in any case so expensive as to be out of reach of most people's pockets.[21] In the commercial theatres too the prices were so high – partly because the actors were grossly overpaid – that even the educated middle classes, let alone the poorer classes, were effectively excluded; hence the small number of theatres by comparison with Berlin.[22] The argument leads to three main conclusions. The theatres should be reorganized to develop specialities, with the Carltheater playing comedies and the Theater an der Wien cultivating the operetta repertoire; any attempt to compete with the Burgtheater should be avoided; and a new genuinely popular theatre, with cheap entry prices and no showy boxes, should be created in an outlying district so far lacking a theatre.[23]

In 1886 Müller-Guttenbrunn became the editor of the cultural section (*Feuilletonredakteur*) of the *Deutsche Zeitung*, and was able to develop his position. One of his complaints in *Wien war eine Theaterstadt* is that Vienna lacked a genuinely independent press (he is particularly critical of the inconsistencies he detects in Speidel);[24] now he had a outlet in which he could give a nationalist slant to the Liberal principles of popular education and argue for the creation of a new 'popular theatre' as part of his ideological programme, so that the idea of the 'Volk' in the term *Volkstheater* now carried German nationalist overtones.

These ideas came together with an older scheme which had been mooted in November 1884 by a group including Ludwig Anzengruber (in Müller-Guttenbrunn's 1885 pamphlet the one redeeming figure connected with the Theater an der Wien),[25] Vincenz Chiavacci, Anton Bettelheim, and the composer Karl Zeller. Their project had been to found a new popular theatre, which they planned to call the 'Raimundtheater', on the Franz-Josefs-Kai, near where Treumann's theatre had burned down in 1863. In June 1886, after various discussions, a group of writers and other interested parties, including Anzengruber and the architect Fellner, resolved

to found a 'popular' theatre for a middle-class public. In the
Deutsche Zeitung Anton Bettelheim demanded that it be explicitly a
'*German* theatre with a German tradition'.[26] Müller-Guttenbrunn
would later complain that despite the name the 'popular' elements
had taken a secondary place in the planning of the repertory, and
also that the emphasis on 'German' had been watered down;[27] but
his was an extremist view. In practice, what emerged as the main
aim was to give priority to local drama, not just continuing the
tradition of dialect comedy but also providing a base for Anzengruber himself (and so for realism, which had been driven from the
theatres since the 1873 crash). Several of Anzengruber's plays had
been performed in the Wiener Stadttheater, and he had hoped
there might be an 'Anzengruber cycle' there, presumably on the
lines of the successful Nestroy cycle in the Carltheater in 1881; but
the fire had dashed that hope.[28] While the building of the new
theatre was in progress, Speidel underlined both the point that
there was now 'no stage for Anzengruber' in Vienna and also the
hope that the Deutsches Volkstheater, as it was to be called, would
fill the gap.[29]

   To fund the building the sum of 530,000 fl. had been raised; a site
had been approved and purchased very cheaply in the Weghuber-
Park, on the edge of what had been part of the open ground between
the walls and the old *Vorstädte*, at the eastern end of the Neustift-
gasse;[30] and by September 1889 the new theatre was complete. The
strict building regulations introduced in reaction to the various
theatre fires now required theatres to be free-standing, as opposed to
the multi-purpose buildings exemplified by the Kai-Theater; this
meant that actual building space was reduced, and the site for the
Deutsches Volkstheater was in any case relatively small (2,472 m²),[31]
less than a third of the size of the site the Opera House had been
built on. But the auditorium (606 m²) was larger than that in the
Wiener Stadttheater, with a capacity of 1,900, and though the décor
was heavily ornate in a pseudo-Baroque style, there were no boxes at
the stalls level and only two tiers above the stalls, and the acoustics
were good.[32] There were no free seats for investors[33] (at least one
lesson had been learned from the difficulties of the Wiener Stadttheater); and though the choice of the first director was fought out
publicly and the initial favourite, Schönthan, eventually withdrew,
and though Anzengruber was worried during the planning lest
commercial interests get the upper hand,[34] in fact once Emerich von

Bukovics was appointed, the programme he organized remained true to the original intentions.

The first production (preceded at the opening on 14 September 1889, in traditionalist spirit, by Beethoven's overture 'The Consecration of the House') was Anzengruber's latest play, *Der Fleck auf der Ehr'* – the last première of his career, as he died three months later, on 12 December. Bukovics continued to put on both dialect plays (Raimund and Nestroy as well as Anzengruber) and also realist drama, including both Ibsen (who attended the Austrian première of *The Wild Duck* in the Deutsches Volkstheater in 1891, seeing Mitterwurzer in one of his most celebrated roles) and Schnitzler (*Das Märchen, Freiwild*). The theatre continued to play an important part in the presentation of modern drama over the next thirty years or so – a story that will be taken up again in Chapters 7 and 8.

Müller-Guttenbrunn, who was an ambitious man, may have been disappointed not to be appointed director of the Deutsches Volkstheater; it is difficult not to suspect sour grapes behind the attack he launched in 1890 in a polemical survey entitled *Das Wiener Theaterleben*, in which he described the Deutsches Volkstheater as having become a mere 'business without artistic principles' and presented the whole theatrical scene as a betrayal of tradition.[35] Both the next major theatres founded in Vienna were associated with him. Both were sited outside the wealthy centre of the city, further from the Ringstrasse than the Deutsches Volkstheater. All three theatres are still standing, though only the Deutsches Volkstheater has continued to be devoted to spoken drama.

By 1893, Müller-Guttenbrunn was director designate of the Raimundtheater, which opened on 28 November of that year in the Wallgasse, just off the outer ring-road (the *Gürtel*). He had got the position despite his lack of practical experience in the theatre, mainly because of the prominence he had attained, through *Wien war eine Theaterstadt*, as a slogan-making opponent of trivial commercialism in the theatre, in particular in the form of operetta and variety. The name chosen for the new theatre was programmatic: it was conceived as a base for dialect drama and local comedy, and it opened with a performance of Raimund's *Die gefesselte Phantasie*, preceded by the obligatory overture 'The Consecration of the House' and in this case a prologue by Berger. As Müller-Guttenbrunn later saw the situation, the idea that had originally inspired the foundation of the Deutsches Volkstheater, 'the thought that we should maintain a healthy modern theatre with popular plays and *popular prices*, informed by the spirit of German writing and acting – this thought was not to be banished'.[36] The siting was intended to catch the kind of audience who felt excluded from the theatres in the centre, and its prices were low, with seats ranging from 2 fl. down to 30 Kreuzer. The Deutsches Volkstheater also had a top price of 2 fl. (that the prices should be low had indeed been one of the conditions of the Emperor's approval in July 1887 of the plan to build it),[37] but in the Carltheater and the Theater an der Wien prices went up to 15 fl., in the Theater in der Josefstadt up to 10 fl., even in the Fürst-Theater in the Prater up to 8 fl. A theatre-bill in the Raimundtheater (just a single sheet with the cast-list: this was still before the days of bulky illustrated programmes) cost 5 kr., half the price charged in other theatres.[38] Nevertheless its position in the farthest south-western corner of the Mariahilf district – not far from one of the main railway stations, the Westbahnhof – made it rather untempting to people living in other districts, and there were bits of ill-luck in the first season which got it off to a bad start: on one evening the safety curtain jammed, on another seats in the stalls collapsed.[39] Furthermore, while Müller-Guttenbrunn had assembled a strong company, with one important new face in Hansi Niese, a young comic actress who enjoyed her first notable success in a production of Anzengruber's *Der Pfarrer von Kirchfeld* in January 1894, there were always tensions between the director and his backers and advisers. Müller-Guttenbrunn was ideologically rigid; at one meeting in 1895 Hermann Bahr, in his capacity of literary adviser, accused him openly of 'anti-Semitic excesses';[40] and the crisis came to a head in February 1896, at an extraordinary general meeting of the theatre organization which ended with a vote, carried by a narrow majority, for Müller-Guttenbrunn's suspension. The charges brought against him were of incompetency and various improprieties; he defended himself in a long oration which dealt mainly with the financial history of the theatre and which he subsequently published as a separate booklet under the title *Der suspendierte Theaterdirektor*. A court later declared the extraordinary general meeting invalid, its decisions null and void;[41] but Müller-Guttenbrunn declined reinstatement and reached a settlement in respect of the unexpired part of his contract, which had originally been for ten years.[42] His successor was Ernst Gettke, a Berliner, who began the new season on 1 September 1896 with a production of *Der Alpenkönig und der Menschenfeind* and remained in charge for eleven years, running an orthodox dramatic repertoire, including dialect comedy: Willy Thaller, for example, who in his twenties had been an acclaimed Schnoferl in the 1881 Carltheater production of *Das Mädl aus der Vorstadt*, appeared as Lips in *Der Zerrissene* in 1898 and as Nebel in *Liebesgeschichten und Heiratssachen* in 1899. From 1908 onwards, however, the Raimundtheater became an operetta theatre, a role from which it was only temporarily rescued between the wars, when it was directed by Rudolf Beer.

In 1897 Müller-Guttenbrunn published a detailed account of the foundation of the Raimundtheater and the course of his own direction, concentrating mainly on his development of the repertory. The book starts off with a repetition of the argument that by the middle of the 1880s theatrical life had descended to the very nadir of intellectual vacuity, and ends with an optimistic assessment of its achievement and potential: when he left the Raimundtheater for the last time on 16 January 1896, it had achieved 'artistic standing and was free of material worries', and he still believed optimistically that 'a good, a noble German popular stage in Vienna' was possible.[43]

3. THE KAISERJUBILÄUMS-STADTTHEATER

Much of the vocabulary of Müller-Guttenbrunn's tracts, the talk of 'healthy' or 'noble' theatre informed by the 'spirit of German writing and acting', is unmistakably in the idiom of the anti-Semitic politics and journalism of the time. In 1898 he had an opportunity to appear openly in his true colours when he was appointed director of a second new foundation on the outer ring-road, the Kaiserjubiläums-Stadttheater on the Währinger Strasse, north-west of the centre. The name commemorated the golden jubilee of the accession of Franz Joseph, and with seating for 1,855 it was one of the largest commercial theatres in Vienna. (The *Neuer Theater-Almanach* for 1900 gives the capacity of the Theater an der Wien at this point as 1,859 and that of the Deutsches Volkstheater as 1,900, by comparison with 1,600 for the Raimundtheater and 1,400 for the Carltheater.)

In the previous year Müller-Guttenbrunn had been approached about a proposal to found a theatre in the third district (Landstrasse); he had dismissed the district as 'dead' and insisted that the only current project to be taken seriously was the 'jubilee theatre'.[44] The appeal lay not just in the location but in the ideology behind the project. The Kaiserjubiläums-Stadttheater was founded explicitly as an 'Aryan' theatre – 'a creation', as Müller-Guttenbrunn summed it up later, 'of the united anti-Semitic and national German parties'.[45] The story of this house is one of the most extraordinary – and most shameful – chapters in Austrian theatre history. Müller-Gutten-brunn's memoirs, which are largely devoted to it, recount how he was approached in April 1896, after he had completed his severance from the Raimundtheater, about the idea of a new anti-'Liberal' theatre in the Währing district, and how he found himself confronted with a 'circle of men who were all full of enthusiasm for the project but had not the least idea of how to set about founding a theatre and were certain of only one thing: that they did not wish to see a Jew on the planning committee, or among the founders, or even, so far as possible, among the audience of the future theatre in Währing'.[46] According to Müller-Guttenbrunn's account of his response, his advice was that it would be possible to ensure a majority of 'Christian' (that is, in the idiom of the time, anti-Semitic) members in the theatre organization and so to ensure that there would be no direct Jewish influence on the theatre, but that it should not be declared 'anti-Semitic', in order not to alienate Jewish influence in artistic and financial circles and in the press[47] – a pragmatic caveat that was rejected. Müller-Guttenbrunn would continue to indulge in transparent sophistry. He published an article in the right-wing *Reichswehr* on 1 November 1896, supporting the idea of an 'anti-Liberal' theatre but insisting that art was not a matter of politics, and feigned surprise that from then on he was regarded by Jewish politicians as anti-Semitic.[48] In March 1903, towards the end of his period in charge of the theatre, he published in the *Österreichische Volks-Presse*, a virulently anti-Semitic newspaper, a declaration re-peating the claim that although the Kaiserjubiläums-Stadttheater had been 'built as a creation of the united anti-Semitic and national German parties', nevertheless the repertory demonstrated that it was an artistic institution to which 'all politics' were alien.[49]

In fact it was closely associated from the first with active members of the Christian Social party, the anti-Semitic party led by the mayor of Vienna, Karl Lueger; furthermore a programme of cultural politics was built into its very statutes. Its statutes laid down that its repertory was to be based on the German *Volksstück*, and on German drama in all its forms (see document 14, p. 257). Works by non-German writers were to be performed only exceptionally; and all works that might in any way endanger patriotic feeling, love of the

German race, or the moral and ethical feeling of the Christian population must, as a matter of principle, always be barred from performance in the theatre. The systematic attempt to construct a 'pro-German' nationalist repertory was underpinned by the institution of performances at reduced prices for the poorer classes ('Volksvorstellungen') and performances of the classics for schoolchildren, in keeping with the educative purpose Müller-Guttenbrunn had formulated in the 1880s. He was able to count on the support of the right-wing press, and his memoirs list the journals that backed him, including the *Deutsche Zeitung*, the *Reichswehr*, the *Deutsches Volksblatt*, the *Reichspost*, *Vaterland*, and the long-running satirical journals *Figaro* and *Kikeriki*, the latter a poisonous vehicle of vulgar anti-Semitism, which Juliette Adam identified all too accurately as 'the most widely read and ... most popular journal in Austria-Hungary'.[50] That the venture attracted the hostility of the Liberal press from the outset goes without saying; more remarkably, by the second season it was also attacked from the Right, including notably in *Kikeriki*, for having a programme that was insufficiently anti-Semitic.[51]

Müller-Guttenbrunn remained in charge of the Kaiserjubiläums-Stadttheater, struggling with a budget in constant deficit, for five years. At the end of December 1902, with insolvency approaching, he wrote a defensive memorandum to Lueger, which he later leaked to Karl Kraus, who printed it in *Die Fackel*. It sets out his grievances about the handicaps under which he had had to operate: 'no Christian financiers' had invested in the theatre, and Christian actors had been scared off by fear of the 'Jewish press' ('aus Furcht vor der Judenpresse'). It puts the blame for the financial crisis that had overtaken the 'liberating reforms' of the enterprise partly on the opposition of the Jewish Liberal press, and partly on the lack of support that had been forthcoming for the ideological function of what he still defined as 'a Christian, an Aryan theatre' ('ein christliches, ein arisches Theater'), which – in contrast to his disclaimers of 'political' motivation in other contexts – would in future be 'celebrated' as one of the most significant achievements of the Christian Social party.[52] It also includes a section (see document 15, pp. 257–8) summing up his pride in the theatre's record as supporting 'Aryan talents' by a programme that was free of immoral material translated ('mostly by Jewish translators') from French, which for thirty years had been 'poisoning' 'healthy' indigenous work.

The claim that the theatre had nurtured indigenous talent that was otherwise being stifled is not supported by the evidence of the repertory, in which such new plays as were produced were all by minor playwrights. After Müller-Guttenbrunn's eventual resignation in summer 1903, Karl Kraus spelled out the self-evident truth that institutions born in a party-political spirit were incapable of survival and that the whole idea of an 'anti-Semitic' theatre was an artistic nonsense, bound to fail.[53] When Rainer Simons, previously director (*Intendant*) of the Stadttheater in Mainz, was nominated as Müller-Guttenbrunn's successor, a heated debate took place at a general meeting of the theatre association (*Generalversammlung des Jubiläums-Stadttheatervereines*), held at the Rathaus on 30 October 1903. Simons's appointment was opposed by the extreme anti-Semites in the Christian Social party; the honorary secretary of the association gave an assurance that Simons had promised to remain true to the 'tradition of the Christian theatre' and not to employ any Jews.[54] What swayed the meeting was a speech by Robert Pattai, a lawyer, originally from Graz, who had been prominent in anti-Semitic politics since the early 1880s and had been a strong supporter of Lueger in the long-drawn-out issue of Lueger's election and appointment as mayor. Pattai, the sole member of the national parliament to take part in the meeting, argued in favour of supporting the theatre under its new director, outflanking the extremists by arguing pragmatically. It was important that anti-Semites should be effectively involved in the cultural sphere in order to counteract the decadence of the theatre, which was corrupted by the 'extraordinary power of the Jewish press'; Simons had committed himself to the anti-Semitic programme; if he achieved a removal of the boycott of the theatre by the Jewish press, so much the better; and failure to agree on his appointment would be playing into the hands of the Jews (see document 16, pp. 258–9). When one questioner (a priest) challenged Simons to commit himself to continuing the theatre as a 'German, Christian, Aryan stage for German artists and German writers', Simons reminded the meeting that the very terms of his contract bound him to upholding the 'Christian' traditions of the theatre.

Though his appointment was ratified, the anti-Semitic forces were not persuaded; when reporting the confirmation of the appointment, the *Deutsches Volksblatt* added a comment to the effect that it was an outcome with which he and his 'Jewish protectors' could be well satisfied. And indeed the days of the 'Aryan theatre' were at an end. Under Simons's direction the financial losses incurred by Müller-Guttenbrunn were reversed, but the price was the gradual conversion of the theatre to one specializing in light opera.

The foundation of the Kaiserjubiläums-Stadttheater in Währing on the basis of a racist ideology is a striking example of how the response of the theatre to political developments in Vienna differed from that in the other big centres. In 1887 André Antoine launched the Théâtre Libre in Paris; in 1890 the Freie Volksbühne was founded in Berlin. Just as there was no Viennese among the leading naturalist dramatists, so there was no Viennese institution born of the *Volksbühne* movement until 1906. With the collapse of Liberalism, the political initiative passed into the hands of the nationalists and anti-Semites, and however briefly Müller-Guttenbrunn's régime lasted, it exemplifies the sinister political energies building up at the turn of the century. In the arguments surrounding his managership, lines of battle were drawn that would re-emerge repeatedly in controversies to come; the menace of anti-Semitism would continue to darken the cultural climate during the period of modernist experiment.

CHAPTER 7

Modernism at the end of the monarchy

I. MODERN DRAMA

The flowering of modernism in turn-of-the-century Vienna is most generally associated with poets and men of letters gathering in coffee-houses, with the artists and architects of the Secession and the Wiener Werkstätte, and with the musicians of the Second Viennese School; but there were also a series of significant events in the theatre which contributed to the new impetus. The importance that was accorded to the theatre is reflected in Stefan Zweig's account of how the middle-class Viennese of the period scanned their newspapers not for political news but for articles about the theatre[1] – a classic illustration of the divorce between intellectual and artistic life and political developments.

One of the catalysts of the modernist movement in Vienna was an 'Ibsen week' in April 1891, when the Norwegian dramatist attended the first night of the Burgtheater production of *The Pretenders* and of the first Austrian performance of *The Wild Duck* in the Deutsches Volkstheater, and there were performances of four plays in all in the Burgtheater and the Deutsches Volkstheater. Just under a year later, the appearance of Eleonora Duse in the Carltheater provided the young Hofmannsthal with 'the most powerful theatrical impression' he had received up to then.[2] One of the roles she played on that first visit was Ibsen's Nora. The Theater an der Wien was the site of a series of important performances by touring celebrities: Sarah Bernhardt appeared there in 1882, 1887, and 1908; Eleonora Duse in 1895, 1900 (she also played in the Burgtheater that year), 1906, and 1907; the Berlin companies of Otto Brahm in 1906 and 1907 and of Max Reinhardt in 1905, 1907, and 1910. As never before, the theatrical life of Vienna was becoming cosmopolitan – flung open not just to popular fashions from Paris, but to the influence of serious modern theatrical experiment. This openness to modern styles was reflected in the reviews and journalistic essays that Zweig and his generation devoured – the work of influential critics across the full political spectrum of the press: Ludwig Speidel in the *Neue Freie Presse* until his death in 1906, later Raoul Auernheimer; Ludwig Hevesi in the *Fremden-Blatt*, another Liberal paper; Julius Bauer in the *Extrablatt*; Jakob Julius David in the *Neues Wiener Journal*; Hermann Bahr in *Die Zeit*; Max Kalbeck and Ludwig Held in the *Neues Wiener Tagblatt*; Alexander von Weilen in the *Montags-Revue*; Albert Leitich in the *Deutsche Zeitung*; Edmund Wengraf in the *Arbeiter-Zeitung*. There was also good specialist coverage in new literary and artistic journals, such as the weekly *Die Wage*, which was founded in 1898, and (from 1902 to 1922) *Der Merker*, of which Hevesi was co-editor. The new internationalism was reflected in the syndication of reviews, a phenomenon that became widespread from about mid-way through the First World War: the reviews written by Felix Salten for the *Fremden-Blatt* appeared also in the *Berliner Tageblatt*; those written by Alfred Polgar for the *Wiener Allgemeine Zeitung* appeared also in the *Vossische Zeitung* and the *Prager Tagblatt*.

After Sonnenthal's interregnum as 'provisional director' of the Burgtheater, a disciple of Laube, August Förster, who had been co-founder of the Deutsches Theater in Berlin, was appointed director in November 1888, but he died suddenly after holding the post for just over a year. For just under five months Sonnenthal had to hold the fort again. The obvious heir apparent was Alfred von Berger, who was close to the pan-German nationalist camp (Müller-Guttenbrunn was sympathetic to his candidature)[3] and who had been 'artistic secretary' under Förster; but he was ruled out because of his marriage to a member of the company, Stella Hohenfels. Instead a surprise appointment was made: on 12 May 1890 a lawyer turned civil servant, Max Burckhard, became director. He held the post for nearly eight years. Though young and inexperienced in the theatre, he was skilful in dealing with Austrian officialdom and bureaucracy, and he also brought a fresh eye to the company (which needed to be rejuvenated), to the repertory, and to the workings and ethos of the theatre. Burckhard introduced Sunday matinées at reduced prices in an attempt to widen the theatre's appeal, and would indeed write later that the less wealthy public attracted in this way was the best and most critically acute he had known.[4] He also had the auditorium remodelled in the spring and summer of 1897. The Opera House was used as an interim theatre; but closing the Burgtheater in mid-season was criticized as an expensive failure – it was this indeed that led to his dismissal on 20 January 1898[5] – and the reconstruction was only partially successful: as late as 1920, writing in the *Neues Wiener Journal*, Friedell was still pouring scorn on the lack of intimate contact between the actors and the audience.[6]

Burckhard added to the company some of the leading actors associated with contemporary drama, notably Mitterwurzer (a past member who rejoined in 1894 after a series of other engagements, including a year as artistic director of the Carltheater in 1884–5) and Adele Sandrock, who in the Deutsches Volkstheater had achieved an outstanding success in the first Viennese production of Ibsen's *Rosmersholm* in 1893 – according to Bahr an even greater success than Eleonora Duse's Nora, 'one of those few truly great pieces of modern acting which remain unfading in the memory'.[7] She joined the Burgtheater in 1895, and played a leading part in the production that signalled the breakthrough of indigenous modern drama, the première of Schnitzler's *Liebelei* on 9 October 1895. Sonnenthal played the part of Weiring, Adele Sandrock that of his daughter, the tragically forsaken Christine, and Mitterwurzer the small but sinister role of the wronged husband whose duel with her lover ends Christine's illusions of happiness.

Liebelei was the first play in Viennese dialect to be performed in the Burgtheater. Bahr wondered whether it did not rather belong in the Raimundtheater (at that time under Müller-Guttenbrunn),[8] and its daring modernity met with a predictably mixed reception. In a review that appeared in the left-wing *Arbeiter-Zeitung* on 11 October 1895, Wengraf questioned the authenticity both of the characterization and of the language, arguing that the play was insufficiently realistic and that the action centred too much on the leisured classes to achieve the accurate fidelity to everyday experience that might be looked for in full-blooded realism. In the right-wing press, on the other hand, it was seen as a daringly realistic, even 'naturalist' work: this was the view taken by Albert Leitich in a review that appeared the same day in the *Deutsche Zeitung*, describing the play as shockingly modern in its closeness to the everyday life of Vienna. The conservatism of this kind of reaction is reflected in an experience recalled years later by Schnitzler's wife: as a young woman she was forbidden to go to a subsequent Schnitzler production, her mother warning her that if a girl was seen at a Schnitzler play, she would get a bad name and would never get a husband.[9]

Burckhard's championing of modern and particularly realist drama – Ibsen, Anzengruber, Schnitzler, staged with star-studded casts – was incongruously out of keeping with the architectural style of the theatre interior, and met with considerable opposition, not least from conservative members of the company who were opposed to the systematic modernizing of the repertory. He was subjected to criticism on almost every front: the introduction of matinées, it was argued, undermined the character of the Burgtheater, which was not meant to have a popularizing function; the unity of the company's style had been lost (this was connected in particular with the dominating influence exercised by Mitterwurzer); the extension of the repertory in keeping with contemporary literary trends had been achieved at the expense of acting standards; and the modern dramas added to the programme (Ibsen, Hauptmann, Sudermann, Schnitzler) had not even all been well produced.[10]

The tension between innovation and conservatism that marks Burckhard's tenure is characteristic of the artistic ambience of Vienna at the time; in hindsight it is clear that in the promotion of modern drama (to some extent in competition with the Deutsches Volkstheater under the direction of Emerich von Bukovics) this was one of the periods of most distinctive achievement in the history of the Burgtheater.

When Paul Schlenther was appointed as Burckhard's successor, it looked as though the Burgtheater were certain to become a major centre of modern drama and modern acting styles. With Brahm and others he had been one of the founders of the *Freie Bühne* in Berlin, and he had promoted the works both of Ibsen and of Hauptmann. When Josef Kainz (who had made guest appearances in 1897) became a permanent member of the company in 1899, this was widely perceived as signalling Schlenther's determination to complete a process of reform that had begun some five years earlier, centring on the acting of Mitterwurzer. Mitterwurzer had died while Burckhard was still director, in 1897; Kainz's engagement had been agreed soon after that – perhaps Burckhard's most important legacy to the company – and he was generally perceived as being intended to take over Mitterwurzer's mantle.[11] Mitterwurzer had had an exceptionally catholic repertoire, but had been celebrated above all as an Ibsen actor; though Kainz had worked both in Meiningen and with Brahm in Berlin, he spoke to a later generation: with his burning eyes, expressive gestures, and musical delivery, he radiated an inward emotional intensity and was the great Tasso of his age (see plate 25). (He would star in a new production in 1906.) Kraus, a romantic conservative in this respect, would compare Kainz's acting unfavourably with the quality of speaking he remembered in the smaller Burgtheater of the 1880s; but his Romeo was another of Bahr's unfadingly 'great pieces of modern acting', and for Hofmannsthal he had long been the actor who most spoke to the neo-Romantics among the 'moderns'.[12]

The promise that Schlenther's appointment as director seemed to hold can be glimpsed in the programme of March 1899, when he had held the post for just over a year. In the first twenty-four days of the month, no fewer than twelve evenings were devoted to plays by the two leading dramatists associated with 'Young Vienna': seven to a programme of one-act plays by Schnitzler, *Paracelsus*, *Die Gefährtin*, and *Der grüne Kakadu* (it is this programme that the young Olga Gussmann was forbidden to attend), one to Schnitzler's *Das Vermächtnis*, and four to Hofmannsthal's *Der Abenteurer und die Sängerin* and *Die Hochzeit der Sobeide*. But this glimpse of classic status in the national theatre was to turn out to be a mirage. Schlenther had twelve years in charge of the Burgtheater, but he was hampered both by the cumbersome censorship arrangements and by the expensiveness which the kind of detail required by naturalist production entailed on the large stage of the new Burgtheater.[13] In the face of these problems he proved cautious and indecisive,[14] and while he kept up Hauptmann performances, he failed to promote the Austrian moderns, with the one exception of Karl Schönherr. He was also rather remote from the actors, and did not maintain the kind of improvement to the company that Burckhard had planned: he dismissed Adele Sandrock, and failed to promote and retain Alexander Moissi, who worked with the company as an extra in the years 1898–1901 and went on to become a central figure in Reinhardt's company in Berlin and Salzburg. Albert Heine, later an outstanding producer and indeed a future director of the theatre, left the company after publicly criticizing Schlenther about the declining quality of the repertory.[15] And as deficits grew, court demands for financial economies led not only to higher prices for premières and guest appearances but also to the stopping of regular Sunday performances at reduced prices.

25 Josef Kainz in costume as Tasso, on the grand staircase of the Burgtheater.

The programme of the Deutsches Volkstheater under Bukovics, who was the director for the first sixteen years of the theatre's existence (1889–1905), centred on the cultivation of Anzengruber, fifteen plays being performed in the first ten years. Tyrolt achieved considerable acclaim in a number of central roles, including Andrä Moser in the première of *Der Fleck auf der Ehr'* in 1889, Steinklopfer-hanns in a revival of *Die Kreuzelschreiber* in 1890, and in the same year the dissolute elder Schalanter in *Das vierte Gebot* (see plate 26), performed for the first time under its original title; and in November 1892 the première took place of the posthumous *Brave Leut' vom Grund*. Otherwise the programme was in many ways conservative, featuring regular productions of the classics (especially Shakespeare and Grillparzer) and also commercially reliable light comedies such as *Im Weißen Rössel* by Oskar Blumenthal and Gustav Kadelburg (1898). But Bukovics was also active in presenting Ibsen, Mitterwurzer's Hjalmar Ekdal in *The Wild Duck* (1891) and Adele Sandrock's Rebecca in *Rosmersholm* (1893) counting among the most influential early performances of Ibsen in Vienna; he also staged plays by Schnitzler and Hauptmann, including *Der Biberpelz*, which had been deemed unsuitable for the Burgtheater, in 1897.

Bukovics's successor, Alfred Weisse, had been a member of the company since 1889, playing leading classical roles (Rudolf II, Shylock, Mephistopheles). He remained in charge until 1916, so providing the Deutsches Volkstheater with an enviable continuity. If anything the programme under Weisse tended to become less adventurous, but it did still include a series of important productions of modern drama. Wedekind's *Frühlings Erwachen* (which had been seen in the Theater an der Wien in 1907, performed by Reinhardt's company from the Deutsches Theater) was produced in May 1908, with Wedekind himself in the cast. In 1909 there was a 'Schnitzler year', which included the première of the one-act satirical comedy *Komtesse Mizzi*. Other premières included the successful one of Schönherr's *Glaube und Heimat* in 1910 and Wildgans's *Armut* in 1915. Weisse's successor, Karl Wallner, was director for only two years, but the programme included the premières of Wildgans's *Liebe* in 1916 and Schnitzler's satirical comedy about journalists, *Fink und Fliederbusch*, in 1917. By this time Schnitzler was aware that the Deutsches Volkstheater had become more important to him than the Burgtheater.[16]

Stability was also a feature of the Theater in der Josefstadt once

26 Rudolf
Tyrolt as the
elder Schalanter
in Ludwig
Anzengruber,
Das vierte Gebot.

Josef Jarno, one of the most energetic figures in the commercial theatre in the early twentieth century, took it over in 1899. He had spent the previous ten years acting in Berlin, including three at the Deutsches Theater; he would remain at the helm in the Josefstadt for no fewer than twenty-four seasons, for part of the time running not only that theatre but also one or both of two others – a management pattern that was to become a major feature of the commercial theatre in the 1920s. One of Jarno's houses was Fürst's old theatre in the Prater, which had lost popularity after Fürst's death in 1882 and had been run for six years in the 1890s (1892–8) by Hermann Jantsch as a summer theatre, eventually under the name Jantschtheater (from 1896), and which Jarno took over in 1905, renaming it the Lustspieltheater. The other was a new theatre in the eighth district, the Neues Wiener Stadttheater, which opened in the Daungasse (between the Skodagasse and the Laudongasse) in 1914 – the last new foundation in Vienna before the outbreak of war. Jarno ran it for four years, and then again after the war in tandem with Wilhelm Karczag, who bought it in 1917. Jarno's plans for the Neues Wiener Stadttheater were influenced by his enthusiastic support of the idea of a *Volksbühne* in Vienna (see below, p. 192): he envisaged it as a family theatre in which serious and even experimental theatre could be played, and he ran it mainly as a separate enterprise. In the Theater in der Josefstadt and the Lustspieltheater (which was only slightly smaller, having a capacity of 785 as against 798 in the Josefstadt at this point, and which he kept open throughout the year) he offered an overlapping programme, employing the one company – an expertly assembled one that included Hansi Niese (Jarno's wife since 1899) – in both houses, with a deputy in charge of day-to-day running of the Lustspieltheater. (From 1912 onwards this deputy was Rudolf Beer, who would become one of the leading figures in the Viennese theatre between the wars.) Jarno's strategy was to make money with light comedies, which allowed him also to put on an adventurous programme of 'literary evenings', featuring dramatists such as Strindberg, Wedekind, Shaw, and Maeterlinck: here, far more than in the Burgtheater or the Deutsches Volkstheater, the theatre-going public of Vienna were brought into touch with the leading trends in contemporary international drama. Productions in the Lustspieltheater that also reflected Jarno's spirit of adventure included the première of Schnitzler's *Zum großen Wurstel* in 1906. One of the biggest successes he mounted in the Josefstadt was the

German-language première of Molnár's *Liliom* in 1913, translated and adapted by Alfred Polgar, with Jarno himself in the title role and Hansi Niese also in the cast.

One other large theatre was for a time harnessed to the modernist cause. This was the Neue Wiener Bühne – the former Orpheum reconstructed as a theatre with a capacity of 1,000 and acquired in 1908 by Robert Wiene, whose intention was to create a literary theatre with a modern repertoire. Under the direction of Adolf Steinert in the three seasons 1908–11 and again under Emil Geyer, director from 1912 to 1922, the Neue Wiener Bühne played host to a series of *Gastspiele* presenting modern drama and realist acting. Albert Bassermann, from Brahm's company, appeared in 1911, 1912, and 1913, playing Hauptmann, Sudermann, and Ibsen. In January and October 1913 Gertrud Eysoldt appeared in Strindberg's *Miss Julie*, Wedekind's *Erdgeist* (Wedekind's biggest success in Vienna, according to the account in the *Neues Wiener Tagblatt*),[17] and Wilde's *Salome*; in 1915 Bassermann returned in Sternheim's *Der Snob*. Geyer defined his goal in terms similar to the strategy pursued by Jarno: it was to mount ambitious and serious theatre, financing it by runs of plays aiming for nothing but entertainment.[18]

The gradual advance of modern drama in these various theatres took place in a climate of continuing anti-Semitism. The same holds good of smaller enterprises, including the Intimes Theater in the Praterstrasse, which opened in 1905 with a seating capacity of 311, directed by Oskar Friedmann, a member of the literary circle around Peter Altenberg and Egon Friedell. The application of anti-Semitism to the theatre was perhaps most systematically argued in an article that first appeared in the *Deutsche Zeitung* in late December 1899. The case put forward is that the theatre was a victim of an international Jewish conspiracy working through the medium of the Jewish press. It was especially vulnerable to 'Jewish terrorism' because of its established function as a 'moral institution'; theatres ought to be inspiring the indigenous population, but instead they were in the hands of paid Jewish hacks and were being reduced to vehicles of propaganda for the Jewish cause.[19] The prejudice underlying this kind of pernicious nonsense accords closely with the motivation behind the foundation of the Kaiserjubiläums-Stadttheater in 1898 (see pp. 173–7, above), and was widely reflected in press reviews.[20] Earlier that year, for example, when the Carltheater presented the first Viennese production of Schnitzler's *Freiwild*, which is about duelling in accordance with the military 'code of honour', the play was attacked not just in pro-military papers but also in the anti-Semitic press: *Kikeriki* published a scurrilous condemnation of it as the product of a 'cowardly Jewish spirit', expressing 'Jewish attitudes' incompetent to treat the honour of Aryan women.[21] Schnitzler's diary the following day records his anger at the 'infamous attacks' to which Jews were being subjected.[22] At the end of that year the Burgtheater production of his next play, *Das Vermächtnis*, prompted further attacks: in the *Deutsche Zeitung* for 1 December 1898, for example, Leitich reported that the work was false to Viennese life, which it presented in a form which had been 'forced' upon it by Jews as 'aliens in the life of our people', and that it had been applauded only by a well-organized claque of 'literary Jews'. The following year, *Kikeriki* carried on 8 May a report on a première in the Carltheater which contrasted the play performed with the 'Jewish botches' of Schnitzler and others and expressed delight that at last the work of a 'Christian German author' had had a turn.

Three years later still, two theatrical flops prompted another outburst of anti-Semitic invective. One was a drama by Carl Bleibtreu, *Weltgericht*, in the Raimundtheater, the other an evening of one-act plays by Antonie Baumberg in the Deutsches Volkstheater, a theatre whose very name always laid it open to criticism for being insufficiently 'national' in its programme. Bukovics withdrew Antonie Baumberg's plays from the repertoire; on 16 April she committed suicide. An article in *Kikeriki* blamed Jewish influence for the 'fate of these two excellent Aryan writers', and stressed that Bleibtreu was far superior to Jewish playwrights (both Schnitzler and Hofmannsthal are among those mentioned by name) and their protégés.[23] Schnitzler in particular continued to be subjected to anti-Semitic abuse in the right-wing press: when he was awarded the Grillparzer Prize in 1908 for his drama *Zwischenspiel*, the *Reichspost* for 16 January 1908 reported that the award was a disgrace explicable only by the Jewish domination of Viennese literary life; after the première of *Das weite Land* in the Burgtheater in 1911, the *Reichspost* printed a cartoon of him as a dancing figure, with a caption in verse about how 'all Israel' had applauded his new play because it loved the 'round dance' of filth.[24]

The combination of Schlenther's lack of vigorous support and the hostility of the critical climate explains why plays by Schnitzler and Hofmannsthal were increasingly premièred not in Vienna but in

Berlin, where Schnitzler had excellent relations with Brahm, and Hofmannsthal with Reinhardt. Reinhardt, a native Austrian who had gone to Berlin in 1894 to join Brahm's company in the Deutsches Theater, was eventually to produce more works by Hofmannsthal than by any other contemporary dramatist, and it was in his productions that Hofmannsthal's major works were introduced to Vienna. The Berlin production of *Elektra* which had brought Hofmannsthal his first big theatrical success in the Kleines Theater in October 1903, with Gertrud Eysoldt in the title role, was one of the works that Reinhardt's company performed in May 1905 in the Theater an der Wien; the prose comedy *Cristinas Heimreise*, first performed in the Deutsches Theater in February 1910, with a cast headed by Moissi, and subsequently shortened by the dramatist in response to criticism of the final act, was in the programme that the company performed in the Theater an der Wien in May that year. Even the morality play *Jedermann*, which would become the centre-piece of the Salzburg Festival after the war, was first produced by Reinhardt in Berlin (on 1 December 1911 in the Zirkus Schumann, again with Moissi). Yet Hofmannsthal was aware that he derived the strongest influences on his work, especially in comedy, from the Burgtheater (both Molière and Bauernfeld, five of whose plays had remained in the repertory when the company moved to the Ring-strasse);[25] and despite his admiration and gratitude for Reinhardt's work he was particularly bitter about his exclusion, as he saw it, from the theatre where he properly belonged. This bitterness was openly expressed in 1918 in two letters to his friend Leopold von Andrian, who had been appointed general director (*Generalintendant*) of the court theatres that summer. The Burgtheater, Hofmannsthal wrote, had 'trampled' on national tradition; his own work had been so neglected there that he felt 'systematically mistreated'.[26]

The tensions between the modernists and an intellectual climate that was heavy with prejudice and in many ways hostile to experi-ment and change were no more marked in the theatre than in the other arts; the best-known disputes concern Klimt's canvas 'Philo-sophy' (the protest petition signed by senior professors of the University of Vienna in 1900), the rejection of Schoenberg's second String Quartet in 1908 after its first performance with the operatic soprano Marie Gutheil-Schoder singing the solo part, the furore about Loos's 'house without eyebrows' on the Michaelerplatz in 1910, the trial of Schiele for indecency in Neulengbach in 1912. In such a climate, the subversive satire of cabaret was bound to flourish. In this again Vienna lagged behind both Paris and Berlin (where Reinhardt had performed in cabaret from the 1898–9 season), but a number of lively cabarets sprang up in the early years of the new century. The first of significance was the short-lived Jung-Wiener Theater zum lieben Augustin, which was organized by Felix Salten in the Theater an der Wien in 1901, with décor by the *Jugendstil* artist Koloman Moser. Both Hansi Niese and Wedekind appeared in it, and it met with a revealingly mixed reception – rejection in the conservative press, support from the avant-garde.[27] Max Burckhard rather waspishly pointed out that despite the name Salten had chosen for his cabaret the writers associated with the 'Jung Wien' movement were not represented on the programme.[28] Other cabarets followed, the most important being the Kabarett Fledermaus, which has a unique place in the history of European cabaret: 'No other European cabaret of the late nineteenth and early twentieth centuries', Segel writes, 'developed, in its totality, in as intimate a relationship with contemporary artistic movements as did the Fledermaus'.[29] It opened in 1907 in the Kärntner Strasse, with a seating capacity of 225, in basement premises designed as a *Gesamtkunstwerk* by Josef Hoffmann and executed by the Wiener Werkstätte with financial support from Fritz Wärndorfer. The very first programme established it in the eyes of Egon Friedell (who would himself be involved as a performer in the second programme, and as a writer from the second season onwards) as 'without doubt the best German cabaret so far'.[30] The programme included texts by Peter Altenberg, Alfred Polgar, and Oskar Kokoschka (the text of *Die träumenden Knaben* was first read there in 1907), and Grete Wiesenthal was among the dancers who appeared. The most famous sketch to have emerged from the enterprise is the scene 'Goethe' by Polgar and Friedell, which was performed some 300 times in the 'Fledermaus', with Friedell in the title role.[31]

In the Burgtheater, Berger, who had been in Hamburg as director of the Deutsches Schauspielhaus, was finally appointed director in 1910, but he held the post only for two and a half years. The two most successful new productions were both of Schnitzler plays: the historical drama *Der junge Medardus* in November 1910, produced by Hugo Thimig, and *Das weite Land* in October 1911. A note in Schnitzler's diary in March 1911 records that after twenty-five performances *Der junge Medardus* was setting a new record for the

„Der Weibsteufel" von Karl Schönherr.

Burgtheaterdirektor Thimig: Komm Karl, laß' dich küssen, Du hast ein echtes Kriegs-Theaterstück geschrieben, hast gespart mit Personen, Kostümen und Dekorationen.

27 *Der junge Medardus* (Schnitzler) and *Der Weibsteufel* (Schönherr).

Burgtheater box-office;[32] but it had a huge cast and was expensive to stage, even lighting costs, as Thimig noted, being noticeably pushed up because of its length.[33] When Thimig succeeded Berger in 1912, he had to operate under an increasingly tight budget, and when Schönherr's *Der Weibsteufel*, which has a cast of three, was premièred in 1915, *Kikeriki* printed a cartoon depicting Thimig as delighted at the contrast (see plate 27). (The cartoon is tinged with anti-Semitism: it was the non-Jewish Schönherr who had written the play suited to wartime conditions.)

In general, the repertory in Thimig's five years as director was marked by an increasing dependence on standard classics (including Shakespeare). Perhaps the most important reform he effected was to do away with the traditional monopoly of the senior actors on production; on the acting side, one performer to come to prominence as a romantic lead was Harry Walden, who had been a member of the company since 1913, and who would take over the direction of the Volksbühne after the war (but died in 1921). In 1917 Thimig was succeeded by Max von Millenkovich, who served for one year only. His strategy was a resolutely nationalist and anti-Semitic one, aiming at limiting the numbers of Jewish actors and Jewish authors – a symptomatic example of the wretched political climate at the end of the monarchy. He brought Girardi into the company, but Girardi would play only two roles, Fortunatus Wurzel in Raimund's *Das Mädchen aus der Feenwelt oder Der Bauer als Millionär* and Weiring in *Liebelei*, before his untimely death in 1918.

In one further way the Viennese theatrical scene in the early years of the twentieth century lagged behind Berlin, even if there was, as Hofmannsthal wrote, 'no tradition in the theatre' there.[34] Not one of the late nineteenth-century foundations in Vienna was linked to naturalism, so that the immediate interests of the broad masses had no outlet in the theatre. This gap led to the founding of a Viennese offshoot of the *Volksbühne* movement. An announcement of the foundation of the Verein 'Freie Volksbühne' appeared in the *Arbeiter-Zeitung* on 29 July 1906. It was linked to an attack on the 'bourgeois' theatres and their public, addicted almost exclusively to a vacuous fare of farcical comedy and operetta. In the new organization, members were to be offered one performance a month in a Viennese theatre, and there was to be a two-tier subscription system. Of the established directors, only Jarno was actively involved; the organization was initially the work of Stefan Grossmann, a journalist on the

Arbeiter-Zeitung and so with contacts with Austrian Socialism. Membership grew to a peak of 25,000 by the end of 1912,[35] but the organization was hampered by lack of money for building its own theatre. Eventually a hall in the Neubaugasse, originally designed as a cinema, became available. It was small, with a total capacity of 798 (599 in the stalls, 168 in the gallery, plus twelve boxes); the stage was 9 x 19 m, the whole auditorium only 30 x 19 m.[36] It opened on 12 December 1912 with a production of Nestroy's *Kampl*, with Rudolf Forster in the title role and a cast including Ernst Deutsch as Herr von Brachfeld. Berta Zuckerkandl wrote in the *Wiener Allgemeine Zeitung* that same day that it had more the character of a smart intimate theatre (*Kammerspiele*) than of a *Volksbühne*, and so did not really meet its social objectives.[37] Though the production of *Kampl* was a success, with twenty-seven performances within three months, the theatre made losses and closed with the outbreak of war.

2. OPERA AND OPERETTA

While Schlenther, Bukovics, and Jarno were in varying degrees advancing the cause of contemporary drama, the Opera House, with Gustav Mahler in charge, was enjoying the ten most brilliant years in its history (1897–1907). Mahler came to Vienna after proving himself a successful director of the opera houses in Budapest (1888–91) and Hamburg (1891–7); he was at this stage less well known as a composer but had a reputation for rigorous perfectionism – the rigour summed up in his famous dictum dismissing tradition as slovenliness ('Tradition ist Schlamperei') – and for creating productions that treated opera as a *Gesamtkunstwerk*. (He himself was responsible for the production of all major additions to the repertory.) Though his productions were costly, he succeeded in wiping out the accumulated deficit of the Opera House. At the same time he raised standards in every aspect of opera production: in singing, in orchestral playing, in acting, and (in collaboration with Alfred Roller as chief designer) in lighting and stage design. It was a period of musical rigour: most of the passages hitherto cut in Wagner were restored, recitatives in Mozart were accompanied on the piano and eventually on the harpsichord. It was also a period of technical and logistical innovations in the service of artistic effect. The auditorium was darkened during performance; the conductor's podium was raised; and a revolve was introduced, which was first used in a production of *Così fan tutte*.[38] The first product of the seminal collaboration between Mahler and Roller, in which they abandoned realistic sets in favour of stylized scenery with suggestive lighting effects, was a production of Wagner's *Tristan und Isolde* in February 1903. Roller would go on to design twenty-one productions in all in the Opera House under Mahler, and later to design the sets for all the first Viennese productions of Richard Strauss's operas from *Elektra* (1909) to *Die ägyptische Helena* (1928). Mahler also engaged a number of young singers (notably the German dramatic soprano Marie Gutheil-Schoder), building up a company that was not only strong vocally but was also skilled in acting; and he engaged two young conductors who would later rise to prominence, Bruno Walter for the Italian repertory, Franz Schalk for the German.

There are many accounts of the intense excitement of Mahler performances;[39] the legendary cultural golden age of Vienna around 1900 took place not least in the Opera House. Yet Mahler too worked under the cloud of anti-Semitic criticism. Against opposition to his appointment such as that of Wagner's widow, who protested against the prospect of a Jew conducting her husband's music in the Opera House, he took the precaution of having himself baptized as a Catholic in Hamburg on 23 February 1897[40] – an opportunist conversion necessary to ensure that the appointment would be a practical possibility at all. But despite his tightening up on 'traditionalist' *Schlamperei* he was constantly attacked in the anti-Semitic press as incompetent,[41] and Pattai's speech to the general meeting of the association of the Kaiserjubiläums-Stadttheater in October 1903 included a passage complaining that in the 'city of Mozart and Beethoven' the Opera House had become 'Jew-ridden'.[42] Other troubles Mahler had to navigate included the censor's rejection of Strauss's *Salome* in 1905, because the text was unacceptable;[43] and especially from early 1907, he was branded as 'destroying the ensemble' of the Opera House. But the heart of the criticism of his directorship was that he was dictatorial and that he failed to meet the demands of pan-German circles for more 'German' operas.[44]

When he finally succumbed to all the pressures and resigned in October 1907, the years that followed could not but be an anticlimax. His immediate successor, from the beginning of 1908, was the conductor Felix Weingartner; he in turn was followed by Hans Gregor, a former actor with the Deutsches Theater in Berlin and a well-known producer, who had been director of the Komische Oper in Berlin, and was director in Vienna from 1911 to 1918. Gregor was criticized for allowing superficial production effects to dominate at the expense of the music, as he had done in Berlin, allegedly applying to opera production techniques appropriate to naturalist drama,[45] and for losing the services of Bruno Walter (who left in 1912) in the process. The major additions to the repertoire during this whole post-Mahler period were Richard Strauss operas, produced with sets and costumes by Roller: *Elektra* in 1909; *Der Rosenkavalier*, with Marie Gutheil-Schoder as Octavian and Richard Mayr as Ochs, in 1911, shortly after Gregor had taken over; and *Ariadne auf Naxos* in 1916 – the première of the revised version, conducted by Franz Schalk, with Maria Jeritza singing the title role, as she had done in the production of the first version in Stuttgart. In the summer of 1918 Richard Strauss, who had just completed ten years as musical director of the court Opera House in Berlin, conducted at a 'Strauss week' in Vienna performances of *Elektra*, *Der Rosenkavalier*, and *Ariadne auf Naxos*, and Andrian seized the opportunity to invite him to succeed Gregor. The appointment was delayed by a number of complications; on 10 November 1918 (the last day of the monarchy), Schalk was nominated as director of the Opera House, and an agreement with Strauss was not completed until 1 March 1919, ushering in a joint direction that lasted until 1924. But as early as October 1918 *Salome* had at last been cleared by the censor for performance in the court Opera House (it was the last new production under the monarchy), with Maria Jeritza singing the title role, in which she subsequently alternated with Marie Gutheil-Schoder. The production of *Salome* in the Opera House seemed to signal an acceptance of modernism, which the appointment of Strauss and Schalk confirmed.

Throughout the early twentieth century, ballet remained subordinate to opera, as it had done in the last years of the nineteenth century. The great events generally involved visiting performers, the most notable examples being the appearances of Diaghilev's Ballets Russes, with Nijinsky, in 1912 and 1913 (the 1912 programme including *Petrushka*). It is symptomatic that the first performance of *Josephs Legende* took place not in Vienna but in Paris, and that when the ballet was eventually staged in Vienna in 1922, with décor by Roller, the role of Potiphar's wife was taken by a leading operatic singer, Marie Gutheil-Schoder.

In the meantime, moreover, the city had acquired a second opera house, in the former Kaiserjubiläums-Stadttheater. Under Rainer

Simons, who remained in office as director until 1917, the programme soon changed in character, with operas added from
September 1904 (*Der Freischütz*, conducted by Alexander Zemlinsky),
and the designation 'Volksoper' was added to its name. This was in
practical response to demand; there had already been a campaign
for a 'Volksoper' in the 1900–1 season.[46] Early productions included
Tosca in 1907 (it had not yet been seen at the Opera House), and by
1908 the theatre had come to specialize entirely in opera, light opera,
and some operetta. Zemlinsky went briefly to the Opera House
under Mahler but after Mahler's resignation returned to the Volksoper until 1911; the première of his own comic opera *Kleider machen
Leute* took place there in 1910. Other important productions under
Simons included the first Viennese performance of *Salome* in December 1910, nearly eight years before the first production in the
Opera House (Richard Strauss himself would conduct a performance
in the Volksoper in April 1911), and an opera based on Schnitzler's
Liebelei by František Neumann (1913).

The transformation of the Kaiserjubiläums-Stadttheater into an
opera theatre for the bourgeoisie was inevitably perceived as an
ideological sell-out; one result was that Müller-Guttenbrunn's regime
began to be viewed more favourably by his erstwhile critics in the
anti-Semitic press, so that when the time came to celebrate his
seventieth birthday, *Kikeriki* was ready to extol him as the pride of
Vienna.[47] In the meantime, operetta, on which he had poured such
contempt, was flourishing. By the end of the nineteenth century, it
had become theatrical big business. Works were designed for export
to other international centres, at the expense of any trace of the
specifically local character inherent in the dialect drama they had
squeezed out of the Viennese commercial theatres. Lehár's breakthrough came in late 1902, with two operettas: *Wiener Frauen*, starring
Girardi, performed in the Theater an der Wien on 21 November,
and *Der Rastelbinder*, performed in the Carltheater a month later, on
20 December. In 1905, Lehár achieved the biggest commercial
success of all with *Die lustige Witwe* in the Theater an der Wien. A
piece which, as Traubner has observed, retained more of 'the glitter
and silliness of nineteenth-century comic opera' than Lehár's later,
more sentimental work, it captured at least the surface image of the
dying monarchy, 'a historical age which has ... been described as
one great operetta itself, with its uniforms, its balls, its political
intrigue, and its intoxicating glamour'.[48] Until about 1915 (the year

of Emmerich Kálmán's biggest success, *Die Csárdásfürstin*), Vienna dominated the international operetta scene, with the number of new operetta productions peaking in 1911.[49] Hit followed hit in the Theater an der Wien into the last years of the monarchy; Lehár operettas premièred there included *Der Graf von Luxemburg* in November 1909, and other composers including Kálmán and Leo Fall followed hard on his heels.

The commercial theatres up to the First World War were indeed largely dominated by operetta: not only the Theater an der Wien and the Carltheater (which was directed from 1907 until his death in 1922 by Siegmund Eibenschütz, who ran it almost entirely as an operetta theatre), but eventually the Raimundtheater, and also new foundations. The Johann-Strauss-Theater in the fourth district (Favoritenstrasse), to the south of the centre,[50] was founded as an operetta theatre in 1908; it was there that *Die Csárdásfürstin* was first performed. Another substantial theatre, the Wiener Bürgertheater, which opened in 1905 in the Vordere Zollamtsstrasse, east of the centre, with a capacity of 1,230 (979 seats plus thirty boxes), went the same way: the programme there had been a predominantly light one from the first (spiced by *Gastspiele*, including one by Girardi, who appeared in L'Arronge's *Mein Leopold* in April 1909); from the 1910–11 season it switched completely to a repertory of operetta. Operetta was also performed in the early years of the century in the Orpheum (the former Harmonie-Theater) in the Wasagasse, and a little later in the Apollotheater in the Gumpendorfer Strasse, which opened in 1904 and was run, mainly as a variety theatre, by one of the most enterprising directors in that field, Ben Tieber, until his death in 1925, and in which a number of operettas, mainly in one act, were produced from 1907 onwards.

Vienna still offered a wide range of theatrical fare. In the first fortnight of December 1912, for example, the programme in the Lustspieltheater included a performance of Anzengruber's rarely seen *Die Trutzige* with Hansi Niese, and another Anzengruber play, *Heimg'funden*, was on in the Deutsches Volkstheater. As well as older classics, the Burgtheater had performances of *Pillars of Society*, *Rosmersholm*, and *Das weite Land*. It was during this fortnight that the Volksbühne in the Neubaugasse opened with *Kampl*. The Neue Wiener Bühne had a matinée reading from Hofmannsthal on 9 December. Operas performed included *Carmen* with Marie Gutheil-Schoder in the Opera House and *Der fliegende Holländer* with Maria

Jeritza in the Volksoper. Nevertheless, the programme as a whole was unmistakably getting ever lighter. The Theater in der Josefstadt, the Neue Wiener Bühne, the Deutsches Volkstheater, and the Residenzbühne (an intimate theatre with a capacity of 500, which had been opened in the Rotenturmstrasse in 1910) were mainly showing comedies of various kinds, and there were operettas in the Theater an der Wien, the Wiener Bürgertheater, the Raimundtheater, the Carltheater, and the Johann-Strauss-Theater – in the latter Kálmán's *Der Zigeunerprimas* with Girardi.

This predominance of operetta and comedy did not change with the outbreak of war. On the contrary: operetta appealed to a new wave of escapism, just as it had done amid the economic and social problems of the 1870s and 1880s; and indeed, light comedy of all kinds had a similar escapist appeal, particularly in the glamour of first nights.[51] The *Arbeiter-Zeitung* commented in March 1918 on the unflagging interest in the theatre that the Viennese showed during the war, and glossed the end of the war in October of the same year with the wry observation that the 'liquidation of the Austrian world' was being conducted amid 'operetta premières and the opening of new operetta theatres'.[52] But the new theatres would not stay open long: the 'Austrian world' as it had been known was indeed in liquidation.

CHAPTER 8

1918-1945

I. ECONOMIC DEPRESSION

As the war drew to its inglorious close, Hofmannsthal was half-way through the composition of *Der Schwierige*, a comedy rooted in the Burgtheater tradition of the *Konversationsstück*. He hoped it would be performed in the Burgtheater, ideally by Max Reinhardt's company. The Burgtheater had been directed since April 1917 by the pan-German nationalist Millenkovich; when Hofmannsthal's old friend Leopold von Andrian was appointed *Generalintendant* in July 1918 (a post that had lain dormant since 1907), his hopes of a new restoration of specifically Austrian traditions rode high. Andrian, a career diplomat, was a convinced Habsburg loyalist; Hofmannsthal shared his scepticism towards the growing power of Germany and glimpsed the possibility that his own works would now establish themselves in the Burgtheater where, he thought, they rightfully belonged. Andrian's success in his new office, his own 'destiny' as a dramatist, and his hopes for a 'rebirth of Austrian theatre from the work of the *only* creative force in this area' [that is, Reinhardt], 'an Austrian with his whole heart and soul', were, so he wrote to Andrian on 27 August 1918, interlinked.[1]

There had even been talk of Reinhardt's succeeding to the direction of the Burgtheater. When there had been similar rumours in 1917 his appointment had been considered inconceivable 'for obvious reasons', so the well-informed *Fremden-Blatt* reported – alluding possibly to his commitments in Berlin but more probably to the strength of anti-Semitic opinion; within a week the same paper carried a leak about the impending appointment of Millenkovich.[2] Now Hofmannsthal gave full vent to his grievance at the neglect of an authentic Austrian voice: this was when he wrote that the Burgtheater had been 'trampling' on its tradition and on the

'Austrian voice', cultivating Gerhart Hauptmann and Otto Ernst ('Hauptmann', he wrote, 'was awarded the Grillparzer Prize *three times!*'), while the responsibilities of a true national theatre had been met by Reinhardt. By his work in Berlin Reinhardt 'was constructing a kind of finer Burgtheater, with a more ambitious repertory, with only one gap – social comedy ('das Gesellschaftsstück')'; and on Reinhardt's behalf he urged that collaboration was possible.[3] Just over a month later he returned to the subject of what he saw as his own 'systematic mistreatment'. In the nineteen years since his first plays had been performed in the Burgtheater, his work had either not been produced there or, in the case of *Jedermann*, had been given only a few performances, by contrast with long runs in German cities such as Munich and Dresden; and this stood in contrast also with performances of practically every play by Hauptmann and Schnitzler (of whom he was always particularly jealous) and the discovery and cultivation of Schönherr. He had long thought of himself as 'a kind of house-dramatist to an imaginary Burgtheater'; this had been the motivation for his adaptations, including *Elektra* and 'various Molière things', work which 'carried on from Schreyvogel, Grillparzer, Halm, and Wilbrandt' and had no meaning in relation to Berlin, 'where there is, after all, no tradition in the theatre'.[4] The traditionalist knowingly evokes the traditions of the court theatre, anxious to preserve its character; but with the end of the war and the fall of the Monarchy in November 1918, all such hopes were dashed.

Andrian had placed a three-man team, effectively headed by Bahr, in charge of the artistic direction of the Burgtheater. Bahr was a recent convert to Catholicism, and the scepticism with which his fervour was regarded by the leading playwrights and producers is captured in a Zasche cartoon (plate 28). Andrian was also sympathetic to a plan advanced by Richard Strauss to establish a network of three court opera houses, to make Vienna a musical capital with a more broadly-based programme than anywhere else in Europe.[5] But his term as *Generalintendant* lasted only four months, until 24 November 1918; with the establishment of the republic what had been court theatres were transferred to state control. Exactly how they were to be run was a much-discussed question, but it was widely accepted that both the Opera House and the Burgtheater must change in character; in the words of the music critic Paul Stefan, they could 'no longer be theatres for the privileged'.[6]

28   Theo Zasche: conference in the Burgtheater.

The immediate consequence for Hofmannsthal and Reinhardt was that they plunged with redoubled commitment into the planning of the Salzburg Festival, which was held for the first time in 1920. Reinhardt had been involved in founding the Salzburger Festspiel-haus-Gemeinde in 1917; he, Schalk, and Richard Strauss had formed an artistic advisory board founded the following year, and Hof-mannsthal and Roller had been co-opted early in 1919. Together, Reinhardt and Hofmannsthal had developed the Festival programme in outline, the characteristic combination of opera and drama, including autochthonic popular plays as well as mystery and morality plays. At the first Festival in August 1920 Reinhardt's production of *Jedermann* was performed in front of the cathedral, and it has remained a focal point of the Festival ever since, being performed again in 1921 and at every subsequent Festival from 1926 onwards, except for the Nazi period (1938–45). Reinhardt did not establish a permanent base in Vienna until 1923, when he took over the Theater in der Josefstadt; the Burgtheater passed into the hands first of Albert Heine and then, in 1921, of Anton Wildgans; and though Hof-mannsthal wrote to Wildgans about *Der Schwierige* almost as soon as he had taken over,[7] the Burgtheater rejected it, and against Hofmannsthal's inclination it had to be premièred in Munich.

Schnitzler, meanwhile, still had closer relations with the Deutsches Volkstheater, which from 1918 to 1924 was under the direction of Alfred Bernau. Not only did the first Austrian production of *Professor Bernhardi* take place in this theatre in 1918; the Kammerspiele in the Rotenturmstrasse (the former Residenzbühne, which had come under the management of the Deutsches Volkstheater after the war) mounted the first Viennese production of *Reigen* on 1 February 1921, so provoking one of the most spectacular theatre scandals of the inter-war years. The production was attacked from the Christian Social camp on grounds of social degeneracy – a campaign con-ducted with open anti-Semitism, and in part a political challenge to the Social Democrat government of Vienna, which had supported the decision to go ahead with the production. In a coordinated demonstration, the performance on 16 February was interrupted, a stink-bomb was thrown, and when the doors were opened to let in fresh air, the theatre was stormed by demonstrators who had gathered in the street. They proceeded to attack the audience and vandalize the theatre, which had to be cleared by police and the fire-brigade, using fire hydrants. The outrage of the Social Democrats was expressed in the *Arbeiter-Zeitung* which referred witheringly on 18 February to 'censorship by stink-bomb' as providing an instant solution to ethical, aesthetic, and constitutional problems.[8] In the right-wing press, by contrast, the police decision to halt further performances was welcomed as a 'success' for the 'Christian youth of Vienna'.[9]

The dire economic plight of the infant republic also brought more basic material problems. Indeed, because of the shortage of fuel for heating after the war (coal had to be imported from what was now the republic of Czechoslovakia) the theatres were closed in early December 1918: the Burgtheater had only ten evening performances that month and remained closed for two evenings a week in January. A full programme was not restored until April 1919, and even then performances were timed early in order to save fuel. There was a further energy shortage in January 1920, when a ban on lighting after 3 p.m. led to a renewed closure for just over a week of all places of evening entertainment, including cinemas and concert-halls as well as theatres, and by September 1920 there were staff cuts in the Deutsches Volkstheater (plus the Kammerspiele), in the Theater an der Wien, and in the Raimundtheater; the crisis was repeated in 1921 as inflation rose. The professional and middle classes could not afford to maintain their regular theatre-going. After attending the première of *Reigen*, Schnitzler noted cryptically in his diary that the audience had been 'unpleasant', with scarcely anyone he knew.[10] The former court theatres were not immune from these problems, as Zasche's cartoon of Richard Strauss conducting in the Opera House in 1920 (plate 29) illustrates: the impoverishment of the middle classes, which had turned theatre-going into a dispensable 'luxury',[11] only compounded the financial pressures arising from the dissolution of the court.

By 1922 the state's commitment to maintaining the Burgtheater and the Opera House was enshrined in two laws guaranteeing terms of service and pension rights; but for a time the possibility of a part-privatization of the Burgtheater was widely canvassed. The repertory had so dwindled that the whole system of subscription was undermined, while the building was so expensive to run that Albert Heine, the director, was drawn to schemes either for abandoning it altogether and using other, cheaper theatres that might be available (the Theater an der Wien and the Volksoper came into question) or else for merging the Burgtheater with the Deutsches Volkstheater.[12] For

29   Theo Zasche: cartoon of an opera performance under Richard Strauss.

expanding the repertory and bringing more flexibility into planning, a second, smaller stage was needed, and from 1919 onwards he made use of the ornate Schönbrunner Schlosstheater (which dates from the mid eighteenth century and had hitherto been used exclusively as a court theatre); but it could be used only in summer and autumn, as it lacked adequate heating. This experiment was continued under subsequent directors until 1924.

In November 1919 the possibility arose of using another small theatre, the Akademietheater in the Künstlerhaus complex, but Heine rejected this because it was available for only three days a week.[13] It was eventually taken on by Max Paulsen, who was director in the season 1922-3 and who recognized its potential (the acoustics are excellent) and put it to good use in expanding the repertory, particularly with financially profitable lighter works.

Paulsen, a long-standing member of the Burgtheater company who lacked only political finesse (he once admitted to Schnitzler that he felt torn between the rival suspicions of the Right and Left),[14] lasted for just one season. He was succeeded by another experienced producer, Franz Herterich, whose seven years in office were overshadowed by the economic stringency in public finances enforced by the Geneva Protocols of 1922. The number of closed performances given (at reduced prices) by arrangement with the cultural sections of the political parties (*Kunststellen*) rose sharply, and the rise in takings gave Herterich a chance to undertake some rebuilding of the company, one of the new actors he engaged being Fred Hennings, later, like Herterich himself, a historian of the Burgtheater – an illustration of the remarkable sense of tradition that has kept on renewing itself within this theatre.

The biggest of the party *Kunststellen* was the Social Democrat one, which was subsidized by the city council as an organ of cultural politics. The underlying intention was to furnish subscribing members (of whom there were about 20,000 in the mid-1920s) with cut-price theatre tickets as part of a programme of cultural education. In practice, however, the system fell short of this idealistic intention, in that many of the productions supported were lightweight plays and operettas, and only a small percentage of the tickets distributed were for the prestige state theatres (3 per cent to the Opera House in 1929, 6 per cent to the Burgtheater).[15] Precisely the fact that the *Kunststellen*, in particular the Social Democrat one, did not support the small but luxuriously appointed Modernes Theater which opened in 1924 in the Johannesgasse was a crucial factor in its financial failure.[16] Among its other activities, the Social Democrat *Kunststelle* also acquired the ailing Carltheater in 1928, intending to mount a programme of left-wing theatre, but financial difficulties proved insuperable, and it closed again after only two productions.

One of the major problems that hung over the whole theatrical scene for most of the twenties was an entertainment tax introduced in Vienna by the city council in 1918. This was a tax with differential rates: in 1918 it was levied at a rate of 4 per cent on spoken theatre, 8 per cent on musical performances, and 10 per cent on cinema and late-night variety; in 1920 the rates for the three bands were raised to 5 per cent (for spoken theatre and opera), 10 per cent (for operetta), and 15 per cent respectively; the rates were doubled from the beginning of 1921, with a ceiling for spoken theatre and opera rising to 20 per cent after a run of fifty performances. The higher tax on operetta theatres was one of the principal factors leading to the temporary closure in 1925 of the Carltheater, the Volksoper, the Neue Wiener Bühne, and the Modernes Theater, and in 1927 the rates were lowered. When the Carltheater under Alfred Bernau first went dark in November 1924, the conclusion of the commentators was that among other factors (including the level of wages) the theatres were simply overtaxed.[17] Though Robert Musil, the most astute of all the theatre critics of the time, idealistically rejected suggestions that the theatre as an institution was in decline,[18] the idea was widely discussed.

To a Social Democrat council engaged actively on an ambitious programme of social reform, the entertainment tax brought in welcome income; but it increased the financial pressures on the commercial theatres, with the result that they were driven down-market in order to attract custom, so that Alfred Polgar was one of those who wrote scornfully of a general 'decline', with actors conniving in offering the most trivial amusement in an attempt to secure the theatres' continued existence.[19] The auditorium of the Kammerspiele, with one small gallery and no boxes – a good example of how far twentieth-century taste had reacted against the old-fashioned style of the nineteenth-century theatre as exemplified by the Carltheater (see plate 30) – was well suited to the intimacy of *Reigen*, in which each of the scenes involves only two characters. But its choice for the première was only partly determined by this consideration; from its time as the 'Residenzbühne' it had been

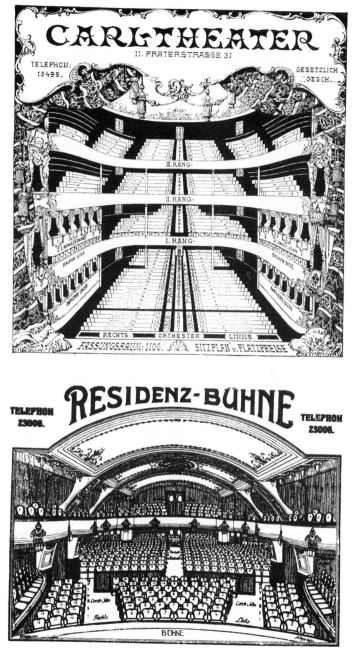

30 Seating plans, Carltheater and Residenzbühne.

known for staging risqué French farces, and so it might hope to draw
in the widest audience at high prices. (In fact even *Reigen* was not
enough of a draw for this to work long, and Bernau had to lower the
prices after the first performance in order not to lose custom.)[20]

An additional factor in the economy of the commercial theatres
was that they were increasingly concentrated in the hands of a few
directors. Jarno remained in charge of the Theater in der Josefstadt
and the Lustspieltheater in the Prater until 1923 and 1927 respectively (the Lustspieltheater was then turned into a cinema); his third
theatre, the Wiener Stadttheater in the eighth district, was acquired
in 1917 by Wilhelm Karczag, who had been director of the Theater
an der Wien since 1901 and the Raimundtheater since 1908, and
who remained at the helm in all three theatres (in the Wiener
Stadttheater in partnership with Jarno) until his death in 1923. In
1925 Jarno took over the Renaissancebühne (the former Volksbühne)
in the Neubaugasse, which he directed until 1931; it had been
reopened after the war, closed by a strike in 1919 because wage
payments were in arrears, and then taken over by Walden, who had
run quickly into financial difficulties; after that the theatre had been
bought out by a Berlin theatre magnate, Eugen Robert, with Walden
remaining as artistic director until 1924. The following year Robert
also took over the Neue Wiener Bühne. Hubert Marischka, Karczag's son-in-law, was director of the Theater an der Wien from 1923
to 1935 and co-owner from 1924; he succeeded Karczag as the
principal shareholder in the Raimundtheater and briefly functioned
as co-director with Rudolf Beer in 1926, and he also directed the
Wiener Stadttheater from 1926. Beer himself directed the Raimundtheater from 1921 to 1932; there was also an offshoot,
'Kammerspiele des Raimundtheaters', for which Beer first got
permission to use the Akademietheater (1922–3) and which played in
1931–2 in the Kammerspiele in the Rotenturmstrasse. From August
1924 until 1932 he was also director of the Deutsches Volkstheater – a
major theatrical empire, with over 3,000 seats to be sold every
evening, so that the support of the party *Kunststellen* was important.

The interdependence of theatres at a time of what was at best
gradual and faltering economic recovery had inherent dangers. This
is clearest in the case of Bernau. For six years (until 1922) he ran the
Deutsches Volkstheater in tandem with the Kammerspiele; the
following year he took over the Carltheater, but by then he was
already in financial difficulties, and in August 1924 he had to cede

the direction of the Deutsches Volkstheater to Beer. By November 1924 his financial position had collapsed again, and the Carltheater closed. An application from the directors of the Theater an der Wien, Hubert Marischka and Emil Steininger, to take over the theatre was rejected by Hugo Breitner, the city councillor (*Stadtrat*) responsible for finances.[21]

Another director to be overtaken by insolvency in 1925 was Siegfried Geyer, who was involved as director or co-director with no fewer than four theatres. One was the Wiener Bürgertheater, of which he was co-director from 1923, and whose programme consisted mainly of operetta. Another was the Neue Wiener Bühne (which he directed on behalf of Eugen Robert, attempting to provide an ambitious programme of contemporary literary theatre). A third was the Modernes Theater, which had been opened in January 1924 by Robert Blum, a close associate of Geyer's, and taken over, heavily in the red, by Geyer eight months later; it went into liquidation after four months. A few days later the same fate befell Geyer's fourth house, the Kammerspiele.

Both the Kammerspiele and the Modernes Theater, the latter under various names, survived until after the Second World War; but economic problems continued to beset Austria throughout the 1920s. The inflation of 1921–2 and the collapse of the Austrian currency were followed by the financial stringency imposed as part of the rescue package agreed in the Geneva Protocols; by the end of the decade, the whole western world was in economic crisis following the Wall Street Crash of 1929. A further threat was presented by the competition provided in the cinema by the rise of talkies. In March 1925, after a spate of bankruptcies and closures, there was a protest meeting, and this drew from Breitner a firm reply, which he published in the *Arbeiter-Zeitung*.[22] Taxes on any profession, he wrote, had to be measured against the greater good of the community as a whole; moreover the entertainment tax on spoken drama had been kept low in the interests of the very people protesting, namely, those working in the theatres, and had not prevented actors' wages from rising. The real causes of the crisis lay elsewhere, not least in poor financial management in the theatres, and in the fact that competition was now damagingly intense. There were simply too many theatres in Vienna: the population had declined by over 300,000 since 1914 (it was now 1,868,000), but with a number of theatres having opened since the beginning of the war the total capacity had risen by 3,463 seats – the equivalent of the Burgtheater, the Theater an der Wien, and the Theater in der Josefstadt put together. At a time when the number of concert halls and cinemas was also rising, there was an 'enormous excess of places of entertainment' ('ein ungeheures Überangebot an Unterhaltungsmöglichkeiten'.

Among the operetta theatres, the Johann-Strauss-Theater enjoyed some major successes, including the première of Lehár's *Paganini* (30 October 1925) and the first performance in Vienna of *Der Zarewitsch* (1928); but the one that flourished best in the 1920s was the Theater an der Wien. Here Kálmán's *Gräfin Mariza* and *Die Zirkusprinzessin* were premièred in 1924 and 1926 respectively; also Eysler's *Die gold'ne Meisterin*, set in sixteenth-century Vienna (première 13 September 1927). Lehár premières took place alternately in Vienna and Berlin, where the principal operetta star of the time, Richard Tauber, was very popular; the biggest hit that Lehár had in Vienna was *Das Land des Lächelns*, a reworking of an earlier work, *Die gelbe Jacke* (Theater an der Wien, 1923): premièred in Berlin in October 1929, it was produced in the Theater an der Wien the following September.

Various strategies were devised in the operetta theatres to counter the economic pressures. Shows would be exchanged between theatres (especially the Theater an der Wien, Raimundtheater, and Wiener Stadttheater when all three were under the direction of Hubert Marischka; so too Beer moved productions of spoken drama between the Deutsches Volkstheater and the Raimundtheater). There was also a tendency to move away from the repertory system, with a frequently-changing programme supported by subscription ticket sales, in favour of long runs of a single show, the strategy that had been established in the London theatre from the mid-1860s: this too Beer adopted in the Kammerspiele. The operetta version of *Im Weißen Rößl* (*White Horse Inn*), with music by Ralph Benatzky and others, which had first been produced in Berlin in 1930, ran for almost 700 performances in the Wiener Stadttheater and saved it from financial ruin in 1931–2, just as the London run kept the Coliseum in being as a theatre.[23] Two other strategies are familiar from the history of the nineteenth-century dialect theatre: both offered illusions of escape from the drabness and rigours of the republic. One was the use of spectacular décor, as in *Gräfin Mariza*, *Die Zirkusprinzessin*, and *Im Weißen Rößl*; the other the exploitation of nostalgia for happier days past. This extended to the show-business of the past, as in *Josefine Gallmeyer* (Wiener Bürgertheater, 1921), with music and libretto by Paul Knepler, who later wrote the libretto for Lehár's *Paganini*; but by the early 1930s what it meant above all was the glamour of the Habsburg Monarchy. The evocative melody of Haydn's anthem was exploited both in *Im Weißen Rößl* and also in Fritz Kreisler's *Sissy*, a work with a book by Ernst and Hubert Marischka which was premièred in the Theater an der Wien on 23 December 1932, with Paula Wessely, who fifty years later would be the undisputed *grande dame* among Austrian actresses, in the title role and Hans Jaray in that of Franz Joseph. Franz Joseph also appears in *Im Weißen Rößl* – a significant addition to the comedy by Blumenthal and Kadelburg on which the libretto is based, inessential for the plot, and serving merely as a peg for musical set pieces.[24]

Despite these strategies for survival, by the mid-1920s the popularity of operetta was fading, even in the Theater an der Wien. As early as 1925, when the erstwhile star of *Die Csárdásfürstin*, Mizzi Günther, retired, one report of her farewell performance in the Johann-Strauss-Theater appeared under the headline 'Viennese operetta is dead'.[25] By the end of the 1920s the operetta theatres were gradually being whittled away in number. After various attempts to keep the Neue Wiener Bühne going, it was closed down in 1928 (it was demolished in 1934, and replaced by flats). The Carltheater – disadvantaged by being in what was now an increasingly run-down part of the city, as Schnitzler noted when walking through the Leopoldstadt in 1922[26] – closed for the last time in 1929. The Johann-Strauss-Theater went into liquidation in February 1931, and became a cinema – the same fate as befell the Lustspieltheater.

There remained the Theater an der Wien, the Raimundtheater, the Wiener Stadttheater in the eighth district, the Wiener Bürgertheater (apart from intermittent closures), and the Volksoper, where the interwar years were a period of almost permanent financial crisis. Felix von Weingartner, who had been director of the Opera House for three years before the war (1908–11), took over as director of the Volksoper in 1919, and remained there for five years, but in December 1924, not long after his resignation, the theatre was forced to close for a time, and in the following fourteen years its survival was in constant doubt. For a time it was renamed the Neues Wiener Schauspielhaus: under Jakob Feldhammer and Otto Preminger, it offered a programme of light comedy and contemporary drama (the opening production of the 1929–30 season was Wedekind's *König Nikolo*), but attendance fell off, and in 1931 it reverted to being an operetta stage under Leo Kraus. Preminger would later produce Nestroy's *Das Haus der Temperamente* in the Burgtheater in 1932 and would then function as Max Reinhardt's deputy in the Josefstadt for two seasons (1933–5), and still later, one of the many Austrians driven into exile in the 1930s, would become famous as a leading Hollywood film director. The Volksoper meanwhile was sustained in the early 1930s by shows like a revival of Lehár's *Friederike* conducted in 1932 by the composer, and Reinhardt's production of Erich Wolfgang Korngold's adaptation of *La Belle Hélène* (6 June 1932).

Even the music-hall theatres (*Variétés*), which attracted audiences from the working class and the lower middle class and had enjoyed enormous popularity at the end of the nineteenth century, were hit by the economic depression as they came under competition from the new mass media, radio and film. The Ronacher, reopened in 1930 under the management of Bernhard Labriola after a three-year closure, with a capacity of 1,546 including newly-added standing places, attracted big audiences by presenting visiting international stars. These included Joséphine Baker, whose appearance in the Johann-Strauss-Theater in 1928 (when the Ronacher was closed) had provoked a stormy debate in the national parliament about moral standards;[27] she appeared in the Ronacher in 1932. A year later she was followed first by Hansi Niese and then by Mistinguett, who at the age of sixty was still so magnetic a box-office draw that Labriola was able to raise his ticket prices, which were generally kept low, to cover her fee. But in many of the smaller and more down-market establishments the programme degenerated into seedy nude shows; and by the end of the 1920s and the early 1930s several of the variety theatres too were turned into cinemas. Among these was even the Apollotheater in the Gumpendorfer Strasse, after the Ronacher the biggest variety theatre in Vienna, which became a cinema in 1929 (and which is still there, having been renovated in 1992–3).

2. THE ART OF THE TWENTIES

Despite the unfavourable economic situation, the postwar years were an exciting time in the theatre. While Richard Strauss was notoriously reluctant to fill the programme of the Opera House with new works, only weeks after he had taken up his office as co-director in 1919 Vienna was provided with its one world première of a Strauss–

Hofmannsthal opera, *Die Frau ohne Schatten*, conducted by Schalk, with Maria Jeritza as the Empress and Lotte Lehmann as Barak's wife. On 14 October 1924, the most celebrated première in the history of the Volksoper took place, that of Schoenberg's *Die glückliche Hand*; three years later the first Viennese performance of Krenek's 'jazz opera' *Jonny spielt auf* in the Opera House on New Year's Eve 1927 was the occasion of virulent objections by Austrian Nazis to allegedly malign Jewish and black influence, with a big anti-Semitic protest meeting organized in a hall in the third district. When Clemens Krauss succeeded Schalk as director of the Opera House in 1929 further new productions included Berg's *Wozzeck* in 1930 and Strauss's *Arabella* in 1933 – major operas added to the repertoire, though neither production was a world première, any more than that of *Jonny spielt auf* had been, despite the Viennese origins of Krenek and Berg and the close connections of Richard Strauss with the Opera House. What was a world première was Lehár's *Giuditta*, with Richard Tauber, in January 1934; but that was a critical flop.

In the spoken theatre there were various controversial attempts to introduce contemporary drama and modern techniques, and for much of the 1920s some of the main commercial theatres were in the hands of two outstanding directors, Rudolf Beer and Max Reinhardt.

The contrast between the two was clear from the first. In the autumn of 1922 Reinhardt's company played for a limited season in the Redoutensaal, then newly redecorated; the works they played included Goethe's *Clavigo* and *Stella* and Hofmannsthal's adaptation of a Calderón play, *Dame Kobold*. This coincided with a season of guest performances organized by Beer in the Raimundtheater, in which Karlheinz Martin, one of the leading expressionist producers in Berlin, produced a series of modern dramas (Strindberg, Wedekind, Bronnen), with guest stars including Fritz Kortner (one of many Viennese exiles based in Berlin) and Tilla Durieux, who appeared in Ibsen's *Rosmersholm*. The press were predictably divided between conservative admiration of the elegance and musicality of Reinhardt's productions and disappointment with their old-fashioned character: Oskar Maurus Fontana, for example, comparing Reinhardt's *Clavigo* and *Dame Kobold* with Martin's intensely expressionistic production of Wedekind's *Hidalla* in the Raimundtheater, wrote that with all respect for Reinhardt's career, his effects seemed *passé*, like the Burgtheater style of yesteryear.[28]

Reinhardt's production style, established in Berlin and later in Salzburg, was based on the ensemble principle, the creation of a harmonious team of actors, working in stage settings which used theatrical décor, often combining realistic and fantastic effects, to achieve suggestive symbolism. His recognition of the primacy of the actor was reflected in the billing of his company in the Theater in der Josefstadt from 1924 onwards as 'The Actors in the Theater in der Josefstadt under the Leadership of Max Reinhardt' ('Die Schauspieler im Theater in der Josefstadt unter der Führung von Max Reinhardt'), a formulation that was retained until 1938, though in practice Reinhardt ran the theatre himself only until the summer of 1926. He made full use of modern technical advances, including the revolve and especially electric spotlights. The use of spotlights was by now an established device in expressionist theatre, which Heine, for example, put to good effect in the Burgtheater in collaboration with Roller and others, notably in a *Hamlet* production in 1920; Reinhardt himself had already exploited it in his earlier, more experimental work, as exemplified in the production of Hofmannsthal's *Elektra* seen in Vienna in 1905.

Among Reinhardt's most scathing critics was Karl Kraus. Believing in the creative primacy of language, Kraus demanded fidelity both to the letter and to the spirit of the text performed. His one-man public readings of an international repertoire of drama, including a succession of Nestroy texts, were conceived as 'theatre without décor' ('dekorationsfreies Theater' – from the mid-1920s he used the title 'Theater der Dichtung'). He read in an impassioned style based on his memories of the Burgtheater company of the 1880s,[29] and his readings were intended as a challenge and a corrective both to the postwar Burgtheater and to the elaborate staging characteristic of Reinhardt, which in Kraus's view was allied in the Salzburg Festival to cynical commercialism.[30]

Negotiations between Reinhardt and Heine about some form of collaboration between Reinhardt's company and the Burgtheater continued until January 1921. In November 1920 Hofmannsthal was still confident that *Der Schwierige* would be played there, produced by Reinhardt, the following spring.[31] What was envisaged, as Hofmannsthal told Andrian on 25 January 1921, was an arrangement whereby Reinhardt's company would be 'guests and more-than-guests, with recurring visits and the expectation of exchange visits and so on'.[32] When Wildgans became director of the Burgtheater in

February 1921, he was confronted with a firm agreement, reached by Heine the previous month; and one of his first tasks was to reverse it. He was willing to see Reinhardt working in the Burgtheater as a producer, but was opposed to productions using the whole of his company because it would have the effect of downgrading the resident company, most of whom, moreover, were bitterly opposed to the scheme.[33] The result was that Wildgans saw himself, so he told Schnitzler a year later, as facing a clique, headed by Hofmannsthal, bent in effect on belittling the Burgtheater in their support of Reinhardt.[34] Reinhardt did conclude a contract for summer productions in the Redoutensaal, but when Paulsen succeeded Wildgans he made it a condition of his appointment that that agreement too be cancelled.[35]

Once all the attempts to bring Reinhardt to the Burgtheater had broken down, the Theater in der Josefstadt, which became available when Jarno ran into financial difficulties, offered him an attractive alternative. It had excellent acoustics, and was well situated within walking distance of the Ringstrasse. With substantial financial backing from a wealthy banker, Camillo Castiglioni, he had the premises (essentially Kornhäusel's 1822 building) reconstructed and refurbished, and reopened the theatre in 1924, its new elegance proclaiming the elitist character of the programme he was launching there. One of the highlights of his first season was the third production, *Der Schwierige*, with Gustav Waldau as Hans Karl, Helene and Hermann Thimig (two of three children of Hugo Thimig who became prominent actors) as Helene Altenwyl and Stani respectively, and Egon Friedell as the academic celebrity Professor Brücke. In the event Reinhardt was unable to resist the lure of Berlin, and after the summer of 1926 returned increasingly to working there; nevertheless, he produced some two dozen plays in the Josefstadt between 1924 and 1937, and he also left a lasting monument in the Max-Reinhardt-Seminar, an acting school which he opened in Schönbrunn in 1928.

Whereas Reinhardt brought a ready-made team of actors to Vienna (to which he was able to add further big names, including Hans Moser, perhaps the most popular Viennese comic actor of his generation), Rudolf Beer, taking over an operetta theatre in the Raimundtheater, had to build a new company from scratch. Among the older actors he engaged in his early years there was Willy Thaller, who had been the leading Nestroy actor in the Deutsches Volkstheater just before the war; among the younger actors Heinrich

Schnitzler (son of the dramatist) and two of the great names of the post-1945 theatre, Paula Wessely and Karl Paryla. Paryla was a member of Beer's company for two seasons (1924–6), acting in productions by Beer and Martin both in the Raimundtheater and in the Deutsches Volkstheater, and appearing with visiting stars, including Alexander Moissi and Elisabeth Bergner.

Beer enjoyed considerable prestige from the 'literary' quality of the programme he put on in the Raimundtheater, especially at the beginning of his direction. It was here that he produced the première of Hofmannsthal's *Der Unbestechliche*, starring Max Pallenberg, in 1923. (This was the season before the Theater in der Josefstadt reopened under Reinhardt, and Hofmannsthal offered the play to Beer with Reinhardt's agreement.)[36]

Beer's determination to produce modern drama was clear in his very first season in the Raimundtheater, which included premières of plays by Georg Kaiser (*David und Goliath*) and Werfel (*Bocksgesang*). Vienna was resistant to the kind of avant-garde experimentation associated with Berlin, and had not proved propitious ground for expressionist drama. This is reflected, for example, in a revealing passage in Polgar's review of a production of Hasenclever's *Der Sohn* in the Volksbühne (Neubaugasse): the play had, he reported, the reputation of being an 'expressionist' work, but though the term aroused prejudices it was worth fighting them.[37] After the war the prejudice was clearly manifest in the failure in December 1919 of Ernst Weiss's *Tanja* in the Deutsches Volkstheater by contrast with the enthusiastic reception of a production in Prague two months earlier.[38] Some of the most conspicuous controversies of the 1920s continued to centre on works by authors who were or had been associated with expressionism. The première of Werfel's *Spiegelmensch*, produced by Herterich in the Burgtheater in April 1920, took place with extra police on duty as a precaution against possible unrest.[39] When Hasenclever's comedy *Ehen werden im Himmel geschlossen*, which had already been performed with success in Berlin, went into rehearsal in the Theater in der Josefstadt in 1929, with Hugo Thimig in the role of the Lord, the *Reichspost* campaigned against the performance of such 'blasphemy', reporting a sermon preached against the play by the Archbishop of Vienna, Cardinal Piffl; as a result the production was dropped.[40]

When Wildgans, who was known as a dramatist on the fringes of expressionism, and whose *Dies irae* had been the second new production of Heine's period as director of the Burgtheater (February 1919), was appointed to succeed Heine, it looked like another programmatic adjustment to modernity; but he lasted only eighteen months (the première of *Spiegelmensch* was the second-last production of his régime), and the theatres where not just expressionism but also other kinds of adventurous contemporary writing were most consistently cultivated were the Neue Wiener Bühne under Siegfried Geyer, and Beer's theatres until Karlheinz Martin returned to Berlin as director of the Volksbühne in 1929. The programme of the Neue Wiener Bühne included standard expressionist works – in 1923, for example, Hasenclever's *Der Sohn*, produced by Geyer in April with Ernst Deutsch in the title part (a production whose significance was strongly underlined by Polgar),[41] and Sternheim's *Die Hose* in December, and also a number of works by Karl Kraus: the première of the epilogue to *Die letzten Tage der Menschheit* in a charity performance in February 1923, and the following year, imported from Berlin with the support of the Social Democrat *Kunststelle*, Berthold Viertel's production of *Traumtheater* and *Traumstück*, the performers including not only Lothar Müthel, who would become director of the Burgtheater during the Second World War, but also the cabaret artist Karl Farkas and (not named in the programme) Kraus himself.[42]

In the autumn of 1924 Vienna hosted a Festival of Music and Theatre which had been organized by David Josef Bach, the leader of the Social Democrat *Kunststelle*, and which was opened on 14 September by the Social Democrat Mayor, Karl Seitz. It was as part of this festival that *Die glückliche Hand* was given its première in the Volksoper; other new productions included the first performance in Vienna of Georg Kaiser's *Kolportage* (Deutsches Volkstheater, 26 September), a Burgtheater production in the Redoutensaal of Hofmannsthal's adaptation of *Le Bourgeois gentilhomme*, with Thaller in the title role (1 October), and the première of Schnitzler's *Komödie der Verführung* (Burgtheater, 11 October), with Raoul Aslan, a future director of the theatre, as Falkenir – according to Musil the saving grace of an affected production.[43]

A feature of the festival was an International Exhibition of New Theatre Technique, designed in the Konzerthaus by Friedrich Kiesler, part of which illustrated experimental developments in stage design unfamiliar in Vienna. The catalogue included an attack on the traditional box-like proscenium structure with fixed painted sets, and argued for its replacement by a more flexible *Raumbühne*, a raised stage without traditional walls, on which the public looked down from raked seats and which provided an expansible space allowing for more versatile forms of theatre.[44] Among the opposition that Kiesler's initiative attracted was a public lecture entitled 'Clarification' given by Kraus on 5 October, in which he rejected all the tricks adopted by 'the pretentious omnipotence usurped by the producer' ('alles Getue einer usurpierten Regieallmacht') as typical modern nonsense derived from the *Kitsch* of the arts and crafts movement. The next day the *Neue Freie Presse* carried an open letter signed by Martin, Fontana, and others, congratulating the organizers of the festival on mounting the exhibition. On 9 November Kraus returned to the attack in a further lecture dismissing Martin's approach as 'Berlin humbug'.[45] Shortly after the festival, Martin produced Wedekind's *Franziska* in the Raimundtheater, with Tilla Durieux in the title role, an example of 'constructivist' theatre on a stage without traditional décor, exploiting various fashionable devices of experimental theatre, including a jazz-band on stage.[46]

This production is one that Beer put on in both his theatres, moving it in February 1925 to the Deutsches Volkstheater, which he had taken over the previous year and to which he subsequently devoted most of his time. Because ultra-modern and avant-garde drama did not square with the history and traditional appeal of the Deutsches Volkstheater, the Raimundtheater remained the principal centre of experimental drama, with Martin functioning as chief producer (*Oberspielleiter*) from the 1924–5 season and as deputy director in 1925–6. During the 1926–7 season, when Marischka was co-director of the Raimundtheater, Beer worked almost entirely in the Deutsches Volkstheater, and was criticized for allowing the Raimundtheater to 'sink' back into being no more than an operetta theatre.[47] But in June 1928 he resumed his function as the sole director of the Raimundtheater, and from 1928 to 1931 (when he also took over the Kammerspiele in the Rotenturmstrasse) he ran the two theatres as a single company.

One way in which Beer's programme in the late 1920s contrasted with the bland fare of the operetta theatres was by cultivating dialect drama. One of the companies that had been keeping dialect drama alive was that of Ferdinand Exl, which was based in Innsbruck but had been appearing since 1907 in summer seasons in Vienna, mainly in the operetta theatres: the Raimundtheater (1907, 1913, 1916, 1917,

1919, 1921, 1924), the Johann-Strauss-Theater (1910), the Theater an der Wien (1911, 1912, 1913, 1920), the Volksoper (1918, 1919, 1920), the Wiener Stadttheater (1920), and the Apollotheater (1923). Exl's company specialized in dialect plays in rural settings, including Anzengruber and especially Schönherr. After Beer had taken over the Raimundtheater, they not only appeared as a guest company in summer 1924: Beer twice appointed Exl as artistic director during the four seasons 1927–31, though outside the summer months the experiment did not prove very popular. Beer's achievements lie rather in his success in mounting productions of modern and experimental drama. Gotthard Böhm has argued that it is the failure of the Neue Wiener Bühne to maintain a programme of contemporary theatre financed by performances by visiting stars, and the succumbing of that theatre to the general rash of closures in the First Republic, that effectively spelled the end of fully unsubsidized independent theatre in Austria.[48] But the true end came later, when in 1932 Beer accepted an appointment to Berlin to run the Deutsches Theater, jointly with Karlheinz Martin. (The following year he returned to Vienna, intending to set up a new dialect theatre in the Johann-Strauss-Theater.) He too had at his peak maintained a mixed repertory combining modern classics (Ibsen, Strindberg, etc.) and examples of the best of contemporary dramatic literature with profitable entertainment, often with guest stars. Notable productions in the Deutsches Volkstheater had included Shaw's *St Joan*, produced by Martin in 1924; Wedekind's *Frühlings Erwachen* with Paula Wessely in March 1928; Schnitzler's last play, *Im Spiel der Sommerlüfte*, with Moissi in December 1929; and one year later Beer's production of Ferdinand Bruckner's *Elisabeth von England*, an example of a vogue for historical drama characteristic of the late 1920s and early 1930s. And towards the end of his direction the Raimundtheater also saw the only Horváth production in a major Viennese theatre during the dramatist's lifetime, *Italienische Nacht* (5 July 1931), and also the first Viennese performance of Brecht's *Mahagonny* in April 1932.

3. AUSTRO-FASCISM AND ANSCHLUSS

The political climate, increasingly dominated in the 1920s and early 1930s by the Christian Social party with the support of pan-German nationalists and the Heimwehr, was inevitably reflected in the Burgtheater. When Wildgans was persuaded against his better

judgement to take over the direction in 1930 again in succession to
Herterich, it was because the then Minister for Education, Heinrich
von Srbik, an established Austrian historian and convinced pan-
German nationalist, was impressed by his 'Rede über Österreich',
and saw the possibility of an essentially patriotic appointment: when
congratulating him, he repeated his 'firm conviction' that no one else
was so ideally suited to fulfil the 'sublime cultural mission of the
Burgtheater as the poet of whom Austria is so proud'.[49] In a tough
economic climate, and in competition both with the Theater in der
Josefstadt and with Beer's theatres, Wildgans tried hard to modernize
the repertoire: it was important, he told Werfel, that the writers
whose cause he was supporting must not let him down.[50] Experimental productions of modern drama were launched in the Akademietheater ('Burgtheaterstudio im Akademietheater'); these would
be continued until 1935. But political tensions increased, and anti-
Semitism was still a major factor in the reception of dramatists such
as Werfel and Schnitzler. From the National Socialist viewpoint,
Wildgans's programme was such as to find favour only with the
'Jewish press';[51] when he agreed to a production of Schnitzler's *Der
Gang zum Weiher* in the Burgtheater, Schnitzler half-expected anti-
Semitic protests to prevent the performance.[52]

Wildgans's second spell in office again lasted only eighteen
months, cut short by ill health. (He died in May 1932, four months
after relinquishing his post.) His successor, Hermann Röbbeling, was
an experienced man of the theatre, who had directed both the
Thalia-Theater and the Deutsches Schauspielhaus in Hamburg. He
modernized practices, and opened up the Burgtheater to more
popular audiences with matinées, a subscription programme for
schools, and an extended repertory of popular classics, showing, as
Herterich recognized, 'everything that had been successful in the
German theatre and all the classics that would repay new productions'[53] – though for the nationalist ideologues this amounted only to
cheap populism, pandering to a corrupt taste; Ernst Lothar, for
example, was invited to produce *König Ottokars Glück und Ende* in
October 1933, but the patriotic Austrian flag-waving of the production was anathema to pan-German thinking, and Röbbeling was
condemned for entrusting Grillparzer productions to the 'Jew'
Lothar.[54] The healthier budget allowed Röbbeling to recruit new
actors, including Hermann Thimig from the Theater in der Josefstadt, and to bring in a number of new producers: these included two

who would become directors of the theatre after the war, Josef Gielen and Adolf Rott.

During Röbbeling's direction, Austria became the 'Corporate State' of Dollfuss and Schuschnigg. With the ending of the party system and the suppression of unions, the actors' professional organization (the 'Bühnenverein') was dissolved and eventually replaced by a guild, the 'Ring der österreichischen Bühnenkünstler', created by Schuschnigg while he was still Minister of Education, and the place of the party *Kunststellen* was taken over by a single national *Kunststelle* set up within the cultural office of the so-called Fatherland Front in order to promote patriotic Austro-German culture by providing low-priced theatre tickets. In 1936 it was augmented by an educational (that is, propaganda) organization called 'Neues Leben', which functioned like the German 'Kraft durch Freude', though less well funded, with membership restricted to members of the Fatherland Front. The monopoly rights of these institutions gave them immense power over the independent theatres, making possible the performance of plays the government wished to promote, such as Hans Naderer's *Lueger der große Österreicher* in the Deutsches Volkstheater (1939), which celebrated the achievements of the founder of the Christian Social party.

After the 1936 July agreement between Austria and Nazi Germany, as part of the Nazis' infiltration of Austrian cultural life and institutions, various groups were founded with the support of pan-German sympathizers to support National Socialist thinking in Austria, including the 'Bund der deutschen Schriftsteller in Österreich', of which Max Mell, a conservative Catholic and former friend of Hofmannsthal's, was appointed chairman, with Mirko Jelusich, a prominent pro-Nazi writer, also on the committee.[55] Another group in which Jelusich was involved, 'Deutsche Bühne', had as its aim the establishment of a 'German' theatre (that is, a theatre free of Jews). The Raimundtheater was available, for no director after Beer had succeeded in running it profitably: Beer's immediate successor had lasted only a year; Carl Rainer Simons, the former director of the Volksoper, then opened a season on 10 November 1933 with a production of Zeller's ever-popular *Der Vogelhändler*, but within a fortnight it closed as the result of a wage dispute. Now it was leased by the 'Deutsche Bühne' group, and Jelusich was designated to run it; but the city administration managed to prevent its opening – avoiding implication in the same mistake as had been made in the creation of the 'Aryan' Kaiserjubiläums-Stadttheater at the end of the nineteenth century, but in National Socialist eyes an act of 'treachery'.[56] By early 1938 there were plans to demolish the Raimundtheater to make way for a garage; it was rescued only by the Anschluss, when it was taken over by the 'Kraft durch Freude' organization, the leisure department of the Deutsche Arbeitsfront.

While the regional drama of the Exl-Bühne continued as before – from 1934 to 1938 Exl leased the Wiener Bürgertheater for four seasons of between four and six months, with Schönherr still central to the programme – in 1935 the direction of the Theater in der Josefstadt passed to Ernst Lothar. The company was full of famous actors whom Reinhardt had helped to develop: Tilla Durieux, Adrienne Gessner, Paula Wessely, Ernst Deutsch, Anton Edthofer, Attila Hörbiger, and Karl Paryla. As a committed communist Paryla had had to return to Austria from Nazi Germany in 1933; his starring roles in Lothar's company included Martin Schalanter in Lothar's production of Anzengruber's *Das vierte Gebot* (1936) and the Elder Brother in a production by Paul Kalbeck of Schönherr's *Kindertragödie* in the Kammerspiele (now affiliated to the Theater in der Josefstadt), also in 1936. Reinhardt himself directed only one more production in the Josefstadt, his last production in Europe, Werfel's *In einer Nacht* (1937).

Lothar's programme was largely orthodox and conformist. For expressions of dissent or politically-charged satire, the Viennese public needed to look not to the major theatres but to cabaret and the small alternative theatres, often in the basements of cafés (*Kellertheater*), with a capacity not in excess of forty-nine seats and so not needing an official theatre licence. The cabaret scene had always been dominated by Jewish artists, the best-known in the 1930s including Fritz Grünbaum and Karl Farkas, who appeared in the 'Simpl' in the Wollzeile (opened in 1912 as the 'Bierkabarett Simplizissimus' and still there today). Literary satire could be found in cabarets such as the 'Lieber Augustin', run by Stella Kadmon in the basement of the Café Prückel on the Stubenring, or 'Literatur am Naschmarkt' in the basement of the Café Dobner, where the contributors to the programme included Hans Weigel and where the best-known play of the left-wing satirist Jura Soyfer, *Der Lechner Edi schaut ins Paradies*, was first performed in 1936.

Fritz Grünbaum appeared in the 'Simpl' for the last time on 10 March 1938, two days before the German invasion of Austria.[57] On

11 March, Zuckmayer's *Bellmann* was in rehearsal in the Theater in der Josefstadt. His memoirs contain a vivid account of the contrast in mood inside and outside the theatre:

On the morning of 11 March I had an experience which had nothing to do with politics and all the more, for that reason, with the imagination, and which in retrospect takes on a tragicomic quality. It was the first full rehearsal of my new play, which was to be produced by Ernst Lothar with the best actors in Vienna, Paula Wessely, Attila Hörbiger, Anton Edthofer. And so it came about that on the morning of the day of disaster a handful of people in the gloom of a dimly-lit playhouse completely forgot the outside world, the political situation, the danger, the crisis on which the fate of us all depended, and for a few hours succumbed completely to the irresistible magic of the theatre, debating and arguing about cuts, positions, alterations, and so on, as though there were nothing more important or of greater consequence in the world. As soon as we left the theatre in the afternoon and stepped out of the artificial light into the dazzling spring sunshine, with paper still whirling about, it was all over. Two hours later, when the sun was setting, Schuschnigg was delivering his last message on the radio: 'I submit to force. May God protect Austria!'...

That evening hell itself broke loose... What was unleashed here was an uprising of envy, of resentment, of bitterness, of blind vindictive malice; and every other voice was condemned to silence... It was a Witches' Sabbath of the rabble, a burial of all the dignity of Man.[58]

After the Anschluss, the whole theatre industry was fully integrated in the cultural politics of the Third Reich (the policy of *Gleichschaltung*). While the Nazis were keen to exploit the reputation of Vienna as a cultural centre, so that subsidies for the state theatres were higher than elsewhere in the Reich, including Berlin,[59] the city was not allowed any independence in the arts (any hint of separatist thinking had to be discouraged). German laws relating to culture and the theatre (the 'Reichskulturkammergesetz' of 1933 and the 'Theatergesetz' of 15 May 1934) were imposed, and all Austrian laws inconsistent with them were annulled. Authority effectively passed to Berlin by July 1938, and the theatre came under the supervision of a department in the Vienna office of the Reich Propaganda Ministry.

Reorganization and 'Aryanization' went ahead very fast. Rolf Jahn, the director of the Deutsches Volkstheater, shed all his Jewish actors on the very day of the Anschluss.[60] Ernst Lothar was forced to resign from the Theater in der Josefstadt; the production of *Bellmann* by the left-wing Zuckmayer never took place. Robert Valberg, who took over administrative control of the theatre on 20 March, was able to announce a complete 'Aryanization' by the end of the month.[61] Meanwhile the first Viennese issue of the *Völkischer Beobachter* on 16 March 1938 had called for the Opera House too to be 'cleansed' of Jewish influence, and in the course of the summer, everyone working in the theatre had to provide documentary evidence of his or her 'Aryan' descent.[62]

The running of the Burgtheater had fallen immediately after the Anschluss in March 1938 to Jelusich – compensation, as it seemed, for the earlier failure to get the planned Aryan theatre in the Raimundtheater off the ground[63] – and by the time he handed over the reins in July he had set in train the addition of suitably *völkisch* dramas to the programme, to replace some of the many pieces, some two-thirds of the repertory,[64] no longer deemed suitable. In the event precisely this company would be joined in 1942 by Horst Caspar, a half-Jewish actor who enjoyed rare special privileges;[65] but in 1938 there were relatively few Jewish actors left in the Burgtheater, so that 'Aryanization' was not regarded as presenting a major problem there.[66] The audience too, however, had to be 'Aryanized', and edicts cancelling Jewish subscriptions were issued in November 1938, when the exclusion of Jews from all theatres, cinemas, and concerts was announced.[67] Earlier that month Jelusich's *Cromwell* had entered the repertory, a prose drama celebrating the idea of strong leadership in the service of a united nation.[68]

Among other measures tying Vienna closer to Germany, and to Berlin in particular, the direction of the Theater in der Josefstadt, which was officially leased by the German Reich, was taken over in September 1938 by Heinz Hilpert, who ran it as a joint venture with the Deutsches Theater in Berlin – the only such pairing, though others were mooted.[69] That summer – a further attempt to cement the unity of pan-German culture – the annual German theatre festival (*Reichstheaterfestwoche*) had been held in Vienna, with performances by visiting companies from Berlin. The festival had been established as an institution in the German Reich since 1934 as an expression of nationalist cultural politics. It opened in Vienna on 12 June, and set in train what was to be a whole series of heavily-subsidized festivals to which the main theatres in Vienna contributed.[70] Among these were a 'Raimund week' in June 1940 (the programme included a public lecture on 'Raimund and the German Nation' given in the Theater in der Josefstadt by the theatre historian Heinz Kindermann, who had just published his monograph, dedicated to the city of Vienna, on Raimund as a 'German folk-dramatist'),[71] a 'Grillparzer week' in January 1941, and a 'Mozart week' in November-December 1941. In June 1944 there was a 'Richard Strauss week' – in fact a Strauss fortnight – in honour of the composer's eightieth birthday, shared between the Opera House and the former Volksoper, which in October 1938 had become a second opera house, the 'Opernhaus der Stadt Wien'. On Strauss's birthday itself Karl Böhm, who had taken over as director of the Opera House at the beginning of the previous year and who was particularly committed to Strauss's operas, conducted a performance of *Ariadne auf Naxos*, with Irmgard Seefried as the Composer. For twenty years Böhm himself, together with Hans Knappertsbusch, was one of the most frequent conductors in the Opera House, and the stability of the company they helped to maintain ensured a continuity of musical standards there, stretching from the mid-1930s to the postwar era.

Under Nazism, experimental theatre, and theatre with any critical function, was impossible, being replaced by old-fashioned theatre of illusion. Theatres were potentially places of propagandist instruction (in the later stages of the war, they served increasingly as bulwarks of the idea of German national culture), but this had to work through the medium of relaxing entertainment: both the Raimundtheater and the Deutsches Volkstheater became 'Kraft durch Freude' theatres, showing operetta and ideologically correct spoken drama respectively. Partly as a concession to local tastes, there were Raimund and Nestroy productions, but throughout this period Nestroy tended often to be reduced to a trivial gaiety at the expense of satirical sharpness; this is most clearly exemplified by the one première in the war years of a hitherto unperformed Nestroy play, a production by Aurel Nowotny of *"Nur keck!"* in 1943 in the Wiener Bürgertheater (which had been reopened under Valberg), in an adaptation by Franz Paul. From a contemporary review it is clear that the text was considerably toned down: the tempo and sparkle of Nestroy's wit had given way to 'a stronger emphasis on Biedermeier cosiness', but the public had 'visibly accepted' this.[72]

The Burgtheater under Lothar Müthel (introduced as director from Berlin) concentrated on orthodox performances of the classics, creating a reassuring sense of secure continuity. And the policy worked; attendances rose. In the second edition of his history of the Burgtheater, Kindermann could point to a 20 per cent rise in attendance in the three years following the Anschluss.[73] This was partly a result of closed performances for the armed forces and munitions workers, but it produced correspondingly high returns: in the four years 1938–42 takings in the state theatres covered up to half of outgoings (the figures ranged between 30 per cent and 58 per cent) – an outcome that can be compared with a typical figure of barely more than 20 per cent in the last twenty years or so.[74] The Opernhaus der Stadt Wien, which offered a standard opera repertory plus operetta and ballet, similarly enjoyed a period of considerable success (99 per cent of the seats were sold in 1942).[75] And in the Wiener Bürgertheater, the production of *"Nur keck!"* ran for no fewer than 355 performances.

Beneath the surface of successful entertainment, however, the theatrical life of Vienna had been impoverished by the Anschluss and the loss not just of those with left-wing sympathies but above all of the Jewish talent that had still been at the heart of much of the most creative work in the era of Dollfuss and Schuschnigg. Many individual careers were interrupted, many lives lost. Space allows only a few representative examples, drawn from names that have already been mentioned in the last two chapters. Among those who took their own lives in 1938 were Rudolf Beer (after being harrassed by the SA) and Egon Friedell (escaping arrest). Among those who died in concentration camps were Jura Soyfer (in Buchenwald in 1939, at the age of twenty-six) and Fritz Grünbaum (in Dachau in 1941). Among the many prominent figures who fled into exile were writers and dramatists, including Molnár, Werfel, Roda Roda, Weigel, Polgar, Salten, and Auernheimer (the latter after first undergoing six months' imprisonment in Dachau); composers, including Emmerich Kálmán, Oscar Straus, Ralph Benatzky, Robert Stolz, Fritz Kreisler, and Erich Wolfgang Korngold; also Alfred Grünwald, the librettist of *Gräfin Mariza*, *Die gold'ne Meisterin*, and *Die Zirkusprinzessin*; producers, including Reinhardt and Ernst Lothar, together with their actress wives, Helene Thimig and Adrienne Gessner; also Heinrich Schnitzler. Performers to be exiled included Elisabeth Bergner, Fritz Kortner (who had returned to Vienna from Germany in 1933), Richard Tauber, Karl Farkas, Stella Kadmon, Ernst Deutsch, and Hans Jaray. Among others associated with Reinhardt's company, Leopold Lindtberg became one of the principal producers at the Schauspielhaus in Zürich. Karl Paryla, who had been objected to by the Swiss authorities in 1936 as an undesirable alien but was allowed to come subject to his abstaining from political activity,[76] also left in 1938 for Zürich, where Austrian works were strongly represented in the repertory and where his fellow-actors included his brother Emil Stöhr and Wolfgang Heinz, both of whom would join him in playing a significant role in the regeneration of theatre in Vienna after the war.

CHAPTER 9

The Second Republic

I. POSTWAR REBUILDING

In the summer of 1944, the President of the Reichskulturkammer issued an order to the effect that as part of the total national commitment to the war effort all theatres were to close: when the new season should have opened at the beginning of September, they all remained dark. By the time of the reopening eight months later, a great deal of damage had been inflicted in the final stages of the war.

The Opera House was bombed on 12 March 1945: the front of the building with the great stairway was not hit, but the auditorium, stage, and workshops were destroyed. The Burgtheater too suffered bomb damage, but was still usable until, unconnected with military action, fire broke out in the stage area on 12 April 1945, and the stage and auditorium were burnt out. The Deutsches Volkstheater was also damaged, but in this case the stage and auditorium escaped (what suffered most was the façade, the foyer, and the cupola), and it could reopen in June.

No sooner had Vienna fallen to the advancing Russian army and a new provisional government been set up at the end of April than the reshaping of theatrical life began. As after the First World War, there were many practical problems to be overcome: public transport services and street lighting were only partly working, and there was a night-time curfew, so that performances had to begin in the late afternoon. Both the Akademietheater and the Volksoper were undamaged and were able to open on 1 May, the latter (now a state theatre, at first still called 'Opernhaus der Stadt Wien') housing the company of the Opera House, who opened the season with a performance of *The Marriage of Figaro*, with Irmgard Seefried as Susanna and Sena Jurinac making her début as Cherubino. The Opera House company played in the Volksoper throughout 1945, including, exceptionally, the whole summer, and in the autumn were able to move into a second house as well. Unused since 1939, the Theater an der Wien had been purchased by the city in June 1940; now it was ceremonially reopened on 6 October, with a performance of *Fidelio*, under the baton of Josef Krips. The Opera House company remained in occupation of both theatres until 1955; they were, however, administered separately from September 1946 onwards. In the 'Staatsoper in der Volksoper', directed until 1955 by Hermann Juch, the programme was a mix of opera and traditional operetta – in effect a new attempt to create a Viennese *Opéra-Comique*. The main base was the Theater an der Wien, where Franz Salmhofer functioned as director from 1945 onwards. This is remembered as a period of classic Mozart productions by Oscar Fritz Schuh, conducted by Krips, and sung – in a house which, being smaller than the Opera House, lent itself much better to Mozart than to Wagner or Strauss – by an ensemble including Erich Kunz (the definitive Papageno of his generation), Irmgard Seefried, Elisabeth Schwarzkopf, and Wilma Lipp. In the ten years the company were exiled from the Opera House, Wilma Lipp sang the Queen of the Night 124 times, Erich Kunz sang Papageno 81 times, Leporello 111 times, and Figaro 146 times, Irmgard Seefried sang Susanna 99 times, and Sena Jurinac sang Cherubino 118 times.[1]

One of the features of the resumption of theatrical life in 1945 was a concern to establish links with the specifically Viennese traditions of the past, to reassert a continuity interrupted by the years of Nazi rule. This is evidenced in the choice of *The Marriage of Figaro* for the first opera performance on 1 May, and by the choice of *Fidelio* for the reopening of the Theater an der Wien, where it had been first performed 140 years earlier. One of the first new productions in the Volkstheater (as the erstwhile Deutsches Volkstheater was now called) was *Des Meeres und der Liebe Wellen* in June; in September the Theater in der Josefstadt presented a new production of *Der Schwierige*. The Burgtheater also acted to preserve its traditions. Eight days after the fire, Raoul Aslan was elected to succeed Müthel as director, and he held the office for three years – one of many examples of a long tradition in the Burgtheater of renewal from within: he had been a member of the company since 1920, playing a series of leading roles, including Rudolf I in Ernst Lothar's 1933 production of *König Ottokars Glück und Ende*. Now, serving without any increase in salary beyond what he was entitled to as an actor,[2] he supervised the resumption of the programme both in the Ronacher, which was taken over as the main house, and in the Akademietheater (with the Redoutensaal being added as a third stage in the autumn). In the Ronacher, which had started life as Laube's Stadttheater, the Burgtheater too reached back to the Austrian past: the first performances were of *Sappho*, played before a simple black backcloth because the old sets had been destroyed; the first new production, with Aslan in the title role and Müthel as producer, was Hofmannsthal's *Jedermann* (13 June 1945): once neglected by the Burgtheater, *Jedermann* was performed 105 times in ten seasons, the fifth most frequently performed piece in the repertory in that time. In the same period Nestroy was the second most frequently performed dramatist in the Burgtheater, headed only by Shakespeare; and the reassertion of national tradition was reflected throughout the Viennese theatres in a sustained upsurge of productions of Grillparzer, Raimund, and especially of Nestroy, classics of specifically Austrian theatre.

Both the Burgtheater and the Opera House had to be rebuilt. This process was overseen by Egon Hilbert, a lawyer and experienced administrator who, having spent the war years as a prisoner in Dachau, served as director of the administration of the state theatres (*Bundestheaterverwaltung*) from autumn 1945 until 1953. The opportunity was taken to introduce radical technical innovations, designed by the technical directors of the two theatres. In both, new turntables were installed and also machinery for raising and lowering the stage, facilitating rapid scene shifts. The Opera House stage area was extended, making it one of the biggest in Europe, and the equipment there did not need a major overhaul again until 1994. In both houses the auditorium was completed in a plainer style, but a conscious gesture to tradition in the Burgtheater was the preservation at first-floor level of the *Festfoyer* with portraits of famous past members of the company: this gallery, together with a second foyer above with more recent portraits, is still in place today.

The Burgtheater, its seating capacity increased by the modernizations from 1,256 to 1,310 (but the standing places reduced from 334 to 210, an overall decrease in capacity of 70), was reopened on 14 October 1955, the Opera House just over three weeks later, on 5 November. It was the year in which Austria's independence had been re-established by the occupying powers; in the Burgtheater, the patriotism of the hour linked with the traditionalism of the theatre in the opening production by Adolf Rott (director since the previous season) of *König Ottokars Glück und Ende*, with the famous speech by Ottokar von Horneck in the third act in praise of Austria spoken by Aslan. This production is the most studied example of the process of reconstructing a national cultural identity. The effect of the conscious emphasis on a distinctively separate 'Austrianness' was that, despite the return to the Burgtheater building on the Ringstrasse, the theatre was in danger of developing a rather provincial quality; and this was not wholly dispelled when Rott was succeeded by Ernst Haeussermann (director from 1959 to 1968), who maintained a strong emphasis on Austrian material (including productions of Raimund with sets by Kokoschka, and no fewer than eight new Grillparzer productions).

The provincialism was part and parcel of the cultural ambience of the time, and was borne out in the mixed reception given to a sharply stylized production by Rudolf Steinboeck of Nestroy's *Der Talisman*, which was first shown at the Bregenz Festival in the summer of 1962 and then in the Akademietheater. With black-and-white décor and costumes, it aimed for a marionette-like effect in the characterization, with Heinrich Schweiger as Titus projecting an aggressiveness which had not otherwise been seen in Nestroy in Vienna since the left-wing productions that had been mounted in the late 1940s and early 1950s in the Neues Theater in der Scala (see below, pp. 235–6) and in some productions by Gustav Manker in the Volkstheater.[3]

There was no risk of provincialism in the Opera House, where Herbert von Karajan became 'artistic director' (*Künstlerischer Leiter*) in 1956 in succession to Böhm, who had been much criticized for protracted absences abroad. Karajan remained as sole director for seven years, then served for one further uneasy year in partnership with Hilbert as co-director, before finally resigning in June 1964.[4] He re-established the Opera House as the unique institution it has remained: open three hundred days a year, with the largest company in the world; still operating a repertory system (rehearsals have to be over by 3 p.m. each day to allow for the décor for the evening's performance to be set up); with a distinctive atmosphere partly attributable to the 567 standing places, eagerly sought after by students especially; and with an orchestra drawn from the members of the Vienna Philharmonic Orchestra. Though Karajan's appearances were limited by his many international commitments, the orchestra played under his baton as it did for no other conductor, and if it was not a time of great new operas, the repertory was enriched by fine new productions both of Italian opera and most notably of Wagner. In all Karajan undertook new productions of seven Wagner operas, including *Tristan und Isolde* in 1959 and the entire *Ring* cycle (1957–60), with a company including Birgit Nilsson, Wolfgang Windgassen, and Hans Hotter.

No director of the Opera House since Mahler had provoked such controversy as Karajan. He had recognized that recordings and television had established a demand for international stars, and that in the age of air travel it was possible to meet this demand. Consequently the company could no longer remain static but must draw in stars from abroad as required.[5] Karajan was reproached for having destroyed the cohesion of the company; but the principle of a coherent 'ensemble' was not restored either in the four years in which Hilbert remained in sole charge as director (1964–8) or under a series of successors, and though it was a task to which Eberhard Waechter committed himself when he was appointed to take over in 1991,[6] he died suddenly in March 1992 and so was unable to see through his plans beyond the first year.

Waechter's plans had included rationalizing the organization of the Opera House and the Volksoper, which he had directed since 1987, bringing them together under a unified direction to ensure maximum cooperation. After the reopening of the Staatsoper, the Volksoper had been directed first by Franz Salmhofer and then from 1963 to 1973 by Albert Moser. A successful production of *Kiss me Kate!* in 1956 had prompted the idea of making it a theatre specializing in musicals; but in the event operetta continued to be the main fare, in a programme which also included popular and also relatively rare operas. This mixture continued under Karl Dönch (director from 1973 to 1987) and under Waechter. Under Dönch, who had been a member of the Staatsoper company since 1947 and remained a soloist in both houses, the adventurous operatic productions included Britten's *Albert Herring* with Sena Jurinac in 1976 and a revival of Zemlinsky's *Kleider machen Leute* in 1985, seventy-five years after its première in the same theatre; and the operettas – some with distinguished soloists such as Lucia Popp, Waechter, and Dönch himself – were supplemented by a number of productions of modern musicals, part of a growing vogue in Vienna: in 1979 *My Fair Lady* (a work with music by a native Viennese, Frederick Loewe), with

Dagmar Koller as Eliza and Heinrich Schweiger as Doolittle; in 1982 *Kiss me Kate!*, starring Dagmar Koller, and *West Side Story* (both with texts adapted by Marcel Prawy, the historian of the Opera House); in 1984 *Hello Dolly!*, again with Dagmar Koller – the last of especial interest in Vienna as the material goes back to Thornton Wilder's adaptation of Nestroy's *Einen Jux will er sich machen*.

Outside the state theatres the operatic diet was extended by the launching in 1953 of a new chamber opera company, the Kammeroper, founded and directed for four decades until his death in 1994 by Hans Gabor. This company performed at first in the Schönbrunner Schlosstheater during the summers, but since 1961 they have had their own permanent theatre in the city centre, just off the Fleischmarkt. Specializing mainly in eighteenth-century and early nineteenth-century *Singspiele* and comic operas (including, for example, a production of Wenzel Müller's *Kaspar der Fagottist* in 1970), they provide a deliberate contrast to the grand opera of the two state-owned companies.

In the spoken theatre, a new generation of actors quickly blended with those who had stayed through the war years and those returning from exile. Some of the most powerful productions of the first twenty years or so after the war centred on partnerships between older and newer stars: Hans Moser as Weiring and a compellingly natural young actress, Inge Konradi, as Christine in *Liebelei* in the Burgtheater in 1954 – 'no one of feeling will ever forget the last great scene between Moser and Konradi', wrote Hans Weigel[7] – or again Moser with Hans Putz (who had been a junior member of the Zürich company during the war) and now proved himself Moser's 'ideal partner'[8] in *Höllenangst* in the Theater in der Josefstadt in 1961. There was soon a lively mix of conservatism and experiment on offer, commented on by a new generation of watchful critics, including Friedrich Torberg and Hans Weigel, both returned from exile. Familiar plays took on new significance: the Jewish hero of Schnitzler's *Professor Bernhardi*, for example, played in the Renaissancebühne in the Neubaugasse in 1947 by Ernst Deutsch, seemed, as Fontana wrote, to 'stand for the hundreds of thousands coming after him who went to the gas chambers if they were not able to save themselves by fleeing'.[9] The works of contemporary dramatists – Dürrenmatt, Frisch, the late plays of Brecht – were discovered, and frequently led to controversy. In the general mood of patriotism, it is perhaps not surprising that when Gustav Manker produced Horváth's bitterly satirical *Geschichten aus dem Wiener Wald*, never before seen in Vienna, in the Volkstheater in 1948, with Inge Konradi as Marianne, it met with incomprehension and rejection;[10] nor that after the restoration in 1955 of Austrian independence in a Europe in which the country bordered to north, east, and south on Communist states, Brecht seemed ideologically suspect.[11]

Many of the more adventurous productions, both of new plays and of old plays rediscovered, took place in small basement theatres. These blossomed again in the postwar years, as did cabarets, with performers often appearing in both. The best-known product of the cabaret of the time is the monologue 'Der Herr Karl' by Helmut Qualtinger and Carl Merz, which provoked a furore of outrage in November 1961 when it was first performed on television by Qualtinger, one of many prominent actors who also appeared in the alternative theatres. These became eligible for subsidy in 1950, and some would prove tenaciously long-lived: the Theater der Courage, for example, a continuation of the Lieber Augustin (it was rechristened only in 1948) which was reopened in 1945, directed for a season from September 1946 by Merz, and then from the following season onwards by Stella Kadmon again; or the Tribüne, which opened in 1953 in the basement of the Café Landtmann on the Ringstrasse, just north of the Burgtheater, and which is still in being. In these small theatres, which could not count on a regular subscribing public, young actors launched their careers, and young producers had more freedom to experiment than in the big established theatres, where there was more at stake in terms both of finances and of publicity: it was precisely for that reason that Leon Epp, the director of the Volkstheater from 1952 to 1968, encouraged one such aspiring producer to stick to working in smaller theatres.[12] Epp had opened a small theatre, the 'Insel', in October 1945 in the premises of the former Modernes Theater in the Johannesgasse, where an ambitious programme included works by various contemporary playwrights. In 1948 he also took over the Renaissancebühne in the Neubaugasse, and put on lighter entertainment there, but it made a loss and Epp had to give up the direction in 1949; in 1957 the premises were taken over by a youth theatre, the Theater der Jugend. Two years after the Insel folded (it was turned into a cinema in 1950) Epp became director of the Volkstheater, where in 1954 a new venture, 'Volkstheater in den Außenbezirken', was launched with financial support both from the city and from the trade unions:

productions toured the outlying districts to play in halls in cinemas, further education colleges, community centres, and the like, a scheme that is still flourishing.

The most adventurous of the larger postwar theatres associated with contemporary drama was the Neues Theater in der Scala, which opened in 1948 in the former Johann-Strauss-Theater in the Favoritenstrasse with a production of Karl Paryla's adaptation of Nestroy's *Höllenangst*, including the famous 'Schicksalsmonolog' which Nestroy drafted in manuscript but did not include in any of his finished plays.[13] Paryla had returned to Vienna and had played the title part in a production of Raimund's *Der Barometermacher auf der Zauberinsel* in March 1946 in the Volkstheater, with Inge Konradi also in the cast; he had then returned to the Theater in der Josefstadt, where he played the leading role in Nestroy's *Der Talisman* that October. He was one of the leading spirits in planning a new democratically-run theatre which he conceived of as an actors' co-operative, aiming at a working-class public, who had never been attracted into the orthodox established theatres with their smartly-dressed audiences.[14] The venture was in effect a would-be educational theatre run by Marxist idealists. When a licence was granted to Wolfgang Heinz to open the theatre in April 1948, the *Arbeiter-Zeitung* reported simply that from 1 September the Scala would be a 'communist propaganda theatre'.[15] Though Heinz was the official licence-holder, the plan was to run it as a society, with the public organized as 'friends of the theatre'. By 1956 there were some eight thousand members, enjoying reduced prices (reduced, moreover, on prices that were in any case some 30–40 per cent lower than in other Viennese theatres); in the 1954–5 season a subscription scheme was also introduced for young persons and students, providing admission at 25 per cent of the box-office price so that they could attend performances for less than the price of a cinema seat.[16] Though finances made it impossible to modernize the theatre thoroughly – the stage was increased in size, and new spotlights were added, but the revolve that Beer had installed in 1933 was not restored to use[17] – an ambitious programme of high quality was maintained. Highlights included a production by Leopold Lindtberg of Brecht's *Mutter Courage* with Therese Giehse in 1948; Paryla's production of Beaumarchais's *Marriage of Figaro* in March 1950, with Paryla himself as Figaro and the young Heinrich Schweiger as Chérubin; visiting performances by the Berliner Ensemble in September of that same year; the first performance in Austria of Brecht's *Die Mutter* in 1953, produced by Manfred Wekwerth in collaboration with Brecht, with Helene Weigel in the title role; and a number of outstanding Nestroy productions, including one by Emil Stöhr of *Einen Jux will er sich machen* in 1952 with Paryla as Weinberl. Despite the quality and the novelty of the programme, the survival of the theatre was often under threat. In September 1950 it was one of five theatres to receive a grant from the city (the others were the Volkstheater, the Theater in der Josefstadt, the Raimundtheater, and the Insel) but though it attracted audiences nearly as big as those in the Josefstadt, it was playing well below its capacity (partly because of inadequate coverage in the anti-communist press), and in July 1951 its grant was stopped. It was not restored until 1955, and even then it was kept comparatively low (60,000 Schilling by comparison with 420,000 and 390,000 Schilling for the Raimundtheater and the Volkstheater respectively).[18] Despite constant support from Viktor Matejka, the City Councillor responsible for cultural affairs (the one Communist councillor, a survivor of Dachau), the licence was renewed only a year at a time, and the theatre finally closed at the end of June 1956, the last production having been Brecht's *Leben des Galilei*, with Paryla as Galileo. The building was demolished the same year. The site was eventually bought by the city; it stood empty until 1977, and in the end flats were built on it.

The Neues Theater in der Scala was only one casualty in a new wave of demolitions. Another famous name to go was the Carltheater. Closed since 1929 and bombed in 1944, the building was finally demolished in 1951. The Wiener Bürgertheater was reopened after the war, with Franz Stoss as director of a strong company, drawn mainly from the Theater in der Josefstadt and including actors who became household names to the modern theatre-going public (Heinz Conrads, Kurt Sowinetz, Vilma Degischer). The accent was mainly on dialect drama including comedy. In 1948 there were 414 performances, including matinées, with a total attendance of just over 214,000; but that represented only 42 per cent of the capacity, slightly below the percentage attained by the Neues Theater in der Scala in 1955.[19] The theatre closed in 1953, and after being used as a radio studio in 1954, it was acquired by a bank and demolished in January 1959. The Wiener Stadttheater in the eighth district (which functioned after the war as a theatre for American troops, the 'Rextheater', then from 1956–7 onwards as a television studio) was demolished in 1961. Other theatres under threat included the Theater an der Wien following its closure in 1955 and again in the mid-1960s, the Raimundtheater, which was nearly demolished in 1967 to make way for a garage, and the Ronacher in the late 1970s and early 1980s.

Amid all the signs of retrenchment, a major boost was given to the performing arts by the growth of the Vienna Festival, which takes place every year in May and June. Egon Hilbert was appointed general manager (*Intendant*) of the festival in 1960, and in that capacity he superintended the renovation and reopening of the Theater an der Wien, which had been rescued from demolition when it was purchased by the city of Vienna. A lot of building work was needed to prevent it falling into a state of ruin like the Carltheater. The auditorium, including the ceiling, was carefully restored to preserve the sensitive acoustics; the improvement of the stage by the addition of a revolve meant rebuilding down to the foundations.[20] The planning of the technical modernization was entrusted to Sepp Nordegg, who had also designed the postwar refurbishment of the stage machinery in the Burgtheater. On 28 May 1962 the Theater an der Wien reopened, and again tradition was served: the first opera to be performed, two days later, was *Die Zauberflöte*, under Karajan, with a cast including both Kunz and Wilma Lipp; eight days later the Burgtheater followed with a production by Lindtberg of *Das Mädl aus der Vorstadt*, performed in the theatre where it had first been seen in 1841; and two days after that, as a Festival production, came the first Austrian performance – six years before the Opera House – of Alban Berg's *Lulu*, produced by Otto Schenk and conducted by Böhm.

2. THE PRESENT

It is always difficult to provide a balanced overview of the current theatre scene, not least because any account is bound to be overtaken by events. To avoid getting bogged down in the kind of ephemeral detail that a comprehensive coverage of the developments in the 1990s would entail, I shall concentrate on outlining three significant aspects of the contemporary scene: the controversial state of affairs in the Burgtheater; examples of innovative new theatres; and the rise of the musical.

By the end of the 1960s, more than half of the Burgtheater's

regular subscribing audience was over fifty.[21] The theatre's appeal
urgently needed to be updated. Gerhard Klingenberg, who took
over as director in 1971 and remained in post for five years, adopted
the strategy of importing visiting international directors; but what
had worked with singers in the Opera House was far more risky in
the Burgtheater, where what was sacrificed was expert control of the
quality of speaking. There had already been danger signals, as when
Ernst Lothar's production of *Der Schwierige* was taken to the Bregenz
Festival in 1963 and a south German reviewer commented that the
Burgtheater's reputation as the guardian of spoken stage German
seemed shaky.[22] During Klingenberg's spell as director, the decline
in the quality of speaking was unmistakable, disrupting a long
tradition in which the cultivation of language had been central. The
same period saw an understandable reaction against the concentration on the Austrian classics in the mid-1950s, a tendency which was
not reversed under Klingenberg's successor as director, Achim
Benning, and which has been exacerbated into neglect under Claus
Peymann, who took over in 1986.

Previously director of the Schauspielhaus in Bochum, Peymann
brought with him a team of *Dramaturgen* in place of the established
staff (one of whom, Reinhard Urbach, went on to take over the
direction of the Theater der Jugend, based in the Neubaugasse).
Discontent in the acting company broke out into the open in the
early summer of 1988 following the publication in the Hamburg
weekly *Die Zeit* on 27 May of an interview Peymann had given to a
journalist, André Müller. There was a complete breakdown in
relations between Peymann and the elected representatives of the
company (*Ensemblevertretung*) on the theatre management committee,
three of whom, Franz Morak, Karlheinz Hackl, and Robert Meyer,
were specialists in Austrian comedy of various kinds, and the crisis
led to a declaration of no confidence by the company.[23]

The case in defence of Peymann is that he has always regarded
himself as having been appointed to reform (that is, to modernize)
the Burgtheater, and as fighting against a traditionalism that threatened to degenerate into moribund provincialism. Specifically, he
championed the iconoclastic work of Thomas Bernhard: one of his
most controversial productions was of *Heldenplatz*, set in Vienna at
the time of the Anschluss and presenting a highly critical picture of
Austria. The première in November 1988 was timed to coincide with
the centenary of the Burgtheater building on the Ringstrasse – a

demonstrative reversal of the kind of patriotic celebration that had marked its reopening in 1955. The production prompted debate about the wisdom of extending Peymann's contract; at the same time, it instantly raised the attendance levels, with forty-seven well-attended performances that season, and it was revived in 1993. When well-known producers have been brought in from outside Vienna, they have tended to come particularly from the former German Democratic Republic (Ruth Berghaus, for example, produced Brecht's *Der kaukasische Kreidekreis* in 1994); one particularly laudable result of this policy was a fine production by Wolfgang Engel of *König Ottokars Glück und Ende* in January 1991, in commemoration of the bicentenary of Grillparzer's birth – a production which starred Morak in the title role and which suggested that the Burgtheater was on its way to establishing a (long-needed) modern style of acting Grillparzer.

The case against Peymann, which has been most consistently presented by Hans Haider in the daily *Die Presse*, rests mainly on three points. First, it has been argued that his direction has been managerially and financially inefficient, with attendances dropping, with the theatre being closed for occasional evenings to create rehearsal time (in January 1993 *Die Presse* was even able to report a week in which it was to close on more evenings than it would open),[24] and with too much of the programme given over to pieces with small casts (including casts of two or even of one), leaving the huge company expensively underused. Secondly, his direction has been seen as involving a systematic politicization of the Burgtheater as an institution: he has depended on support within the ruling Austrian Social Democrat party to remain in office despite all the controversy and criticism his work has generated, in particular in the renewal of his contract in 1992 and its further extension in 1994 by the Minister for Education and the Arts, Rudolf Scholten.[25] Defending his continued support of Peymann, Scholten argued that he had raised standards and maintained a more varied programme than in any German-speaking theatre of comparable size; his critics were running the risk of seeming narrow-minded or even provincial.[26] But in 1992 Scholten had to survive a motion of no confidence proposed in parliament by representatives of the right-wing populist FPÖ for his support of the 'notorious denigrator of Austria',[27] and the elected representatives of the company (*Ensemblevertretung*), who still included Morak and Meyer, resigned in protest against his reappointment as director. When the audit office raised questions in 1993 about the financial management of the theatre, the FPÖ again made political capital out of the issue, attacking the government for its continued support of Peymann. Thirdly, it has been argued that the increasing use of visiting producers who have brought their own star actors with them has endangered the ensemble principle (precisely Wildgans's objection against the idea of performances by Reinhardt's company after the First World War), and with it the autonomy of the repertory, without any long-term gain to the Burgtheater:[28] the most celebrated productions (including a *Richard III* which was demonstratively applauded in Peymann's first season, an indication of the support he attracted, and *Macbeth* in 1992) were built round a star actor, Gerd Voss, who left again for Berlin in 1993.

In sum, Peymann stands charged with destroying the integrity of Burgtheater tradition. Part of the trouble is clearly rooted in political differences: Morak, his most outspoken critic within the company, was elected to parliament in October 1994 as a candidate of the conservative People's Party (ÖVP) and became their spokesman on the arts. Nevertheless, the artistic effect is plain to see not just in the relative neglect of the Austrian classics (Grillparzer, Nestroy, Schnitzler, Hofmannsthal) by comparison with the repertory of, say, twenty or thirty years ago but also, when productions have been attempted, in their unsympathetic character: a gloomy *Der Schwierige*, for example, produced by Jürgen Flimm for the Salzburg Festival in 1991 and subsequently taken into the Burgtheater repertory, or a self-indulgently shapeless *Der Talisman* produced by Benning in November 1993 and lasting three and a half long hours. The departure of Voss in 1993 occasioned a widespread sense that the whole character and identity of the theatre had been lost sight of;[29] within a few months a former director, Gerhard Klingenberg, was quoted as stressing its historical character as a specifically Austrian theatre and warning that experimentation needed to be carried out with caution.[30]

Tradition has been more securely guarded in the Theater in der Josefstadt, under a succession of postwar directors, including Haeussermann and Stoss, who between them were in charge, either jointly or separately, for over thirty years (1953–84) and most recently Schenk (since 1988). Schenk has attracted to the company leading Viennese actors, refugees from Peymann's Burgtheater (Karlheinz Hackl, Helmut Lohner), and continuity seems to be assured in that he is to be succeeded as artistic director in the autumn of 1997 by Lohner, who has declared his commitment to maintaining an emphasis on the Viennese classics, including Nestroy and Schnitzler, in the Josefstadt and a programme of lighter comedies in the Kammerspiele.[31] The cultivation of nineteenth-century dialect drama, including Nestroy, has also been taken up by a number of (mainly outdoor) summer theatres in various places in Lower Austria (Melk, Krems, Laxenburg, Reichenau, Bisamberg, Liechtenstein), often using well-known actors from the principal Viennese theatres. One of the most remarkable of these summer ventures has been an annual Nestroy production in Rannersdorf, on the eastern outskirts of Vienna. These 'Nestroy-Spiele' have taken place every year since 1973, performed by amateur actors from Schwechat but produced throughout that period by Peter Gruber, who is now established as one of the best-known Austrian producers.

Contemporary drama, including social drama, has featured in the programme both of the Burgtheater under Peymann and of the Volkstheater under successive directors (including the current incumbent, Emmy Werner, who has been in post since 1988). In Peymann's first season, one addition to the programme in the Akademietheater was a production by the iconoclastic George Tabori, the première of his 'farce' *Mein Kampf*; and the programme there has continued to include productions of contemporary Austrian writers, e.g. Felix Mitterer's *Sibirien*, produced by Morak in 1990, Elfriede Jelinek's *Totenauberg* (1992), and Peter Turrini's *Alpenglühn*, produced by Peymann in 1993. Austrian dramatists produced in the Volkstheater in the last twenty-five years have included Mitterer, Wolfgang Bauer, and Turrini, whose first première, *Rozznjogd*, in 1971 was one of the most contentious productions of the ten years Manker was director of the theatre (1969–79); and one of the best-received productions of 1994 was the first Austrian one of Turrini's *Grillparzer im Pornoladen* in the Theater in der Josefstadt's studio theatre, the Rabenhof in the Third District.

But it is a feature of the theatrical life of big cities that a high proportion of the more adventurous and experimental work is done in smaller theatres. Many of those are ephemeral. Among the little theatres in postwar Vienna, one that exemplifies the precariousness of experiment is the Ensemble Theater of Dieter Haspel: founded in 1967, the company has specialized in premières of works by young Austrian authors and has played in numerous different small theatres (most recently on the Petersplatz). Two others that were also founded over twenty years after the end of the war and have become well established and have built up a distinctive reputation may serve as examples of the range and importance of the whole phenomenon of smaller experimental theatres.

The entrance to the Schauspielhaus in the Porzellangasse, in the ninth district, has a mural with the programmatic motto 'Art Triumphant over Good Taste'. Founded in a former cinema in 1978 under Hans Gratzer, who has directed it throughout its existence except for a spell in the late 1980s under Tabori, it has developed a programme – inevitably, not always financially successful – which in principle is devoted exclusively to contemporary writers. Among these there have been numerous translations of foreign works, but German-language works premièred there have notably included Wolfgang Bauer's *Ach, armer Orpheus!* (1991) – a play rejected by the Burgtheater, which not only proved a box-office success but also, in Hans Haider's judgement, re-established the Schauspielhaus in the first rank of Viennese theatres.[32] The theatre of the 'Gruppe 80', in the Gumpendorfer Strasse, is even smaller, with seating for 163. The company, which was launched in 1981 with a production of Nestroy's *Der Talisman*, has been particularly successful in producing local classics. The theatre in the Gumpendorfer Strasse was opened in October 1983 with Raimund's *Der Alpenkönig und der Menschenfeind*, and under the joint direction of Helga Illich and Helmut Wiesner it has continued to cultivate the Viennese repertory, with a number of Raimund, Nestroy, Grillparzer, and Schnitzler works in the programme, including an adventurous production of *Die Ahnfrau* in modern dress in May 1991, the scene transferred to a down-market café; this was followed up the following year with a (less successful) modern *Sappho*.

In the 1870s the social *Volksstück* competed with operetta; in the early twentieth century naturalist and expressionist plays were again in competition with operetta. In present-day Vienna, the place of operetta has been taken by the musical. In 1963 a production of *My Fair Lady* by the company of the Theater des Westens (Berlin) was shown in the Theater an der Wien and ran for four months. When Rolf Kutschera was appointed director of the theatre in 1965 (a post he held until 1983), he established a plan for a repertoire of musicals there. A succession of American and British musicals followed, including in 1968 *Hello, Dolly!* (with Marika Rökk, who had begun her career in the Ronacher in 1931); then more recent musicals, including the works of Andrew Lloyd Webber, the longest-running hit of all being *Cats* (1983), with specifically local interest catered for in 1992 by Sylvester Levay's *Elisabeth* (libretto by Michael Kunze), produced by the well-known opera producer Harry Kupfer.

Cats was the first production in the theatre under the direction of Peter Weck, a former Burgtheater actor. In 1986 a new umbrella organization, the 'Vereinigte Bühnen Wien Ges.m.b.H.', was set up, with Weck as director (*Intendant*), managing the Theater an der Wien, the Raimundtheater, and the Ronacher. The Ronacher had closed as a theatre in 1960 and had been used from then until 1976 by ORF, the Austrian national radio and television service, as a studio. After a long period of negotiation, in which demolition of the neglected and increasingly tumbledown building often seemed the likely outcome but was strongly opposed by the city, it was saved as a listed building and reopened in 1986 for a summer season with a production by Hans Gratzer of Johann Strauss's *Cagliostro in Wien*.

By 1990 Vereinigte Bühnen Wien were publicizing their programme in three theatres under the slogan 'Vienna, the Metropolis of Musicals'. When Weck retired as director of the group in 1992, what his successor, Rudi Klausnitzer, who came from the world of television, was taking over was a well-established musicals empire. The management strategy was based on long runs, with the possibility of shifting productions from one theatre to another. In September 1988, when *Les Misérables* opened in the Raimundtheater, *Cats* (originally staged in the Theater an der Wien) was on in the Ronacher, and the Theater an der Wien was showing *Phantom of the Opera*, which later moved to the Raimundtheater. Transferring shows between theatres was not a new device: it was used by Karl Carl when he owned both the Theater an der Wien and the Theater in der Leopoldstadt in the late 1830s and early 1840s, and by Marischka and Beer in the 1920s, always with the intention of extending the potential audience. In the 1980s and 1990s, the Raimundtheater has attracted a more youthful audience than the Theater an der Wien, and has also drawn in people from the outlying districts, while the more centrally-placed Theater an der Wien has attracted a rather wealthier public. Despite the rationalization of their planning and despite the long runs they have achieved, the theatres of the Vereinigte Bühnen Wien continue to rely heavily on subsidies from the public purse. In 1993 the Raimundtheater (with a published

31   Etablissement Ronacher: the restored building, 1994.

capacity of 1,186 when an orchestra is playing) and the Theater an der Wien (with a capacity of 1,143 including 70 standing places) received subsidies from the city of over 220,000,000 Schilling. The Ronacher, which required three years' thorough repair and refurbishment, was privatized, being leased for five years to a Berlin impresario, Peter Schwenkow (initially in partnership with a financial expert, Stefan Seigner), for a nominal rent, against a return to the city of 15 per cent of profits. It was reopened on 16 October 1993, its exterior beautifully restored (see plate 31), and with a maximum seating capacity of 1,239 plus twenty standing places (eighty years earlier the total capacity had been as many as 3,000). Concentrating on bills of international variety, the theatre made a profit from the first, in part by applying modern management principles to reduce overheads (a very small staff was retained, supplemented by short-term contracts, and with service facilities such as the buffet and cloakrooms contracted out).[33]

The assertion of business management principles and the long runs of imported musicals are part of a steady process of internationalization, which has been at work in the Viennese theatre throughout the history of the last two and a quarter centuries (for example, in the reliance on the Parisian *comédie-vaudeville* in the 1830s and 1840s, the domestication of operetta in the 1870s, the growing interdependence of theatres in Berlin and Vienna in the first half of the twentieth century). It is a process that will undoubtedly continue; it is an indication that the theatrical life of Vienna is not stagnating. And indeed interest in the theatre there shows no signs of abating. The city is a major centre of theatre research, with a heavily oversubscribed university department, important archives and libraries, and a theatre museum with the largest collection in the world (see Appendix 2, pp. 260–3). As for live theatre, the passions displayed in the disputes about the direction of the Opera House and most recently the Burgtheater, the cultivation of tradition in the Theater in der Josefstadt, the large number of small theatres showing contemporary writing: all these are sure indications that the vitality and individuality of Viennese theatre will survive, a constant disproof of Müller-Guttenbrunn's consignment to the past tense of its cherished status as a 'city of theatre'.

Appendix 1: Documents

1. Josef Kurz: *Eine neue Tragödie, Betitult: Bernardon die Getreue Prinzeßin Pumphia, und Hanns-Wurst Der tyrannische Tartar-Kulikan, Eine Parodie in lächerlichen Versen*, s.l.s.a. (Vienna: Stadt- und Landesbibliothek, Druckschriftensammlung, shelf-mark A13.440): 'Avertissement', signed 'Joseph Kurtz, Comicus Bernardon':

Ich nenne dieses kleine Werk eine *Critique*, oder *Parodie*, über die sonst von vielen Teutschen Truppen sehr übel vorgestellten *Tragoedien*. Genug, unser Hanns-wurst stellet dabey den Kulican, und ich, welcher sonst die lustigen *Caracteurs* agire, die Prinzeßin Pumphia vor . . .
. . . Schließlich sage ich, daß sich meine *Critique* nicht so gut wird lesen lassen, als man sie auf dem Theater wird sehen, und hören können, dann ich habe das Vergnügen unter einer Gesellschaft auserlesener *Acteurs* zu seyn, welche meistens ihre Rollen ausnehmend gut vorstellen . . .

2. Franz Karl Hägelin: memorandum setting out ground rules for censorship in Hungary (1795), incorporating principles effective in Vienna, *Jahrbuch der Grillparzer-Gesellschaft* 7 (1897), 298–340 (excerpt from pp. 301–2):

Fürs dritte verstehet es sich von selbst, daß die Theatralzensur viel strenger seyn müsse als die gewöhnliche Zensur für die bloße *Lecture* der Druckschriften, wenn leztere auch in Dramen bestehen. Dieses ergibt sich schon aus dem verschiedenen Eindruck, den ein in lebendige Handlung bis zur Täuschung gesetztes Werk in den Gemüthern der Zuschauer machen muß, als derjenige seyn kann, den ein blos am Pulte gelesenes gedrucktes Schauspiel bewirckt. – Der Eindruck des erstern ist unendlich stärcker als jener des leztern, weil das erstere Augen und Ohren beschäftigt und sogar in den Willen des Zuschauers treten soll, um die beabsichtigten Gemüthsbewegungen hervorzubringen, welches die bloße *Lecture* nicht leistet. Die Bücherzensur kann Lesebücher restringiren und folglich solche nur einer gewissen Gattung von Lesern gestatten, da hingegen das Schauspielhaus dem ganzen Publikum offen stehet, das aus Menschen von jeder Klasse, von jedem Stande und von jedem Alter bestehet.

3. Declaration by Karl Carl (signed 'Der k. baiersche Hofschauspieler und Director des k. Theaters am Isarthor in München *Carl*'), *Allgemeine Theaterzeitung und Unterhaltungsblatt für Freunde der Kunst, Literatur und des geselligen Lebens*, 18 August 1825 (no. 99), p. 408:

Theater-Nachricht. Da morgen die Gastvorstellungen auf dem k.k. priv. Theater an der Wien beginnen, so hält es der Unterzeichnete für seine Pflicht, vorher dem hochverehrten Publikum seine Ansichten darüber zu entwickeln …

Sein Vorhaben ist für diese Zeit ein *théatre de varietés*, im edler[n] Sinne zu begründen; das Drama, das feine Lustspiel, das romantische Schauspiel und die Local-Posse sollen sich im bunten Reigen folgen; die Oper und die Pantomime fehlen nur deßhalb, weil sie in dem früheren Wirkungskreise in München nicht zum Ressort dieser Anstalt gehörten, und es nicht möglich gewesen wäre, sie in dieser kurzen Zeit, und *für* diese kurze Zeit würdig herzustellen.

Bey den Vorstellungen beabsichtet die Direction besonders ein kräftiges Ensemble. Es gilt nicht sowohl *Einzelne* glänzen zu lassen, als das Werk mit möglichster Rundung zu geben, und ein *Ganzes* aufzustellen, daher auch die Regisseurs, und ersten Mitglieder der Bühne, wenn es nöthig ist, die kleinsten Rollen übernehmen, um das Ensemble zu sichern.

Die Direction ist weit entfernt mit irgend einer der hier bestehenden, oder früher bestandenen Kunstanstalten wetteifern zu wollen; – bey einem so kunstsinnigen Publikum, wie das der Kaiserstadt, würde sich solch ein Dünkel schnell und streng bestrafen. Ganz anspruchlos tritt das neue Unternehmen auf.

4. Letter from Karl Carl to Adolf Bäuerle, 15 November 1840 (Wiener Stadt- und Landesbibliothek, Handschriftensammlung, H.I.N. 34.455).

An Herrn Adolf von Bäuerle, Schriftsteller

Wohlgeborner Herr!
Ich ertheile Ihnen hierdurch die Versicherung, daß ich Ihnen für die, zur freien Benützung der unter meiner Leitung stehenden Bühnen, mir überlassenen zwey *Manuscripte*, als: *Rococo*, Lustsp. in 2 Aufz. und der Sonderling in Wien Posse in 4 Aufz. eine *[sic]* Honorar für beide Stücke zusammen von fünfhundert Gulden *CM.* bezahle, unter der ausdrücklichen Bedingung jedoch: daß diese beiden erwähnten Stücke die hohe *Censurs*-Genehmigung zur Aufführung erhalten, Euer Wohlgeboren so gefällig seyn werden, die zwischen uns mündlich besprochenen

Abänderungen darin vorzunehmen, keines dieser beiden Manuscripte vor Ablauf von Drey Jahren vom Tage der ersten Aufführung eines jeden der beiden benannten Stücke auf meinen Bühnen gerechnet, im Druck erscheinen dürfen und endlich, daß Euer Wohlgeboren diese beiden *Manuscripte* wärend der angeführten drey Jahre nur mir zum Gebrauche für *meine* Bühnen und keiner anderen hierortigen *Direction* überlassen. Mit Hochachtung verharrt Euer Wohlgeboren

ergebenst
Carl

Wien d. 15ten Nov. [1]840

5. ch l—— [= Wilhelm Schlesinger?], review of *Die beiden Rauchfangkehrer, oder: Welcher ists? Das ist die Frage?* by Josef Kilian Schickh after an original by F. Soulié [Theater an der Wien, 16 April 1841], *Der Humorist*, 19 April 1841 (no. 78), pp. 318–19:

> ... Wir bleiben dabei, daß die jetzige so sehr um sich greifende Wuth, *par force* aus französischen Romanen, Vaudevilles, Operntexten, Balletprogrammes deutsche, oder vielmehr *österreichische Possen* herauszubacken, nicht nur die unbegrenzte, trostlose Erfindungsarmuth unserer Lokaldichter am Handgreiflichsten bezeichnet, sondern, daß sie auch der letzte, verderblichste Stoß ist, den unsere Possenmuse überhaupt hätte erhalten können. Man mag über die französischen Dichter schimpfen so viel man will, man wird ihnen doch nicht Geist, Grazie, Leichtigkeit, Elastizität streitig machen können, und man mag unsere Possendichter in Schutz nehmen, so viel man kann, man wird es ihrem größten Theile doch nicht aufbürden können, daß sie diese unbestrittenen Gaben der französischen Poeten in ihre deutsche[n] Lokalprodukte hineinarbeiten, und so bleiben uns von dem ewigen Nachbilden, Uebersetzen, Bearbeiten nur zwei Dinge: Erstens die leichtbeflügelte, französische Frivolität in plumpe deutsche Zweideutigkeit übertragen, und Zweitens das gänzliche Aufgeben des eigenen Schaffens und Erfindens, die Resignation auf Originalität, unaufhörliches Uebertragen und Nacharbeiten, ewige Kopisten!

6. M.G. Saphir, review of première of *Der Zeitgeist, oder: Der Besuch aus der Vorstadt* by Carl Haffner with music by Adolf Müller [Theater an der Wien, 15 May 1841], *Der Humorist*, 15 May 1841 (no. 99), p. 398–9 (excerpt from p. 398):

> Es mag für ein *Theater* recht angenehm, recht bequem sein, ein und dasselbe Stück zum 'achtzigsten Mal,' zum 'sechsunddreißigsten Mal' ankündigen und geben zu können, für das *Publikum*, für die *Theaterbesucher* und für die Juste milieu zwischen Seligen und Verdammten: für *Rezensenten* ist es höchst langweilig, höchst abgeschmackt, höchst ledern! 'Novitäten! Novitäten!' das ruft der Theatermagen des Publikums

unaufhörlich, und lieber alle Tage eine *andere Gattung Mehlspeise*, als alle Tage oder sechzig Mal hintereinander *Zuckerbrot*!

Dieser Hungerschrei des ewighungerigen, ewigzermalmenden Theaterpublikum-Magens berücksichtigt Niemand so sehr, als Hr. Direktor *Carl*. Wir haben seit einigen Monaten eine solche Masse von Novitäten auf diesen Bühnen ('Wien' und 'Leopoldstadt') vorüberschreiten sehen, daß uns eher die *Abwechslung* als die *Monotonie* ermüdete. *Vieles, Vielerlei, Varietäten, Novitäten* zu bringen, das ist die erste Bedingung einer Direktion, welche Kunst, Publikum, Dichter und das allgemeine Amüsement im Auge hat.

7. K. Arnold, 'Ueber den Verfall der Volkstheater', *Österreichische Blätter für Literatur und Kunst, Geografie, Geschichte, Statistik und Naturkunde*, 30 March 1847 (no. 76), pp. 301–2 (p. 301):

Die Volksbühne ist ihrer Natur nach auf ein kleines Theater angewiesen und das Theater an der Wien war deshalb nie dafür geeignet. Seine Bestimmung ist Oper, Ballet und große Spektakelstücke, und wenn es jetzt dahin zurückgekehrt ist, so hat es nur Recht gethan ... Die ausschließende Basis eines Volkstheaters muß immer das eigentliche Volksstück bleiben, dessen Horizont ohnedies heut zu Tage bedeutend erweitert ist.

8. *Die Grenzboten* (Leipzig), June 1847, p. 407: 'Tagebuch. IV. Aus Wien. Mai: "Nestroy als Tendenzmann"' [on the success of Nestroy's *Der Schützling*]:

Wir haben jetzt ein Theater weniger, das in der Leopoldstadt, welches Director Carl niederreißen lie[ß], um an seiner Stelle ein größeres zu erbauen. Es hat in letzterer Zeit die Aufmerksamkeit durch die beiden neuesten Stücke Nestroy's: 'der Unbedeutende' und 'der Schützling' auf sich gezogen, der in dem ersten die Fragen des Sozialismus und Communismus, in dem zweiten Protection und Nepotismus, diese beiden Grundübel unserer Verhältnisse in's Gebiet der Wiener Posse ziehen wollte. Eine Wiener politische Localposse! Wahrlich wunderbar. Soll diese vielleicht ein Bild des Wiener Lebens abgeben, des politischen Lebens der untern Volksclassen? Die Herren und Damen der höhern Stände haben sich recht gut dabei unterhalten, sie haben wenigstens klatschen können ohne sich schämen und über die Zoten obligat erröthen zu müssen ... Ein Volkstheater, und das Volk geht nicht hinein!

9. M.G. Saphir, 'Der Rezensent in dem Gasluster des neuen Carl-Theaters', II, *Der Humorist*, 11, no. 300 (16 December 1847), pp. 1197–9 (excerpt from p. 1199):

Aber es drängt sich uns der Zweifel auf, ob das 'Volksstück' ... in dem Rahmen des jetzigen 'Carl-Theaters' eine solche *ausschließliche* Alleinherrschaft und Totalwirkung machen würde. Das 'Carl-Theater' ist

mit dem Sammtmantel um die stolzen Glieder nicht mehr der
geeignete Dollmetsch des bloßen Volksstückes; das 'Carl-Theater' muß
mit den goldenen Epaulettes nicht bloß den Jokusstab schwingen,
sondern auch die Muse Thalia, und besonders das Drama, 'le grand
drame' kultiviren! In solchen Räumen, in solchem Rahmen, in solchem
Luxus soll nicht der Aschenbrödl Volksstück *allein* logiren! Herr
Direktor Carl soll das Vaudeville ebenfalls kultiviren, das Vaudeville,
gegen das wir selbst einst aufgetreten sind, denn andere Verhältnisse
erzeugen andere Bedürfnisse. Hauptsächlich muß Herr Carl ein
Drama, ein gutes Schauspiel bilden und schaffen.

10. Nestroy: Submission dated 22 March 1851 concerning the cen-
    sor's objections to his comedy *Mein Freund*. Archiv für Nieder-
    österreich: Akten der Wiener Polizeidirektion (Theaterzensur,
    Karton 1, Zl. 922 ex 1851):

Hochwohlgeboren K.K. Herr Statthalter von Nieder-Österreich.

Nachdem die von mir verfaßte Posse 'Mein Freund' der K.K.
Stadthauptmannschaft zur Beurtheilung unterlegt wurde, sind mir von
dem K.K. Stadthauptmannschaftsober Commissär Herrn v. *Janota*
mehrere Stellen und Worte aus beygefügten Gründen als beanständet
kundgegeben worden. Ich erlaube mir das Beanständete sammt den
angegebenen Gründen, wie auch meine Gegenbemerkungen gehor-
samst zu unterbreiten.

Beanständet wurde *pag* 18. wo
Einer den Plan faßt ein
Illustriertes Blatt zu gründen, die
Worte '*illustrirt*' und '*Carrikatur*'
– und zwar aus dem Grunde,
weil in Österreich keine
Concession auf ein *illustriertes* Blatt
ertheilt wird.

Daß in der Österreichischen
Monarchie keine *Concession* auf ein
illustriertes Blatt ertheilt wird, kann
u[n]möglich schon den Wortlaut
'Illustriertes Blatt' zu etwas
Verpöntem machen, denn Erstens
spielt das Stück nicht *directe* in
Österreich, sondern in jeder
beliebigen großen Stadt, und hat
durchaus keine politische Tendenz
oder irgend eine *Local*-Beziehung,
und Zweitens, liegen ja selbst in
Österreich, nahmentlich in Wien an
allen öffentlichen Orten illustrierte
Blätter, auch mit Carrikatur-
zeichnungen unschädlicher Natur,
auf, nehmlich die '*Fliegenden Blätter*',
die '*Illustrierte Zeitung*' *ectr* was doch
gewiß nicht ohne Bewilligung der
Behörde geschehen könnte.

Beanständet wurde ferner *pag.* 58, u. 59 die Scene des '*Stuzl.*' Es erscheint darin ein kleiner Junge, welcher für seinen Bruder in der Leihbibliothek 'wühlerische Bücher' verlangt, wofür ihm der alte *Commis* der Bibliotheck verdientermaßen den Schopf beuteln will.

Ferner wurde beanständet: *pag.* 98, die Stelle: – 'Es ist Luxus vom Schicksal, daß es Pfeile schleudert, an seinen Fügungen sieht man ohnedem, daß es das Pulver nicht erfunden hat.' – aus dem Grunde, weil diese Stelle im Widerspruch mit der religiösen Ergebenheit stehe.

Ferner wurde beanständet: *pag* 106 die Stelle, – 'es kann unmöglich *schwer* seyn, Etwas Geringes in die Höh' zu heben.' – und zwar aus dem Grunde, weil dieß als eine Anspielung auf Herrn Minister *Bach* genommen werden könnte.

Diese Scene hat, nach meiner Meinung gerade das Gute, daß sie die in der Jugend *grassierenden* üblen und verkehrten Grundsätze geisselt. Das Lächerlichmachen ist in solchen Dingen das wircksamste Mittel den in der Menschennatur wurzelnden Reitz des Verbothes zu *neutralisieren.* Das Lächerlichmachen des Bösen und Schlechten ist die einzige moralische Wircksamkeit der Komick, ich glaube, man sollte sie gerade darin am wenigsten beschräncken.

Das 'Hadern mit dem Schicksal', glaube ich, kann durchaus nichts Anstößiges haben, denn es *existiert* gar kein Stück, wo derley nicht in allen *Nuancen* vorkömmt. *Raisonnements* über Schicksal, blinden Zufall, Glückslaunen, Verhängniß *ectr* machen den größten Theil der Reflexionen aller Stücke aus, und sind zu keiner Zeit als *collidierend* mit der Christlichen Religion – welche sämmtliches Obbenannte *ignoriert,* und nur eine Vorsehung *statuiert* – betrachtet worden. Übrigens darf man nur in dieser Stelle das Wort 'Fügungen' weglassen, und 'Taten' dafür setzen, so ist auch der leiseste Anklang vermieden.

Es ist in dieser Scene von einem jungen Baron die Rede, welcher ein Mädchen von geringem Stande zu sich emporheben will, somit auf die, mit Schließung einer *Maisalliance* verbundenen Mißlichkeiten, hingedeutet. Dem *Context* nach ist also eine Anspielung auf Herrn Minister *Bach* nicht denckbar. Aber auch in dem Wortlaut 'Geringes erheben' kann diß nicht liegen, denn alle verdienstvollen Männer, die zu hohen Würden gelangten, sind früher etwas Geringeres gewesen; es giebt keinen *Praesidenten* der nicht früher *Concepts*-Praktikant, keinen *General*, der nicht früher *Cadett* war *ectr*. Spezielle Anspielung auf Herrn Minister *Bach*, ist aber auch von dieser Seite nicht zu *deducieren*.

pag 141 ist eine Stelle, als verletzend für den Bauernstand, beanständet.

In dieser Stelle darf nur bey den Worten, 'daß er sich aus was eine Ehr' macht' das Wörtlein 'so' eingeschoben werden, dann heißt es: 'daß er sich aus *so* was, eine Ehr' macht,' wonach das Verletzende wegfällt.

Ferner wurde beanständet:, *pag* 160 – die Stelle, wo *Schlicht* zu *Schippl* sagt, er wolle ihm eine Fabel erzählen. – und zwar aus dem Grunde, weil dieß als eine Anspielung auf den Litteraten *Ebersberg* genommen werden könnte.

Fabeln wurden von vielen Dichtern geschrieben, und wenn man von Fabeln überhaupt spricht, so ist dieß eine Anspielung auf einen Zweig der Dichtkunst, aber nicht auf den Dichter derselben; nahmentlich aber hat Herr *Ebersberg* nur 'politische Fabeln' geschrieben, gerade von dieser Gattung ist aber hier nicht die Rede, folglich eine Beziehung auf Herrn *Ebersberg* durchaus nicht anzunehmen.

Beanständet wurde *pag* 163 das Wort 'Umsatteln.'

Es ist, wie Sinn und Zusammenhang zeigt, dieses Wort hir gar nicht in politischer Beziehung gebraucht.

Es wurden ferners mehrere einzelne Worte als *pag* 3, 97, 119, 159. beanständet, weil es Worte der politischen Zeitungssprache seyen.

Alle diese Worte sind hir ohne politischer Beziehung in ihrer natürlichen Bedeutung hingestellt, und es dürfte überhaupt beynahe u[n]möglich seyn, im *Dialog* jedes Wort zu vermeiden, welches zufällig auch ein in der Zeitungspolitick gebrauchter Ausdruck ist. Übrigens sehe ich aus der erschienenen *Annonce* der *Saphir'schen Acadamie*, daß selbst der modernste politische Ausdruck '*freye Conferenzen*' kein für die Bühne verpönter seyn kann.

Endlich wurde beanständet *pag* 20, eine Stelle, und zwar aus dem Grunde, weil es eine Zote wäre.

Ich berühre diesen Punct zuletzt, weil ich dagegen mit der größten Entschiedenheit protestieren muß. Der *Context* weist deutlich darauf hin, daß keine Zote beabsichtigt ist. Übrigens sind Zoten, welche einstens unläugbar gerade beym elegantesten Theile des Publikums als Modeartikel sehr beliebt waren, jetzt gänzlich aus der Mode, ich glaube nicht leicht, daß ein Dichter jetzt derley beabsichtigen wird, indem damit durchaus kein Effect zu erzielen ist, sondern im Gegentheil das Zotenschreiben in seinem eigenen Fleische wühlen hieße. Übrigens, wenn man Zoten finden will, dann ist auch jeder Satz eine Zote. Die Worte 'Vater, Mutter, Sohn, Tochter' sind lauter Zoten, weil man, wenn man will, dabey an den unerläßlich damit verbundenen Zeugungs*act* dencken kann.

Mit der Bitte, meine hir unterbreiteten Bemerckungen einer gütigen Berücksichtigung, weniger für jetzt als für künftighin, würdigen zu wollen, zeichne ich mit vorzüglicher Hochachtung

Euer Hochwohlgebohren

gehorsamster

J. Nestroy

Wien, den 22. März [1]851.

Janota commented on this in a memorandum dated 24 March 1851, which he submitted for a decision from higher authority. In this he summarizes the play and introduces his own counter-arguments:

Es handelt sich sonach bei dieser fortlaufenden Entgegenstellung eines moralischen Licht- und Schattenpoles lediglich um ein psüchologisches Charaktergemälde, das nicht nur der Tendenz sondern auch der äußeren Form nach von politischen Anstößigkeiten und Beziehungen gänzlich ferne gehalten ist, und man würde sonach auf die Ertheilung der hochortigen Aufführungsbewilligung eingerathen haben, wenn die Direkzion einige angedeuteten Abänderungen vorgenommen hätte.

Nachdem diese geweigert wurden, so werden nunmehr die diesfälligen Gründe sammt den Gegenbemerkungen des hierortigen Referenten zur hohen Entscheidung vorgelegt.

There then follows a detailed rebuttal, point by point, including the following:

ad p. 58/9. Hier wäre ich mit der Bemerkung des Verfaßers ganz einverstanden, wenn in der ganzen Scene irgend eine Moral läge. So ist es aber bloß darauf abgesehen, dem kleinen Repräsentanten des radikalen Elementes Beifall zu verschaffen und ihn allenfalls zur Fortschreitung auf dieser Bahn aufzumuntern. Überhaupt sollte die theatralische Schaustellung entgegengesezter politischen Prinzipien gänzlich vermieden werden, weil dadurch Parteileidenschaften angeregt und Demonstrazionen hervorgerufen werden.

ad p. 98. Es handelt sich hier nicht nur um bloßes Hadern mit dem Schiksal sondern um eine atheistische, das christlich-religiöse Gefühl beleidigende Ansicht, welche noch dazu mit scheinbarer, humoristischer Ruhe vorgetragen wird, und durch den Ausdruk 'deine Blize leuchten nicht' eine direkte Beziehung auf das höchste Wesen nach biblischer Anschauung nimmt. Der Gegenstand ist zu ernst, zu heilig, und die Profanazion de[ss]elben könnte von gefährlicher und verderblicher Wirkung sein . . .

ad p. 141 Die Geringschätzung, die ein Adeliger gegen den Bauernstand hegt, und die zornige Replik des Betheiligten können wohl nie einen passenden Gegenstand zum Scherze auf der Bühne abgeben, da hiedurch nur kommunistische Affekte, analog jenen, die sich in dem Rufe 'Nieder mit den Aristokraten' verewigten, angeregt und aufgestachelt werden . . .

Daß übrigens *Nestroy* beim Niederschreiben dieser Posse an die Tagespolitik nicht gedacht haben soll, ist kaum zu glauben, indem dies eine allzugroße Selbstverleugnung voraussezen ließe, die von dem Verfaßer der berüchtigten 'Freiheit in Krähwinkel' welche im Jahre 848 ungeheuren Skandal verursachte, nicht zu erwarten wäre.

ad p. 20. Die ganze Argumentazion gegen das Zotenwesen grenzt an Unverschämtheit, da *Nestroy* mit seinen Stüken wesentlich zur Entsittlichung des wiener Volkes beigetragen, und bis auf den heutigen Tag nur zu oft die harmlosesten Worte durch sein Mienen- und Händespiel zur gemeinsten Zote werden. Man braucht nur die '12 Mädchen in Uniform' zu sehen, um das Gesagte sattsam gerechtfertigt zu finden.

Wie wenig Sinn *Nestroy* für ein loyales Streben hat, beweist der Umstand, daß er von seiner alten Gewohnheit, dem Extemporiren, nicht laßen kann, und erst in der letzten Zeit bei Gelegenheit der Aufführung des *Kaiser*'schen Charakterbildes 'Frauenstärke und Männerschwäche' wegen Extemporirens radikaler Floskeln von dem betreffenden Bezirkskommissariate in die gesezlichen Schranken gewiesen werden mußte, nachdem er zuvor meiner mündlichen Aufforderung keine Folge gegeben hat.

However, a second official, Karl Hölzl, reporting on 27 March, came down on Nestroy's side:

... Da nun bei einer dramatischen Posse ohne genaue Beobachtung der Regeln des höhern Lustspiels und mit Vernachläßigung der Charaktere und des Ineinandergreifens der Szenen die Situationen de[m] gemeinen Leben angehören, so muß sich Dichter und Darsteller in Sprache, Geberde und Costüme mit mehr als gewöhnlicher Freiheit bewegen, durch lächerliche Übertreibungen theils belustigen, theils auch ernsthafte Thorheiten verspotten, aber doch immer die Gränzlinie beobachten, um nicht selbst zu sehr ins Possenhafte, Übertriebene, Gemeine und Platte zu versinken, und anstatt lächerlich zu machen, lächerlich zu werden; daher derlei komische Scherze im Gegensatze zum feinern Lustspiele in der Posse gestattet werden können, in so fern sie nämlich nicht gegen die Sittlichkeit, den Anstand, den Geschmack und die Gesellschaft anstoßen.

Ich glaube demnach, daß die vorliegende Posse mit den vom Verfaßer selbst angetragenen Veränderungen, übrigens mit Beibelaßung aller andern von Statthaupt. H^{rn} *Commissair* beanständeten Stellen zur Aufführung – versteht sich ohne Extemporationen – sich eignen dürfte, um so mehr den falschen, häuchlerischen Freund die verdiente Strafe ereilt, dem Reichen die Lehre gegeben wird, in der Wahl des Bräutigams vorsichtig zu seyn und dem Mädchen des Proletariers die Warnung nicht entgehen kann, sich mit einem Manne aus ihrem Stande zu verbinden, und den lockenden Verführungen junger Wüstlinge und Gauner zu widerstehen.

Wien am 27. März 1851
Hölzl
k.k.Rath

11. 'Das Testament des Theaterdirectors Carl', *Wiener allgemeine Theaterzeitung*, 31 August 1854 (no. 198), pp. 817–19, and 1 September 1854 (no. 199), pp. 821–2 (excerpts from pp. 818):

V. Rücksichtlich des mir gehörigen Carl Theater-Gebäudes Nr. 511 in der Leopoldstadt verordne ich ausdrücklich, daß das Theater Directions-Geschäft bei diesem Theater weder von meinen Erben in ihrer Gesammtheit noch von einem Einzelnen meiner Erben, sei es als Eigenthümer oder Pachter, oder in was immer für einen Namen habenden Eigenschaft, weder öffentlich noch stillschweigend, weder allein oder in Compagnie mit einer fremden nicht zu meinen Erben gehörigen Person, selbst geleitet und betrieben werden darf. Diejenigen meiner Erben, welche gegen dieses mein *ausdrückliches Verbot* handeln, sollen der ihnen nach diesem meinem Testamente zufallenden

Erbtheile für *immer verlustig sein* ... Aus dem strengen Nachdrucke, womit ich die genaue Befolgung dieses meines ausdrücklichen, ernsten Willens angeordnet habe, werden meine Erben, deren Wohl mir so sehr am Herzen liegt, unzweifelhaft erkennen, daß ich durch meine so überaus langjährige Erfahrung die Leitung eines Theater-Geschäftes als das schwerste, unsicherste und darum gefährlichste industrielle Geschäft kennen gelernt habe; ohne Ruhmredigkeit spreche ich hier offen aus, daß ich zweifle, es werde bald wieder ein Mensch auftauchen, der so wie *ich* durch und durch, nach allen Richtungen geschaffen sein wird, ein *solches* Geschäft auf die Art und Weise, wie ich es verstand, mit glücklichem Erfolge zu führen; ein Blick auf die Resultate aller europäischen und überseeischen Theater-Unternehmungen aus *Privat*mitteln erhalten, wird *meine Ansicht* bewahrheiten ... Hierbei mache ich meine Erben darauf aufmerksam, daß ich die Engagements-Verträge mit sämmtlichen Mitgliedern meines Theaters ohne Ausnahme in der Art abgeschlossen habe, daß meine *Erben* berechtigt sind, diese Verträge alsogleich nach meinem Tode auflösen zu können, welche Vertrags-Clausel von meinen Erben im Auge zu halten ist, um sie nach Maßgabe der Sachlage (besonders mit Rücksichtsnahme, ob die Zeit meines Ablebens zur *Sommer-* oder *Winter*zeit eingetreten ist) zu benützen und daraus bei der Verpachtung oder Veräußerung des Theatergebäudes den bestmöglichsten Vortheil zu ziehen und jeden Schaden von sich abzuwenden. Auch bemerke ich meinen Erben noch, daß die Auflösung meiner Directions-Führung meine Erben oder *Nachfolger* in der Directions-Führung gleichfalls zur alsogleichen Auflösung der bei meinem Carl-Theater bestehenden Engagements-Verträge berechtiget – und daß überhaupt alle diese Engagements-Verträge mit kurzer Kündigungzeit von *meiner* Seite abgeschlossen wurden, mit Ausnahme des alleinigen Vertrages mit dem Schauspieler und Dichter Herrn Johann *Nestroy.*

12. Friedrich Kaiser, 'Wenzel Scholz. Ereignisse und Denkwürdigkeiten aus seinem Leben', *Die Morgenpost*, March-April 1858, Part 15 (*Morgenpost*, no. 86):

Im Jahre 1842 erlitten die Volksposse und ihre Vertreter, welche doch Carl zu einem reichen Manne gemacht hatten, von diesem eine arge Kränkung. Er hatte nämlich Frau *Brüning*, welche im Theater in der Josefstadt mit großen *[sic]* Erfolge gastirt hatte, für seine Bühne gewonnen. Die Neuheit ihrer Darstellungsweise erregte auch im Theater an der Wien große Sensation, einige aus dem Französischen übertragene Stücke, welche mit eingelegten Liedern ausgestattet waren, und, zwar nicht ganz entsprechender Weise als *Vaudevilles* bezeichnet wurden, erlebten viele Wiederholungen, Carl, welcher mit Frau Brüning die Hauptrollen darstellte, gefiel sich ganz besonders in dem neuen Genre, und sprach sich schon ganz offen aus, daß die Volksposse sich gänzlich überlebt habe.

13. L.Sp. [= Ludwig Speidel], 'Eine Krisis des Burgtheaters', *Neue Freie Presse*, 6 January 1889 (no. 8753, morning edn), pp. 1–2 (p. 2).

Die unglaubliche Thatsache, die man betonen muß, liegt darin, daß ein paar hundert Schritte vom alten Burgtheater ein neues Gebäude aufgeführt wurde, welches auf Geist und Tradition des berühmten Bühnen-Instituts nicht die geringste Rücksicht nahm. Es wurde ein großer Bühnenraum und ein weiter und hoher Zuschauerraum hergestellt, die beide nicht für einander taugten. Der Bühnenraum legt der Erzeugung des Wortes Schwierigkeiten auf, läßt es mit seiner Eisenconstruction hallen und nicht klingen, und an vielen Stellen des Zuschauerraumes zerflattert das Wort und wird undeutlich. Feines Sprechen, sonst der Vorzug des Burgtheaters, ist unmöglich geworden, weil zu viel Lungenkraft in Anspruch genommen wird, um die Rede verständlich zu machen. Durch diese Anstrengung wird das Tempo langsamer und das Gespräch gedehnt.

14. Statutes of the Kaiserjubiläums-Stadttheater, § 2, reprinted *Deutsches Volksblatt*, 31 October 1903, p. 11:

In erste Linie ist das deutsche Volksstück zu stellen, neben dem das deutsche Drama in allen seinen Arten gepflegt werden soll. Werke *nichtdeutscher* Schriftsteller dürfen nur ausnahmsweise aufgeführt werden. Bei allen Aufführungen jedoch muß als Grundsatz festgehalten werden, daß allen Werken, deren Tendenz geeignet wäre, das patriotische Gefühl zu verletzen, die Liebe zum deutschen Stammesvolk zu beeinträchtigen oder das ethische und moralische Gefühl der christlichen Bevölkerung in irgend einer Weise zu erschüttern, die Bühne dieses Theaters verschlossen bleibt.

15. Adam Müller-Guttenbrunn: submission to the Mayor of Vienna, Karl Lueger, on the plight of the Kaiserjubiläums-Stadttheater, December 1902; reprinted in *Die Fackel* 146, 11 November 1903, pp. 12–21 (excerpt from pp. 18–19):

Durch die Gründung dieses Schauspielhauses sollte der Beweis erbracht werden, daß die deutsche Literatur reich genug ist, das deutsche Theater zu versorgen und daß wir der internationalen Mode-Literatur und der zumeist durch jüdische Übersetzer eingeschleppten französischen Unsitten-Stücke, die das gesunde Gefühl unseres Volkes verpesten, entraten können; durch dieses Theater sollte die vom jüdischen Journalismus vollständig überwucherte und entmutigte heimische Produktion, die seit drei Jahrzehnten fast versiegt schien, wieder geweckt werden; auf dieser Bühne sollte den *arischen Talenten* auf dem Gebiete der Literatur und der Schauspielkunst der Weg geebnet, durch den Bestand dieses Theaters sollte Bresche gelegt werden in den Ring, der das gesamte deutsche Künstlerleben unterjocht und dasselbe zu seiner geschäftlichen Domäne gemacht hat.

Und dies ist schon in seinen Anfängen gelungen. Wie haben *nur christliche Schauspieler*, wir führen nur Werke *christlicher Schriftsteller* auf, unser Theater hat diesen Autoren bereits 110.000 Kronen Tantièmen bezahlt und ihre Werke, die früher unbeachtet blieben, werden jetzt auch an anderen Bühnen gespielt. Der unversöhnliche Haß gegen dieses so reformatorisch und befreiend wirkende Theater, der namentlich in den auswärtigen Korrespondenzen oft zum Durchbruch kommt (um unsere Stücke und Schauspieler bei den reichsdeutschen Direktoren zu diskreditieren), dieser Haß beweist, daß man auf gegnerischer Seite die prinzipielle Bedeutung unseres Theaters ganz genau kennt.

Und Eines ist für mich gewiß: Neben den großen wirtschaftlichen Schöpfungen, welche die christlichsoziale Partei unter der genialen und wahrhaft staatsmännischen Führung Dr. Lueger's geschaffen, wird man unser Theater einst als eines der bedeutsamsten Werke dieser Partei feiern.

16. From Robert Pattai's speech at the general meeting of the association of the Kaiserjubiläums-Stadttheater ('Generalversammlung des Jubiläums-Stadttheatervereines'), 30 October 1903; reported *Deutsches Volksblatt*, 31 October 1903 (no. 5323), pp. 9–12 (p. 10):

Von vornherein bin ich der Idee gewesen, daß die antisemitische Bewegung nicht eine bloße Bewegung des Gewerbes und der Landwirtschaft ist, sondern in wesentlicher Beziehung auf die Höhen der geistigen Aufgaben sich erstrecken soll. Obwohl wir in politischer Beziehung antisemitisch sehr weit vorgeschritten sind, geht unsre Gesellschaft einer fortschreitenden Verjudung entgegen, insbesondere die Hochschulen und die Kunstwelt. Es ist das für Wien, die Kunststadt und insbesondere erste Musikstadt, betrübend. *Trotzdem sehen wir infolge einer Clique und der außerordentlichen Macht der Judenpresse mehr und mehr die vaterländische Kunst verkümmern und den populärsten Teil, das Theater, mehr und mehr auf die andre Seite hinübergehen.* Das ist eine riesige Gefahr für unser geistiges Leben . . .

Jetzt tritt der neue Direktor an Sie heran. Was macht man ihm zum Vorwurf? Man traut ihm nicht recht in der Parteisache, man glaubt, er möchte ins andre Fahrwasser hinübersegeln. Wir haben gehört, was er für Verpflichtungen eingegangen ist. Wir haben vorläufig keinen Anlaß, zu glauben, daß er die Verpflichtungen nicht halten wird. Wenn er es verstanden hat, mit der Judenpresse so weit zu kommen, daß das Theater nicht boykottiert wird, so ist das Geschäftssache. In der letzten Zeit waren weder Juden noch Christen im Theater . . .

Warum ist Wien als Theaterstadt so gesunken? Das hat seinen Grund teils in der Dekadenz des Mittelstands, zum größten Teil aber in der Verjudung des Theaters ...

Wenn diese Versammlung auseinandergeht und nicht das Resultat einer Einigung erzielt, wissen Sie, wer die größte Freude haben wird? Es wäre damit im Interesse des auserwählten Volks gearbeitet, sie würden sich die Hände reiben und sagen: Die Christen sind nicht fähig, einig zu sein, selbst wenn es sich um ihr Geld handelt.

Appendix 2: Research resources

Vienna is not just a city of live theatre tradition; it is also a centre for academic research in theatre history, with a number of important collections.

1. THEATRE STUDIES IN THE UNIVERSITY

Theatre history as a separate academic discipline is relatively young; the oldest specialized societies and collections in German-speaking Europe date back only to the beginning of the twentieth century. The early development of the discipline is charted in a survey by Helmar Klier, 'Theaterwissenschaft und Universität. Zur Geschichte des Fachs im deutschsprachigen Raum', in Helmar Klier (ed.), *Theaterwissenschaft im deutschsprachigen Raum. Texte zum Selbstverständnis* (Wege der Forschung, 548), Darmstadt: Wissenschaftliche Buchgesellschaft 1981, pp. 327–43. The Institut für Theaterwissenschaft in the University of Vienna was founded in 1943, the first holder of the chair being Heinz Kindermann; he was reinstated in 1954. The Institute is accommodated in the former Imperial Palace, overlooking the Michaelerplatz. By the end of the 1970s it offered the most comprehensive course of study in German-speaking Europe. Since 1955 the journal *Maske und Kothurn* has been edited within the Institute; and its research productivity is well exemplified in the Bibliography to this book, both in the many dissertations listed and also in the publications of its staff. These include notably four current holders of professorial chairs, Wolfgang Greisenegger, Hilde Haider-Pregler, Johann Hüttner, and Ulf Birbaumer.

2. THE AUSTRIAN THEATRE MUSEUM

The Österreichisches Theatermuseum is now housed in the Palais Lobkowitz, on the Lobkowitzplatz. Built in the 1690s, the house was originally the Palais Dietrichstein. Under the Lobkowitz family, important Beethoven concerts were held there, including the first performance in December 1804 of the Eroica Symphony (the first public performance in the Theater an der Wien followed a few months later, on 7 April 1805). One of the showpieces of the house is the large and ornately decorated room known as the *Eroicasaal*, now used for exhibitions. The building has been put to a wide variety of uses, and after the Second World War it was for a long time the home of the French Cultural Institute. It was acquired by the state in 1979, refurbished in 1985–91, and opened in its present function as a theatre museum in 1991. The most extensive theatre collection in German-speaking Europe, its holdings include a very large collection of illustrative pictorial material of all kinds. In this its stock is usefully complemented by the collection of the Historisches Museum der Stadt Wien, which has been housed since 1959 in a modern building on the Karlsplatz and has a large room set aside for research study.

3. ARCHIVES AND LIBRARIES

Over and above the archives of individual theatres, there is a wealth of material in the collections of the central libraries and archives.

The Theatre Collection (Theatersammlung) of the Austrian National Library was founded in 1921. For an account of its early development see Joseph Gregor, 'Die Theatersammlung der Nationalbibliothek in den Jahren 1922–1932', in Franz Hadamowsky, *Das Theater in der Wiener Leopoldstadt 1781–1860* (1934), pp. 7–36. Housed in the Hofburg until 1991, it is now accommodated in the Österreichisches Theatermuseum building, with a modern reading-room. Like all other sections of the National Library, it is closed every year for the first three weeks of September. The holdings were originally founded on the collection of Hugo Thimig, the largest specialized private collection in Vienna, which was acquired by the National Library in 1922, together with libraries and/or archives from the Theater an der Wien, the Carltheater, the Theater in der Josefstadt, and the Deutsches Volkstheater, all acquired in 1922–3. Steadily extended by further purchases, bequests, and gifts, the stock contains a large collection of plays (printed texts and manuscripts, including play-sets both from the Theater an der Wien from its foundation to the time of the Pokornys and also from the Carltheater under Karl Carl), press cuttings, and theatre bills and posters. The most comprehensive collection of nineteenth-century theatre bills is in the archive of the Gesellschaft der Musikfreunde.

The Wiener Stadt- und Landesbibliothek (in the Rathaus) contains the most comprehensive collection of reference material on the history and institutions of the city of Vienna, together with a good range of newspapers and journals published there (these holdings are not comprehensive, however, and can usefully be supplemented from the collection of the National Library). A further useful reference amenity in the Wiener Stadt- und Landesbibliothek is an index to newspaper items concerning Vienna since 1900. The theatrical material in the Library includes the large collection of Fritz Brukner, which was purchased in 1954; it is also here that the majority of autograph manuscripts by Grillparzer, Raimund, Nestroy, and other important theatrical figures, including Costenoble and Carl, are held. It closes for the first three weeks in August every year. The Music Collection (Musiksammlung) of the Wiener Stadt- und Landesbibliothek (in the Bartensteingasse, near the Rathaus) and that of the National Library (housed in the Albertina, in the Augustinerstrasse) both have substantial holdings of scores of Viennese theatre music, including manuscripts.

Documents on the court and state theatres are held in the State Archives (Österreichisches Staatsarchiv, section Haus-, Hof- und Staatsarchiv [Minoritenplatz]). It is not known precisely how many police files with records concerning censorship in the commercial theatres were destroyed in 1927 in the fire in the Palace of Justice; but since censorship was administered under the provincial government, there is a great deal of material in the Niederösterreichisches Landesarchiv (Herrengasse), going back to the late eighteenth century. The City Archive (Wiener Stadt- und Landesarchiv), in the Rathaus, also houses records relating to the city administration, especially in the period since Vienna became a separate province in 1922.

A useful summary of the distribution of archival material relating to the theatres from 1776 to 1918 is given in Franz Hadamowsky, *Wien. Theatergeschichte* (1988), pp. 813–17. An introductory outline of source material on commercial theatre up to the late nineteenth century is given by Franz Hadamowsky, 'Zur Quellenlage des Wiener Volkstheaters von Philipp Hafner bis Ludwig Anzengruber', in Herbert Zeman (ed.), *Die Österreichische Literatur. Ihr Profil im 19. Jahrhundert (1830–1880)*, Graz: Akademische Druck- und Verlagsanstalt 1982, pp. 579–88. The holdings of the

Wiener Stadt- und Landesbibliothek in relation to early-nineteenth-century commercial theatre are outlined by Walter Obermaier, 'Um Raimund und Nestroy. Die Handschriftensammlung der Wiener Stadt- und Landesbibliothek als Quelle zur Geschichte des Wiener Volkstheaters in der ersten Hälfte des 19. Jahrhunderts', *Biblos* 35, no. 3 (1986), 253–60.

Notes

References to works listed in the Bibliography are given here in shortened form; readers cross-referring should note that the names of some authors and editors are to be found in more than one section of the Bibliography.

1: THE ESTABLISHMENT OF THE 'CITY OF THEATRE'

1   Heinrich Laube, *Schriften zum Theater* (1959), p. 75.
2   See Antonio Cesti, *Il pomo d'oro. (Music for Acts* III and v from Modena, Biblioteca Estense, Ms. Mus. E. 120), ed. Carl B. Schmidt (Recent Researches in the Music of the Baroque Era, 42), Madison: A-R Editions 1982, pp. xii-xv. Illustrations of Burnacini's designs are given in Otto Rommel, *Die Alt-Wiener Volkskomödie* (1952), pp. 51–3.
3   Quoted in Rommel, *Die Alt-Wiener Volkskomödie*, p. 209.
4   *Letters from the Right Honourable Lady Mary Wortley Montagu 1709 to 1762*, ed. R. Brimley Johnson, London: Dent n.d., p. 66 (letter of 14 September 1716). Illustration in Ernst Wangermann, *The Austrian Achievement 1700–1800* (1973), p. 50.
5   Quoted in *Wiener Haupt- und Staatsaktionen*, ed. Rudolf Payer von Thurn, 2 vols. (Schriften des Literarischen Vereins in Wien, vols. 10 and 13, 1908–10), I, XXVI.
6   *Letters from the Right Honourable Lady Mary Wortley Montagu 1709 to 1762*, p. 67.
7   The text is reprinted in *Barocktradition im österreichisch-bayrischen Volkstheater*, ed. Otto Rommel (Deutsche Literatur in Entwicklungsreihen), 6 vols., Leipzig: Reclam 1935–39, I, 85–133.
8   See Otto G. Schindler, 'Das Publikum des Burgtheaters in der Josephinischen Ära' (1976), pp. 34, 84.
9   Schindler, 'Das Publikum des Burgtheaters in der Josephinischen Ära', p. 90.
10 J. von Sonnenfels, *Briefe über die wienerische Schaubühne* [1768] (1884), p. 202.
11 See Johann Hüttner, 'Das Burgtheaterpublikum in der ersten Hälfte

des 19. Jahrhunderts' (1976), p. 165; Rudolf Tyrolt, *Chronik des Wiener Stadttheaters* (1889), p. 128.

12 Philipp Hafner, 'Brief eines Komödienschreibers an einen Schauspieler'.

13 Sonnenfels, *Briefe über die wienerische Schaubühne*, p. 343.

14 Quoted in David G. John, 'From extemporization to text' (1990), p. 124.

15 Quoted in Bodo Plachta, *Damnatur – Toleratur – Admittitur* (1994), Part III: *Dokumentation* (microfiche), p. 101.

16 Carl Glossy, 'Zur Geschichte der Wiener Theatercensur. 1' (1897), 299: 'Nach der Hauptregel soll das Theater eine Schule der Sitten und des Geschmackes seyn.'

17 Laube, *Schriften zum Theater*, p. 177.

18 Sonnenfels, *Briefe über die wienerische Schaubühne*, pp. 10–29.

19 *Joseph II. als Theaterdirektor*, ed. Rudolf Payer von Thurn (1920), p. 16; Franz Hadamowsky, *Die Josefinische Theaterreform* (1978), p. 16.

20 See Johann Heinrich Friedrich Müller, *Theatererinnerungen eines alten Burgschauspielers*, ed. Richard Daunicht (1958), pp. 56–7.

21 The Schröders were engaged at a joint salary of 4,000 fl. See Oscar Teuber in Alexander von Weilen *et al.*, *Die Theater Wiens*, 2.2.1 (1903), pp. 23, 30–1.

22 See decree by Count Rosenberg-Orsini, 26 February 1789, quoted in Eduard Wlassack, *Chronik des k.k. Hof-Burgtheaters* (1876), p. 63.

23 See Franz Hadamowsky, 'Die Schauspielfreiheit, die "Erhebung des Burgtheaters zum Hoftheater" und seine "Begründung als Nationaltheater" im Jahr 1776' (1976), p. 16; *Die Josefinische Theaterreform* (1978), pp. XXI–XXII.

24 Letter of Hofrat Baron Michael von Kienmayer, 3 July 1777, quoted by Oscar Teuber in Alexander von Weilen *et al.*, *Die Theater Wiens*, 2.2.1, p. 39.

25 The libretto is generally ascribed to Paul Weidmann; Otto Michtner, *Das alte Burgtheater als Opernbühne* (1970), p. 355, advances evidence that payment was in fact made to Josef Weidmann.

26 Mozart, *Briefe und Aufzeichnungen. Gesamtausgabe*, ed. Wilhelm A. Bauer and Otto Erich Deutsch, 7 vols., Kassel: Bärenreiter 1962–75, III, 138.

27 See letter of 16 May 1788 to Count Rosenberg-Orsini: 'La musique de Mozard est bien trop difficile pour le chant': *Joseph II. als Theaterdirektor* (1920), p. 75.

28 Egon Komorzynski, *Emanuel Schikaneder* (1951), p. 249.

29 Max Burckhard, *Das Theater* (1907), p. 82.

30 'Die Sprache sei von der Natur, aber nicht vom Pöbel genommen': quoted in Kurt Kahl, *Die Wiener und ihr Burgtheater* (1974), p. 22.

31 Kahl, *Die Wiener und ihr Burgtheater*, p. 21, quoting Sonnenfels.

32 Franz Hadamowsky, *Die Josefinische Theaterreform*, p. 32.

33 See Peter Branscombe, *W. A. Mozart: 'Die Zauberflöte'* (1991), pp. 29–34.

34 *Handbook for Travellers in Southern Germany* (1837), p. 133.
35 Ilsa Barea, *Vienna* (1966), p. 90.
36 *Handbook for Travellers in Southern Germany*, p. 133.
37 Quoted in Franz Hadamowsky, *Wien. Theatergeschichte* (1988), p. 510.
38 See Hadamowsky, *Wien. Theatergeschichte*, p. 310.
39 Nestroy, *Stücke 23/1* (HKA), 51 (*Unverhofft*, II, 13).

2: CENSORSHIP

1 Carl Glossy, 'Zur Geschichte der Wiener Theatercensur. I' (1897), p. 300.
2 Quoted in Johann Hüttner, 'Das Burgtheaterpublikum in der ersten Hälfte des 19. Jahrhunderts' (1976), p. 146.
3 Karl Glossy, 'Zur Geschichte der Theater Wiens', I (1915), p. 35.
4 Glossy, 'Zur Geschichte der Wiener Theatercensur. I', p. 333: 'Von dem Worte "Aufklärung" ist auf dem Theater eben so wenig Erwähnung zu machen als von der Freiheit und Gleichheit.'
5 Quoted in Ernst Wangermann, 'Grillparzer und das Nachleben des Josephinismus', *Anzeiger der phil.-hist. Klasse der Österreichischen Akademie der Wissenschaften* 128 (1991), 55–73 (p. 55).
6 *Erinnerungen von Ludwig August Frankl*, ed. Stefan Hock (Bibliothek Deutscher Schriftsteller aus Böhmen, 29), Prague: Calve 1910, p. 315.
7 To Adolf Foglar, 11 August 1844: *Grillparzers Gespräche* (1904–16), III, 332.
8 *Bilder und Träume aus Wien* (1836), II, 133–4.
9 Carl Ludwig Costenoble, *Aus dem Burgtheater* (1889), II, 263: diary entry dated 13 February 1836.
10 Costenoble, *Aus dem Burgtheater*, II, 195: entry for 2 June 1834.
11 Costenoble, *Aus dem Burgtheater*, II, 265–6 (11 March 1836), 268 (22 March 1836).
12 *Bilder und Träume aus Wien*, I, 177.
13 Glossy, 'Zur Geschichte der Theater Wiens', III (1930), p. 112.
14 Glossy, 'Zur Geschichte der Theater Wiens', I (1915), p. 258.
15 Glossy, 'Zur Geschichte der Theater Wiens', II (1920), p. 33.
16 Glossy, 'Zur Geschichte der Wiener Theatercensur. I', p. 326.
17 Franz Grillparzer, *Sämtliche Werke* (1909–48), I/13, 176.
18 See Hägelin, in Glossy, 'Zur Geschichte der Wiener Theatercensur. I', pp. 313, 325; Friedrich Reischl, *Wien zur Biedermeierzeit* (1921), p. 182.
19 John Russell Stephens, *The Censorship of English Drama 1824–1901* (1980); for a useful outline see Johann Hüttner, 'Theatre censorship in Metternich's Vienna' (1980).
20 Friedrich Kaiser, *Unter fünfzehn Theater-Direktoren* (1870), p. 167.
21 Transcribed in Eugen Kilian, 'Schreyvogels Shakespeare-Bearbeitungen' (1903), p. 105.

22 Iffland, letter of 10 February 1799: Schiller, Nationalausgabe, Vol. 38/1 (Weimar: Böhlau 1975), p. 35.

23 Jakob Zeidler, 'Ein Censurexemplar von Grillparzer's: *König Ottokars Glück und Ende*' (1898), p. 291.

24 Nestroy, *Stücke 5* (HKA), 300; *Stücke 13* (HKA), 195, 229; Österreichische Nationalbibliothek, Theatersammlung (Österreichisches Theatermuseum), shelf-mark Cth H 31ª.

25 John Russell Stephens, *The Profession of the Playwright* (1992), p. 188.

26 Ludwig Tieck, *Kritische Schriften* (1848–52), IV, 24.

27 Charles Sealsfield, *Austria As It Is* (1828), pp. 195, 212.

28 'Instruktion für die Theaterkommissäre in den Vorstädten von Wien', dated 5 December 1803, in Glossy, 'Zur Geschichte der Theater Wiens', I, 59–64.

29 See Christian Grawe, 'Grillparzers Dramatik als Problem der zeitgenössischen österreichischen Theaterzensur' (1992), p. 171, quoting Börne on Darmstadt in 1830.

30 Glossy, 'Zur Geschichte der Wiener Theatercensur. I', pp. 326–7.

31 Glossy, 'Zur Geschichte der Theater Wiens', III, 101–3.

32 Costenoble, *Aus dem Burgtheater*, II, 243.

33 Glossy, 'Zur Geschichte der Theater Wiens', III, 105.

34 Zeidler, 'Ein Censurexemplar von Grillparzer's: *König Ottokars Glück und Ende*' (1898), p. 308.

35 Glossy, 'Zur Geschichte der Wiener Theatercensur. I', p. 303; see Rudolph Lothar, *Das Wiener Burgtheater* (1934), p. 55; Hüttner, 'Theatre censorship in Metternich's Vienna' (1980), p. 65.

36 Tieck, *Kritische Schriften*, IV, 33–7 (p. 34); Adalbert Stifter, *Sämtliche Werke*, ed. Hansludwig Geiger, 3 vols. (Tempel-Klassiker), Wiesbaden: Vollmer n.d., II, 820–2.

37 Glossy, 'Zur Geschichte der Theater Wiens', I, 5.

38 Heinrich Anschütz, *Erinnerungen aus dessen Leben und Wirken* (1866), pp. 339–40; cf. Franz Hadamowsky, *Schiller auf der Wiener Bühne 1783–1959* (1959), pp. 99–100.

39 Glossy, 'Zur Geschichte der Wiener Theatercensur. I', p. 313.

40 Glossy, 'Zur Geschichte der Theater Wiens', I, 121–2.

41 Glossy, 'Zur Geschichte der Theater Wiens', I, 173–8.

42 Glossy, 'Zur Geschichte der Theater Wiens', II, 56.

43 Eduard Genast, *Aus Weimars klassischer und nachklassischer Zeit*, p. 247.

44 See Evelyn Schreiner, 'Nationalsozialistische Kulturpolitik in Wien 1938–1945' (1980), p. 167.

45 Johann Hüttner, 'Das Burgtheaterpublikum in der ersten Hälfte des 19. Jahrhunderts' (1976), p. 177.

46 Costenoble, *Aus dem Burgtheater*, I, 38; Glossy, 'Zur Geschichte der Theater Wiens', I, 189, 253. The parable of the rings was not excluded altogether: in 1836 Costenoble records the effectiveness of Anschütz's delivery of it (Costenoble, *Aus dem Burgtheater*, II, 265).

47 Costenoble, *Aus dem Burgtheater*, I, 29–30.
48 See Karl Pörnbacher (ed.), *Erläuterungen und Dokumente. Franz Grillparzer: 'König Ottokars Glück und Ende'* (1969), pp. 64–81, for full documentation.
49 Franz Grillparzer, *Sämtliche Werke* (1909–48), I/18, 18–19.
50 Grillparzer, *Sämtliche Werke*, III/1, 300.
51 August Sauer, *Gesammelte Reden und Aufsätze zur Geschichte der Literatur in Österreich und Deutschland* (1903), p. 91–2: 'Möchte es Ihnen doch gefallen, bei der Wahl Ihrer Sujets einige Rücksicht auf unsere politischen und kirchlichen Verhältnisse zu nehmen!' See also Glossy's note in *Josef Schreyvogels Tagebücher 1810–1823* (1903), II, 423.
52 Grillparzer, *Sämtliche Werke*, I/16, 175.
53 See *Grillparzers Gespräche*, II, 234–5.
54 Grillparzer, *Sämtliche Werke*, I/16, 180.
55 Grillparzer, *Sämtliche Werke*, I/16, 176; see I/18, 27.
56 Grillparzer, *Sämtliche Werke*, I/18, 31.
57 Details in Zeidler, 'Ein Censurexemplar von Grillparzer's: *König Ottokars Glück und Ende*' (1898), 292–304.
58 Grillparzer, *Sämtliche Werke*, I/16, 179.
59 See Zeidler, 'Ein Censurexemplar von Grillparzer's: *König Ottokars Glück und Ende*', pp. 290, 311.
60 Zeidler, 'Ein Censurexemplar von Grillparzer's: *König Ottokars Glück und Ende*', pp. 310–11. On the content of the reviews see W. E. Yates, 'Grillparzer und die Rezensenten' (1994), pp. 20–3.
61 Grillparzer, *Sämtliche Werke*, III/2, 17–19 (letter dated 5 March 1828).
62 Sealsfield, *Austria As It Is*, pp. 209–10.
63 It sought 'Erlassung eines Zensurgesetzes' and 'Gründung eines wirksamen Rekurszuges in Zensurangelegenheiten': *Eduard von Bauernfelds Gesammelte Aufsätze* (1905), pp. 1–27 (quotations from p. 15), 349–51.
64 Nestroy, *Stücke 13* (HKA), 225–9.
65 Glossy, 'Zur Geschichte der Wiener Theatercensur. I', p. 319.
66 Lothar, *Das Wiener Burgtheater* (1934), p. 169.
67 Wiener Stadt- und Landesbibliothek, Handschriftensammlung, shelfmark H.I.N. 33.351.
68 Drawn from Nestroy, *Stücke 5* (HKA), 478–92; *Stücke 7/II* (HKA), 323–9; *Stücke 8* (HKA) (in preparation); *Stücke 14* (HKA), 283–4; *Stücke 22* (HKA) (in preparation).
69 Nestroy, *Stücke 5* (HKA), 485, 487 ('NB. In der Abschrift für die Censur ist dieses Lied folgendermaßen zu schreiben'), 482.
70 Nestroy, *Stücke 17/I* (HKA), 343.
71 Friedrich Kaiser, *Unter fünfzehn Theater-Direktoren*, p. 178.
72 Nestroy, *Stücke 26/I* (HKA), 26–7 (*Freiheit in Krähwinkel*, I, 14).
73 See Friedrich Kaiser, *Unter fünfzehn Theater-Direktoren*, 184–5; see also Bauernfeld, *Aus Alt- und Neu-Wien* (1873), pp. 289–93.
74 Letter of 16 July 1851 to Charlotte Birch-Pfeiffer, quoted in Susan Doering, *Der wienerische Europäer* (1992), p. 83.

75 See Anton Bettelheim, *Neue Gänge mit Ludwig Anzengruber* (1919), pp. 125–8.
76 Quoted in Franz Hadamowsky and Heinz Otte, *Die Wiener Operette* (1947), p. 84.
77 See Hadamowsky and Otte, *Die Wiener Operette*, pp. 85–7.
78 Lothar, *Das Wiener Burgtheater* (1934), pp. 280–4.
79 Hans Wagner, 'Die Zensur am Burgtheater zur Zeit Direktor Schlenthers 1898–1910' (1961), pp. 412, 407.
80 *Hugo Thimig erzählt* (1962), p. 195.
81 Maria-Christine Werba, 'Das Wiener Kabarett im Zeichen des Jugendstils' (1976), ii, 362–3.
82 Gotthard Böhm, 'Geschichte der Neuen Wiener Bühne' (1965), i, 51–63.
83 Reinhard Urbach, *Schnitzler-Kommentar* (1974), p. 186. See W. E. Yates, 'The tendentious reception of *Professor Bernhardi*' (1990).
84 *Neues Wiener Journal*, 21 January 1910; see Böhm, 'Geschichte der Neuen Wiener Bühne', i, 56.
85 *Arbeiter-Zeitung*, 30 October 1912; *Reichspost*, 3 December (article signed 'H.B.').
86 Karl Glossy, *Vierzig Jahre Deutsches Volkstheater* (1929), pp. 76, 90–5, 158.
87 'Jede Zensur ist als dem Grundrechte der Staatsbürger widersprechend als rechtsungültig aufgehoben'; quoted in Johannes Schober, 'Zensur. Eine aktuelle Betrachtung', *Neue Freie Presse*, 4 April 1926 (morning edition, no. 22111), pp. 10–11.
88 Schnitzler, *Tagebuch 1917–1919* (1985), p. 196.
89 See John McCormick, *Popular Theatres of Nineteenth-Century France* (1993), p. 110.
90 A similar condition was imposed in Berlin in 1909 when new verses for satirical songs in Nestroy's *Zu ebener Erde und erster Stock* were approved: see Jürgen Hein, 'Nestroy-Theatermanuskripte in der Zensurbibliothek des Landesarchivs Berlin', *Nestroyana* 13 (1993), 121–9 (pp. 121–2).
91 Alfred Pfoser, Kristina Pfoser-Schewig, and Gerhard Renner, *Schnitzlers 'Reigen'. Zehn Dialoge und ihre Skandalgeschichte* (1993), i, 260–8.
92 Johannes Schober, 'Zensur. Eine aktuelle Betrachtung', *Neue Freie Presse*, 4 April 1926 (morning edition, no. 22111), pp. 10–11.
93 Franz Dirnberger, 'Theaterzensur im Zwielicht der Gesetze (1918–1926)' (1983), p. 249. See also Alfred Pfoser *et al.*, *Schnitzlers 'Reigen'* (1993), i, 378–84.
94 Dirnberger, 'Theaterzensur im Zwielicht der Gesetze', pp. 259–60.

3: THE 'OLD' BURGTHEATER

1 Quoted by Alexander von Weilen in Alexander von Weilen *et al.*, *Die Theater Wiens*, 2.2.1 (1903), p. 180.
2 Franz Dirnberger (ed.), *Burgtheater in Dokumenten* (1976), p. 29.

3 Grillparzer, *Sämtliche Werke* (1909–48), 1/16, 132–3.
4 *Grillparzers Gespräche* (1904–16), VI, 54 (February 1871).
5 Frances Trollope, *Vienna and the Austrians* (1838), I, 246.
6 Eduard Wlassack, *Chronik des k.k. Hof-Burgtheaters* (1876), pp. 158–9.
7 Heinz Kindermann, 'Josef Schreyvogel und sein Publikum' (1976), p. 238.
8 See Konrad Zobel and Frederick E. Warner, 'The old Burgtheater: a structural history' (1972–3), pp. 36–43.
9 *Josef Schreyvogels Tagebücher 1810–1823* (1903), II, 102 (19 April 1815), 106 (15 and 23 May 1815), 168 (29 March 1816).
10 Zedlitz, 'Joseph Schreyvogel' (1835), p. 134. According to Costenoble this article nearly fell victim to the censor because it was insufficiently flattering to Czernin: Carl Ludwig Costenoble, *Aus dem Burgtheater* (1889), II, 224 (entry dated 17 April 1835).
11 Heinrich Anschütz, *Erinnerungen aus dessen Leben und Wirken* (1866), p. 240.
12 Letter to K. Th. Winkler (Theodor Hell), 25 November 1825, quoted in August Sauer, *Gesammelte Reden und Aufsätze zur Geschichte der Literatur in Österreich und Deutschland* (1903), p. 85: 'Die Regiegeschäfte bei dem Hoftheater, sowie bei dem Theater an der Wien sind nach und nach ganz in die Hände der Schauspieler gekommen... Ich ... nütze die Muße ... zur Verbesserung des Repertoires, worauf doch am Ende die Erhaltung jeder Bühne beruht.'
13 *Josef Schreyvogels Tagebücher 1810–1823*, II, 220, 224, 225: entries for 2, 16, and 20 December 1816.
14 E.g. *Josef Schreyvogels Tagebücher 1810–1823*, II, 224, 335: entries for 18 December 1816 and 1 October 1819.
15 Bauernfeld, *Aus Alt- und Neu-Wien* (1873), pp. 166–7.
16 See Dirnberger, *Burgtheater in Dokumenten*, pp. 29–30.
17 *Josef Schreyvogels Tagebücher 1810–1823*, II, 349 (entry for 3 June 1820); Anschütz, *Erinnerungen*, p. 218; Karl Glossy, 'Zur Geschichte der Theater Wiens', I (1915), 265.
18 *Josef Schreyvogels Tagebücher 1810–1823*, II, 366 (entry for 7 April 1821); Kindermann, 'Josef Schreyvogel und sein Publikum', p. 240.
19 *Handbook for Travellers in Southern Germany* (1837), p. 133.
20 *Josef Schreyvogels Tagebücher 1810–1823*, II, 161: 21 February 1816.
21 Bauernfeld, *Aus Alt- und Neu-Wien*, p. 165.
22 *Josef Schreyvogels Tagebücher 1810–1823*, II, 105: 9 May 1815.
23 I. F. Castelli, *Memoiren meines Lebens* (1914 edn), II, 284.
24 Ludwig Tieck, *Kritische Schriften* (1848–52), IV, 25.
25 Tieck, *Kritische Schriften*, IV, 26, 33.
26 Grillparzer, *Sämtliche Werke*, 1/16, 123.
27 Grillparzer, *Sämtliche Werke*, 1/16, 118.
28 Frances Trollope, *Vienna and the Austrians*, I, 288; Heinrich Laube, *Schriften zum Theater* (1959), p. 358; Ludwig Speidel, *Schauspieler* (1911), p. 238.

29 *Grillparzers Gespräche*, III, 14–15.

30 Grillparzer, *Sämtliche Werke*, II/8, 296 (diary note no. 1626).

31 Grillparzer, *Sämtliche Werke*, II/10, 188 (diary note no. 3262, May 1837); *Grillparzers Gespräche*, III, 194–5 (to Foglar, December 1839); *Sämtliche Werke*, I/16, 214.

32 Zedlitz, 'Joseph Schreyvogel', p. 135.

33 *Gesammelte Schriften von Thomas und Karl August West* (1829), II/2, 65–79: 'Dramaturgische Briefe. Siebenter Brief'.

34 Grillparzer, *Sämtliche Werke*, I/16, 196. Schreyvogel too had underlined the disadvantage for Schiller of the interruption in his direct contact with the theatre: *Gesammelte Schriften von Thomas und Karl August West*, II/2, 68.

35 Laube, *Schriften zum Theater*, p. 375.

36 Tieck, *Kritische Schriften*, IV, 35–6.

37 Anschütz, *Erinnerungen*, p. 234.

38 See 'Aus Bauernfelds Tagebüchern' (1895), p. 61 (entry for 30 May 1832).

39 Bauernfeld, *Aus Alt- und Neu-Wien*, p. 164.

40 Costenoble, *Aus dem Burgtheater*, II, 110.

41 Bauernfeld, *Gesammelte Aufsätze* (1905), pp. 214–15.

42 Grillparzer, *Sämtliche Werke* (1909–48), II/10, 141 (diary entry no. 3168).

43 Ludwig Böck and Wilhelm Englmann (eds), *Grillparzers Selbstbiographie und Bildnisse* (1923), p. 241.

44 See *Grillparzers Gespräche*, II, 261–62; VI, 168; *Sämtliche Werke* (1909–48), I/18, 27.

45 Grillparzer, *Sämtliche Werke*, I/18, 28.

46 See Grillparzer, *Sämtliche Werke*, III/2, 65; I/18, 49; III/4, 72; I/18, 55.

47 Wiener Stadt- und Landesbibliothek, H.I.N. 36.851, 34.375; see Otto Rommel, *Johann Nestroy* (1930), p. 57; see also Oskar Pausch (ed.), *Theaterkult in Wien* (Biblos-Schriften, 121), Vienna: Österreichisches Theatermuseum 1983, no. 176.

48 *Josef Schreyvogels Tagebücher 1810–1823*, II, 179, 380; Kindermann, 'Josef Schreyvogel und sein Publikum', p. 240.

49 See Anschütz, *Erinnerungen*, p. 219.

50 Wlassack, *Chronik des k.k. Hof-Burgtheaters*, pp. 157–8.

51 *Josef Schreyvogels Tagebücher 1810–1823*, II, 105 (entry for 12 May 1815).

52 Bauernfeld, 'Die Wiener Volksbühne', 2 (1853), p. 100: 'Die Stücke ... sind nichts – die Persönlichkeit der Schauspieler ist Alles'; Speidel, *Schauspieler*, p. 237 (first published *Neue Freie Presse*, 15 May 1887); Comte Paul Vasili, *La Société de Vienne* (1885), p. 342; Stefan Zweig, *Die Welt von gestern* (1941), p. 22; Egon Friedell, *Wozu das Theater?* (1966), p. 143.

53 Laube, *Schriften zum Theater*, p. 161; Costenoble, *Aus dem Burgtheater*, II, 254–8.

54 *Das Sonntagsblatt* (Vienna, 1807–09), I, 93; I/2, 190; *Gesammelte*

Schriften von Thomas und Karl August West, II/I, 69, 138–9, 157–8; II/2, 187. Grillparzer, *Sämtliche Werke*, II/7, 361 (diary entry no. 933); I/14, 121.

55 *Handbook for Travellers in Southern Germany*, p. 133.
56 *Bilder und Träume aus Wien* (1836), I, 179.
57 See 'Aus Bauernfelds Tagebüchern', p. 61: June 1832.
58 Costenoble, *Aus dem Burgtheater*, II, 115: entry for 14 June 1832.
59 See Rudolph Lothar, *Das Wiener Burgtheater* (1934), p. 56.
60 See Johann Hüttner, 'Das Burgtheaterpublikum in der ersten Hälfte des 19. Jahrhunderts' (1976), pp. 170–7.
61 Laube, *Schriften zum Theater*, p. 609. See also *Hugo Thimig erzählt* (1962), pp. 198–9 (diary, 1 June 1911).
62 Anschütz, *Erinnerungen*, p. 234.
63 L.Sp., 'Eine Krisis des Burgtheaters', *Neue Freie Presse*, 6 January 1889 (no. 8753, Morgenblatt), pp. 1–2 ('Die Schaubude war verschwunden, man befand sich mitten in der besten Gesellschaft').
64 See Lothar, *Das Wiener Burgtheater* (1899), p. 191; Stefan Zweig, *Die Welt von gestern* (1941), p. 22.
65 For Costenoble's account of the production and its reception see Costenoble, *Aus dem Burgtheater*, II, 265–72. The three reviews by Saphir, published in the *Theaterzeitung* on 26 and 28 March 1835, 9–10 September 1835, and 26 March 1836, are reprinted in *M. G. Saphirs Schriften*, Volksausgabe, 26 vols., Brünn, Vienna, Leipzig: Karafiat, n.d. [1887–89], IV, 27–58.
66 Saphir, 'Der Rezensent in dem Gasluster des neuen Carl-Theaters', Part 2, *Der Humorist*, 16 December 1847 (no. 300), pp. 1197–9 (p. 1198).
67 Grillparzer, *Sämtliche Werke* (1909–48), II/9, 217 (diary entry no. 2304).
68 See W. E. Yates, 'Nestroy und die Rezensenten' (1987), 36–9.
69 See Costenoble, *Aus dem Burgtheater*, II, 222–4, 236, 241, 335.
70 See *Morgenblatt für gebildete Leser*, 3 March 1843 (no. 53), pp. 211–12 (Korrespondenz-Nachrichten).
71 Grillparzer, while by this time not a frequent theatre-goer, was clear that by 1844 there was a paucity of outstanding acting talents by comparison with the Burgtheater of the past: see *Grillparzers Gespräche* (1904–16), III, 311.
72 Karl Gutzkow, *Wiener Eindrücke* (1845), pp. 296–301.
73 Dirnberger, *Burgtheater in Dokumenten*, p. 54; see also Lothar, *Das Wiener Burgtheater* (1934), p. 135.
74 See Heinrich Reschauer and Moritz Smets, *Das Jahr 1848* (1872), II, 44–5.
75 *Allgemeine Theaterzeitung*, 7 April 1848 (no. 84), p. 339; reprinted in Nestroy, *Stücke 26/1* (HKA), 120–1.
76 Anschütz, *Erinnerungen*, pp. 428–9.
77 Laube outlined his plans in a letter of 25 April 1848 to Dietrichstein, quoted in Ludwig Speidel, 'Theater' (1888), p. 351.

78 See Ferdinand von Seyfried, *Rückschau in das Theaterleben Wiens seit den letzten fünfzig Jahren* (1864), p. 36.

79 See Laube, *Schriften zum Theater*, p. 195; Lothar, *Das Wiener Burgtheater* (1934), pp. 133–4.

80 J. K. Ratislav, 'Laubes Kampf um die Subvention des Burgtheaters' (1944), pp. 44–60.

81 Quoted in Lothar, *Das Wiener Burgtheater* (1934), pp. 212–13.

82 Laube, *Schriften zum Theater*, p. 177.

83 Laube, *Schriften zum Theater*, pp. 357–8.

84 Laube, *Schriften zum Theater*, pp. 385, 291.

85 Laube, *Schriften zum Theater*, pp. 331, 177.

86 Laube, *Schriften zum Theater*, p. 216.

87 Dirnberger, *Burgtheater in Dokumenten*, p. 57.

88 Laube, *Schriften zum Theater*, pp. 382–3.

89 Laube, *Schriften zum Theater*, p. 549.

90 Laube, *Schriften zum Theater*, pp. 378, 401, 391.

91 Quoted in Lothar, *Das Wiener Burgtheater* (1934), pp. 205–12.

92 Dirnberger, *Burgtheater in Dokumenten*, p. 65.

93 Laube, *Schriften zum Theater*, p. 391.

94 See Alexander von Weilen in Alexander von Weilen *et al.*, *Die Theater Wiens*, 2.2.2, p. 210.

95 See A. von Sternberg [= Alexander Freiherr von Ungern-Sternberg], *Ein Fasching in Wien* (1851), quoted in Fritz Fuhrich, 'Burgtheater und Öffentlichkeit' (1976), pp. 337–8.

96 Laube, *Schriften zum Theater*, p. 637.

97 Max Martersteig, *Das deutsche Theater im neunzehnten Jahrhundert* (1904), quoted in Fuhrich, 'Burgtheater und Öffentlichkeit', p. 356.

98 Ludwig Hevesi (1894), quoted in Fuhrich, 'Burgtheater und Öffentlichkeit', p. 365.

99 Eduard Genast, *Aus Weimars klassischer und nachklassischer Zeit*, p. 247; Tieck, *Kritische Schriften*, IV, 23.

100 Laube, *Schriften zum Theater*, p. 632.

101 Laube, *Schriften zum Theater*, p. 179.

102 Speidel, 'Theater', p. 379.

103 Dirnberger, *Burgtheater in Dokumenten*, p. 62.

104 Speidel, 'Theater', p. 383.

105 Lothar, *Das Wiener Burgtheater* (1934), pp. 234, 239.

106 Richard Smekal (ed.), *Das alte Burgtheater (1776–1888)* (1916), p. 188.

107 Adolf Wilbrandt, quoted in Smekal, *Das alte Burgtheater*, p. 187.

108 Ludwig Speidel, *Schauspieler* (1911), pp. 47–62 (reviews first published in the *Neue Freie Presse*, 29 September and 4 November 1875).

109 Anschütz, *Erinnerungen*, p. 239.

110 Speidel, *Schauspieler*, p. 241; Ludwig Hevesi, quoted in Fritz Fuhrich, 'Burgtheater und Öffentlichkeit' (1976), p. 365.

111 Speidel, *Schauspieler*, p. 281.

112 Laube, *Schriften zum Theater*, p. 164.
113 *Aus der Briefmappe eines Burgtheaterdirektors* (1925), p. 257: letter of 27 June 1872 to Kathi Fröhlich.
114 Submission dated 25 March 1872, quoted in Karl Kaderschafka, '*Ein Bruderzwist in Habsburg* auf der Bühne' (1924), p. 230.
115 Emil Kuh, *Wiener Zeitung*, 29 November 1872. The critical reception is documented in Grillparzer, *Sämtliche Werke* (1909–48), I/21, 326–48.
116 Ludwig Speidel, *Neue Freie Presse*, 23 January 1873, morning edition.
117 Smekal (ed.), *Das alte Burgtheater*, pp. 215–17.
118 'Aus Adolf Wilbrandts Burgtheater-Erinnerungen', in Heinrich Glücksmann (ed.), *Zu Adolf Wilbrandts 100. Geburtstag* (1937), pp. 51–99 (p. 72).
119 *Aus der Briefmappe eines Burgtheaterdirektors*, p. 285: letter of 2 April 1872.
120 Text in Smekal (ed.), *Das alte Burgtheater*, pp. 225–8. At her own request Charlotte Wolter was buried in the costume she wore in the part of Iphigenie: see Speidel, *Schauspieler*, p. 277.
121 Cf. letter of 4 November 1898 from Alfred von Berger to Rudolph Lothar, quoted in Lothar, *Das Wiener Burgtheater* (1934), pp. 284–7 (p. 285).
122 Rudolf Tyrolt, *Vom Lebenswege eines alten Schauspielers* (1914), p. 210.
123 Entries for 1 October, 5 October, and 25 November 1888, quoted in Fred Hennings, *Zweimal Burgtheater* (1955), pp. 67–8; Lothar, *Das Wiener Burgtheater* (1934), p. 271.
124 Karl Kraus, 'Das Denkmal eines Schauspielers', *Die Fackel* 391–392 (1914), pp. 31–40.
125 Schnitzler, *Tagebuch 1909–1912* (1981), p. 193: entry for 16 November 1910.
126 *Hugo Thimig erzählt*, p. 214: diary, 4 November 1912.
127 Quoted in Lothar, *Das Wiener Burgtheater* (1934), pp. 353–7.

4: COMMERCIAL THEATRES IN 'OLD VIENNA'

1 See Johann Hüttner, 'Baugeschichte und Spielplan des Theaters am Franz Josefs Kai' (1970), p. 87.
2 Friedrich Kaiser, *Unter fünfzehn Theater-Direktoren* (1870), pp. 15–17.
3 Heinz Kindermann, 'Josef Schreyvogel und sein Publikum' (1976), p. 238.
4 See review, *Allgemeine Theaterzeitung*, 30 August 1825 (no. 104), pp. 426–7.
5 Karl Glossy, 'Zur Geschichte der Theater Wiens', II (1920), 108.
6 The text of Meisl's adaptation is given in the programme of the Burgtheater production (Programmbuch no. 60, 1989/90); that of Kringsteiner's original in *Ein Jahrhundert Alt-Wiener Parodie*, ed. Otto Rommel, Vienna and Leipzig: Österreichischer Bundesverlag 1930, pp. 41–72, and in *Parodien des Wiener Volkstheaters*, ed. Jürgen Hein, Stuttgart: Reclam 1986, pp. 29–66.
7 Charles Mathews, *Othello, the Moor of Fleet Street (1833)*, ed. Manfred

Draudt, Tübingen and Basle: Francke 1993; see also Manfred Draudt, ' "Committing outrage against the Bard" ' (1993).

8 Nestroy, *Briefe* (HKA), p. 57: letter of 14 March 1842.

9 See Raimund, *Sämtliche Werke* (1924–34), IV, 25.

10 Bauernfeld, *Aus Alt- und Neu-Wien* (1873), p. 49. The comparison with Virginie Déjazet was commonly made; see Ignaz Franz Castelli, *Memoiren meines Lebens* (1914), I, 274.

11 Castelli, *Memoiren meines Lebens*, I, 274.

12 Bernhard Bauer, *Komödiantin – Dirne? Der Künstlerin Leben und Lieben im Lichte der Wahrheit*, Vienna and Leipzig: Fiba-Verlag 1927, p. 280.

13 *Sonntags-Blätter*, 29 January 1843, p. 103. Excerpted in Grillparzer, *Sämtliche Werke* (1909–48), I/20, p. 30.

14 M. G. Saphir, *Theaterzeitung*, 30 September 1835 (no. 195), p. 779 (reviewing *Zu ebener Erde und erster Stock*); Dr. Wagner, 'Die Lokalposse jüngerer Zeit', *Sonntags-Blätter*, 12 November 1843 (no. 46), pp. 1093–5, reprinted in Nestroy, *Stücke 20* (HKA), 167–9: 'Was ist in diesen auf den Kopf gestellten Tragödien noch volksthümlich...?' (p. 1094).

15 Eduard von Bauernfeld, 'Die Wiener Volksbühne', 2 (1853), p. 100; *Aus Alt- und Neu-Wien*, p. 53.

16 See *Sternstunden im Theater an der Wien* (1962), p. 20.

17 Grillparzer, *Sämtliche Werke* (1909–48), I/10, 46.

18 See Anton Bauer, *150 Jahre Theater an der Wien* (1952), p. 107.

19 Jürgen Hein, 'Grabbe's *Don Juan und Faust* in Wien' (1992). Some of the cuts were almost certainly made in response to the censorship conventions (see p. 39).

20 Karl Glossy, 'Zur Geschichte der Theater Wiens', II (1920), pp. 59–60.

21 Glossy, 'Zur Geschichte der Theater Wiens', II, 63.

22 See W. E. Yates, 'Grillparzer und die Rezensenten' (1994), pp. 22–3.

23 Franz Hadamowsky, *Das Theater an der Wien* (1962), p. 33; see also Anton Bauer, *150 Jahre Theater an der Wien*, pp. 117–24; Johann Hüttner, 'Theater als Geschäft', I, 199; II, 463.

24 Hüttner, 'Theater als Geschäft' (1982), I, 198.

25 Hüttner, 'Theater als Geschäft', I, 199.

26 Glossy, 'Zur Geschichte der Theater Wiens', II, pp. 98–100.

27 *Der Wanderer*, 20 November 1837 (no. 276), p. 1104; reprinted in Nestroy, *Stücke 13* (HKA), 206–8 (p. 208).

28 *Josef Schreyvogels Tagebücher 1810–1823* (1903), II, 106: entries for 18 and 22 May 1815.

29 See Peter Branscombe, 'The Connexions between Drama and Music in the Viennese Popular Theatre' (1976), pp. 145–6.

30 Wiener Stadt- und Landesbibliothek H.I.N. 131.607. Quoted in Branscombe, 'The Connexions between Drama and Music in the Viennese Popular Theatre', pp. 142–3.

31 The text is given in Hansjörg Schenker, 'Theaterdirektor Carl und die Staberl-Figur' (1986), pp. 296–366.

32   See reports in *Der Humorist*, 14 March 1838 (no. 42), p. 167 (signed: ch l— [= Wilhelm Schlesinger?]), and *Wiener Telegraph*, 14 March 1838 (no. 32), p. 134. Reprinted in Nestroy, *Stücke 14* (HKA), 170–5.

33   The text is reproduced in Anton Bauer, *150 Jahre Theater an der Wien*, pp. 138–9; see Karl Gutzkow, *Wiener Eindrücke* (1845), p. 294.

34   *Die Grenzboten* (Leipzig), 6 (1847) (1. Semester, Vol. 2), no. 20, p. 310 (signed o——o).

35   *Der Humorist*, 13 December 1847 (no. 297), p. 1186.

36   Hüttner, 'Theater als Geschäft', 1, 226–8.

37   See Nestroy, *Stücke 12* (HKA), 148–57; on the audience see in particular the account by M. G. Saphir, *Der Humorist*, 21 January 1837 (no. 9), p. 36 (*Stücke 12*, p. 153); on Nestroy's reaction see the *Theaterzeitung*, 19 January 1837 (no. 14), p. 59 (*Stücke 12*, p. 150).

38   See Carl Ludwig Costenoble, *Aus dem Burgtheater* (1889), 1, 134 (entry dated 28 August 1821); also Gottfried Riedl (ed.), *Raimund. Bilder aus einem Theaterleben* (1990), p. 26.

39   See *Der Sammler*, 17 October 1842 (no. 166), pp. 688–9; reprinted in Nestroy, *Stücke 18/1* (HKA), 138–9.

40   *Handbook for Travellers in Southern Germany* (1837), p. 133.

41   When he died he left a bequest to an illegitimate daughter born in 1848, and his will also mentions a previous gift to another daughter, born in 1844: 'Das Testament des Theaterdirectors Carl' (1854), pp. 818–19 (§ ix).

42   *Allgemeine Theaterzeitung*, 28 November 1842 (no. 284), p. 1250, review (signed 'Hth'): '...wenn man sie, wäre ihr unser Dialekt geläufig, die zweite *Krones* nennen könnte, so kommt ihr, wie sie jetzt ist, der Name der deutschen *Dejazet* unstreitig mit besserem Rechte zu.'

43   Walter Pöll, 'Der Wiener Theaterdichter Friedrich Kaiser' (1947), p. 33.

44   See Jeanne Benay, 'Das Wiener Volkstheater als Intention und Strategiedramaturgie' (1988), pp. 130–2. Nestroy's sources are summarized in Jürgen Hein, *Johann Nestroy* (1990), 70–98; over and above those given by Hein, *Die beiden Herrn Söhne* is also based on a *vaudeville* text.

45   Kaiser, *Unter fünfzehn Theater-Direktoren* (1870), p. 177.

46   See Johann Hüttner, 'Machte sich Nestroy bezahlt?' (1979), p. 8.

47   Friedrich Kaiser, 'Wenzel Scholz. Ereignisse und Denkwürdigkeiten aus seinem Leben' (1858), Part 17; Ferdinand Ritter von Seyfried, *Rückschau in das Theaterleben Wiens seit den letzten fünfzig Jahren* (1864), p. 108.

48   See Nestroy, *Stücke 26/1* (HKA), 190–202, 255–9.

49   See Otto Rommel, *Johann Nestroy* (1930), p. 542–8.

50   See Kaiser, 'Wenzel Scholz', Part 20.

51   See Hüttner, 'Machte sich Nestroy bezahlt?', p. 13.

52   Kaiser, 'Wenzel Scholz', Part 8.

53   Friedrich Kaiser, *Theater-Director Carl* (1854), pp. 65–8.

54 Kaiser, *Theater-Director Carl* (1854), p. 57.
55 Rommel, *Johann Nestroy* (1930), pp. 56–7, 541–64. See also Kaiser, *Theater-Director Carl*, pp. 65–8, and Jeanne Benay, *Friedrich Kaiser (1814–1874) et le théâtre populaire en Autriche au XIXe siècle* (1993), 1, 443–6. For a contemporary defence see *Der Wanderer*, 16 April 1845 (no. 91), pp. 362–4, reprinted in Nestroy, *Stücke 23/1* (HKA), 107–14.
56 Letter of 15 November 1840 to Bäuerle (Wiener Stadt- und Landesbibliothek, H.I.N. 34.455).
57 Wiener Stadt- und Landesbibliothek, H.I.N. 24.756; transcription in Rommel, *Johann Nestroy* (1930), pp. 563–4.
58 Hüttner, 'Machte sich Nestroy bezahlt?', p. 13; 'Theater als Geschäft', I, 253.
59 Rommel, *Johann Nestroy*, p. 549.
60 Kaiser, 'Wenzel Scholz', Part 8.
61 Ferdinand von Seyfried, *Rückschau in das Theaterleben Wiens*, p. 77.
62 See Rommel, *Johann Nestroy*, p. 559.
63 'Das Testament des Theaterdirectors Carl', p. 821 (§ xv).
64 Wiener Stadt- und Landesbibliothek, H.I.N. 10.043.
65 *Theaterzeitung*, 8 August 1854 (no. 175), p. 744.
66 See Johann Hüttner, 'Johann Nestroy im Theaterbetrieb seiner Zeit' (1977), p. 234.
67 See Nestroy, *Stücke 32* (HKA), 249; Johann Hüttner, 'Theater im Zeitalter Kaiser Franz Josephs' (1984), pp. 348–9.
68 See Johann Hüttner, 'Volkstheater als Geschäft' (1986), pp. 140–1.
69 Kaiser, *Theater-Director Carl*, p. 74.
70 Kaiser, 'Wenzel Scholz', Part 10.
71 See Hüttner, 'Theater als Geschäft', I, 196–229; Schenker, 'Theaterdirektor Carl und die Staberl-Figur', pp. 105–15.
72 See Schenker, 'Theaterdirektor Carl und die Staberl-Figur', pp. 90–1. This also affected later accounts: see Hüttner, 'Theater als Geschäft', I, 207.
73 Kaiser, 'Wenzel Scholz', Part 15.
74 Bauer, *150 Jahre Theater an der Wien*, p. 137.
75 Nestroy, *Briefe* (HKA), pp. 68–9: letter of 22 May 1846 to Moriz Märzroth.
76 Bauernfeld, *Großjährig. Lustspiel in zwei Aufzügen und dem Nachspiel: Ein neuer Mensch*, Vienna: Gerold 1849, p. x: 'Aber sie honoriren blos *Manuscripte*! Dabei hat der Autor den Nachtheil, daß er sein neues Stück, welches etwa "einschlug", erst *nach Jahren* drucken lassen kann...'
77 Nestroy, *Briefe* (HKA), pp. 34–5 (letter of 14 January 1836), 38 (letter of 23 May 1836 to Heinrich Börnstein), 98 (letter of 20 April 1852).
78 See Susan Doering, *Der wienerische Europäer* (1992), pp. 80–4; Jeanne Benay, *Friedrich Kaiser (1814–1874) et le théâtre populaire en Autriche*, I, 420–9.

79 See Jürgen Hein, 'Frühere Verhältnisse und Alte Bekanntschaften' (1989–90), p. 53.

80 See Peter Schmitt, *Schauspieler und Theaterbetrieb* (1990), pp. 194–202.

81 Bernhard Gutt in *Bohemia*, 27 May 1847 (no. 84), p. [1]. On Nestroy's *Gastspiele* see Wolfgang Neuber, *Nestroys Rhetorik. Wirkungspoetik und Altwiener Volkskomödie im 19. Jahrhundert* (Abhandlungen zur Kunst-, Musik und Literaturwissenschaft, 373), Bonn: Bouvier 1987, pp. 182–203.

82 See Nestroy, *Stücke 18/1* (HKA), 139–49.

83 See Rommel, *Johann Nestroy*, p. 512.

84 Grillparzer, *Sämtliche Werke* (1909–48), II/10, 98 (diary note, 27 May 1836).

85 On Carl's tour see *Der Sammler*, 14 September 1840 (no. 147), p. 588, and 28 July 1840 (no. 120), p. 479; also Kaiser, *Unter fünfzehn Theater-Direktoren*, pp. 119–20.

86 See Nestroy, *Stücke 21* (HKA), 125–6.

87 See John Russell Stephens, *The Profession of the Playwright* (1992), pp. 84–95.

88 See Murray G. Hall, *Österreichische Verlagsgeschichte 1918–1938*, 2 vols., Vienna, Cologne, Graz: Böhlau 1985, I, 28–37.

89 See Stephens, *The Profession of the Playwright*, pp. 97–8.

90 See Nestroy, *Stücke 21* (HKA), 121–5. This is not a phenomenon limited to Vienna; in Berlin the *Vossische Zeitung* printed Franz Wallner's 'Pariser Theaterbriefe' in 1854: see Hein, 'Frühere Verhältnisse und Alte Bekanntschaften', p. 55.

91 Glossy, 'Zur Geschichte der Theater Wiens. II', pp. 35–6; *Josef Schreyvogels Tagebücher*, II, 381–2, 534.

92 Ferdinand von Seyfried, *Rückschau in das Theaterleben Wiens*, pp. 83–4.

93 *Allgemeine Theaterzeitung*, 31 March 1846 (no. 77), p. 307.

94 E.g. Max Schmidt, *Österreichisches Morgenblatt*, 19 March 1838 (no. 34, p. 136 (reviewing Nestroy's *Glück, Mißbrauch und Rückkehr*); reprinted in Nestroy, *Stücke 14* (HKA), 181.

95 E.g. *Morgenblatt für gebildete Leser*, 15 January 1838 (Nr. 13), p. 52, on *Das Haus der Temperamente*, reprinted in W. E. Yates, 'Nestroy im Morgenblatt', *Nestroyana*, 12 (1992), 81–6 (p. 83); 20 July 1838 (Nr. 173), p. 692.

96 E.g. *Morgenblatt für gebildete Leser*, 25 February 1839 (Nr. 48), p. 192: 'Einen großen Theil der Schuld dieses Verfalls der Volksbühne trägt der Theaterdirektor Carl.'

97 *Wiener Zeitschrift für Kunst, Literatur, Theater und Mode*, 2 May 1833 (no. 53), pp. 435–6; reprinted in Nestroy, *Stücke 5* (HKA), 359–61.

98 E.g. *Der Wanderer*, 19 January 1837 (no. 16), p. 63, reviewing *Eine Wohnung ist zu vermieten*, reprinted in Nestroy, *Stücke 12* (HKA), 150; *Der Humorist*, 27 March 1843, pp. 250–1, reviewing *Liebesgeschichten und Heiratssachen*, reprinted *Stücke 19* (HKA), 154–6 (see p. 155); *Wiener*

Zeitschrift..., 20 November 1843 (no. 231), pp. 1843–4, review of *Nur Ruhe!*, signed 'Stbe.' (=Emanuel Straube), reprinted *Stücke 20* (HKA), 178–9 (p. 179).

99 On the use of French material see *Der Sammler*, 27 November 1841 (no. 189), pp. 774–6, and *Österreichisches Morgenblatt*, 27 November 1841 (no. 142), p. 587; on alleged 'indecency' see Emanuel Straube, *Wiener Zeitschrift...*, 27 November 1841 (no. 189), pp. 1510–11 (signed 'Stbe.'); L. Viola, *Der Wiener Zuschauer*, 1 December 1841 (no. 144), pp. 1440–1.

100 Performances in the Kärntnertortheater: 9 December 1844 and 25 January 1845; see review in *Allgemeine Theaterzeitung*, 11 December (no. 297), pp. 1214–15.

101 See *Der Humorist*, 28 February 1845 (no. 51, p. 202); *Sonntagsblätter*, 2 March 1845 (no. 9), p. 213–14 [Beilage] (review by Dr. Wagner); *Der Zuschauer*, 5 March 1845 (no. 28), pp. 299–300.

102 *Der Humorist*, 12 March 1842 (no. 51), pp. 206–7, reviewing *Einen Jux will er sich machen*, reprinted in Nestroy, *Stücke 18/1* (HKA), 125–7; *Der Humorist*, 5–6 January 1844, p. 22, reviewing *Eisenbahnheiraten*, reprinted in Nestroy, *Stücke 20* (HKA), 270–2 (p. 272).

103 Franz V. Schindler, *Österreichisches Morgenblatt*, 1 March 1845 (no. 26, pp. 102–3 (p. 102)).

104 *Theaterzeitung*, 24 September 1840 (no. 230), p. 1062.

105 Nestroy, *Stücke 17/1* (HKA), 59 (*Der Talisman*, II, 24).

106 Kaiser, *Theater-Director Carl*, pp. 51–2.

107 See Nestroy, *Stücke 17/1* (HKA), 325–6.

108 H. Adami, *Theaterzeitung*, 5 May 1846 (no. 107), p. 426.

109 K. Arnold, 'Ueber den Verfall der Volkstheater', *Österreichische Blätter für Literatur und Kunst, Geografie, Geschichte, Statistik und Naturkunde*, 30 March 1847 (no. 76), pp. 301–2.

110 E.g. E. Norbert, *Die Gegenwart*, 12 April 1847 (no. 83), pp. 386–7.

111 A. F. Draxler, *Der Wanderer*, 1 May 1847 (no. 104), pp. 413–14.

112 Eduard Breier, *Wiener Zeitschrift...*, 10 April 1847 (no. 72), pp. 186–87; 12 April 1847 (no. 73), pp. 290–1.

113 *Wiener Bote* (*Sonntagsblätter*, Beilage), 11 April 1847 (no. 15), p. 119.

114 M. G. Saphir, 'Der Rezensent in dem Gasluster des neuen Carl-Theaters' (1847), p. 1198.

115 Friedrich Kaiser, *Der Rastelbinder*, Vienna: Wallishauser 1850, p. 84; *Sie ist verheiratet*, Vienna: Wallishausser 1846, p. 38; *Junker und Knecht*, Vienna: Wallishausser 1850, p. 39.

116 See Erwin Rieger, *Offenbach und seine Wiener Schule* (1920), p. 31.

117 M. G. Saphir, 'Des Wiener Volksstücks Glück und Ende' (1847), especially pp. 451, 465.

118 'Dem Erbauer des Carl-Theaters', *Die Gegenwart*, 28 December 1847 (no. 299), p. 1281: 'Und freundlich öffnet sich das Haus der Pracht / Den neu verjüngten Volkstheatermusen.'

119 Quoted in Johann Hüttner, 'Volk sucht sein Theater' (1988), p. 34.

120 *Der Theater-Mayr*, ed. Karl Michael Kisler (1988), p. 233 (Michael Mayr, diary entry dated 31 December 1842).

121 E.g. *Wiener Zeitschrift...*, 14 February 1842 (no. 32), p. 255 (review signed 'Stbe.' [= Emanuel Straube]). See W. E. Yates, 'Nestroy und die Rezensenten' (1987), p. 34.

122 Ferdinand von Seyfried, *Rückschau in das Theaterleben Wiens*, p. 63.

123 See *Der Humorist*, 1 September 1845 (no. 209), pp. 835–6 (signed H—r. [= Jakob Hausner]).

124 See *Der Humorist*, 1–3 November 1845 (no. 262–3), p. 1048 (signed H—r. [Jakob Hausner]).

125 *Bilder und Träume aus Wien* (1836), 1, 207.

126 See Anton Bauer and Gustav Kropatschek, *200 Jahre Theater in der Josefstadt* (1988), p. 60.

127 Dr. Wagner, 'Theater-Wochenbericht', *Sonntagsblätter*, 5 April 1846 (no. 14), p. 336.

128 Ludwig Speidel, 'Theater', p. 401.

129 Kaiser, 'Wenzel Scholz', Parts 15, 18.

130 Kaiser, *Unter fünfzehn Theater-Direktoren*, p. 262.

131 Kaiser, *Unter fünfzehn Theater-Direktoren*, pp. 263–6; Ferdinand von Seyfried, *Rückschau in das Theaterleben Wiens*, p 131.

132 See Franz Hadamowsky and Heinz Otte, *Die Wiener Operette* (1947), pp. 41–3, 52–3.

133 Hadamowsky and Otte, *Die Wiener Operette*, p. 82.

134 *Der Zwischen-Akt*, 10 May 1867; quoted in Hans Pemmer, 'Das Harmonietheater in der Wasagasse' (1966), p. 26.

135 Nestroy, *Stücke 31* (HKA), 18 (*Kampl*, 1, 11).

136 See Kaiser, *Unter fünfzehn Theater-Direktoren*, p. 190.

137 Ludwig Anzengruber, *Briefe* (1902), 1, 289 (letter of 30 October 1876 to Julius Duboc).

138 Text of the prologue, *Fremden-Blatt*, 3 January 1881 (no. 2), p. 6, reprinted in W. E. Yates, 'Nestroy und Bauernfeld' (1994), pp. 19–20.

5: OPERA AND OPERETTA

1 Mozart, *Briefe und Aufzeichnungen*. Gesamtausgabe, ed. Wilhelm A. Bauer and Otto Erich Deutsch, 7 vols., Kassel: Bärenreiter 1962–75, III, 102 (letter no. 586, 4 April 1781).

2 Charles Sealsfield, *Austria As It Is* (1828), p. 202.

3 Frances Trollope, *Vienna and the Austrians* (1838), II, 20.

4 See Tim Carter, *W. A. Mozart: 'Le nozze di Figaro'* (1987), pp. 122–5.

5 See O. E. Deutsch, *Schubert. Die Dokumente seines Lebens* (1964), pp. 100–9, 212–19.

6 Grillparzer, *Sämtliche Werke* (1909–48), III/5, 254.

7 *Handbook for Travellers in Southern Germany* (1837), p. 133.

8 Frances Trollope, *Vienna and the Austrians*, 1, 283.

9 *Wiener allgemeine Musik-Zeitung*, 19 August 1847 (no. 99), p. 398.

10 See Marc Baer, *Theatre and Disorder in Late Georgian London* (1992), pp. 210–14.

11 Sealsfield, *Austria As It Is*, p. 203.

12 See O. E. Deutsch, *Schubert. Die Dokumente seines Lebens*, p. 207: letter to Franz von Schober, 30 November 1823.

13 See Eduard Hanslick, 'Musik' (1888), p. 312.

14 *Der Sammler*, 19 June 1827 (no. 73), p. 291 (F.: 'Mozart. Nach Anhörung seiner "Entführung"'); 12 March 1842 (no. 41), p. 165 (signed: —ng—).

15 See *Der Sammler*, 10 November 1827 (no. 135), p. 539.

16 Heinrich Adami, *Allgemeine Theaterzeitung*, 13 January 1842 (no. 11), p. 50: 'Wenn die Opern von Anno 41 nicht ziehen wollen, probiert man es mit einer von Anno 90.'

17 H—r. [Jakob Hausner], *Der Humorist*, 13 January 1842 (no. 9), p. 39.

18 See Franz Hadamowsky, *Wien. Theatergeschichte* (1988), pp. 325–6.

19 Riki Raab, 'Das Wiener Opernballett' (1986), p. 212.

20 See Adam Müller-Guttenbrunn, *Das Wiener Theaterleben* (1890), pp. 68–9.

21 See Nestroy, *Stücke 14* (HKA), 263–79.

22 Cf. Nestroy, *Briefe* (HKA), p. 41: letter of 29 September 1836 to Josef Pellet.

23 'Künstler-Silhouetten aus Wien' (1843), p. 1139.

24 *Wiener Theaterzeitung*, 24 October 1858 (no. 245), p. 980.

25 See Franz Hadamowsky and Heinz Otte, *Die Wiener Operette* (1947), pp. 51–3.

26 See Ludwig Speidel, 'Theater' (1888), p. 404.

27 See P. Walter Jacob, *Jacques Offenbach in Selbstzeugnissen und Bilddokumenten* (1969), p. 81.

28 Speidel, 'Theater', p. 402.

29 See Gottfried Kraus (ed.), *Musik in Österreich* (1989), p. 250.

30 Beatrix Schiferer, *Girardi* (1975), p. 23–4.

31 *Die Fackel* 462–471 (9 October 1917), pp. 180–4 (pp. 182–3).

32 Franz Dirnberger (ed.), *Burgtheater in Dokumenten* (1976), p. 66.

33 *Neue Freie Presse*, 29 June 1869 (signed 'Ed.H.'); quoted in Theodor Jauner, *Fünf Jahre Wiener Opertheater 1875–1880* (1962), p. 26.

6: THE LATE NINETEENTH CENTURY: NEW FOUNDATIONS

1 Heinrich Laube, *Schriften zum Theater* (1959), p. 550.

2 Johann Hüttner, 'Theater als Geschäft' (1982), ii, 639–43.

3 'Von den Vorstadttheatern', *Blätter für Musik, Theater und Kunst* [Vienna], 15 and 20 February 1855. The full text is reprinted in Nestroy, *Stücke 33* (HKA), 149–53.

4 Laube, *Schriften zum Theater*, pp. 552–3.

5 See Franz Hadamowsky, *Wien. Theatergeschichte* (1988), p. 694.

6 Rudolf Tyrolt, *Chronik des Wiener Stadttheaters* (1889), p. 39.
7 Laube, *Schriften zum Theater*, p. 645.
8 Tyrolt, *Chronik des Wiener Stadttheaters*, p. 9.
9 Laube, *Schriften zum Theater*, p. 555.
10 Tyrolt, *Chronik des Wiener Stadttheaters*, pp. 9–15; Laube, *Schriften zum Theater*, p. 651; Ludwig Speidel, 'Theater' (1888), pp. 390–1; 'Aus Adolf Wilbrandts Burgtheater-Erinnerungen', in Heinrich Glücksmann (ed.), *Zu Adolf Wilbrandts 100. Geburtstag* (1937), pp. 51–99 (p. 57).
11 Tyrolt, *Chronik des Wiener Stadttheaters*, pp. 55, 58–9, 65.
12 Tyrolt, *Chronik des Wiener Stadttheaters*, pp. 3–5, 13.
13 See Tyrolt, *Chronik des Wiener Stadttheaters*, pp. 26, 42–3; Speidel, 'Theater', pp. 392–3.
14 Laube, *Schriften zum Theater*, pp. 632 (this is where Laube writes of 'Besucher des rezitierenden Schauspiels'), 642–3, 656.
15 Tyrolt, *Chronik des Wiener Stadttheaters*, p. 46.
16 Laube, *Schriften zum Theater*, p. 643.
17 Tyrolt, *Chronik des Wiener Stadttheaters*, pp. 50–3.
18 See Johann Hüttner, 'Theater im Zeitalter Kaiser Franz Josephs' (1984), p. 350.
19 Adam Müller-Guttenbrunn, *Wien war eine Theaterstadt* (1885), pp. 6–7.
20 Müller-Guttenbrunn, *Wien war eine Theaterstadt*, p. 8.
21 Müller-Guttenbrunn, *Wien war eine Theaterstadt*, pp. 12, 17, 19–20.
22 Müller-Guttenbrunn, *Wien war eine Theaterstadt*, pp. 17, 28.
23 Müller-Guttenbrunn, *Wien war eine Theaterstadt*, pp. 15–16, 35–7.
24 Müller-Guttenbrunn, *Wien war eine Theaterstadt*, pp. 29–34.
25 Müller-Guttenbrunn, *Wien war eine Theaterstadt*, p. 8.
26 Quoted in Maria Kinz, *Raimundtheater* (1985), p. 6.
27 Adam Müller-Guttenbrunn, *Deutsche Zeitung*, 20 October 1887, quoted in Johann Hüttner, '1889–1918: Die Direktionen Emerich von Bukovics, Adolf Weisse, Karl Wallner' (1989), p. 17; *Das Wiener Theaterleben* (1890), p. 94.
28 See Anzengruber, *Briefe* (1902), II, 186–7 (letters of 26 April 1884 to Wilhelm Bolin and 22 May 1884 to Peter Rosegger).
29 Speidel, 'Theater', p. 408.
30 See Karl Glossy, *Vierzig Jahre Deutsches Volkstheater* (1929), p. 3; Johann Hüttner, 'Die Gründung des "Deutschen Volkstheaters" in Wien' (1981), p. 4.
31 Hadamowsky, *Wien. Theatergeschichte*, p. 726.
32 See Glossy, *Vierzig Jahre Deutsches Volkstheater*, pp. 4–6.
33 Hüttner, 'Die Gründung des "Deutschen Volkstheaters" in Wien', p. 4.
34 See letter to Adam Müller-Guttenbrunn, 20 October 1887, quoted in Nagl/Zeidler/Castle, *Deutsch-österreichische Literaturgeschichte*, IV (1937), p. 1644. The letter is not included in the edition of Anzengruber's letters (*Briefe*, 1902).

35 Adam Müller-Guttenbrunn, *Das Wiener Theaterleben* (1890), p. 113 ('eine Erwerbsquelle ohne künstlerische Grundsätze').

36 Müller-Guttenbrunn, *Das Wiener Theaterleben*, p. 95.

37 See Hadamowsky, *Wien. Theatergeschichte*, p. 724–5.

38 Kinz, *Raimundtheater*, p. 15; Lutz Eberhardt Seelig, *Ronacher. Die Geschichte eines Hauses* (1986), p. 19; Ulrike Riss, 'Theatergeschichtliche Aspekte 1880–1916' (1987), p. 213.

39 Kinz, *Raimundtheater*, p. 17.

40 Quoted in Kinz, *Raimundtheater*, p. 22; see also Hadamowsky, *Wien. Theatergeschichte*, p. 739.

41 Adam Müller-Guttenbrunn, *Das Raimund-Theater. Passionsgeschichte einer deutschen Volksbühne* (1897), pp. 151–8.

42 See Hadamowsky, *Wien. Theatergeschichte*, pp. 739–40; Adam Müller-Guttenbrunn, *Der suspendierte Theaterdirektor* (1896), p. 11.

43 Müller-Guttenbrunn, *Das Raimund-Theater*, p. 150.

44 Letter of 9 February 1897, quoted in Hans Pemmer, *Das Wiener Bürgertheater* (1967), p. 2.

45 *Österreichische Volks-Presse*, 1 March 1913, p. 6.

46 Adam Müller-Guttenbrunn, *Erinnerungen eines Theaterdirektors* (1924), p. 15.

47 Müller-Guttenbrunn, *Erinnerungen eines Theaterdirektors*, pp. 15–16.

48 Müller-Guttenbrunn, *Erinnerungen eines Theaterdirektors*, p. 25.

49 *Österreichische Volks-Presse*, 1 March 1903, p. 6: 'Das Kaiserjubiläums-Stadttheater ist als Bau eine Schöpfung der vereinigten antisemitischen und nationalen deutschen Parteien, doch ist dem Hause als Kunstinstitut, wie Sie unserem Spielplan entnehmen mögen, *jegliche Politik fremd.*'

50 Müller-Guttenbrunn, *Erinnerungen eines Theaterdirektors*, p. 40; Comte Paul Vasili, *La Société de Vienne* (1885), p. 244.

51 See Richard S. Geehr, *Adam Müller-Guttenbrunn and the Aryan Theater of Vienna* (1973), pp. 135–6.

52 *Die Fackel* 146 (11 November 1903), 12–21 (quotations from pp. 12–13, 18–19).

53 *Die Fackel* 145 (28 October 1903), 23.

54 *Deutsches Volksblatt*, 31 October 1903, p. 9 ('keine Juden in das Theater aufzunehmen und an den Traditionen des christlichen Theaters fortzuhalten').

7: MODERNISM AT THE END OF THE MONARCHY

1 Stefan Zweig, *Die Welt von gestern* (1941), p. 22.

2 Hugo von Hofmannsthal, *Briefe 1890–1901*, Berlin: S. Fischer 1935, p. 42: letter to Felix von Oppenheimer.

3 Adam Müller-Guttenbrunn, *Das Wiener Theaterleben* (1890), p. 54.

4 Max Burckhard, *Das Theater* (1907), p. 63.

5 Richard Specht, *Zehn Jahre Burgtheater* (1899), pp. 19–20.

6 Egon Friedell, *Wozu das Theater?* (1966), p. 183.

7 Hermann Bahr, *Wiener Theater* (1899), p. 223.

8 Arthur Schnitzler – Richard Beer-Hofmann, *Briefwechsel 1891–1931*, ed. Konstanze Fliedl, Vienna: Europaverlag 1992, p. 67 (Schnitzler's letter of 20 October 1894).

9 Olga Schnitzler, *Spiegelbild der Freundschaft* (1962), p. 18.

10 Specht, *Zehn Jahre Burgtheater*, pp. 12, 14, 16, 19–20.

11 See Karl Kraus, 'Zum Gastspiel des "Deutschen Theaters"', *Die Fackel* 10 (July 1899), pp. 16–20 (p. 19).

12 Hugo von Hofmannsthal – Arthur Schnitzler, *Briefwechsel*, ed. Therese Nickl and Heinrich Schnitzler, Frankfurt a.M.: Fischer Taschenbuch Verlag 1983, p. 18: letter of 19 March 1892.

13 See Hans Wagner, 'Die Zensur am Burgtheater zur Zeit Direktor Schlenthers' (1961), p. 417; Franz Herterich, 'Die szenische Entwicklung des neuen Burgtheaters' (1926), p. 38.

14 Specht, *Zehn Jahre Burgtheater*, p. 21.

15 See Max Burckhard, *Theater. Kritiken, Vorträge und Aufsätze* (1905), II, 113–14.

16 Schnitzler, *Tagebuch 1917–1919* (1985), p. 73 (entry for 17 August 1917).

17 *Neues Wiener Tagblatt*, 24 January 1913; quoted in Gotthard Böhm, 'Geschichte der Neuen Wiener Bühne' (1965), I, 144.

18 *Fremden-Blatt*, 21 February 1918; quoted in Böhm, 'Geschichte der Neuen Wiener Bühne', I, 129–30.

19 'Judentheater und Theaterjuden' (signed 'W.R.v.P.'), *Deutsche Zeitung*, 30 December 1899, evening edn (no. 10057), pp. 3–4.

20 This climate and the examples given in the following section are discussed more fully in W. E. Yates, *Schnitzler, Hofmannsthal, and the Austrian Theatre* (1992), pp. 77–87.

21 *Kikeriki*, 10 February 1898 (no. 12), p. 2: 'Unbeschnittene Theaterberichte des Dr. Hahn', reviewing ' "Freiwild." Sauspiel von Aaron Schnitzler'.

22 Schnitzler, *Tagebuch 1893–1902* (1989), p. 278.

23 J.J., 'Carl Bleibtreu und A. Baumberg', *Kikeriki*-Anzeiger, 20 April 1902, p. 3.

24 *Reichspost*, 22 October 1911; reproduced in W. E. Yates, *Schnitzler, Hofmannsthal, and the Austrian Theatre*, p. 85.

25 *Bekenntnisse, Bürgerlich und Romantisch, Krisen, Aus der Gesellschaft*, and *Landfrieden*.

26 Hugo von Hofmannsthal – Leopold von Andrian, *Briefwechsel* (1968), pp. 271, 287–8 (letters of 28 August and 2 October 1918).

27 E.g. A. L—ch [Albert Leitich], *Deutsche Zeitung*, 19 November 1901; H.B. [Hermann Bahr], *Neues Wiener Tagblatt*, 17 November 1901; L. H—i [Ludwig Hevesi], *Fremden-Blatt*, 17 November 1901; Berta Zuckerkandl, *Wiener Allgemeine Zeitung*, 19 November 1901. See Maria-

Christine Werba, 'Das Wiener Kabarett im Zeichen des Jugendstils' (1976), 1, 134.

28 Burckhard, *Theater. Kritiken, Vorträge und Aufsätze*, I, 339.

29 Harold B. Segel, *Turn-of-the-Century Cabaret* (1987), p. 219.

30 Egon Friedell, 'Kabarett Fledermaus', *Die Schaubühne* (Berlin), 7 November 1907, pp. 454–5 (p. 454).

31 The text is reprinted in Egon Friedell, *Wozu das Theater?*, pp. 197–208, and in Alfred Polgar, *Kleine Schriften* (1982–6), VI, 447–60.

32 Schnitzler, *Tagebuch 1909–1912* (1981), pp. 227–8 (entry for 21 March 1911).

33 *Hugo Thimig erzählt* (1962), p. 195 (diary, 4 November 1912).

34 Hofmannsthal – Andrian, *Briefwechsel*, p. 288 (letter of 2 October 1918).

35 Ingrid Pötz, 'Zur Geschichte des Theaters in der Neubaugasse' (1986), p. 45.

36 Pötz, 'Zur Geschichte des Theaters in der Neubaugasse', pp. 61–3.

37 B.Z., 'Volksbühne', *Wiener Allgemeine Zeitung*, 12 December 1912 (no. 10406), pp. 3–4 (p. 3).

38 Paul Stefan, *Das neue Haus* (1919), p. 55.

39 E.g. Olga Schnitzler, *Spiegelbild der Freundschaft*, p. 21.

40 Franz Willnauer, *Gustav Mahler und die Wiener Oper* (1979), pp. 38–9.

41 E.g. *Kikeriki*, 24 April 1902 (no. 33), p. 4: cartoon 'Unangenehmes Abenteuer Mahler's in der Secession', showing Klinger's figure of Beethoven hitting out at Mahler from his chair, with Beethoven saying in the caption 'Hab' ich Dich endlich! Na wart, Du Symphonie-verhunzer!'.

42 *Deutsches Volksblatt*, 31 October 1903, quoted in Richard S. Geehr, *Adam Müller-Guttenbrunn and the Aryan Theater of Vienna* (1973), p. 381.

43 See Willnauer, *Gustav Mahler und die Wiener Oper*, pp. 240–2.

44 See Marcel Prawy, *Die Wiener Oper* (1969), p. 74; Willnauer, *Gustav Mahler und die Wiener Oper*, pp. 246–7.

45 Paul Marsop, 'Die Theaterstadt Wien und ihre Zukunft. Offener Brief an Richard Specht', *Der Merker* 2, no. 3 (10 November 1910), pp. 89–97 (p. 91); Stefan, *Das neue Haus*, pp. 68–70.

46 See Gottfried Kraus (ed.), *Musik in Österreich* (1989), p. 284.

47 *Kikeriki*, 29 October 1922 (no. 42), p. 7.

48 Richard Traubner, *Operetta* (1989), pp. 244, 249.

49 Martin Lichtfuss, *Operette im Ausverkauf* (1989), pp. 30, 171.

50 Favoritenstr. 8, built after plans by Eduard Prandl on the corner Neumanngasse/Mozartgasse/Mozartplatz.

51 See Ludwig Hirschfeld, 'Abends im Theater. Premiereneindrücke', *Neue Freie Presse*, 19 November 1916. Quoted in Elisabeth Pablé, 'Anton Wildgans und das Wiener Theater' (1958), p. 46.

52 *Arbeiter-Zeitung*, 28 March and 14 October 1918, quoted in Lichtfuss, *Operette im Ausverkauf*, p. 41.

8: 1918–1945

1 Hugo von Hofmannsthal – Leopold von Andrian, *Briefwechsel* (1968), p. 268.
2 *Fremden-Blatt*, 1 April 1917, p. 12 ('Wer wird Burgtheaterdirektor?'); 7 April 1917, p. 7.
3 Hofmannsthal – Andrian, *Briefwechsel*, p. 271: letter of 28 August 1918.
4 Hofmannsthal – Andrian, *Briefwechsel*, pp. 287–8: letter of 2 October 1918.
5 See Andrian's later account of his direction (1928), reproduced in Rudolph Lothar, *Das Wiener Burgtheater* (1934), pp. 407–31 (pp. 424–6 on Strauss's proposals).
6 Paul Stefan, *Das neue Haus* (1919), p. 72.
7 Hugo von Hofmannsthal – Anton Wildgans, *Briefwechsel*, ed. Norbert Altenhofer, Heidelberg: Stiehm 1971, pp. 30–1 (letter of 14 February 1921).
8 Quoted in Alfred Pfoser, Kristina Pfoser-Schewig, and Gerhard Renner, *Schnitzlers 'Reigen'* (1993), I, 148.
9 *Wiener Stimmen*, 17 February 1921; *Reichspost*, 17 February 1921. See Alfred Pfoser *et al.*, *Schnitzlers 'Reigen'*, I, 145; I, 374–7.
10 Arthur Schnitzler, *Tagebuch 1920–1922* (1993), p. 137.
11 Felix Salten, 'Lebensfrage des Theaters', *Neue Freie Presse*, 3 October 1920; quoted in Wolfgang Greisenegger, 'Überlebensstrategien' (1989), p. 246.
12 See letter of May 1933 to Rudolph Lothar, quoted in Lothar, *Das Wiener Burgtheater*, pp. 442–51 (pp. 448–50).
13 Franz Dirnberger (ed.), *Burgtheater in Dokumenten* (1976), p. 93.
14 Schnitzler, *Tagebuch 1920–1922*, pp. 365–6 (entry for 10 October 1922).
15 See Helmut Gruber, *Red Vienna* (1991), pp. 96–7.
16 See Heidemarie Brückl-Zehetner, 'Theater in der Krise' (1988), p. 126.
17 E.g. *Neues Wiener Tagblatt*, 28 November 1924 (no. 327), p. 6: 'Der Zusammenbruch im Carltheater'.
18 Robert Musil, *Theater. Kritisches und Theoretisches* (1965), p. 181.
19 Alfred Polgar, 'Wiener Theater', *Die Weltbühne*, 17, no. 48 (1 December 1921), pp. 557–8 (p. 557).
20 See Schnitzler, *Tagebuch 1920–1922*, p. 137: entry for 1 February 1921.
21 See *Neues Wiener Abendblatt*, 28 November 1924 (no. 327).
22 Hugo Breitner, 'Lustbarkeitsabgabe und Theaterkrise', *Arbeiter-Zeitung*, 29 March 1925 (no. 87), p. 9.
23 See Martin Lichtfuss, *Operette im Ausverkauf* (1989), pp. 44–5; Richard Traubner, *Operetta* (1989), p. 327.
24 See Lichtfuss, *Operette im Ausverkauf*, pp. 139–47; also Helmut Arntzen, 'Vom Lustspiel zum Singspiel. Bemerkungen zu der Operette *Im weißen Rößl* als Ausdruck der dreißiger Jahre', in Helmut Arntzen (ed.), *Komödiensprache. Beiträge zum deutschen Lustspiel zwischen dem 17. und dem 20.*

Jahrhundert (Literatur als Sprache, 5), Münster: Aschendorff 1988, pp. 111–27.

25   *Neues 8-Uhr-Blatt*, 28 February 1925: 'Die Wiener Operette ist tot'.

26   Schnitzler, *Tagebuch 1920–1922*, p. 370 (entry for 23 October 1922).

27   See Alfred Pfoser, *Literatur und Austromarxismus* (1980), p. 196.

28   *Berliner Börsen-Courier*, 3 October 1922; reprinted in Oskar Maurus Fontana, *Das große Welttheater* (1976), pp. 65–9 (pp. 66–8).

29   See Edward Timms, *Karl Kraus, Apocalyptic Satirist: Culture and Catastrophe in Habsburg Vienna*, New Haven and London: Yale University Press 1986, pp. 178–9.

30   See especially 'Nestroy und das Burgtheater', *Die Fackel* 676–678, pp. 1–40; 'Vom großen Welttheaterschwindel', *Die Fackel* 601–607 (November 1922), pp. 1–7; 'Bunte Begebenheiten', *Die Fackel* 622–631 (June 1923), pp. 65–7. Kraus's campaign against Reinhardt culminated in 1935 in the essay 'Die Handschrift des Magiers', *Die Fackel* 912–915, pp. 34–62.

31   Letter of 27 November 1920 to Anders Österling; quoted in Martin Stern, 'Hofmannsthals *Der Schwierige* in Paris. Neue Briefe und Fakten zu Paul Géraldys Übersetzung *L'Irrésolu*', *Etudes Germaniques* 48 (1993), 129–46 (p. 130).

32   Hofmannsthal – Andrian, *Briefwechsel*, p. 319.

33   Lilly Wildgans, *Anton Wildgans und das Burgtheater* (1955), pp. 30–6; see also Franz Hadriga, *Drama Burgtheaterdirektion* (1989), pp. 32–9.

34   Schnitzler, *Tagebuch 1920–1922*, p. 290 (entry dated 14 March 1922).

35   See Franz Dirnberger, 'Von den Hoftheatern zu den Bundestheatern' (1982), p. 255.

36   See letter of 22 December 1922 to Christiane von Hofmannsthal, in Hofmannsthal, *Sämtliche Werke*, Kritische Ausgabe, ed. Rudolf Hirsch *et al.*, Frankfurt a.M.: S. Fischer 1975– , XIII (1986), 241.

37   Alfred Polgar, 'Wiener Theater', *Die Schaubühne* 13/1 (1917), no. 10 (8 March 1917), p. 231.

38   See Klaus-Peter Hinze, 'Ernst Weiss: the novelist as dramatist' (1993), pp. 95–7.

39   Dirnberger, *Burgtheater in Dokumenten*, p. 95.

40   See Pfoser, *Literatur und Austromarxismus*, pp. 197–8.

41   *Der Tag* (Vienna), 21 April 1923; reprinted in Alfred Polgar, *Kleine Schriften* (1982–86), v, 289–91.

42   See Gotthard Böhm, 'Geschichte der Neuen Wiener Bühne' (1965), II, 6, 50.

43   Robert Musil, *Theater. Kritisches und Theoretisches*, p. 180.

44   See Dieter Bogner and Barbara Lesák, 'Die Internationale Ausstellung neuer Theatertechnik (1924)' (1985); illustrations pp. 668 and 671.

45   'Klarstellung', *Die Fackel* 668–675 (December 1924), pp. 60–3 (p. 62); *Neue Freie Presse*, 6 October 1924 (no. 21577, morning edn), p. 6; 'Das Mangobaumwunder', *Die Fackel* 668–675, pp. 88–93.

46 See review by Oskar Maurus Fontana, *Berliner Börsen-Courier*, 3 January 1925, reprinted in Fontana, *Das große Welttheater*, pp. 86–90. Martin's stage design is illustrated in the catalogue section accompanying Dieter Bogner and Barbara Lesák, 'Die Internationale Ausstellung neuer Theatertechnik', p. 679.

47 *Neue Freie Presse*, 18 April 1926; quoted in Elisabeth Breslmayer, 'Die Geschichte des Wiener Raimundtheaters von 1893 bis 1973' (1975) I, 204.

48 Böhm, 'Geschichte der Neuen Wiener Bühne', II, 79.

49 Anton Wildgans, *Ein Leben in Briefen* (1947), III, 384 (letter of 29 August 1930 from Heinrich von Srbik). See Hadriga, *Drama Burgtheaterdirektion*, pp. 75–8.

50 Wildgans, *Ein Leben in Briefen*, III, 383 (letter of 11 August 1930 to Franz Werfel).

51 Heinz Kindermann, *Das Burgtheater* (1944), p. 217.

52 Arthur Schnitzler, *Briefe 1913–1931*, ed. Peter Michael Braunwarth *et al.*, Frankfurt a.M.: S. Fischer 1984, p. 739 (letter of 8 January 1931 to Otto P. Schinnerer).

53 Franz Herterich, *Das Burgtheater und seine Sendung* [1946], p. 91.

54 Kindermann, *Das Burgtheater*, pp. 218–20.

55 See Klaus Amann, *Der Anschluß österreichischer Schriftsteller an das Dritte Reich* (1988), pp. 156–8.

56 Kindermann, *Das Burgtheater*, p. 223.

57 *Sag beim Abschied...* (1992), p. 170.

58 Carl Zuckmayer, *Als wär's ein Stück von mir*, p. 87. The reference to 'paper still whirling about' is to pamphlets urging people to vote in the plebiscite Schuschnigg had called.

59 See Evelyn Schreiner, 'Nationalsozialistische Kulturpolitik in Wien 1938–1945' (1980), p. 144.

60 Schreiner, 'Nationalsozialistische Kulturpolitik in Wien', p. 161.

61 Schreiner, 'Nationalsozialistische Kulturpolitik in Wien', p. 162.

62 Schreiner, 'Nationalsozialistische Kulturpolitik in Wien', pp. 64, 160.

63 Kindermann, *Das Burgtheater*, p. 223.

64 Brückl-Zehetner, *Theater in der Krise*, p. 219.

65 He also worked in Bochum, Munich, and Berlin before he was moved to Vienna. See Friedrich Michael and Hans Daiber, *Geschichte des deutschen Theaters* (1990), p. 125.

66 Kindermann, *Das Burgtheater*, p. 223.

67 Dirnberger, *Burgtheater in Dokumenten*, p. 101; *Sag beim Abschied...*, p. 27.

68 Cromwell's last speech ends with the words: 'Sie mögen mich segnen oder verfluchen – meine Tat können sie mir nicht nehmen; die lebt und bleibt und wird sie alle überdauern: die geeinte, einige, große Nation – die Nation!' (Mirko Jelusich, *Cromwell. Schauspiel in fünf Aufzügen*, Vienna and Leipzig: Speidel 1934, p. 176).

69 See Schreiner, 'Nationalsozialistische Kulturpolitik in Wien', pp. 177–82.

70 See Schreiner, 'Nationalsozialistische Kulturpolitik in Wien', pp. 147–8, 309–11, 316.
71 Heinz Kindermann, *Ferdinand Raimund. Lebenswerk und Wirkungsraum eines deutschen Volksdramatikers*, Vienna and Leipzig: Luser 1940.
72 Zeno von Liebl, 'Nestroy im Bürgertheater', *Neues Wiener Tagblatt*, 4 July 1943 (no. 182), p. 3; reprinted in Nestroy, *Stücke 34* (HKA), 132–3.
73 Kindermann, *Das Burgtheater*, p. 266.
74 Schreiner, 'Nationalsozialistische Kulturpolitik in Wien', pp. 145–6.
75 Erika Gieler, 'Die Geschichte der Volksoper in Wien' (1961), I, 260.
76 *Fluchtpunkt Zürich* (1994), pp. 95–6.

9: THE SECOND REPUBLIC

1   Hubert Hackenberg and Walter Herrmann, *Die Wiener Staatsoper im Exil 1945–1955* (1985), pp. 169, 174, 191.
2   Kurt Kahl, *Die Wiener und ihr Burgtheater* (1974), p. 123.
3   See Evelyn Deutsch-Schreiner, 'Der verhinderte Satiriker' (1994), p. 111.
4   Documentation in Ernst Haeussermann, *Herbert von Karajan* (1978), pp. 127–88.
5   Marcel Prawy, *Die Wiener Oper* (1969), pp. 186–7.
6   See Gottfried Kraus (ed.), *Musik in Österreich* (1989), p. 418.
7   Hans Weigel, *Tausendundeine Premiere* (1961), p. 155.
8   Friedrich Torberg, *Das fünfte Rad am Thespiskarren*, Vol. I (1966), 201.
9   *Welt am Abend*, 25 September 1947, reprinted in Oskar Maurus Fontana, *Das große Welttheater* (1976), pp. 347–8 (p. 348).
10 See Traugott Krischke (ed.), *Materialien zu Ödön von Horváths 'Geschichten aus dem Wiener Wald'* (1978), pp. 138–44.
11 E.g. Hans Weigel, *Tausendundeine Premiere*, pp. 103–4 (reviewing *Das Leben des Galilei*, Neues Theater in der Scala).
12 Herbert Lederer, *Bevor alles verweht...* (1986), p. 84.
13 Wilhelm Pellert, *Roter Vorhang, rotes Tuch* (1979), p. 40: see Nestroy, *Gesammelte Werke*, ed. Otto Rommel, 6 vols., Vienna: Schroll 1948–49, V, 253.
14 See Evelyn Deutsch-Schreiner, *Karl Paryla* (1992), p. 78.
15 *Arbeiter-Zeitung*, 14 April 1948; quoted in Pellert, *Roter Vorhang, rotes Tuch*, p. 24.
16 See Pellert, *Roter Vorhang, rotes Tuch*, p. 31.
17 Pellert, *Roter Vorhang, rotes Tuch*, p. 35.
18 Pellert, *Roter Vorhang, rotes Tuch*, pp. 57, 74, 78.
19 See Hans Pemmer, *Das Wiener Bürgertheater* (1967), p. 32, Pellert, *Roter Vorhang, rotes Tuch*, p. 78.
20 See Attila E. Láng, *Das Theater an der Wien* (1976), illustration facing p. 41.
21 See Kurt Kahl, *Die Wiener und ihr Burgtheater*, p. 134.

22 Rolf Lehnhardt, *Schwäbische Zeitung* (Laupheim), 31 July 1963, reprinted in Douglas A. Joyce, *Hugo von Hofmannsthal's 'Der Schwierige': A Fifty-Year Theater History* (1993), p. 292.

23 Documented in 'Streit um Peymann', *Theater heute*, July 1988, pp. 1–11.

24 *Die Presse*, 5 January 1993, p. 16.

25 See Hans Haider, 'Peymanns Poker-Spiel um die politische Gunst als Stationendrama', *Die Presse*, 2–3 July 1994, p. 3.

26 See *Die Presse*, 25 January 1992, p. 12.

27 See *Die Presse*, 28 February 1992, p. 1.

28 See Wolfgang Herles, 'Das Dilemma Peymanns und seines Hauses', *Der Standard* (Vienna), 26 February 1992. The comparison between Wildgans and Peymann is made, in Wildgans's favour, by Franz Hadriga, *Drama Burgtheaterdirektion* (1989), pp. 113–15.

29 See Barbara Petsch, interview with Gerd Voss, *Die Presse*, 17 March 1993; Alfred Pfoser, 'Peymann, der Star in der Defensive', *Salzburger Nachrichten*, 26 March 1993.

30 Barbara Petsch, interview with Gerhard Klingenberg, *Die Presse*, 2–4 April 1994, p. 18.

31 See Elisabeth Hirschmann-Altzinger, 'Jedermann wird seßhaft', *Bühne*, December 1993, pp. 16–18.

32 Hans Haider, 'Orpherl und die wilden Tiere. Eine Wolfgang-Bauer-Uraufführung im Wiener Schauspielhaus', *Die Presse*, 4–5 May 1991, p. 12.

33 See Andrea Hodoschek, 'Manager als Theatermacher', *Kurier*, 25 April 1994, p. 17. Current capacities as given in *Deutsches Bühnen-Jahrbuch* 1992/93, pp. 626–7.

Bibliography

The following Bibliography lists the principal published works on theatre history and the main background reference works drawn on in the book. It excludes manuscripts and archival sources, titles of the daily, weekly, and monthly journals consulted, and works (including press articles) referred to on single occasions only.

It is divided into four sections: the first gives primary sources, then comes secondary material on theatre in Vienna (section 2) and elsewhere (section 3), and the final section lists works of general reference. Some authors and editors are listed in more than one section.

All quotations from manuscripts and ephemeral journalistic items are given specific references in the Notes. The character of the principal archives is outlined in Appendix 2 (pp. 260–3, above); journals concerned with the theatre are listed by Franz Hadamowsky in his article 'Wiener Theater-Periodica' (1952), listed below in Section 2.

I. PRIMARY SOURCES

(Memoirs, letters, collections of reviews, theatre yearbooks, and editions containing substantial documentation)

Almanach für Freunde der Schauspielkunst [from Vol. 18: *Deutscher Bühnenalmanach*], ed. L. Wolff (1837–46), A. Heinrich (1847–59), L. Schneider (1860–1), A. Entsch (1862–83), Th. Entsch (1884–93), 57 vols., Berlin 1837–93.

Anschütz, Heinrich: *Erinnerungen aus dessen Leben und Wirken. Nach eigenhändigen Aufzeichnungen und mündlichen Mittheilungen*, Vienna: Leopold Sommer 1866.

Anzengruber, Ludwig: *Briefe*, ed. Anton Bettelheim, 2 vols., Stuttgart and Berlin: Cotta 1902.

Bahr, Hermann: *Wiener Theater (1892–1898)*. Berlin: S. Fischer 1899.

Rezensionen. Wiener Theater 1901 bis 1903, Berlin: S. Fischer 1903.

Glossen. Zum Wiener Theater (1903–1906), Berlin: S. Fischer 1907.

[Bauernfeld, Eduard von]: 'Aus Bauernfelds Tagebüchern, 1 (1819–1848)', ed. Karl Glossy, *Jahrbuch der Grillparzer-Gesellschaft* 5 (1895), 1–217.

Bauernfeld, Eduard von: 'Die Wiener Volksbühne', *Österreichische Blätter für*

291

Literatur und Kunst. Beilage zur Wiener Zeitung, 18 and 25 April 1853, pp. 93 and 99–101.

Aus Alt- und Neu-Wien, in Bauernfeld, *Gesammelte Schriften*, 12 vols., Vienna: Braumüller 1871–3, Vol. xii (1873).

Gesammelte Aufsätze, ed. Stefan Hock (Schriften des Literarischen Vereins in Wien, 4), Vienna: Literarischer Verein in Wien 1905.

Böhm, Hans (ed.): *Die Wiener Reinhardt-Bühne im Lichtbild. Erstes Spieljahr 1924/1925*, Zürich, Leipzig, Vienna: Amalthea 1926.

Burckhard, Max: *Theater. Kritiken, Vorträge und Aufsätze*, 2 vols., Vienna: Manz 1905.

[Carl, Karl]: 'Das Testament des Theaterdirectors Carl', *Wiener allgemeine Theaterzeitung*, 31 August 1854 (no. 198), pp. 817–19, and 1 September 1854 (no. 199), pp. 821–22.

Castelli, I.F.: *Memoiren meines Lebens. Gefundenes und Empfundenes, Erlebtes und Erstrebtes*, ed. Josef Bindtner, 2 vols. (Denkwürdigkeiten aus Alt-Österreich, 9–10), Munich: Georg Müller n.d. [1914].

Costenoble, Carl Ludwig: *Aus dem Burgtheater. 1818–1837. Tagebuchblätter*, 2 vols., Vienna: Konegen 1889.

Deutsch, Otto Erich: *Schubert. Die Dokumente seines Lebens*, Kassel: Bärenreiter 1964.

[Dingelstedt, Franz von]: *Aus der Briefmappe eines Burgtheaterdirektors (Franz von Dingelstedt)*, ed. Karl Glossy, Vienna: Schroll 1925.

Dirnberger, Franz (ed.): *Burgtheater in Dokumenten. Katalog der Theaterausstellung, Sept. 1976-März 1977*, Vienna: Haus-, Hof- und Staatsarchiv 1976.

Fontana, Oskar Maurus: *Das große Welttheater. Theaterkritiken 1909–1967*, Vienna: Amalthea 1976.

Friedell, Egon: *Wozu das Theater? Essays, Satiren, Humoresken*, ed. Peter Haage, Munich: Beck 1966.

Genast, Eduard: *Aus Weimars klassischer und nachklassischer Zeit*. Erinnerungen eines alten Schauspielers, ed. Robert Kohlrausch, Stuttgart: Lutz n.d.

[Glassbrenner, Adolf]: *Bilder und Träume aus Wien*, 2 vols., Leipzig: Volckmar 1836.

Glossy, Carl: 'Zur Geschichte der Wiener Theatercensur. 1', *Jahrbuch der Grillparzer-Gesellschaft* 7 (1897), 238–340.

'Zur Geschichte der Theater Wiens', i (1800–1820), ii (1821–1830), iii (1831–1840), *Jahrbuch der Grillparzer-Gesellschaft* 25 (1915), 1–334; 26 (1920), 1–155; 30 (1930), 1–152.

Grillparzer, Franz: *Sämtliche Werke*, hist.-krit. Ausgabe, ed. August Sauer and Reinhold Backmann, 42 vols., Vienna: Gerlach & Wiedling and Schroll 1909–48.

Grillparzers Gespräche und die Charakteristiken seiner Persönlichkeit durch die Zeitgenossen, ed. August Sauer, 6 vols. (Schriften des Literarischen Vereins in Wien, 1, 3, 6, 12, 15, 20), Vienna: Literarischer Verein in Wien 1904–16.

Grillparzers Selbstbiographie und Bildnisse, ed. Ludwig Böck and Wilhelm Englmann, Vienna: Wiener Drucke 1923.

Gutzkow, Karl, *Wiener Eindrücke*, in Gutzkow, *Gesammelte Werke. Vollständig umgearbeitete Ausgabe*, 12 vols., Frankfurt a.M.: Literarische Anstalt (J. Rütten), 1845–6, III, 269–335.

Hadamowsky, Franz: *Die Josefinische Theaterreform und das Spieljahr 1776/77 des Burgtheaters. Eine Dokumentation* (Quellen zur Theatergeschichte, 2) (*Jahrbuch der Wiener Gesellschaft für Theaterforschung* 22), Vienna: Verband der wissenschaftlichen Gesellschaften Österreichs 1978.

Hafner, Philipp: 'Brief eines neuen Komödienschreibers an einen Schauspieler', in *Philipp Hafners Gesammelte Werke*, ed. Ernst Baum, Vol. I (Schriften des Literarischen Vereins in Wien, 19), Vienna: Literarischer Verein in Wien 1914, pp. 1–10.

Hanslick, Eduard: 'Musik', in *Wien 1848. Denkschrift zum 2. December 1888*, 2 vols., Vienna: Konegen 1888, II, 301–42 (pp. 306–23: 'Die Oper in Wien').

[Heine, Albert]: 'Aus den Erinnerungen des Burgtheaterdirektors Albert Heine (1918–1921)', *Jahrbuch der Gesellschaft für Wiener Theaterforschung* 1951/1952 [1955], 147–69.

Hofmannsthal, Hugo von, and Leopold von Andrian: *Briefwechsel*, ed. Walter H. Perl, Frankfurt a.M.: S. Fischer 1968.

Joyce, Douglas A.: *Hugo von Hofmannsthal's 'Der Schwierige': A Fifty-Year Theater History*, Columbia, SC: Camden House 1993.

Kaiser, Friedrich: *Theater-Director Carl. Sein Leben und Wirken – in München und Wien, mit einer entwickelten Schilderung seines Charakters und seiner Stellung zur Volksbühne*, Vienna: Sallmayer 1854.

'Wenzel Scholz. Ereignisse und Denkwürdigkeiten aus seinem Leben, nach seinen hinterlassenen Schriften und den Mittheilungen seiner Witwe, zusammengestellt von Friedrich Kaiser', *Morgenpost*, 14 March–19 April 1858 [28 parts, bound together in the Wiener Stadt- und Landesbibliothek, shelf-mark B 6.422].

Friedrich Beckmann. Heiteres – Ernstes – Trauriges aus seinem Leben. Erinnerungen, Vienna: Wallishausser (Josef Klemm) 1866.

Unter fünfzehn Theater-Direktoren. Bunte Bilder aus der Wiener Bühnenwelt, Vienna: Waldheim 1870.

Krischke, Traugott (ed.): *Materialien zu Ödön von Horváths 'Geschichten aus dem Wiener Wald'* (edition suhrkamp, 533), 2nd edn, Frankfurt a.M.: Suhrkamp 1978.

'Künstler-Silhouetten aus Wien', *Der Adler*, 13 November 1843 (no. 267), pp. 1094–5; 16 November 1843 (no. 270), pp. 1107–8; 18 November 1843 (no. 272), p. 1114; 20 November 1843 (no. 273), p. 1120; 25 November 1843 (no. 278), pp. 1138–9.

Laube, Heinrich: *Schriften zum Theater*, ed. Eva Stahl-Wisten, Berlin: Henschelverlag 1959.

Erinnerungen 1841–1881, in *Heinrich Laubes gesammelte Werke in 50 Bänden*, ed. Heinrich Hubert Houben, Leipzig: Hesse 1908–9, LXI, 1–238.

Max Mell als Theaterkritiker, ed. Margret Dietrich, Vienna: Österreichische Akademie der Wissenschaften 1983.

[Mayr, Michael]: *Der Theater-Mayr. Aus den Biedermeiertagebüchern des Theater-malers Michael Mayr*, ed. Karl Michael Kisler, Vienna and Eisenstadt: Edition Roetzer, 1988.

Müller, Johann Heinrich Friedrich: *Theatererinnerungen eines alten Burgschau-spielers*, ed. Richard Daunicht, Berlin: Henschelverlag 1958.

Müller-Guttenbrunn, Adam: *Wien war eine Theaterstadt* (Gegen den Strom, 2), Vienna: Graeser 1885.

Das Wiener Theaterleben, Leipzig and Vienna: Spamer 1890.

Der suspendierte Theaterdirektor, Leipzig: Georg Heinrich Meyer 1896.

Das Raimund-Theater. Passionsgeschichte einer deutschen Volksbühne, Vienna: Verlag der *Neuen Revue* 1897.

Erinnerungen eines Theaterdirektors, ed. Roderich Meinhart, Leipzig: Staack-mann 1924.

Musil, Robert: *Theater. Kritisches und Theoretisches*, ed. Marie-Louise Roth, Reinbek bei Hamburg: Rowohlt 1965.

Nestroy, Johann: *Sämtliche Werke*, hist.-krit. Ausgabe, ed. Jürgen Hein, Johann Hüttner, Walter Obermaier, and W. Edgar Yates, Vienna: Jugend und Volk 1977– . References are given to individual volumes, e.g. *Briefe* (HKA), *Stücke 14* (HKA) etc.

Neuer Theater-Almanach, Vols 1–15, Berlin 1890–1914; continued as *Deutsches Bühnen-Jahrbuch*, Vols 26–101, Berlin 1915–92/3.

Payer von Thurn, Rudolf (ed.): *Joseph II. als Theaterdirektor. Ungedruckte Briefe und Aktenstücke aus den Kinderjahren des Burgtheaters*, Vienna and Leipzig: Heidrich 1920.

Polgar, Alfred: *Kleine Schriften*, ed. Marcel Reich-Ranicki and Ulrich Wein-zierl, 6 vols., Reinbek bei Hamburg: Rowohlt 1982–6, Vols. v–vi.

Pörnbacher, Karl (ed.): *Erläuterungen und Dokumente. Franz Grillparzer: 'König Ottokars Glück und Ende'* (Universal-Bibliothek, 8103), Stuttgart: Reclam 1969.

Raimund, Ferdinand: *Sämtliche Werke*, hist.-krit. Säkularausgabe, ed. Fritz Brukner and Eduard Castle, 6 vols., Vienna: Schroll 1924–34.

Riedl, Gottfried (ed.): *Nestroy. Bilder aus einem Theaterleben*, Vienna: Sonderzahl 1988.

Raimund. Bilder aus einem Theaterleben, Vienna: Sonderzahl 1990.

Rühle, Günther: *Theater für die Republik 1917–1933 im Spiegel der Kritik*, Frankfurt a.M.: S. Fischer 1967.

Saphir, M.G.: 'Des Wiener Volksstücks Glück und Ende', *Der Humorist*, 12–13 May 1847 (no. 113–14), pp. 449–51; 15 May 1847 (no. 116), pp. 461–2; 17 May 1847 (no. 117), pp. 465–8.

'Der Rezensent in dem Gasluster des neuen Carl-Theaters', *Der Humorist*, 15 December 1847 (no. 299), pp. 1193–5; 16 December 1847 (no. 300), pp. 1197–9.

Schnitzler, Arthur: *Tagebuch*, 10 vols., ed. Werner Welzig *et al.*, Vienna: Österreichische Akademie der Wissenschaften 1981– .

Schnitzler, Olga: *Spiegelbild der Freundschaft*, Salzburg: Residenz 1962.

[Schreyvogel, Josef]: *Gesammelte Schriften von Thomas und Karl August West*, 4 vols., Braunschweig: Vieweg 1829.

Josef Schreyvogels Tagebücher 1810–1823, ed. Karl Glossy, 2 vols. (Schriften der Gesellschaft für Theatergeschichte, 2–3), Berlin: Gesellschaft für Theatergeschichte 1903.

Sealsfield, Charles: *Austria As It Is: or, Sketches of Continental Courts. By an Eye-Witness*, London: Hurst, Chance 1828.

Seyfried, Ferdinand Ritter von: *Rückschau in das Theaterleben Wiens seit den letzten fünfzig Jahren*, Vienna: Selbstverlag 1864.

Smekal, Richard (ed.): *Das alte Burgtheater (1776–1888). Eine Charakteristik durch zeitgenössische Darstellungen*, 2nd edn, Vienna: Schroll 1916.

Sonnenfels, J.v.: *Briefe über die wienerische Schaubühne* [1768], repr. (Wiener Neudrucke, 7) Vienna: Konegen 1884.

Speidel, Ludwig: 'Theater', in *Wien 1848–1888. Denkschrift zum 2. December 1888*, 2 vols., Vienna: Konegen 1888, II, 343–408.

Schauspieler (Ludwig Speidels Schriften, Vol. IV), Berlin: Meyer & Jessen 1911.

[Thimig, Hugo]: *Hugo Thimig erzählt von seinem Leben und dem Theater seiner Zeit. Briefe und Tagebuchblätter*, ed. Franz Hadamowsky, Graz and Cologne: Böhlau 1962.

Tieck, Ludwig: *Kritische Schriften*, 4 vols., Leipzig: Brockhaus 1848–52, Vol. IV (*Dramaturgische Blätter*, 2. Theil).

Torberg, Friedrich: *Das fünfte Rad am Thespiskarren. Theaterkritiken*, 2 vols., Munich and Vienna: Langen Müller 1966–7.

Trollope, Frances, *Vienna and the Austrians, with Some Account of a Journey through Swabia, Bavaria, the Tyrol, and the Salzbourg*, 2 vols., Paris: Baudry 1838.

Tyrolt, Rudolf: *Chronik des Wiener Stadttheaters 1872–1884. Ein Beitrag zur deutschen Theatergeschichte*, Vienna: Konegen 1889.

Aus dem Tagebuche eines Wiener Schauspielers 1848–1902. Erinnerungen und Betrachtungen, Vienna and Leipzig: Braumüller 1904.

Vom Lebenswege eines alten Schauspielers, Vienna: Schworella & Heick 1914.

Ueber den Verfall der Volkstheater. Ein Wort zu seiner Zeit, gesprochen von einem Volksdichter, Vienna: A. Strauß's sel. Witwe & Sommer 1847.

Vasili, Comte Paul: *La Société de Vienne. Augmenté de lettres inédites*, 6th edn, Paris: Nouvelle Revue 1885.

Weigel, Hans: *Tausendundeine Premiere. Wiener Theater 1946–1961*, Vienna: Wollzeilen Verlag 1961; revised version: *1001 Premiere. Hymnen und Verrisse*, 2 vols., Graz, Vienna, Cologne: Styria 1983.

Wertheimer, Paul (ed.): *Alt-Wiener Theater. (Schilderungen von Zeitgenossen)*, Vienna: Paul Knepler n.d. [c. 1921].

Wildgans, Anton, *Ein Leben in Briefen*, ed. Lilly Wildgans, 3 vols., Vienna: Frick 1947.

Zedlitz, [Joseph Christian von]: 'Joseph Schreyvogel', *Oesterreichische Zeitschrift für Geschichts- und Staatskunde*, 29 April 1835 (no. 34), pp. 133–6.

Zuckmayer, Carl: *Als wär's ein Stück von mir. Horen der Freundschaft*, Frankfurt a.M.: S. Fischer 1971.
Zweig, Stefan: *Die Welt von gestern. Erinnerungen eines Europäers*, London: Hamish Hamilton; Stockholm: Bermann Fischer 1941.

2. VIENNESE THEATRE

Alth, Minna von: *Burgtheater 1776–1976. Aufführungen und Besetzungen von zweihundert Jahren*, 2 vols., Vienna: Ueberreuter n.d. [1976].
Bahr, Hermann: *Josef Kainz*, Vienna and Leipzig: Wiener Verlag 1906.
Bauer, Anton: *150 Jahre Theater an der Wien*, Zürich, Leipzig, Vienna: Amalthea 1952.
Opern und Operetten in Wien (Wiener Musikwissenschaftliche Beiträge, 2), Graz: Böhlau 1955.
Bauer, Anton, and Gustav Kropatschek: *200 Jahre Theater in der Josefstadt 1788–1988*, Vienna: Schroll 1988.
Bauer, Roger: *La Réalité, royaume de Dieu. Etudes sur l'originalité du théâtre viennois dans la première moitié du XIXe siècle*, Munich: Hueber 1965.
Laßt sie koaxen, Die kritischen Frösch' in Preußen und Sachsen! Zwei Jahrhunderte Literatur in Österreich, Vienna: Europaverlag 1977, pp. 119–35: 'Wiener Volkstheater: Noch nicht und (oder) doch schon Literatur?'.
Benay, Jeanne: 'Das Wiener Volkstheater als Intention und Strategiedramaturgie. Ein Beispiel: Friedrich Kaiser und seine französischen Vorlagen', in Jean-Marie Valentin (ed.), *Das österreichische Volkstheater im europäischen Zusammenhang 1830–1880* (Contacts, Série 1: Theatrica, 5), Berne: Lang 1988, pp. 107–32.
Friedrich Kaiser. Gesamtprimärbibliographie seiner dramatischen Produktion zwischen 1835–1874 (Nachlass 1875) (Contacts, Série 1: Theatrica, 9), Berne: Lang 1990.
Friedrich Kaiser (1814–1874) et le théâtre populaire en Autriche au XIXe siècle, 2 vols. (Contacts, Série 1: Theatrica, 14), Berne: Lang 1993.
Bettelheim, Anton: *Neue Gänge mit Ludwig Anzengruber*, Vienna, Prague, Leipzig: Strache 1919.
Birbaumer, Ulf: ' "Die Insel". Wiener Theater nach 1945', in Kristian Sotriffer (ed.), *Das größere Österreich. Geistiges und soziales Leben von 1880 bis zur Gegenwart*, Vienna: Edition Tusch 1982, pp. 392–6.
Blümml, Emil Karl, and Gustav Gugitz: *Alt-Wiener Thespiskarren. Die Frühzeit der Wiener Vorstadtbühnen*, Vienna: Schroll 1925.
Bogner, Dieter, and Barbara Lesák: 'Die Internationale Ausstellung neuer Theatertechnik (1924)', in *Traum und Wirklichkeit. Wien 1870–1930* (catalogue, 93. Sonderausstellung des Historischen Museums der Stadt Wien), Vienna: Museen der Stadt Wien 1985, pp. 664–71 (catalogue entries pp. 677–80).
Böhm, Gotthard: 'Geschichte der Neuen Wiener Bühne', 2 vols., Diss., University of Vienna 1965 [1966].

Branscombe, Peter: 'Music in the Viennese popular theatre of the eighteenth and nineteenth centuries', *Proceedings of the Royal Musical Association*, 1971–2, pp. 101–12.

'The Connexions between Drama and Music in the Viennese Popular Theatre from the Opening of the Leopoldstädter Theater (1781) to Nestroy's Opera Parodies (ca. 1855), with Special Reference to the Forms of Parody', Diss., University of London 1976.

W.A. Mozart: 'Die Zauberflöte', Cambridge: Cambridge University Press 1991.

Breslmayer, Elisabeth: 'Die Geschichte des Wiener Raimundtheaters von 1893 bis 1973. 80 Jahre Wiener Raimundtheater', 2 vols., Diss., University of Vienna 1975.

Brückl-Zehetner, Heidemarie: 'Theater in der Krise. Sozialgeschichtliche Untersuchungen zum Wiener Theater der ersten Republik', Diss., University of Vienna 1988.

Brusatti, Otto, and Wilhelm Deutschmann (eds): *FleZiWiCsá & Co. Die Wiener Operette* (catalogue, 91. Sonderausstellung des Historischen Museums der Stadt Wien), Vienna: Museen der Stadt Wien 1985.

Buschbeck, Erhard: *Raoul Aslan und das Burgtheater*, Vienna: Erwin Müller 1946.

Calaitzis, Elke: 'Das Burgtheater-Publikum von Wilbrandt bis zum Dreier-kollegium', in Margret Dietrich (ed.), *Das Burgtheater und sein Publikum*, Vol. 1 (1976), pp. 369–477.

Carter, Tim: *W.A. Mozart: 'Le nozze di Figaro'*, Cambridge: Cambridge University Press 1987.

Das neue Volkstheater. Festschrift, herausgegeben aus Anlaß der Renovierung 1980/81, Vienna 1981.

David, J.J.: *Mitterwurzer* (Das Theater, 13), Berlin and Leipzig: Schuster & Loeffler n.d.

Deleglise, Oscar (ed.): *Das Schönbrunner Schloßtheater*, Vienna: H. Bauer 1947.

Deutsch, Otto Erich: *Das Freihaustheater auf der Wieden 1787–1801*, 2nd edn, Vienna and Leipzig: Deutscher Verlag für Jugend und Volk 1937.

Deutsch-Schreiner, Evelyn: *Karl Paryla. Ein Unbeherrschter*, Salzburg: Otto Müller 1992.

'Der verhinderte Satiriker. Aspekte zu Nestroy im Wiederaufbau', *Nestroyana* 14 (1994), 104–24.

Deutschmann, Wilhelm (ed.): *Wiener Theater. Bilddokumente 1660–1900 aus der Theatersammlung des Historischen Museums* (exhibition catalogue), Vienna: Historisches Museum der Stadt Wien 1971.

Theatralische Bilder-Gallerie. Wiener Theater in Aquarellen von Johann Christian Schoeller (Die bibliophilen Taschenbücher, 175), Dortmund: Harenberg 1980.

Deutschmann, Wilhelm, in collaboration with Edith Marktl and Reingard Witzmann: *Therese Krones. Zum 150. Todestag* (catalogue, 68. Sonderaus-stellung des Historischen Museums der Stadt Wien), Vienna: Museen der Stadt Wien 1980.

Dietrich, Margret: *Jupiter in Wien oder Götter und Helden der Antike im Altwiener Volkstheater*, Graz, Vienna, Cologne: Böhlau 1967.

'Karl Franz Akács (Aktás), called Grüner', *Theatre Research – Recherches Théâtrales* 9, no. 3 (1968), 147–56.

Dietrich, Margret (ed.): *Das Burgtheater und sein Publikum*, Vol 1. (Veröffentlichungen des Instituts für Publikumsforschung, 3), Vienna: Österreichische Akademie der Wissenschaften 1976.

Dirnberger, Franz: 'Theatergeschichte und Theaterlegende. Bemerkungen zum Schriftgut der Theaterverwaltung', *Mitteilungen des Österreichischen Staatsarchivs* 28 (1975) (Festschrift Walter Goldinger), 210–25.

'Von den Hoftheatern zu den Bundestheatern. Besitz- und Rechtskonflikte 1918–1926', *Mitteilungen des Österreichischen Staatsarchivs* 35 (1982), 238–81.

'Theaterzensur im Zwielicht der Gesetze (1918–1926)', *Mitteilungen des Österreichischen Staatsarchivs* 36 (1983), 237–60.

Doering, Susan: *Der wienerische Europäer. Johann Nestroy und die Vorlagen seiner Stücke* (Literatur aus Bayern und Österreich, 5), Munich: W. Ludwig 1992.

Eberstaller, Gerhard: *Zirkus und Variété in Wien*. Vienna and Munich: Jugend und Volk 1974.

Ronacher. Ein Theater in seiner Zeit, Vienna: Edition Wien 1993.

Ellenberger, Hugo: *Das Burgtheater. Ein Führer durch das Haus mit besonderer Berücksichtigung der Fassaden und der Feststiegen* (Österreich-Reihe, 41), 2nd edn, Vienna: Bergland 1958.

Ferraris, Francesca: 'Die Wiener Theaterverhältnisse und Ludwig Anzengruber im Spiegel seiner Briefe – eine Bestandsaufnahme', in Herbert Zeman (ed.), *Die österreichische Literatur. Ihr Profil von der Jahrhundertwende bis zur Gegenwart (1880–1980)*, 2 vols., Graz: Akademische Druck- und Verlagsanstalt 1989, 1, 257–71.

Fritz, Otto: *95 Jahre Wiener Volksoper. Vom Stadttheater zur Staatsbühne 1898–1993*, Vienna: Österreichischer Bundestheaterverband 1993.

Fuerst, Norbert: *Grillparzer auf der Bühne. Eine fragmentarische Geschichte*, Vienna and Munich: Manitiuspresse 1958.

Fuhrich, Fritz: 'Burgtheater und Öffentlichkeit: Von Laube bis Dingelstedt', in Margret Dietrich (ed.), *Das Burgtheater und sein Publikum*, Vol. 1 (1976), pp. 335–67.

Fuhrich-Leisler, Edda: '"The miracle of survival": the Theater in der Josefstadt under Ernst Lothar (1935–1938)', in Kenneth Segar and John Warren (eds), *Austria in the Thirties: Culture and Politics*, Riverside, Ca.: Ariadne Press, 1991, pp. 219–33.

Futter, Edith: *Die bedeutendsten Schauspielerinnen des Leopoldstädter Theaters in der Zeit von 1800 bis 1830* (Dissertationen der Universität Wien, 48), 2 vols., Vienna: Notring 1970.

Geehr, Richard S.: *Adam Müller-Guttenbrunn and the Aryan Theater of Vienna: 1898–1903. The Approach of Cultural Fascism* (Göppinger Arbeiten zur Germanistik, 114), Göppingen: Kümmerle 1973.

Gieler, Erika: 'Die Geschichte der Volksoper in Wien von Rainer Simons bis 1945', 2 vols., Diss., University of Vienna 1961.

Glossy, Blanka, and Gisela Berger: *Josefine Gallmeyer. Wiens größte Volksschauspielerin*, Vienna: Waldheim-Eberle n.d.

Glossy, Karl: 'Aus der Gründungszeit des Burgtheaters', in *Hundertfünfzig Jahre Burgtheater 1776–1926* (1926), pp. 9–21.

Vierzig Jahre Deutsches Volkstheater. Ein Beitrag zur deutschen Theatergeschichte, Vienna: Deutsches Volkstheater n.d. [1929].

Glücksmann, Heinrich (ed.): *Zu Adolf Wilbrandts 100. Geburtstag. Festschrift* (Beigabe zum 34. Jg. des *Jahrbuchs der Grillparzer-Gesellschaft*), Vienna: Perles n.d. [1937].

Grawe, Christian: 'Grillparzers Dramatik als Problem der zeitgenössischen österreichischen Theaterzensur', in August Obermayer (ed.), *'Was nützt der Glaube ohne Werke ...'. Studien zu Franz Grillparzer anläßlich seines 200. Geburtstages* (Otago German Studies, 7), Dunedin: Department of German, University of Otago 1992, pp. 162–90.

Gregor, Joseph: *Das Theater in der Wiener Josephstadt*, Vienna: Wiener Drucke 1924.

Greisenegger, Wolfgang: 'Überlebensstrategien. Wiener Theater in der Zwischenkriegszeit', in Herbert Zeman (ed.), *Die österreichische Literatur. Ihr Profil von der Jahrhundertwende bis zur Gegenwart (1880–1980)*, 2 vols., Graz: Akademische Druck- und Verlagsanstalt 1989, 1, 245–55.

Gugitz, Gustav: 'Joachim Perinet. Ein Beitrag zur Wiener Theatergeschichte', *Jahrbuch der Grillparzer-Gesellschaft* 14 (1904), 170–223.

Der Weiland Kasperl (Johann La Roche). Ein Beitrag zur Theater- und Sittengeschichte Alt-Wiens, Vienna, Prague, Leipzig: Strache 1920.

'Das alte Landstraßer Theater', *Jahrbuch der Gesellschaft für Wiener Theaterforschung* 13 (1961), 52–71.

Guglia, Eugen: *Friedrich Mitterwurzer*, Vienna: Gerold 1896.

Hackenberg, Hubert, and Walter Herrmann: *Die Wiener Staatsoper im Exil 1945–1955*, Vienna: Österreichischer Bundesverlag 1985.

Hadamowsky, Franz: 'Das Carltheater unter der Direktion Johann Nestroys', *Jahrbuch der österreichischen Leo-Gesellschaft* 1926, 196–241.

Das Theater in der Wiener Leopoldstadt 1781–1860 (Bibliotheks- und Archivbestände in der Theatersammlung der Nationalbibliothek) (Kataloge der Theatersammlung der Nationalbibliothek in Wien, 3), Vienna: Höfels 1934.

'Wiener Theater-Periodica. Mit einem Verzeichnis der Wiener Theaterzeitschriften', *Das Antiquariat* 8, no. 13/18 [*Festschrift für Josef Stummvoll, Alois Kisser, Ernst Trenkler zum 50. Geburtstag*] (July-September 1952), pp. 35–8.

Schiller auf der Wiener Bühne 1783–1959, Vienna: Wiener Bibliophilen-Gesellschaft 1959.

Das Theater an der Wien, Vienna: Jugend und Volk 1962.

Die Wiener Hoftheater (Staatstheater) 1776–1966. Verzeichnis der aufgeführten Stücke mit Bestandsnachweis und täglichem Spielplan, Part 1: *1776–1810*, Vienna: Prachner 1966.

Die Wiener Hoftheater (Staatstheater). Ein Verzeichnis der aufgeführten und eingereichten Stücke mit Bestandsnachweisen und Aufführungsdaten, Part 2: *Die Wiener Hofoper (Staatsoper) 1811–1974*, Vienna: Hollinek 1975.

'Die Schauspielfreiheit, die "Erhebung des Burgtheaters zum Hoftheater" und seine "Begründung als Nationaltheater" im Jahr 1776', *Maske und Kothurn* 22 (1976), 5–19.

Wien. Theatergeschichte. Von den Anfängen bis zum Ende des Ersten Weltkriegs (*Geschichte der Stadt Wien*, 3), Vienna: Jugend und Volk 1988.

Hadamowsky, Franz, and Heinz Otte: *Die Wiener Operette. Ihre Theater- und Wirkungsgeschichte* (Klassiker der Wiener Kultur, 2), Vienna: Bellaria-Verlag 1947.

Hadriga, Franz: *Drama Burgtheaterdirektion. Vom Scheitern des Idealisten Anton Wildgans*, Vienna: Herold 1989.

Haeussermann, Ernst: *Herbert von Karajan*, 2nd edn, Vienna: Molden 1978.

Haider, Hilde: 'Das Zürcher Schauspielhaus und das Theater in Österreich', in Dieter Bachmann and Rolf Schneider (eds), *Das verschonte Haus. Das Zürcher Schauspielhaus im Zweiten Weltkrieg*, Zürich: Ammann 1987, pp. 55–85.

Haider-Pregler, Hilde: 'Die Schaubühne als "Sittenschule" der Nation. Joseph von Sonnenfels und das Theater', in Helmut Reinalter (ed.): *Joseph von Sonnenfels* (Veröffentlichungen der Kommission für die Geschichte Österreichs, 13), Vienna: Österreichische Akademie der Wissenschaften 1988, pp. 191–244.

'Die Wiener "Nationalschaubühne" (1776–1794): Idee und Institution', in Roland Krebs and Jean-Marie Valentin (eds), *Théâtre, nation & société en Allemagne au XVIIIᵉ siècle*, Nancy: Presses Universitaires de Nancy 1990, pp. 167–92.

Hanslick, Eduard: 'Musik', in *Wien 1848–1888. Denkschrift zum 2. December 1888*, 2 vols., Vienna: Konegen 1888, II, 301–42 (pp. 306–23: 'Die Oper in Wien').

Häussler, Franz, and Michael Wagner (eds): *Etablissement Ronacher. Stand und Perspektiven*, Vienna: Consulting Büro Wagner 1991.

Hein, Jürgen: *Ferdinand Raimund* (Sammlung Metzler, 92), Stuttgart: Metzler 1970.

'*Frühere Verhältnisse* und *Alte Bekanntschaften*. Eine Berliner Posse als Vorlage eines Nestroy-Stückes', *Nestroyana* 9 (1989–90), 51–9.

Johann Nestroy (Sammlung Metzler, 258), Stuttgart: Metzler 1990.

Das Wiener Volkstheater. Raimund und Nestroy (Erträge der Forschung, 100), 2nd edn, Darmstadt: Wissenschaftliche Buchgesellschaft 1991.

'Grabbes *Don Juan und Faust* in Wien. Ein Vorstadttheater-Spektakel im Vormärz', in '*– und nichts als nur Verzweiflung kann uns retten!*' (Grabbe-Jahrbuch, 11), Bielefeld: Aisthesis 1992, pp. 31–61.

Hennings, Fred: *Zweimal Burgtheater. Vom Michaelerplatz zum Franzensring*, Vienna: Kremayr & Scheriau 1955.

Herles, Helmut: 'Nestroy und die Zensur', in Jürgen Hein (ed.), *Theater und*

Gesellschaft. Das Volksstück im 19. und 20. Jahrhundert, Düsseldorf: Bertelsmann Universitätsverlag 1973, pp. 121–32.

Herterich, Franz: 'Die szenische Entwicklung des neuen Burgtheaters', in *Hundertfünfzig Jahre Burgtheater 1776–1926* (1926), pp. 37–41.

Das Burgtheater und seine Sendung, Vienna: Neff n.d. [*c*. 1946].

Hilmar, Ernst: 'Die Nestroy-Vertonungen in den Wiener Sammlungen', *Maske und Kothurn* 18 (1972), 38–98.

Hinze, Klaus-Peter: 'Ernst Weiss: the novelist as dramatist', in Edward Timms and Ritchie Robertson (eds), *Theatre and Performance in Austria: From Mozart to Jelinek* (Austrian Studies, 4), Edinburgh: Edinburgh University Press, 1993, pp. 93–101.

Hundertfünfzig Jahre Burgtheater 1776–1926. Eine Festschrift. Herausgegeben von der Direktion des Burgtheaters, Vienna: Krystall-Verlag 1926.

Hüttner, Johann: 'Wiener Nestroyaufführungen vom Tode des Autors bis zum Ende des zweiten Weltkrieges', 2 vols., Diss., University of Vienna 1964.

'Baugeschichte und Spielplan des Theaters am Franz Josefs Kai', *Jahrbuch der Gesellschaft für Wiener Theaterforschung* 17 (1970), 87–161.

'Literarische Parodie und Wiener Vorstadtpublikum vor Nestroy', *Maske und Kothurn* 18 (1972), 99–139.

'Sensationsstücke und Alt-Wiener Volkstheater'. Zum Melodrama in der ersten Hälfte des 19. Jahrhunderts', *Maske und Kothurn* 21 (1975), 263–81.

'Das Burgtheaterpublikum in der ersten Hälfte des 19. Jahrhunderts', in Margret Dietrich (ed.), *Das Burgtheater und sein Publikum*, Vol. 1 (1976), pp. 123–84.

'Johann Nestroy im Theaterbetrieb seiner Zeit', *Maske und Kothurn* 23 (1977), 233–43.

'Machte sich Nestroy bezahlt?', *Nestroyana* 1 (1979), 3–25.

'Theatre censorship in Metternich's Vienna', *Theatre Quarterly* 10, no. 37 (1980), 61–9.

'Vor- und Selbstzensur bei Johann Nestroy', *Maske und Kothurn* 26 (1980), 234–48.

'Die Gründung des "Deutschen Volkstheaters" in Wien', in [Georg Robor (ed.)], *Das neue Volkstheater. Festschrift* (1981), pp. 1–7.

'Leben und Sterben eines Wiener Theaters', *wien aktuell magazin* 1981, no. 5, pp. XXVI–XXVIII.

'Das theatrale Umfeld Nestroys', *Nestroyana* 3 (1981), 140–55.

'Theater als Geschäft. Vorarbeiten zu einer Sozialgeschichte des kommerziellen Theaters im 19. Jahrhundert aus theaterwissenschaftlicher Sicht. Mit Betonung Wiens und Berücksichtigung Londons und der USA', 2 vols., Diss. (Habilitationsschrift), University of Vienna 1982.

'Theater im Zeitalter Kaiser Franz Josephs', in *Das Zeitalter Kaiser Franz Josephs*, Part 1: *Von der Revolution zur Gründerzeit 1848–1880* (Katalog des Niederösterreichischen Landesmuseums, new series, 147), Vol. 1: *Beiträge*, Vienna: Amt der NÖ Landesregierung, Abt. III/2 (Kulturabteilung) 1984, pp. 346–51.

'Der ernste Nestroy', in W.E. Yates and John R.P. McKenzie (eds), *Viennese Popular Theatre* (1985), pp. 67–80 (notes p. 157).

'Volkstheater als Geschäft: Theaterbetrieb und Publikum im 19. Jahrhundert', in Jean-Marie Valentin (ed.), *Volk – Volksstück – Volkstheater im deutschen Sprachraum des 18.–20. Jahrhunderts (Jahrbuch für Internationale Germanistik*, Reihe A: Kongressberichte, 15), Berne: Lang 1986, pp. 127–49.

'Volk sucht sein Theater. Theater suchen ihr Publikum: Das Dilemma des Wiener Volkstheaters im zweiten Drittel des 19. Jahrhunderts', in Jean-Marie Valentin (ed.), *Das österreichische Volkstheater im europäischen Zusammenhang 1830–1880* (Contacts, Série 1: Theatrica, 5), Berne: Lang 1988, pp. 33–53.

'Zum Wiener Theater 1815–1848', in *Bürgersinn und Aufbegehren. Biedermeier und Vormärz in Wien 1815–1848* (catalogue, 109. Sonderausstellung des Historischen Museums der Stadt Wien), Vienna: Jugend und Volk 1988, pp. 412–17.

'Das Theater als Austragungsort kulturpolitischer Konflikte' and '1889–1918: Die Direktionen Emerich von Bukovics, Adolf Weisse, Karl Wallner. Zwischen Stadttheater und Volkstheater', in Evelyn Schreiner (ed.), *100 Jahre Volkstheater* (1989), pp. 10–15, 16–31.

Jarka, Horst (ed.): *The Legacy of Jura Soyfer 1912–1939. Poems, Prose and Plays of an Austrian Antifascist*, Montreal: Engendra Press 1977 (Introduction, pp. 1–67).

Jauner, Theodor: *Fünf Jahre Wiener Operntheater 1875–1880. Franz Jauner und seine Zeit*, Vienna: Selbstverlag 1962.

Johann Christian Schoeller. Karikatur und Satire in Biedermeier und Vormärz (catalogue, 54. Sonderausstellung des Historischen Museums der Stadt Wien), Vienna: Museen der Stadt Wien 1978.

John, David G.: 'From extemporization to text: observations on an unpublished Viennese manuscript', in Linda Dietrick and David G. John (eds), *Momentum dramaticum. Festschrift für Eckehard Catholy*, Waterloo, Ont.: University of Waterloo Press 1990, pp. 123–34.

Jones, Michael R.: 'Censorship as an obstacle to the production of Shakespeare on the stage of the Burgtheater in the nineteenth century', *German Life and Letters*, new series, 27 (1973–4), 187–94.

Kaderschafka, Karl: '*Ein Bruderzwist in Habsburg* auf der Bühne', in Oskar Katann (ed.), *Grillparzer-Studien*, Vienna: Gerlach & Wiedling 1924, pp. 221–43.

Kahl, Kurt: *Die Wiener und ihr Burgtheater*, Vienna and Munich: Jugend und Volk 1974.

Keil-Budischowsky, Verena: *Die Theater Wiens*, Vienna and Hamburg: Zsolnay 1983.

Keppelmüller, Elisabeth: 'Die künstlerische Tätigkeit der Exl-Bühne in Innsbruck und Wien von 1902 bis 1945', Diss., University of Vienna 1947.

Kilian, Eugen, 'Schreyvogels Shakespeare-Bearbeitungen. Ein Beitrag zur Bühnengeschichte der Shakespeareschen Dramen in Deutschland', *Jahrbuch der Deutschen Shakespeare-Gesellschaft* 39 (1903), 87–120.

Kindermann, Heinz: *Das Burgtheater. Erbe und Sendung eines Nationaltheaters*, 2nd edn, Vienna: Wiener Verlag 1944.

Hermann Bahr. Ein Leben für das europäische Theater, Graz and Cologne: Böhlau 1954.

Shakespeare und das Burgtheater (Österreichische Akademie der Wissenschaften, Phil.-hist. Klasse, Sitzungsberichte, Vol. 245, no. 1), Graz, Vienna, Cologne: Böhlau 1964.

'Josef Schreyvogel und sein Publikum', in Margret Dietrich (ed.), *Das Burgtheater und sein Publikum*, Vol. 1 (1976), pp. 185–333.

Kinz, Maria: *Raimundtheater*, Vienna and Munich: Jugend und Volk 1985.

Komorzynski, Egon: *Emanuel Schikaneder. Ein Beitrag zur Geschichte des deutschen Theaters*, Vienna: Doblinger 1951.

Kretschmer, Helmut: *Verschwundene Wiener Theater* (Veröffentlichungen des Wiener Stadt- und Landesarchivs, Reihe B: Ausstellungskataloge, 20), Vienna: Wiener Stadt- und Landesarchiv (MA 8) 1988.

Kupfer, Hermann: 'Franz Pokorny und das Theater an der Wien', Diss., University of Vienna 1979 [1980].

Láng, Attila E.: *Das Theater an der Wien. Vom Singspiel zum Musical*, Vienna and Munich: Jugend und Volk 1976.

Lang, Berthold: 'Zirkus und Kabarett', in Franz Kadrnoska (ed.), *Aufbruch und Untergang. Österreichische Kultur zwischen 1918 und 1938*, Vienna: Europaverlag 1981, pp. 301–23.

Lederer, Herbert: *Bevor alles verweht... Wiener Kellertheater 1945 bis 1960*. Vienna: Österreichischer Bundesverlag 1986.

Leitner, Josef: 'Die Anfänge der Wiener Theaterkritik und der Kritiker Wilhelm Hebenstreit', *Jahrbuch der Grillparzer-Gesellschaft* 31 [1932], 115–37.

Lichtfuss, Martin: *Operette im Ausverkauf. Studien zum Libretto des musikalischen Unterhaltungstheaters im Österreich der Zwischenkriegszeit*, Vienna, Cologne: Böhlau 1989.

Lothar, Rudolph: *Das Wiener Burgtheater* (Dichter und Darsteller, 2), Leipzig and Berlin: Seemann; Vienna: Gesellschaft für graphische Industrie 1899.

Das Wiener Burgtheater. Ein Wahrzeichen österreichischer Kunst und Kultur, Vienna: Augartenverlag 1934.

McMullen, Sally: 'From the armchair to the stage: Hofmannsthal's *Elektra* in its theatrical context', *Modern Language Review* 80 (1985), 637–51.

Mantler, Anton: *Adolf Bäuerle und das Alt-Wiener Volkstheater* (catalogue, 201. Wechselausstellung der Wiener Stadt- und Landesbibliothek), Vienna: Stadt Wien (MA 9) 1984.

Ferdinand Raimund und die Nachwelt (catalogue, 207. Wechselausstellung der Wiener Stadt- und Landesbibliothek), Vienna: Stadt Wien (MA 9) 1986.

May, Erich Joachim: *Wiener Volkskomödie und Vormärz*, Berlin: Henschelverlag 1975.

Mayerhöfer, Josef (ed.): *50 Jahre Akademietheater 1922–1972* (Biblos-Schriften, 72), Vienna: Österreichische Nationalbibliothek 1972.

Wiener Theater des Biedermeier und Vormärz. Ausstellungs-Katalog (Biblos-Schriften, 97), Vienna: Österreichisches Theatermuseum 1978.

Operette in Wien. Ausstellungs-Katalog (Biblos-Schriften, 107), Vienna: Österreichisches Theatermuseum 1979.

Meister, Monika: 'Theater im Vorkriegswien: Jura Soyfer und der Widerstand', in Kristian Sotriffer (ed.), *Das größere Österreich. Geistiges und soziales Leben von 1880 bis zur Gegenwart*, Vienna: Edition Tusch 1982, pp. 317–20.

Michtner, Otto: *Das alte Burgtheater als Opernbühne. Von der Einführung des deutschen Singspiels (1778) bis zum Tod Kaiser Leopolds II. (1792)* (*Theatergeschichte Österreichs*, III/1), Vienna: Böhlau 1970.

Obermaier, Walter: 'Nestroy und Ernst Stainhauser', in W.E. Yates and John R.P. McKenzie (eds), *Viennese Popular Theatre* (1985), pp. 41–54 (notes pp. 154–6).

'Zensur im Vormärz', in *Bürgersinn und Aufbegehren. Biedermeier und Vormärz in Wien 1815–1848* (catalogue, 109. Sonderausstellung des Historischen Museums der Stadt Wien), Vienna and Munich: Jugend und Volk 1987, pp. 622–7.

'Nestroyaufführungen in Wien 1938–1945', *Nestroyana* 7 (1987), 52–64.

Hans Weigel. Leben und Werk. Zum 80. Geburtstag (catalogue, 213. Wechselausstellung der Wiener Stadt- und Landesbibliothek), Vienna: Stadt Wien (MA 9) 1988.

'Nestroy-Pflege in Österreich', *Nestroyana* 7 (1988), 117–29.

'Der Einfluß des französischen Theaters auf den Spielplan der Wiener Vorstadtbühnen in den 50er Jahren des 19. Jahrhunderts, insbesondere die Offenbachrezeption Nestroys', in Jean-Marie Valentin (ed.), *Das österreichische Volkstheater im europäischen Zusammenhang 1830–1880* (Contacts, Série 1: Theatrica, 5), Berne: Lang 1988, pp. 133–53.

'Nestroy und die Presse', in Gerald Stieg and Jean-Marie Valentin (eds): *Johann Nestroy 1801–1862. Vision du monde et écriture dramatique*, Asnières: Institut d'Allemand d'Asnières (Paris III) and Paris: U.R.A. 1282 (Paris IV) 1991, pp. 109–18.

Oellers, Norbert: 'Heinrich Laube als Direktor des Wiener Burgtheaters', in Herbert Zeman (ed.): *Die österreichische Literatur. Ihr Profil im 19. Jahrhundert (1830–1880)*, Graz: Akademische Druck- und Verlagsanstalt 1982, pp. 23–45.

Pablé, Elisabeth: 'Anton Wildgans und das Wiener Theater', *Jahrbuch der Gesellschaft für Wiener Theaterforschung* 1954/1955 [1958], 3–68.

Pellert, Wilhelm: *Roter Vorhang, rotes Tuch. Das Neue Theater in der Scala (1948–1956)* (In Sachen, 8), Vienna: Arbeitsgemeinschaft für Sozialwissenschaftliche Publizistik 1979.

Pemmer, Hans: 'Das Harmonietheater in der Wasagasse', in *Das Harmo-*

nietheater. 14. Sonderausstellung des Heimatmuseums Alsergrund (Beiträge zur Heimatkunde des IX. Bezirks, 1), Vienna: Heimatmuseum Alsergrund 1966, pp. 5–42.

Das Wiener Bürgertheater (Festwochensonderheft des Landstraßer Heimatmuseums, 4) Vienna 1967.

Pfoser, Alfred, Kristina Pfoser-Schewig, and Gerhard Renner: *Schnitzlers 'Reigen'. Zehn Dialoge und ihre Skandalgeschichte. Analysen und Dokumente,* 2 vols., Frankfurt a.M.: Fischer Taschenbuch Verlag 1993.

Pirchan, Emil, Alexander Witeschnik, and Otto Fritz: *300 Jahre Wiener Operntheater. Werk und Werden,* Vienna: Fortuna-Verlag 1953.

Pöll, Walter: 'Der Wiener Theaterdichter Friedrich Kaiser', Diss., University of Vienna 1947.

Pott, Gertrud: *Die Spiegelung des Sezessionismus im österreichischen Theater* (Wiener Forschungen zur Theater- und Medienwissenschaft, 3), Vienna and Stuttgart: Braumüller 1975.

Pötz, Ingrid: 'Zur Geschichte des Theaters in der Neubaugasse (Volksbühne – Renaissancebühne)', Diplomarbeit (Mag. phil.), University of Vienna 1986.

Prawy, Marcel: *Die Wiener Oper. Geschichte und Geschichten.* Vienna, Munich, Zürich: Molden 1969.

Raab, Riki: 'Das Wiener Opernballett', in Andrea Seebohm (ed.), *Die Wiener Oper. 350 Jahre Glanz und Tradition* (1986), pp. 211–36.

Ratislav, J.K.: 'Laubes Kampf um die Subvention des Burgtheaters (Mit einem "Memoire" Laubes an das Finanzministerium)', *Jahrbuch der Gesellschaft für Wiener Theaterforschung* 1944, 41–62.

[Ratislav, Josef Karl, *et al.*]: *175 Jahre Burgtheater 1776–1951. Fortgeführt bis Sommer 1954.* Vienna: [Direktion des Burgtheaters] n.d. [1954].

Reichert, Herbert W.: 'Some causes of the Nestroy renaissance in Vienna', *Monatshefte* 47 (1957), 221–30.

Reischl, Friedrich: *Wien zur Biedermeierzeit. Volksleben in Wiens Vorstädten nach zeitgenössischen Schilderungen,* Vienna: Gerlach & Wiedling 1921, pp. 146–89: 'Sensationen im Theater an der Wien'.

Rieger, Erwin: *Offenbach und seine Wiener Schule* (Theater und Kultur, 4), Vienna and Berlin: Wiener Literarische Anstalt 1920.

Riss, Ulrike: 'Theatergeschichtliche Aspekte 1880–1916', in *Das Zeitalter Kaiser Franz Josephs,* Part 2: *1880–1916. Glanz und Elend* (Katalog des Niederösterreichischen Landesmuseums, new series, 186), Vol. 1: *Beiträge,* Vienna: Amt der NÖ Landesregierung, Abt. III/2 (Kulturabteilung) 1987, pp. 205–13.

[Robor, Georg (ed.)]: *Das neue Volkstheater. Festschrift – herausgegeben aus Anlaß der Renovierung 1980/81,* Vienna and Munich: Jugend und Volk 1981.

Rommel, Otto: 'Ludwig Anzengruber als Dramatiker', in *Ludwig Anzengrubers sämtliche Werke,* ed. Rudolf Latzke and Otto Rommel, 17 vols., Vienna: Schroll 1920–2, II, 333–607.

Johann Nestroy. Ein Beitrag zur Geschichte der Wiener Volkskomik, in Nestroy,

Sämtliche Werke, ed. Fritz Brukner and Otto Rommel, 15 vols., Vienna: Schroll 1924–30, Vol. xv (1930).

Die Alt-Wiener Volkskomödie. Ihre Geschichte vom barocken Welt-Theater bis zum Tode Nestroys, Vienna: Schroll 1952.

[Ronge, Irene (ed.)]: *1889–1964. 75 Jahre Volkstheater*, Vienna: Volkstheater [Selbstverlag] n.d. [1964].

Rosner, Leopold: *Fünfzig Jahre Carl-Theater (1847–1897). Ein Rückblick*, Vienna: Schworella & Heick 1897.

Rub, Otto: *Das Burgtheater. Statistischer Rückblick auf die Tätigkeit und die Personalverhältnisse während der Zeit vom 8. April 1776 bis 1. Januar 1913. Ein theaterhistorisches Nachschlagebuch*, Vienna: Knepler 1913.

Sag beim Abschied... Wiener Publikumslieblinge in Bild & Ton. Sammlung Robert Sachs (catalogue, 158. Ausstellung des Historischen Museums der Stadt Wien), Vienna: Museen der Stadt Wien 1992.

Salten, Felix: 'Wiener Theater (1848 bis 1898)', in *Die Pflege der Kunst in Österreich 1848–1898*, Wien: Perles 1900, pp. 60–85.

Sauer, August: *Gesammelte Reden und Aufsätze zur Geschichte der Literatur in Österreich und Deutschland*, Vienna and Leipzig: Fromme 1903, pp. 81–101: 'Zur Geschichte des Burgtheaters. Aus Josef Schreyvogels Papieren' [1888].

Scheichl, Sigurd Paul: 'Alfred Polgar als Wiener Theaterberichterstatter der *Schaubühne* und der *Weltbühne*', *Cahiers d'études germaniques* (Aix-en-Provence), 24 (1993), 149–62.

Schenker, Hansjörg: 'Theaterdirektor Carl und die Staberl-Figur. Eine Studie zum Wiener Volkstheater vor und neben Nestroy', Diss., University of Zürich 1986.

Schiferer, Beatrix: *Girardi – Der Wiener aus Graz*, Vienna and Munich: Jugend und Volk 1975.

Schimscha, Beatrix Renate: 'Das Josefstädtertheater als Opernbühne', Diss., University of Vienna 1965 [1966].

Schindler, Otto G.: 'Der Zuschauerraum des Burgtheaters im 18. Jahrhundert. Eine baugeschichtliche Skizze', *Maske und Kothurn* 22 (1976), 20–53.

(in collaboration with Herbert Matschinger): 'Das Publikum des Burgtheaters in der Josephinischen Ära. Versuch einer Strukturbestimmung', in Margret Dietrich (ed.), *Das Burgtheater und sein Publikum*, Vol. 1 (1976), pp. 11–95.

Schinnerer, Otto P.: 'The History of Schnitzler's *Reigen*', *Publications of the Modern Language Association of America* 46 (1931), 839–59.

Schnabel, Werner Wilhelm, '*Professor Bernhardi* und die Wiener Zensur. Zur Rezeptionsgeschichte der Schnitzlerschen Komödie', *Jahrbuch der Deutschen Schillergesellschaft* 28 (1984), 349–83.

Schreiner, Evelyn: 'Nationalsozialistische Kulturpolitik in Wien 1938–1945 unter spezieller Berücksichtigung der Wiener Theaterszene', Diss., University of Vienna 1980 [1981].

'Nationalsozialistische Kulturpolitik und die Auswirkungen auf das Wiener Theater', 'Das Deutsche Volkstheater wird "Kraft durch Freude"-Theater', and '1938–1954: Direktion W.B. Iltz', in Evelyn Schreiner (ed.): *100 Jahre Volkstheater* (1989), pp. 106–37.

Schreiner, Evelyn (ed.): *100 Jahre Volkstheater. Theater. Zeit. Geschichte*, Vienna and Munich: Jugend und Volk 1989.

Schrott, Margarethe: 'Shakespeare im Alt-Wiener Volkstheater', *Maske und Kothurn* 10 (1964), 282–300.

Schwarz, Helmut H.: 'Wiener Theater in Stock und Keller', *Jahrbuch der Gesellschaft für Wiener Theaterforschung* 1951/1952 [1955], 170–90.

Seebohm, Andrea (ed.): *Die Wiener Oper. 350 Jahre Glanz und Tradition*, Vienna: Ueberreuter 1986.

Seelig, Lutz Eberhardt: *Ronacher. Die Geschichte eines Hauses*, Vienna, Cologne, Graz: Böhlau 1986.

Singer, Herta: 'Die Akustik des alten Burgtheaters. Versuch einer Darstellung der Zusammenhänge zwischen Aufführungsstil und Raumakustik', *Maske und Kothurn* 4 (1958), 220–9.

Specht, Richard: *Zehn Jahre Burgtheater. Eine Studie*. Vienna: Rosner 1899.

Stefan, Paul: *Das neue Haus. Ein Halbjahrhundert Wiener Opernspiel und was voranging*. Vienna and Leipzig: Strache 1919.

Sternstunden im Theater an der Wien. Eine Rückschau anläßlich der Wiedereröffnung (Österreichische Musikzeitschrift, Sonderband), Vienna: Verlag Österreichische Musikzeitschrift 1962.

Straubinger, O. Paul: 'Grillparzer in der Parodie des Alt-Wiener Volkstheaters', *Jahrbuch der Grillparzer-Gesellschaft*, 3rd series, 3 (1960), 115–26.

Swoboda, Helmut: '"Der Humorist". Ein Beitrag zur österreichischen Pressegeschichte', Diss., University of Vienna 1948.

Tschulik, Norbert: *Musiktheater in Österreich. Die Oper im 20. Jahrhundert*, Vienna: Österreichischer Bundesverlag 1984.

Urbach, Reinhard: *Die Wiener Komödie und ihr Publikum. Stranitzky und die Folgen*, Vienna and Munich: Jugend und Volk 1973.

Schnitzler-Kommentar. Zu den erzählenden Schriften und dramatischen Werken, Munich: Winkler 1974.

Wagner, Hans: 'Die Zensur am Burgtheater zur Zeit Direktor Schlenthers 1898–1910', *Mitteilungen des Österreichischen Staatsarchivs* 14 (1961), 394–420.

Wagner, Renate, and Brigitte Vacha: *Wiener Schnitzler-Aufführungen 1891–1970* (Studien zur Kunst des neunzehnten Jahrhunderts, 17), Munich: Prestel 1971.

Walla, Friedrich: 'Johann Nestroy und der Antisemitismus. Eine Bestandaufnahme', *Österreich in Geschichte und Literatur* 29 (1985), 37–51.

'Johann Nestroy und die Zensur. Krokodil am Geistesstrom oder Die jüngere Schwester der Inquisition', *Nestroyana* 9 (1989), 22–34.

'Aus eins mach zwei, aus zwei mach eins: Zur Entstehungsgeschichte und Chronologie von Nestroys Stücken der Jahre 1833 und 1834', *Nestroyana* 13 (1993), 91–109.

'Die Theaterzensur am Beispiel des *Lumpacivagabundus*', in W. Edgar Yates (ed.), *Vom schaffenden zum edierten Nestroy*, Vienna: Jugend und Volk 1994, pp. 45–68.

Warren, J.D.A.: 'Viennese theatre in the First Republic', in B.O. Murdoch and M.G. Ward (eds), *Studies in Modern Austrian Literature*, Glasgow: Scottish Papers in Germanic Studies 1981, pp. 56–73.

Warren, John: 'Max Reinhardt and the Viennese Theatre of the Interwar Years', *Maske und Kothurn* 29 (1983), 123–36.

'Austrian theatre and the Corporate State', in Kenneth Segar and John Warren (eds), *Austria in the Thirties: Culture and Politics*, Riverside, Ca.: Ariadne Press 1991, pp. 267–91.

'Friedrich Kiesler and theatrical modernism in Vienna', in Edward Timms and Ritchie Robertson (eds), *Theatre and Performance in Austria: From Mozart to Jelinek* (Austrian Studies, 4), Edinburgh: Edinburgh University Press 1993, pp. 81–92.

Weilen, Alexander von, Oscar Teuber, Josef Bayer, and Richard Wallaschek: *Die Theater Wiens*, 4 vols. in 6 parts, Vienna: Gesellschaft für vervielfältigende Kunst 1894–1909.

Werba, Maria-Christine: 'Das Wiener Kabarett im Zeichen des Jugendstils', 3 vols., Diss., University of Vienna 1976.

Werba, Christine: 'Cabaret viennois. "Herr Karl" und die Folgen', in Kristian Sotriffer (ed.), *Das größere Österreich. Geistiges und soziales Leben von 1880 bis zur Gegenwart*, Vienna: Edition Tusch 1982, pp. 443–7.

Wiener Volksoper. Die Direktion Karl Dönch. 1. September 1973 bis 31. August 1987, Vienna: Österreichischer Bundestheaterverband / Direktion der Wiener Volksoper [1987].

Wildgans, Lilly: *Anton Wildgans und das Burgtheater*, Vienna: Kremayr & Scheriau 1955.

Willnauer, Franz: *Gustav Mahler und die Wiener Oper*, Vienna and Munich: Jugend und Volk 1979.

Witeschnik, Alexander: *Wiener Opernkunst. Von den Anfängen bis zu Karajan*, Vienna: Kremayr & Scheriau 1959.

Wladika, Otto: 'Von Johann Fürst zu Josef Jarno. Die Geschichte des Wiener Pratertheaters', 3 vols., Diss., University of Vienna 1960 [1961].

Wlassack, Eduard: *Chronik des k.k. Hof-Burgtheaters. Zu dessen Säcular-Feier im Februar 1876*, Vienna: Rosner 1876.

Yates, W.E.: ' "Die Jugendeindrücke wird man nicht los …": Grillparzer's Relation to the Viennese Popular Theatre', *Germanic Review* 48 (1973), 132–49.

'An object of Nestroy's satire: Friedrich Kaiser and the *Lebensbild*', *Renaissance and Modern Studies* 22 (1978), 45–62.

'The idea of the "Volksstück" in Nestroy's Vienna', *German Life and Letters*, new series, 38 (1984–5), 462–73.

'Nestroy und die Rezensenten', *Nestroyana* 7 (1987), 28–40.

'Nestroys Weg zur klassischen Posse', *Nestroyana* 7 (1987) [1988], 93–109.

'The tendentious reception of *Professor Bernhardi*: documentation in Schnitzler's collection of press cuttings', in Edward Timms and Ritchie Robertson (eds), *Vienna 1900: From Altenberg to Wittgenstein* (Austrian Studies, 1), Edinburgh: Edinburgh University Press 1990, pp. 108–25.

Schnitzler, Hofmannsthal, and the Austrian Theatre, New Haven and London: Yale University Press 1992.

'The Biedermeier Mozart', in Martin Swales (ed.), *London German Studies*, v (Publications of the Institute of Germanic Studies, 57), London: University of London Institute of Germanic Studies 1993, pp. 19–33.

'Nestroy in 1847: *Der Schützling* and the decline of Viennese popular theatre', *Modern Language Review* 88 (1993), 110–25.

'Nestroy und Bauernfeld', *Nestroyana* 14 (1994), 11–22.

'Grillparzer und die Rezensenten', in Hilde Haider-Pregler and Evelyn Deutsch-Schreiner (eds): *Stichwort Grillparzer* (Grillparzer-Forum 1), Vienna, Cologne, Weimar: Böhlau 1994, pp. 17–28.

Nestroy and the Critics, Columbia, SC: Camden House 1994.

Yates, W.E., and John R.P. McKenzie (eds): *Viennese Popular Theatre. A Symposium – Das Wiener Volkstheater. Ein Symposion*, Exeter: University of Exeter 1985.

Zechmeister, Gustav: *Die Wiener Theater nächst der Burg und nächst dem Kärntnerthor von 1747 bis 1776 (Theatergeschichte Österreichs, III/2)*, Vienna: Böhlau 1971.

Zeidler, Jakob: 'Ein Censurexemplar von Grillparzer's: *König Ottokars Glück und Ende*. (Ein Beitrag zur Wiener Theatergeschichte)', in *Ein Wiener Stammbuch. Dem Director der Bibliothek und des historischen Museums der Stadt Wien Dr. Carl Glossy zum 50. Geburtstage, 7. März 1898, gewidmet von Freunden und Landsleuten*, Vienna: Konegen 1898, pp. 287–311.

Zobel, Konrad, and Frederick E. Warner: 'The old Burgtheater: a structural history, 1741–1888', *Theatre Studies* 19 (1972–3), 19–53.

3. THEATRE OUTSIDE VIENNA
(London, Paris, Berlin, Meiningen, Salzburg, Zürich)

Baer, Marc: *Theatre and Disorder in Late Georgian London*, Oxford: Clarendon 1992.

Booth, Michael R.: *English Melodrama*, London: Herbert Jenkins 1965.

Victorian Spectacular Theatre 1850–1910, Boston, London, Henley: Routledge & Kegan Paul 1981.

Theatre in the Victorian Age, Cambridge: Cambridge University Press 1991.

Brazier, Nicolas: *Chroniques des petits théâtres de Paris. Depuis leur création jusqu'à ce jour* [1837], ed. Georges d'Heylli, 2 vols., Paris: Rouveyre and Blond 1883.

Draudt, Manfred: ' "Committing outrage against the Bard": nineteenth-century travesties of Shakespeare in England and Austria', *Modern Language Review* 88 (1993), 102–9.

Fluchtpunkt Zürich. Zu einer Stadt und ihrem Theater. Schauplätze der Selbstbehaup-tung und des Überlebens 1933–1945, compiled by Ute Cofalka and Beate Schläpfer (exhibition catalogue, Österreichisches Theatermuseum, Vienna), 1994.

Freydank, Ruth: *Theater in Berlin. Von den Anfängen bis 1945*, Berlin: Henschel-verlag 1988.

Fuhrich, Edda, and Gisela Prossnitz: *Die Salzburger Festspiele. Ihre Geschichte in Daten, Zeitzeugnissen und Bildern*, Vol. 1: *1920–1945*, Salzburg: Residenz 1990.

Gautier, Théophile: *Histoire de l'art dramatique en France depuis vingt-cinq ans*, 6 vols., Paris: Hetzel 1858–9.

Gidel, Henri: *Le Vaudeville* (Que sais-je, 2301), Paris: Presses Universitaires de France 1986.

Hemmings, F.W.J.: *The Theatre Industry in Nineteenth-Century France*, Cam-bridge: Cambridge University Press 1993.

Jackson, Russell (ed.): *Victorian Theatre*, London: Black 1989.

Kaindl-Hönig, Max (ed.): *Resonanz. 50 Jahre Kritik der Salzburger Festspiele*, Salzburg: SN Verlag 1971.

Kaut, Josef: *Festspiele in Salzburg*, Salzburg: Residenz 1969.

Latour, Geneviève, and Florence Claval (eds): *Les Théâtres de Paris* (exhibi-tion catalogue), Paris: Délégation à l'action artistique de la Ville de Paris 1991.

Leroy, Dominique: *Histoire des arts du spectacle en France. Aspects économiques, politiques et esthétiques de la Renaissance à la Première Guerre mondiale*, Paris: L'Harmattan 1990.

McCormick, John: *Popular Theatres of Nineteenth-Century France*, London and New York: Routledge 1993.

Osborne, John: *The Meiningen Court Theatre 1866–1890*, Cambridge: Cam-bridge University Press 1988.

Riess, Curt: *Sein oder Nichtsein. Zürcher Schauspielhaus: Der Roman eines Theaters*, Zürich: Ex Libris 1963; revised edn: *Das Schauspielhaus Zürich. Sein oder Nichtsein eines ungewöhnlichen Theaters*, Munich: Langen Müller 1988.

Rowell, George: *The Victorian Theatre 1792–1924*, 2nd edn, Cambridge: Cambridge University Press 1978.

Silvain, Eugène: *Frédérick Lemaître*, new edn, Paris: Alcan 1930.

Stephens, John Russell: *The Censorship of English Drama 1824–1901*, Cambridge: Cambridge University Press 1980.

The Profession of the Playwright: British Theatre 1800–1900, Cambridge: Cambridge University Press 1992.

Trussler, Simon: *The Cambridge Illustrated History of British Theatre*, Cambridge: Cambridge University Press 1994.

Wahnrau, Gerhard: *Berlin. Stadt der Theater. Der Chronik 1. Teil*, Berlin: Henschelverlag 1957.

Yates, W.E.: 'Grillparzer als Theaterbesucher in Paris und London', *Anzeiger der phil.-hist. Klasse der Österreichischen Akademie der Wissenschaften* 128 (1991), 75–95.

4. GENERAL AND REFERENCE

Ackerl, Isabella, *et al.*: *Die Chronik Wiens*, Dortmund: Chronik Verlag 1988.

Amann, Klaus: *Der Anschluß österreichischer Schriftsteller an das Dritte Reich. Institutionelle und bewußtseinsgeschichtliche Aspekte*, Frankfurt a.M.: Athenäum 1988.

Arlt, Herbert (ed.): *Jura Soyfer und Theater*, Frankfurt a.M.: Lang 1992.

Aust, Hugo, Peter Haida, and Jürgen Hein: *Volksstück. Vom Hanswurstspiel zum sozialen Drama der Gegenwart*, Munich: Beck 1989.

Barea, Ilsa: *Vienna: Legend and Reality*, London: Secker and Warburg 1966.

Baumann, Carl-Friedrich: *Licht im Theater. Von der Argand-Lampe bis zum Glühlampen-Scheinwerfer*, Stuttgart: Steiner 1988.

Bayerdörfer, Hans-Peter: 'Probleme der Theatergeschichtsschreibung', in Renate Möhrmann (ed.), *Theaterwissenschaft heute. Eine Einführung*, Berlin: Dietrich Reimer 1990, pp. 41–64.

Bergman, Gösta M.: *Lighting in the Theatre*, Stockholm: Almqvist & Wiksell International; Totowa, N.J.: Rowman and Littlefield 1977.

Bland, Alexander: *A History of Ballet and Dance in the Western World*, London: Barrie & Jenkins 1976.

Brandstätter, Christian, Günter Treffer, *et al.* (eds): *StadtChronik Wien. 2000 Jahre in Daten, Dokumenten und Bildern*, Vienna: Brandstätter 1986.

Braulich, Heinrich: *Max Reinhardt. Theater zwischen Traum und Wirklichkeit*, Berlin: Henschelverlag 1969.

Brauneck, Manfred, and Gérard Schneilin (eds): *Theaterlexikon: Begriffe und Epochen, Bühnen und Ensembles*, Reinbek bei Hamburg: Rowohlt 1986.

Breuer, Dieter: *Geschichte der literarischen Zensur in Deutschland* (Uni-Taschenbücher, 1208), Heidelberg: Quelle & Meyer 1982.

Brown, Maurice J.E.: *The New Grove Schubert*, with a work-list by Eric Sams, London: Macmillan 1982.

Bruford, W.H.: *Theatre, Drama and Audience in Goethe's Germany*, London: Routledge & Kegan Paul 1950.

Burckhard, Max: *Das Theater* (Die Gesellschaft, 18), Frankfurt a.M.: Rütten & Loening 1907.

Chandler, Tertius, and Gerald Fox: *3000 Years of Urban Growth*, New York and London: Academic Press 1974.

Czeike, Felix: *Geschichte der Stadt Wien*, Vienna: Molden 1981.

Historisches Lexikon Wien, 5 vols., Vienna: Kremayr & Scheriau 1992– .

Czeike, Felix (ed.): *Das große Groner Wien Lexikon*, Vienna: Molden 1974.

Deppisch, Walter: *Richard Strauss* (Rowohlts Monographien, 146), Reinbek bei Hamburg: Rowohlt 1991.

Devrient, Eduard: *Geschichte der deutschen Schauspielkunst*, ed. and continued by Willy Stuhlfeld, Berlin and Zürich: Eigenbrödler-Verlag 1929.

Eisenberg, Ludwig: *Großes Biographisches Lexikon der deutschen Bühne im XIX. Jahrhundert*, Leipzig: Paul List 1903.

Fiedler, Leonhard M.: *Max Reinhardt* (Rowohlts Monographien, 228), Reinbek bei Hamburg: Rowohlt 1975.

Fischer-Lichte, Erika: *Kurze Geschichte des deutschen Theaters* (Uni-Taschen-bücher, 1667), Tübingen and Basle: Francke 1993.

Fleischmann, Benno: *Max Reinhardt. Die Wiederentdeckung des Barocktheaters*, Vienna: Neff 1948.

Frenzel, Herbert A.: *Geschichte des Theaters. Daten und Dokumente 1470–1840*, Munich: Deutscher Taschenbuch Verlag 1979.

Fuhrich, Edda, and Gisela Prossnitz (eds): *Max Reinhardt. 'Ein Theater, das den Menschen wieder Freude gibt . . .'. Eine Dokumentation*, Munich: Langen Müller 1987.

Gartenberg, Egon: *Johann Strauss: The End of an Era*, New York: Da Capo Press 1979.

Giebisch, Hans, and Gustav Gugitz: *Bio-bibliographisches Literaturlexikon Österreichs. Von den Anfängen bis zur Gegenwart*, Vienna: Hollinek 1963.

Gregor, Joseph: *Geschichte des österreichischen Theaters. Von seinen Ursprüngen bis zum Ende der Ersten Republik*, Vienna: Donau-Verlag 1948.

Groner, Richard: *Wien wie es war. Ein Auskunftsbuch für Freunde des alten Wien*, revised edn, ed. Otto Erich Deutsch, Vienna: Franz Hain n.d. [1934].

Gruber, Helmut: *Red Vienna: Experiment in Working-Class Culture 1919–1934*, New York and Oxford: Oxford University Press 1991.

Hadamowsky, Franz: *Bücherkunde deutschsprachiger Theaterliteratur*, 2 vols (*Maske und Kothurn*, Beihefte 5 and 6), Vienna: Böhlau 1982–8.

Hammond, Bryan, and Patrick O'Connor: *Joséphine Baker*, Boston, Toronto, London: Little, Brown 1988.

Handbook for Travellers in Southern Germany, London: John Murray 1837.

Herlosssohn, K[arl]; H[ermann] Marggraff, *et al.* (eds): *Allgemeines Theater-Lexikon oder Encyklopädie alles Wissenswerthen für Bühnenkünstler, Dilettanten und Theaterfreunde*, new edn, 7 vols., Altenburg, Leipzig: Expedition des Theater-Lexikons, 1839–46.

Jacob, P. Walter: *Jacques Offenbach in Selbstzeugnissen und Bilddokumenten* (Rowohlts Monographien, 155), Reinbek bei Hamburg: Rowohlt 1969.

Jacobs, Margaret, and John Warren (eds): *Max Reinhardt: The Oxford Symposium*, Oxford: Oxford Polytechnic 1986.

Junk, Victor: *Handbuch des Tanzes*, Stuttgart: Klett 1930.

Kleindel, Walter: *Österreich. Daten zur Geschichte und Kultur*, Vienna: Ueber-reuter 1978.

Klotz, Volker: *Bürgerliches Lachtheater, Komödie, Posse, Schwank, Operette*, Munich: Deutscher Taschenbuch Verlag 1980.

Operette. Porträt und Handbuch einer unerhörten Kunst, Munich and Zürich: Piper 1991.

Knepler, Henry: *The Gilded Stage. The Lives and Careers of Four Great Actresses: Rachel Félix, Adelaide Ristori, Sarah Bernhardt and Eleonora Duse*, London: Constable 1968.

Koch, Hans-Albrecht: *Das deutsche Singspiel* (Sammlung Metzler, 133), Stuttgart: Metzler 1974.

Koegler, Horst: *Friedrichs Ballettlexikon*, Velber bei Hannover: Friedrich 1972; revised edn: *The Concise Oxford Dictionary of Ballet*, London, New York, Toronto: Oxford University Press 1977.

Kosch, Wilhelm, and Ingrid Bigler-Marschall: *Deutsches Theater-Lexikon. Biographisches und bibliographisches Handbuch*, Vols. I and II, Klagenfurt and Vienna: Kleinmayr 1953–60; Vol. III, Berne: Francke 1992.

Kraus, Gottfried (ed.): *Musik in Österreich. Eine Chronik in Daten, Dokumenten, Essays und Bildern*, Vienna: Brandstätter 1989.

Leacroft, Richard, and Helen Leacroft: *Theatre and Playhouse: An Illustrated Survey of Theatre Building from Ancient Greece to the Present Day*. London: Methuen 1984.

Macartney, C.A.: *The Habsburg Empire 1790–1918*, London: Weidenfeld and Nicolson 1968.

Maske und Kothurn 8 (1962), no. 2: *Regie in Österreich*.

Michael, Friedrich, and Hans Daiber: *Geschichte des deutschen Theaters* (suhrkamp taschenbuch, 1665), Frankfurt a.M.: Suhrkamp 1990.

Nagl, Johann Willibald, Jakob Zeidler, and Eduard Castle (eds): *Deutsch-Österreichische Literaturgeschichte. Ein Handbuch zur Geschichte der deutschen Dichtung in Österreich-Ungarn*, 4 vols., Vienna: Fromme 1899–1937.

Pfoser, Alfred: *Literatur und Austromarxismus*, Vienna: Löcker 1980.

Plachta, Bodo: *Damnatur – Toleratur – Admittitur: Studien und Dokumente zur literarischen Zensur im 18. Jahrhundert* (Studien und Texte zur Sozialgeschichte der Literatur, 43), Tübingen: Niemeyer 1994.

Probszt, Günther: *Österreichische Münz- und Geldgeschichte. Von den Anfängen bis 1918*, 3rd edn, Vienna, Cologne, Weimar: Böhlau 1994.

Reed, John: *Schubert*, London: Dent 1987.

Reschauer, Heinrich, and Moritz Smets: *Das Jahr 1848. Geschichte der Wiener Revolution*, 2 vols., Vienna: Waldheim 1872.

Reyna, Ferdinando: *A Concise History of Ballet*, translated by Pat Wardroper, London: Thames and Hudson 1965.

Rieckmann, Jens: *Aufbruch in die Moderne: Die Anfänge des Jungen Wien. Österreichische Literatur und Kritik im Fin de Siècle*, Königstein/Ts.: Athenäum 1985.

Sadie, Stanley (ed.): *The New Grove Dictionary of Opera*. 4 vols., London: Macmillan Press 1992.

Schmitt, Peter: *Schauspieler und Theaterbetrieb. Studien zur Sozialgeschichte des Schauspielerstandes im deutschsprachigen Raum 1700–1900* (Theatron, 5), Tübingen: Niemeyer 1990.

Segel, Harold B.: *Turn-of-the-Century Cabaret*, New York: Columbia University Press 1987, pp. 183–219: 'Vienna: nightlights and bats'.

Spemanns goldenes Buch des Theaters. Eine Hauskunde für Jedermann, Berlin and Stuttgart: Spemann 1902.

Styan, J.L.: *Max Reinhardt*, Cambridge: Cambridge University Press 1982.

Theater in Österreich – Theatre in Austria – Le Théâtre en Autriche (Notring-Jahrbuch 1965), Vienna: Notring 1965.

Traubner, Richard: *Operetta: A Theatrical History*, New York and Oxford: Oxford University Press 1989.

Unruh, Walther: *Theatertechnik. Fachkunde und Vorschriftensammlung*, Berlin and Bielefeld: Klasing 1969.

Wangermann, Ernst: *The Austrian Achievement 1700–1800*, London: Thames and Hudson 1973.

Warrack, John, and Ewan West: *The Oxford Dictionary of Opera*, Oxford: Oxford University Press 1992.

Weiss, Karl: *Geschichte der Stadt Wien*, 2 vols., Vienna: Lechner 1872.

Willett, John: *The Theatre of the Weimar Republic*, New York: Holmes and Meier 1988.

Wurzbach, Constant von: *Biographisches Lexikon des Kaiserthums Oesterreich*, 60 vols., Vienna: Verlag der k.k. Hof- und Staatsdruckerei etc. 1856–91.

Yates, W.E.: 'Cultural life in early nineteenth-century Vienna', *Forum for Modern Language Studies* 13 (1977), 108–21; reprinted in Peter Branscombe (ed.): *Austrian Life and Literature 1780–1938*, Edinburgh: Scottish Academic Press 1978, pp. 12–25.

Zielske, Harald: *Deutsche Theaterbauten bis zum zweiten Weltkrieg. Typologisch-historische Dokumentation einer Baugattung* (Schriften der Gesellschaft für Theatergeschichte, 65), Berlin: Gesellschaft für Theatergeschichte 1971.

Index

2. GENERAL

3. PLAYS, OPERAS ETC.